W9-AEB-650

Political Culture and Secession in Mississippi

POLITICAL CULTURE AND SECESSION IN MISSISSIPPI

Masculinity, Honor, and the
Antiparty Tradition,
1830–1860

Christopher J. Olsen

OXFORD
UNIVERSITY PRESS

2000

OXFORD

UNIVERSITY PRESS

Oxford   New York
Athens   Auckland   Bangkok   Bogotá   Buenos Aires   Calcutta
Cape Town   Chennai   Dar es Salaam   Delhi   Florence   Hong Kong   Istanbul
Karachi   Kuala Lumpur   Madrid   Melbourne   Mexico City   Mumbai
Nairobi   Paris   São Paulo   Shanghai   Singapore   Taipei   Tokyo   Toronto   Warsaw

and associated companies in
Berlin   Ibadan

Copyright © 2000 by Oxford University Press, Inc.

Published by Oxford University Press, Inc.
198 Madison Avenue, New York, New York 10016

Oxford is a registered trademark of Oxford University Press.

All rights reserved. No part of this publication may be reproduced,
stored in a retrieval system, or transmitted, in any form or by any means,
electronic, mechanical, photocopying, recording or otherwise,
without the prior permission of Oxford University Press.

Library of Congress Cataloging-in-Publication Data
Olsen, Christopher J.
Political culture and secession in Mississippi :
masculinity, honor, and the antiparty tradition, 1830–1860 / Christopher J. Olsen.
p.   cm.
Includes bibliographical references and index.
ISBN 0-19-513147-9
1. Mississippi—Politics and government—To 1865.   2. Political culture—
Mississippi—History—19th century.   3. Political parties—
Mississippi—History—19th century.   4. Secession—Mississippi.
I. Title.
F341.O47   2000
306.2'09762'09034—dc21   99-049213

1 3 5 7 9 8 6 4 2
Printed in the United States of America
on acid-free paper

For Mom and Dad,
with love and thanks

Acknowledgments

I take great pleasure in thanking the many people whose generous gifts of time and talent made this a better work. It began as a dissertation at the University of Florida under the direction of Ronald P. Formisano, who was both a demanding and a patient critic. His suggestions on countless drafts challenged me and made the final product more subtle and satisfying. Bertram Wyatt-Brown was just as exacting, perceptive, and supportive. From the beginning they both inspired and motivated me to make my work the best it could be. I hope this book draws on and expands some of their best insights about antebellum history and would be especially satisfied if it meets their high standards and follows their path-breaking examples.

I spent several enjoyable months in Jackson, Mississippi, at the Mississippi Department of Archives and History. Its dedicated archivists made it easier for me to navigate the piles of dusty election returns and county records. I am also indebted to the staffs at the Southern Historical Collection of the University of North Carolina at Chapel Hill and at the Perkins Library at Duke University. The interlibrary loan folks at the University of Florida and Virginia Wesleyan College made possible both the dissertation and revisions for the book by finding me dozens of obscure county histories, articles, and old newspapers. The Graduate School, the College of Liberal Arts and Sciences and the Department of History at the University of Florida, Professor Wyatt-Brown and the Milbauer Chair of History, and Virginia Wesleyan College all generously supported the research for this study. While writing the dissertation, I was energized by the competitive but friendly atmosphere created by my friends at Florida: dutch, snuggles, ignatius, brains, and grandad. Many of the revisions were completed between 1996 and 1999 while I was at Virginia Wesleyan College, where my colleagues — Clay Drees, Stephen Mansfield, Dan Graf, and Ben Berry — were extremely supportive.

Many people read parts of the manuscript, and it is better because of their suggestions. I owe special thanks to Christopher Morris, Daniel Kilbride, Stan Deaton, Mark Greenberg, A. Glenn Crothers, Andrew Chancey, Jeffrey Adler, Jeffrey Needell, Richard K. Scher, Kirsten Wood, Jonathan Wells, Ted Vial, and Jennifer Olsen. A special thanks to Kenneth Winkle, my advisor at the University of Nebraska, for his help with quantitative methods and political culture. Thank you to Christina DeFendi, who helped complete some additional research, and to Amy Amies, in the Indiana State University office of Media Technologies and Resources, for help with the map of 1850s Mississippi. Finally, many people at Oxford University Press helped make the book a reality. Thanks especially to Susan Ferber, Thomas LeBien, Will Moore, copy editor Roberta Clarke for a very careful and thoughtful reading, and the anonymous readers who made many helpful suggestions.

Most of all I thank my family, many of whom have lived with this project as long as I have. My sisters Catherine, Elizabeth, and Constance and my in-laws, Bob and Janet Ross, all stayed interested and provided many types of support. My parents, Richard and Jean Olsen, have done so much that there is no way to thank them enough. The best I can say is that I owe them everything and hope they are proud of the finished product. Finally, my wife and best friend, Jennifer, made this book possible through her constant encouragement and better through her editing. It may not be dedicated to her, but it would not be worthwhile without her. Kayshea did nothing to help me finish the book, in fact she probably delayed it. But that's okay.

Terre Haute, Indiana   C. J. O.
February 2000

Contents

Political Culture and Secession in Mississippi

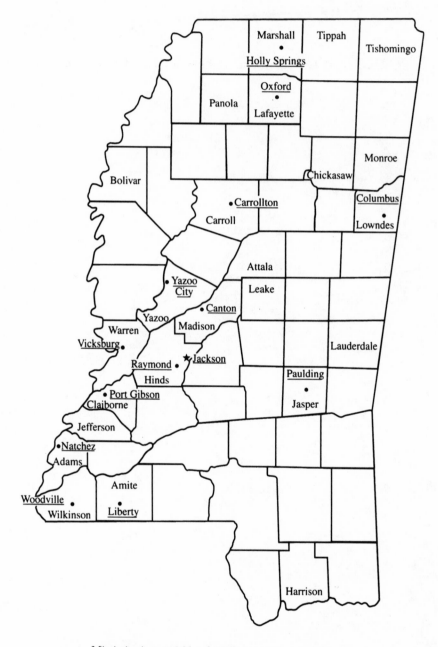

Mississippi, ca. 1855, selected counties and towns.

Introduction

It was late October, 1855, in Handsboro, Mississippi. A typical afternoon barbecue turned tense and violent when Democrat Robert Saffold drew a loaded pistol, aimed, and threatened to shoot his opponent for the state senate, prominent attorney Roderick Seal (figure 1.1). The trouble began when, along with a crowd of several hundred others, Saffold and Seal listened to a speech by Know-Nothing Isaac Martin, a local Harrison County politician. In the course of his remarks, Martin claimed that President Thomas Jefferson had once directed his postmaster general to bar all foreigners from post office patronage. This order, he implied, demonstrated that the Democratic Party had discriminated against foreigners in the past, making its current complaints about the Know Nothings' nativist platform hypocritical and dishonest. When Saffold demanded proof of Jefferson's actions, Martin admitted he did not have a copy of the order. Seal then rose to defend his colleague, Martin, and chastized Saffold for interrupting the speech. This was the critical moment. Seal made a quick, but subtle, transition from partisan rhetoric to personal insult: he "declared that Saffold had given Martin the lie twice." This loaded phrase (also known as the "Lie Direct") implied that Saffold had charged Martin with willful and personal dishonesty. It constituted an important step in the ritualized protocol leading to a duel, the affair of honor that settled disputes among gentlemen. With his accusation, Seal conflated the partisan and the personal, interpreting Saffold's rather mundane partisan question as a dangerous slur against Martin's personal character.[1]

Defending himself, Saffold "denied having given Martin the lie . . . [and avowed] he did not intend to question his veracity, that he had only asked for proof as he had a right to do, without intending offence." Martin, apparently satisfied, continued his speech after "order was restored." Only a few min-

3

FIGURE 1.1. Roderick Seal, lawyer and politician. *Source: Biographical and Historical Memoirs of Mississippi; Embracing an Authentic and Comprehensive Account of the Chief Events in the History of the State, and a Record of the Lives of Many of the Most Worthy and Illustrious Families and Individuals* (Chicago: The Goodspeed Publishing Company, 1891). Courtesy of the Earl Gregg Swem Library, The College of William and Mary.

utes later, though, Saffold protested that Martin had exceeded his allotted time, a complaint overheard by Seal, who warned those within earshot that he would "deal with" anyone who interfered with Martin again. In response to an angry question from Saffold, Seal made good on his threat and "gave Saffold the Damned Lie." The Damned Lie moved beyond the Lie Direct; it impugned a man's honesty and character, his claim to public integrity and honor. So it was at this point that Robert Saffold knocked his opponent in the mouth, depositing him on his political backside, and drew a loaded pistol, which he leveled on the prostrated attorney. "When Seal was recovered and upon his feet, Saffold asked him if he was armed" and declared that he "would not shoot an unarmed man." If Seal was armed (naturally he was), then he should draw his weapon; alternatively, he should "go and arm himself, [as] he Saffold was ready." Apparently, friends stopped the confrontation at this point and persuaded the two candidates to settle their differences in the proper manner, away from the women and children.[2]

That these two men nearly fired at one another over offhand comments made in a routine speech presents an interesting study in political culture. Though Robert Saffold identified himself with the Democratic Party—or at least with Thomas Jefferson, one of its patriarchs—he interpreted Martin's and Seal's comments within a personal, not institutional, framework. Each man claimed membership in a political party (though both switched sides more than once during their careers), but their responses to partisan rhetoric indicated their adherence to a personal code different from that of much of the country. They did not assess language from within a personality structure that conformed to institutional patterns of thought. In other words, their culture was not grounded in civil and social institutions—including political parties—that work to restrain individual behavior and encourage a greater degree of emotional control. These institutional relationships necessitate a delayed and controlled response from individuals who operate within their structures, whereas a noninstitutional personality draws an immediate, personal inference and reacts, as Saffold did, instinctively.[3] Most Mississippians spoke and acted in this way, suggesting they, too, considered politics and rhetoric personal matters. Men's actions consistently betrayed their preference for face-to-face relationships that preserved an institutionally weak, antiparty political culture. The personal implications they perceived in every political exchange meant that men could not ignore insults submitted in any political forum (or form), an attitude that infused the whole system with violence, as the many duels between politicians and editors evince. In the Upper South and the North, by contrast, antipartyism had faded by midcentury and parties had become permanent, widely accepted institutions that depersonalized language and allowed men more easily to dismiss the customary partisan taunts.

Mississippi's antiparty political culture distinguished it (and, I suspect, much of the Lower South) from other regions and explains why men denounced the Republican Party's Free Soil program with such vehemence. In his study of Mississippi secession, historian William Barney underlines the "spontaneous reaction" that greeted Lincoln's election: "Everyone expected that something had to be done," even "conservatives." The reasons for that spontaneous response lay in male gender roles, which conditioned voters to choose aggressive resistance to any insult, and in Mississippi's political culture. The ultimate response, secession, was inspired by virtues of southern honor and masculinity, but Mississippi's noninstitutional political culture provided the basis for its popularity. Thus, the sectional controversy became so emotionally charged and was taken so personally because it engaged men where they measured themselves—with and against their peers—and because it linked their understanding of masculinity and honor with the formal political system through which they effected secession.[4]

Since 1861 Americans have struggled to solve the great historical riddle of secession. Even before the final crisis, politicians and journalists speculated about why southerners would consider leaving the vigorous, thriving nation they did so much to create. Many historians have related the narrative of events leading to secession in the individual Confederate states, training their attention on party politics, and national elections and politicians. Some others have looked, instead, to the underlying tensions or anxieties within southern society that pushed certain groups toward disunion, and which were brought to the surface in a crisis atmosphere that enveloped the fateful summer, and election, of 1860. I believe the best approach is one that combines both of these outlooks. Certainly secession, a political act, occurred within the mostly male world of formal politics: campaigns, elections, candidates, and speech making. But it was more deeply rooted than the short-term crisis suggests; men in the Deep South had considered secession before — in 1832 and in 1850. The final act of disunion resulted from consequences of the long-term interaction between the political culture, especially how men thought about politics, and the deeply held, pervasive values of southern male culture.[5]

While many fine works analyze in detail the party maneuvers and ideologies of national and state leaders, they primarily explain how a minority of white men thought and behaved — editors, professional politicians, and core party activists. However, reaching beyond national and state elections, beyond correspondence between presidents, senators, and governors, and focusing instead on the behavior and attitudes of rank-and-file voters can help explain why so many ordinary Mississippians endorsed secession rather than even consider accepting Abraham Lincoln as president. Something in the Republican message, or, rather, in their interpretation of it, prompted voters in seven states to react, nearly as a unit, with such a drastic measure. To understand the motivation behind that decision we need to lay bare the political culture that shaped the perspective of most voters.

Numerous studies confirm the narrow outlook of antebellum people, who saw little immediate relevance to what happened in Washington, D. C. or even in their state capital. County politics, I suggest, are crucial to understanding Mississippi's nineteenth-century political culture, especially its voters' attitudes toward party organization. Until they embraced parties in local races, when voters could choose between candidates as friends, neighbors, or kinsmen and did not have to follow party labels, the political culture must be considered *antiparty* or, at most, *deferential-participant*.[6] Rejecting the legitimacy of parties created an attitude or political style that became a habit, a way of thinking that treated political rhetoric as a personal exchange. This attitude separated Mississippians from people in much of the country, including many fellow southerners in the Upper South; it provides a contrast that helps us understand the two-stage course of secession. A product of men's collective attitudes and culture, it was the final chapter to the political drama written during the antebellum years.

Therefore, rather than returning to the more well-covered ground of partisan ideology and national or state issues, in this work I place renewed emphasis on the purely local, nonpartisan, and nonideological nature of most Mississippi politics. In doing so, I hope to add to party studies by exploring what commonplace, familiar political actions meant to the great majority of ordinary folks — actions linking the preeminent, everyday political culture of the antebellum era to its climactic moment. This dominant, defining aspect of the political culture constituted a system embedded in the values and experiences of all Mississippi's white men. The wellspring of secession logic, it drew upon evangelical Protestantism, family and community identity, and patron-client relations — all of which were shaped by slavery and honor. In addition to secession, then, this study seeks to understand what politics and the act of voting meant to men in antebellum Mississippi and deals with a number of related issues: the intersection of gender and politics, southern class relations, and the effects of mobility in a stratified, hierarchical social system.

By choosing to study southern political culture and secession, I enter one of the most contested and vital debates in all of American historiography. Since the 1960s and 1970s, a number of historians have suggested that divisions within the South contributed significantly to the drive toward secession and civil war. They perceive a conflict, or potential conflict, between the white slaveowning and nonslaveowning classes. The slaveholding minority doubted that their less wealthy neighbors had a firm commitment to slavery and the southern way of life. They worried about the rising cost of slaves and land, and about soil exhaustion and erosion — all of which threatened access to the plantation dream. Thus, the argument runs, a ruling elite of masters engineered secession to unify southern white society and provide cheap land for southern farmers, which would help maintain the planters' hegemony over regional culture and economy.[7] Another version, or aspect, of this internal crisis theory(ies) contends that many southerners, especially nonslaveholders, became anxious about socioeconomic changes that were drawing them into a market economy and threatening their self-sufficient independence. Fearful of an intrusive, hostile world symbolized by an activist, Free Soil Republican Party, they eagerly supported secession to preserve "white liberty" — a combination of freedom from government or modernization and a bulwark against racial warfare or "amalgamation."[8]

Other historians who emphasize internal divisions but see them as stumbling blocks to secession argue (or at least imply) that some group — usually designated fire-eaters or secessionists — precipitated the climactic crisis in 1861. Secession, they conclude, though it was probably supported by most voters, resulted from a confrontation managed by ambitious and sometimes scheming, if well-meaning, politicians.[9] Still others portray secession as a sort of southern "Machiavellian moment," a crisis of republican government.

According to this reading, secessionists, convinced that the national government and political parties had become hopelessly corrupted, led a regional purge in "a revolution against politics." And many scholars contend that fire-eaters revived and exploited antiparty sentiment after 1856–1857 in order to generate secessionist frenzy.[10]

Finally, a number of studies argue that the explanation of secession lies in the actions of politicians and the structure of politics and party competition. They conclude that control of the apparently all-powerful Democratic Party in the Lower South was the deciding factor: secession was possible because local Democratic leaders and many of the party's rank-and-file committed to it, and the remainder of voters were carried along. In the Upper South, conversely, there were significant opposition parties to moderate Democratic rhetoric and offer alternative courses. Historian Michael Holt, in particular, insightfully argues that Upper-South voters had more confidence in parties and in their ability to fashion a sectional compromise because there were two long-lasting political organizations in those states.[11]

Like the authors of these studies, I emphasize the existence of two distinct political cultures within the South. But instead of seeing one overpowering party in the Lower South, I argue that there was no real party tradition there at all. Persistent two-party competition over time in the Upper South was important, mainly because it helped foster a political culture that accepted parties as natural. That acceptance created more than a moderating platform; it also helped voters make a fundamental transition to thinking in institutional terms. In Mississippi, some faithful Democrats undoubtedly did support separate-state secession out of partisan loyalty, or simply habit. But the state's party spokesmen portrayed Republicanism as a personal affront because most men interpreted politics within in a tradition of honor; this included "Cooperationists," who made the same assessment, although some of them disagreed about the gravity of the insult or the appropriate form of resistance.

Rather than a product of internal class conflict or economic changes, secession was the result of a clash between antagonistic societies or, at least, what most white men regarded as such. Because of this sectional difference, Republican attacks against southern values and institutions precipitated the final break. Most offensive of all was the implicit, and sometimes explicit, accusation that southerners' way of life was morally less worthy than that of their northern countrymen. It was the Republican attack on southerners themselves—and on their slave-based culture—that was the most important factor forcing the crisis. (As historians of antebellum northern politics have demonstrated, antisouthernism, and not antislavery or even Free Soil, was often the touchstone of Republican partisanship.)[12] For Mississippi's men, therefore, secession became a popular crusade to vindicate themselves from the Republicans' sectional critique and insistence on the Free Soil program. In voting for secession, Mississippians reacted, as they saw it, to years of northern moral and political condemnation culminating in a suddenly popular antislavery party and the election of its candidate in 1860.

Bound by a regional ethic of honor — the lingua franca of southern sectionalism — Mississippi voters challenged one another to defend their communities as they believed men should. That ethic was the principal reason that politicians used the language of honor when speaking about the sectional crisis; they did not manipulate honor to become popular or gain votes but, rather, employed it with unself-conscious conviction, uniting with one another to safeguard their families, neighborhoods, and, ultimately, their regional way of life. Southern men were struggling to vindicate their own, as well as their society's reputation and character. This "manly imperative" was more important to them than preserving the Union and, ultimately, more important than simply extending slavery into the western territories. Yet slavery was inseparable from their regional identity, and it helped define southern masculinity and perpetuate honor. Like a cancer, slavery underlay variations among white Americans, spreading its malignant effects to warp southern gender norms, class relations, evangelical religion, and virtually every other cultural trait.

A number of factors ultimately convinced formerly hesitant men to support secession: fear of class or racial warfare spread by "Black Republicans"; economic hopes, dreams, and nightmares; and party loyalty. Upper South voters, too, delayed action for many reasons: fewer slaves in the region, more numerous economic and personal ties with northerners, and fear of war and destruction in their own backyards. But in Mississippi, and perhaps in the entire Deep South, the noninstitutional political culture provided the critical atmosphere that joined together these individual motives and facilitated, even demanded, manly action. It was the lens through which voters gauged the Republican threat and northern insults; in the Upper South, they had a different lens. Steeped in an ethos of public violence and conditioned by their fateful, antiparty political culture, Mississippi voters considered Lincoln's victory a personal attack. Secession and its possible consequences — death in defense of reputation — offered the only proper response for men who saw themselves as grievously insulted.

Political culture remains a popular term among historians. Over the last twenty years, many scholars have used it explicitly, others implicitly, both as something to be studied or explained and as a methodology or means to study social or cultural ethics. In this study, the term *political culture* includes both attitudes about politics and more tangible aspects of the political system: how votes were cast, the disposition of actual ballots and timing of elections, disqualification of voters, who voted for whom, and patronage. These elements, sometimes called *implicit orientations* or the *taken-for-granteds* of politics, are things so commonplace and ordinary that men seldom notice them in operation. They reveal as much, or more, about a society as rhetoric, because they rest on assumptions so basic that they remain unspoken and, usually, unquestioned. Political culture, then, is more than editorials and speeches; it includes voting, running for office, and the voting process itself, among other taken-for-granteds. The intersection of language and behavior is a — perhaps the — crucial feature of political culture because words, like all aspects of politics, can only be understood when grounded in the everyday lives of human beings. Considering behavior along with rhetoric, of course, also makes it possible to examine seriously the attitudes of illiterate and otherwise historically inarticulate people.[13]

If, in addition, we consider elections and politics from a ritualistic perspective, as social historians have done with many other public events, we broaden our understanding of what politics meant to ordinary folks. This effort can also let us see beyond the voters, since political rituals often encompassed the entire community — just as Clifford Geertz's famous Balinese cockfight involved more than just the gamblers — and delivered important messages about power and class, gender and race, and the culture in which those basic principles were negotiated.[14] Thus, I would argue, using political culture as a methodology provides insights into values and attitudes that may not always be articulated or even consciously considered by many people. This approach rests on the potency of taken-for-granteds and the power of discourse, especially when leaders articulate values, assumptions, and convictions *for* (not *to*) the masses.

Public exchanges reveal issues and concerns that are most salient to voters and leaders alike — which does not preclude the possibility that followers may act independently of their leaders (or vice versa) — because leaders primarily articulate what ordinary citizens think. In short, there is a reciprocal relationship between the symbols and rhetoric employed by community leaders and the values held by their "inarticulate" listeners. While politicians often operate at a more urbane and informed level, both the elite and masses are part of a common political culture.[15] Mississippi Representative Reuben Davis perfectly captured this relationship when he described his resignation speech before Congress in 1860: "I spoke bitterly and with some angry vehemence," Davis remembered, "because I *felt myself the mouthpiece of a wronged and outraged people, and their righteous indignation poured itself through me.*"[16]

Finally, like several recent works, this one combines the study of political culture and gender, what one historian has called "the politics of gender and the gendering of politics." In other words, it considers gender norms part of political culture and looks for the connections between gender and electoral politics. Conceptually, however, it differs from other studies in two respects: first, rather than in the household or family roles, I maintain that southern men measured themselves in public rivalries with one another.[17]

Masculinity required them constantly to prove themselves because, as David Gilmore concludes: "the state of being a 'real man' or 'true man' [is] uncertain or precarious, a prize to be won or wrested through struggle." From the perspective of women and slaves, white men certainly enjoyed privileges from their birth, but the struggle for "real" manhood could only be measured against other men. This emphasis, of course, did (and does) not dispute or invalidate the relational qualities of masculinity: what was not feminine or childish was manly. And like race and class, gender norms were constructed over time — shaped, to an extent, by variables such as age, marital status, class, race, education, and ethnicity — and dependent on the perspectives of individual men and women. But southern white men were always united by common principles, and they largely took for granted their superiority over women, children, and slaves, granting ultimate approval only to their peers. This process placed great emphasis on the public arena, especially politics. Thus, white men's perspective on masculinity is decisive for our examination of antebellum political culture because they saw electoral politics — ultimately the source of seccession — as a purely masculine forum. Of course, women participated in public political events, entering the "male sphere" to attend barbecues and speeches or even, on rare occasions, to debate issues in the partisan press. But what stands out in the political culture of antebellum Mississippi are its obsessively masculine and competitive qualities. Most of all, men prized physical courage, aggressiveness, and individual power; but they also valued reliability and loyalty to neighbors, kin, and other men in the community. When they invoked the household as a metaphor, for example, it was in the context of defending it better than, or at least as well as, other men did.[18]

The two most important factors that sustained this obsession with male rivalry and the importance of public reputation were slavery and the ethic of honor. The qualities of honor, a set of cultural virtues that lent structure to social relations and offered guidelines for human behavior, varied across time, space, and class; honor in medieval Spain necessarily differed from that of the Old South. Yet everywhere the ancient code held sway its defining mechanism was the same: a person's inner self-worth was determined by one's peers; every man submitted his reputation and good character to the community, which either affirmed or denied his claim after careful scrutiny of his family background and public comportment. "Honour was a quality, the contents of which eluded positive definition," writes historian Ute Frevert, and "was discernible solely through the perceptions of others." It was "a matter of interchanges between the individual and the community . . . meaning was imparted not with words alone, but in courtesies, rituals, and even deeds of personal and collective violence." This mechanism, then, placed extraordinary value on outward appearance, style, and language. Most important, the community's judgment was internalized by individuals, which gave the code its exceptional power to unite public behavior and social scrutiny with a man's personal, emotional, and psychological self-worth.[19]

Finally, while honor operated most basically at the individual level, it remained intimately connected with the community. The community, after all, conferred status on the individual. Thus insults leveled against the community called into question a man's own personal honor, validated as it was by his peers. Conversely, questioning a man's reputation undermined the collective honor of everyone who sanctioned him. In other words, each individual and his community were bound by honor in a mutually sustaining relationship demanding that each defend the reputation of the other. "Honor and shame are reciprocal moral values," concludes one student of the ethic, "representing primordial integration of individual to 'group.'" Thus, the dictates of honor underscored loyalty to clan and community and the importance of personal courage and manly dependability.[20]

Slavery also required white men to demonstrate physical power and proclaimed the functional importance of violence to maintaining discipline. It placed a premium on courage, loyalty, and the reliability of all the white men of the community. Slavery also reinforced men's preoccupation with public reputation, especially physical courage, because southerners "defined a slave as a person without honor," as someone cowardly who would not, and could not, risk his life for family or principles. Slaves could be called and considered liars and cowards and have no recourse, while free men of honor reacted fiercely to such slurs. Thus, the combined effects of honor and slavery mutually sustained a regional obsession with aggressive, competitive masculinity, but also with loyalty to other white men.[21]

The second way the present work differs from many studies of gender and politics is that it joins gender analysis with such time-honored methods of political history as analysis of voting returns and taken-for-granteds. I am therefore advocating a model of political culture that combines some of the insights of anthropology and of gender and ritual studies with evidence and methods more familiar to political historians and political scientists. Combining diverse sources — some unused before now — and an approach that surveys the entire state of Mississippi gives the work, I believe, a broad perspective. Written evidence, of course, is always biased toward the elite. In politics, this record favors party activists and those most concerned with state or national issues, particularly men who corresponded across county and state lines. Relying on state organs written by party leaders also gives undue attention to state and national elections. Finally, concentrating on one county sometimes magnifies the distortion, since historians typically choose counties with good manuscript collections and towns large enough to support competing partisan newspapers. All these factors exaggerate the importance of parties and issues among the mass of voters and overstate the driving power of state and national concerns.[22]

Instead, therefore, of focusing principally on state and national politics, I emphasize the manuscript returns from thousands of local and county elections across the state. They demonstrate that residency was the decisive factor in voter behavior; consistently high turnout at all levels testifies to the importance men placed on local offices. Moreover, although it utilizes statewide party organs, this study relies more heavily on rural newspapers, which often presented a different picture of the issues that were important to Mississippi readers. When combined with testimony from the county boards of police (the basic unit of local government), these sources sketch a rich, diverse, and hotly contested world of local politics — filled with some colorful, even comic, characters — in which parties played no meaningful role. A statewide perspective also reveals a complex and varied political culture. It registers the impact of towns and partisan newspapers, population density, socioeconomic diversity, and the evolution of rural neighborhoods. Finally, Mississippi's antebellum experience reminds us that political culture did not take a linear, consistent path from hierarchy to democracy or from antiparty to strong parties. Rather, it often ebbed and flowed unevenly.

At the foundation of Mississippi's political culture was a suspicion of political parties and professional politicians that was expressed in speeches, public letters and pamphlets, editorials, and private correspondence. Despite these paeans to antiparty principles, though, most historians contend that Whigs and Democrats enjoyed an intense emotional commitment from voters who operated within identifiable belief systems traceable to state and local elections. Many studies of states in the North and the Upper South offer strong support for this position. By the 1840s and 1850s, antipartyism had become a marginal, or sporadic, part of public discourse as both leaders and rank-and-file voters demonstrated a consistent faith in party organization. Most important, men apparently carried their partisan identifications into county and even local contests. Thus, concludes one recent study, "the key difference by 1838 was that . . . high interest and commitment and strong party institutions fed by intense partisanship became permanent [and] deeply rooted," and all Americans demonstrated a "widespread acceptance of the party role in American politics."[23] In large parts of the country, yes, but not in Mississippi.

Mississippi's parties did have support, especially from editors, national politicians, and some core activists. There were certainly elements of modern parties — electioneering and hundreds of campaign rallies, for instance. Men recorded their party identification by wearing pins and buttons, marching with coonskin caps and dragging miniature log cabins through town; women sewed banners and "civilized" a hundred parades with their inevitably "graceful" presence. People, in short, shouted "huzzah" for their party in a thousand different ways. But what did it mean to them? Evidence suggests that most voters became Whigs or Democrats because of family heritage or community tradition and that most people considered party events to be primarily social, community functions. Most crucially, as the opening vignette implies, most voters identified with candidates as individual men, not as the impersonal representative of a cause. In short, men could be Democrats or Whigs but still not think in institutional terms because they were never reconciled to the supposed benefits or inevitability of party organization.

Far from fanatical devotion, Mississippians' language and behavior evinced a shallow and weak partisan culture. Most voters paid more than lip service to antiparty principles; they avoided parties whenever possible, and many switched loyalties with no apparent anxiety. In national or state races in which few voters could know candidates personally, they were often forced to follow party labels, though they still complained loudly about the evils of party organization. Furthermore, even at that level, contemporaries acknowledged that thousands of new or uncommitted voters would determine each contest, an expectation also borne out by election returns. Because of geographic mobility, natural demographic turnover, and voter choice, uncertainty characterized the whole party "system." Mississippi's Whigs, in particular, barely qualified as a coherent party. Below the state level, parties had almost no impact: party activists failed to bring about county nominations, control access to most public offices, or connect party opinion with local races. Thus, perhaps the crucial measurement of public opinion was the fact that whenever they had the opportunity voters rejected parties. That does not mean that there were no parties or that voters did not, at times, respond to party leaders or slogans. But it does reflect a political culture that was noninstitutional and preferred personal relationships; one could be a Whig or a Democrat without actually believing in the virtue of parties.

Instead, most politics revolved around networks of friends and neighbors, a set of community bonds driven by face-to-face relationships. In such a personal political culture, men relied on their own or their families' reputations and resources. It was an ideal system for men whose lives were defined by public image and perception, but it only worked as long as parties remained marginal and ineffective, especially at the local level.[24] Candidates for numerous county and precinct officers reflected the prevailing social hierarchy, suggesting that most Mississippians knew, or quickly learned, where they stood in the pecking order. As one of several important male public rituals, politics allowed voters to assert their proper place and status within the community. Family influence and honor also allowed planters to extend their power and prestige to the next generation. Thus, the political culture provided a crucial bridge between the seemingly irreconcilable traits of widespread geographic and, sometimes, social mobility and a hierarchical society based on honor and slavery that accepted, even celebrated, inequality. In short, an exploration of how politics operated in the neighborhood suggests that it was much less democratic or ideological than is often assumed and highlights the importance of personal power and position in the community.

This antiparty, ritualistic political culture combined with southern notions of masculinity and honor to precipitate secession. In 1860 most Mississippi voters concluded they could not accept a Republican victory. Rather than "bow in craven submission" to the "yoke" of Yankee insults, they rallied to assert their own masculinity, their family and community honor, and to answer the public slur of Free Soil. Conditioned by their political culture, men like Robert Saffold interpreted (Republican) partisan rhetoric as a personal insult. Prickly about their masculinity and honor, most Mississippians responded with predictable outrage and, eventually, with violence. Thus, a set of deeply held convictions about honor and the duty of men to protect themselves and their community from insult led to a fracturing of the Republic — because of the state's political culture. When community leaders articulated the sectional controversy in terms of "craven submission" or "manly resistance," they meant that docile acquiescence would be personally humiliating. Political parties of a modern tenor, with their bureaucratic machinery and sets of impersonal candidates, could have defused the potent language of manliness and honor; insults offered through the institutionalized anonymity of effective parties might have been ignored. But in the absence of that partisan tradition, secession represented the natural interaction of southern honor, men's visceral anger, and the state's antiparty, community-based political culture.

This work takes both a narrative and a topical organization. Chapter 1 details Mississippi's evolution in the 1830s and early 1840s, tracing the state's rapid growth and describing its emerging political system. The chapter also outlines the development of an intensely masculine public culture under frontier conditions and, later, within a slave society. As men learned to value ferocity, physical courage, loyalty, and dependability, they fashioned a personal, face-to-face political culture based on those values and the country's celebrated heritage of white man's democracy. Sectional conflict and the possibility of secession form the background of chapter 2, which examines the crisis of 1849–1851. It demonstrates the weakness of party ties and the ease with which voters abandoned supposedly strong commitments. It also clarifies the importance of honor and manliness to the language of sectionalism and to the regional political culture. Chapters 3 and 4 trace the politics of antipartyism through popular rhetoric and voting behavior. Both Whigs and Democrats painted their opponents as professional "demagogues" and slaves to "rigid organization." These appeals, I argue, signaled a widespread popular distrust of political parties and demonstrated that most voters still considered them an unnatural and, hopefully, unnecessary part of political life. Not only did Mississippians talk a good antiparty game, but quantitative evidence indicates that as voters they rejected party organization whenever possible.

Chapter 5 discusses neighborhoods as the foundation of the state's political culture. County and local politics revolved around rural residency patterns, and voters typically supported neighborhood candidates. Indeed, the neighborhood so thoroughly defined rural politics that state and county governments, respecting the force of community will, codified it into law. The ritualistic functions of politics are the subject of chapter 6. The election process—that is, voting and running for office—stabilized class relationships and allowed men who prized and benefitted from geographic and social mobility to restore a hierarchical, even deferential, society. Mississippi's localized political culture helped define and perpetuate the community power structure, permitting planter families to maintain power over time. In short, it reconciled American democracy and egalitarianism with the hierarchical values inherent in honor and slavery.

In chapter 7 I analyze the most fascinating aberration of Mississippi's antebellum political culture, the Know-Nothings. For two years, even at the local level, many voters began to embrace parties; for the first time, the state's political culture moved toward partisan. Allowed to develop, a viable two-party system like that in the Upper South and the North might have evolved. Such a fundamental reordering of the political culture could have changed the attitude of Mississippi's voters and conditioned them—like their counterparts farther north—to think in institutional terms. Theoretically, such a change might have stopped secession. The Know-Nothings, however, were divided in 1856—a crucial moment—and Mississippians became more and more united in the face of Republican opposition to slavery and the South's political power. Politics in the late 1850s and secession, the subjects of chapter 8, manifested the ultimate power of personal politics and the violent consequences of honor and manliness. It was an unfortunate, indeed lethal, combination.

Finally, although this work treats only one state, Mississippi was representative of the Deep South. Its social, economic, and demographic profile were similar to other states in the region, and it eventually took the lead, with South Carolina, in the movement for southern unity and disunion. But whereas South Carolina had a uniquely undemocratic political system, Mississippians enjoyed almost unparalleled power at the ballot box, making it an ideal subject for study of the interaction between popular politics and southern social ethics. Secession was a political action driven by forces deep within southern culture, and nowhere were these forces more clearly manifested than in Mississippi. The state's voters listened to northerners "threaten" and "insult" them for more than a decade. They responded as their culture, and their political culture, taught: with direct action and violence.

1

A SAVAGE PLACE

*The Mississippi Frontier, Masculinity, and
Political Culture in the 1830s*

"The present inhabitants," wrote Judge Ephraim Kirby upon his arrival in frontier Mississippi, "are illiterate, wild and savage, of depraved morals." One hopes he exaggerated, but Kirby's judgment captures the spirit of many early settlers struggling to tame the state's savage conditions. Mostly a wilderness, much of the state belonged to American Indians until the 1820s and 1830s, when a succession of treaties cleared the way for white settlement. Even at the time of secession, many areas still resembled a frontier. Another early resident spoke for thousands when he recalled "that the times then tried the stuff men were made of."[1] Part of the settlement heritage, reinforced and sustained by slavery and scattered residence, was a glorification of certain manly virtues: physical courage and aggressiveness, but also reliability and loyalty to neighbors and kin. Confirmed in public, face-to-face encounters between men, these values defined masculinity and reinforced the demands of honor, linking individual men with their peers in the community. After 1830 rapid immigration sparked social and economic development and created a more complex society. Settlers began to enjoy greater social stability, more coherent and supportive neighborhoods, and some outward signs of "civilization."

In the 1830s a nascent political culture also took shape. Founded in the state's rural communities, it celebrated and enshrined white male democracy and operated within local networks of friends, neighbors, and kinsmen. Because most candidates and voters knew each other, personal reputation and face-to-face contacts were the most important ingredients of political success. This political culture allowed men to demonstrate both personal independence as sovereign voters and loyalty to fellow members of the community by supporting local candidates. It thus conformed to, and helped men satisfy, the requirements of honor and manliness. It only worked, however, when the bureaucracy and anonymity of institutional parties were absent; it needed to remain highly personal, conducted through public encounters that depended on, and helped confirm, reputation and status within the community. The state's antebellum conditions (few roads, isolated communities, and the need to police a slave society) as well as a number of divisive and confusing state issues in the 1840s, the Mexican War, and the possibility of secession in 1850, also undermined party development and competition. In short, men's foremost values and ethics, socioeconomic conditions, and the state's history all fostered and sustained a political culture that discredited and sabotaged the development of effective parties.

Looking back over his career, Judge John C. Burrus described Bolivar County as it was during his childhood in the 1850s. He recalled it as a land of "primeval forests," virtually "a wall of living green" covered in cane breaks, a wilderness inhabited by black bears, cougars, and spotted panthers. When the settlers labored to clear the rich land for cotton, there were almost no roads; only rudimentary trails connected the isolated plantations along the Mississippi River. Years later, Matilda Clark Sillers remembered Bolivar in 1854 as still "almost a wilderness with [only] clearings along the river front." Her brother Charles, later a Civil War governor, greeted her at his plantation, "Doro," when she arrived on the steamboat *Bulletin,* the only means of transportation. Early settlers in Harrison County, too, recalled thickets and swamps and woods full of deer, turkeys, and more exotic animals. As late as 1843, one Covington County resident shot and killed a "verry large tiger [panther?]" as it made "an awful spring . . . directly for me." The animal surprised the hapless hunter, who expected a much-less-threatening (to say the least) deer. In the 1840s many residents of the state still made their own clothes and eked out a meager subsistence.[2]

Living quarters reflected the hard life. "Most of the houses," Judge Burrus reminisced, "were built of hewn logs with stick and dirt chimneys." The first Bolivar County courthouse consisted of a single room with benches made of "cypress puncheons, or slabs with holes bored and wooden pegs for legs." Judge Joseph McGuire, a planter and county pioneer, "furnished food and sleeping quarters for those who attended the [circuit] court." Most slept on the floor or outside. McGuire's own residence "was of the most primitive style; the interstices between the logs poorly chinked with clay or mud." John and Polly Colvin settled in Mississippi and for two years inhabited a "very old and dilapidated double log house," later adding a more "modern" frame structure. Even in town, residents lived in little more comfort. In 1822 Columbus, Reverend George Shaeffer remembered, the grandest house belonged to Judge Cocke. It sat on the point of a hill and had four rooms in each story. Built with rough-hewn logs, the judge "called it 'the big pile of logs.'" The town's "academy" occupied a "small frame house 30 by 40,

not ceiled nor plastered; this was [also] the preaching place for all denomi-
nations." As late as 1856, New York's Frederick Law Olmsted complained
that there were no toilet facilities in any of Jackson's hotels.[3]

Much of antebellum Mississippi resembled these frontier descriptions.
Civilization—in the form of roads, brick homes, churches, and schools—
came slowly. The notorious early trails forced George Rogers to ride with
his coach doors open to avoid being smothered in mud if the vehicle sank
or overturned. Others described traveling single file, a slave leading the column to hold back tree branches. In Bolivar County, women "contented
themselves by exchanging notes, recipes, and patterns" during the winter
because only men dared test the local paths. Other travelers complained of
tree stumps and roots, boulders that broke wheels and axles or overturned
wagons, and Black Belt clay so clinging it actually "sucked horseshoes off."[4]
Better roads could transform life. In Columbus introduction of mail service
in 1821 and a new post road to Jackson meant that residents "could now
communicate with their families and neighbors," a luxurious sign "that the
rigors and deprivations of frontier life were fast passing away." In the early
1840s, John F. H. Claiborne noted the quality of Mrs. Ray's "spacious Inn
at the junction of the Gallatin and Monticello roads," where he enjoyed a
dinner of "oysters and chicken salad, turkeys, terrapin and champagne!"
These changes happened first near the growing towns and long-settled cotton lands. Nonetheless, except for outposts of progress around Vicksburg,
Natchez, Jackson, and Columbus, much of the state remained but sparsely
settled.[5]

Not surprisingly, early settlers were a rough bunch who showed few
signs of gentility. Satirist Joseph Baldwin, who immortalized 1830s Mississippi in his *Flush Times* vignettes, mocked the residents' feckless manners.
"The condition of society may be imagined," noted the Virginia-born Baldwin with thinly veiled contempt: "vulgarity—ignorance—fussy and arrogant
pretension—unmitigated rowdyism—bullying insolence, if they did not rule
the hour, *seemed* to wield unchecked dominion." He derided the comical,
and to Baldwin pathetic, efforts of backwoods farmers in their Sunday best:
"Bur-*well* Shines ... *was* sworn and directed to take the stand. He was a
picture! ... He wore ... nankeen pants that struggled to make both ends
meet, but failed, by a few inches, in the legs, yet made up for it by fitting a
little better than the skin every where else; his head stood upon a shirt collar
that held it up by the ears, and a cravat something smaller than a table-cloth,
bandaged his throat."[6] In 1861 London's William Howard Russell described
Governor John Pettus as abrupt, ill-mannered, and stained with tobacco
juice. The executive mansion was "ragged," covered with mildew, and notable mainly for its broken windows. In the Piney Woods, manners apparently
changed more slowly than even Baldwin could have imagined. One mis-
placed college professor described the locals in 1902 as "among the crudest

people it has ever been my good or bad fortune to know. . . . they often had their own standards [of proper behavior]," and "human life at the time was quite cheap."[7]

This evolving civilization proceeded unevenly across the South and the state of Mississippi. William Henry Sparks claimed migrants from the Atlantic seaboard fled to 1850s Mississippi as "refugees from a growing civilization," seeking a wilderness and solitude unavailable at home. Claiborne marveled at the thinly settled Piney Woods, where "houses on the road [stood] from ten to twenty miles apart." Like Bolivar, other Delta counties seemed like a frontier, even in 1860. Elsewhere, however, as in Lowndes County, settlers had conquered much of the wilderness by 1840 and Columbus had become a thriving merchant town.[8] The transition from wilderness to civilization also went in both directions. When northern Mississippi was opened to white settlement in the 1830s, thousands flocked to its better soil from such older southern counties as Greene, Pike, and Lawrence. "Lawrence may be called the mother county of North Mississippi," concluded one resident, because "it has planted its little colonies throughout the northern and middle counties." The north Mississippi land rush brought renewed isolation to many settlements and created ghost towns across the southern counties.[9]

Although life usually offered a bit more than Hobbes's state of nature, it remained nasty, brutish, and threateningly short. Danger from wild animals, disease, and (not least of all) one's fellow settlers contributed to the evolution of a society that revered physical courage and valor. Men celebrated their ability to carve a life out of wilderness and gloried in stalking wolves and black bear. Some whites, probably exaggerating the danger for literary effect, noted the presence of "savage" American Indians in the late 1830s and early 1840s. Horace Fulkerson remarked that bands of Choctaws occasionally strolled "menacingly" through his town of Rodney. These graphic descriptions suggest a whole society of Thomas Sutpens struggling with grim and ruthless determination to wrench a life from the primeval forests.[10]

Given the isolated settlements and threatening conditions, periodic gatherings fostered a nearly mythic cult of male bonding. Men sought the company of other men for safety, but also to relieve boredom and loneliness. William Faulkner's classic patriarch lived in the Mississippi wilderness "eight miles from any neighbor, in masculine solitude." Sutpen hosted parties of local men who hunted by day, played cards at night, and slept "in blankets in the naked rooms of his embryonic formal opulence." Real life Mississippians remembered scenes that confirmed Faulkner's Spartan portrait. John Burrus hosted neighborhood hunters who "frequently [brought] their friends with them and [found] shelter in the overseers' homes or [slept] in tents." Travelers rarely failed to comment on the unending passion for hunting, drinking, and gambling—a sort of southern male holy trinity that seemed forever linked.[11]

Needing one another for survival and companionship, every household relied on the cooperation and support it received from neighbors. Jesse Wilkins remembered how the men in one Wayne County neighborhood along Buckatunna Creek responded to a rumored Creek uprising. First they "decided that a fort should be built . . . for the protection of all families in the community." Completed in a week, "Patton's Fort" was a success. Still, "about fifteen families becoming dissatisfied with the discomforts of fort life . . . abandoned the place and returned to their farms" and planned their own defense. "When the duties of the day were over, these families would repair to some designated house in the community, around which sentinels would be posted for the night." Each day "another house would be selected as a place of meeting, at which all would assemble at the appointed time." The men also created their own scouting service. With the neighborhood secured, "these Buckatunna farmers enjoyed the freedom of country life and kept up their farm work." Men thus learned to recognize the "real men" — what another early settler called "the efficient men of the place" — on whom they could rely. Anthony Rotundo characterizes this emphasis on duty and loyalty to others as "communal manhood," a value system that thrived in small, close-knit rural settlements in which people intimately related with and depended on each other.[12]

Whether mostly recreational, like hunting, or concerned more directly with survival, group activities helped establish mutual loyalty among men living in isolated, hostile conditions. Rather than turn to the government, settlers relied on neighbors, who were often extended kin. They created a definition of masculinity that valued ferocity, physical courage, dependability, and loyalty above all other traits. As one Mississippian remembered, "It required courage to brook the disorders and exposures of the wild life they had led in the first settlement of the country, and this courage then displayed, had marked their characters as they grew older." And, he might have added, it fostered a culture of masculinity that was handed down to later generations.[13]

Even after the most Hobbesian period of settlement ended and conflict with American Indians no longer presented a constant threat, the state's rural situation and peculiar institution perpetuated the obligations of communal manhood, aggressive masculinity, and neighborhood solidarity. Mississippi's small, face-to-face communities were critical, of course, in sustaining the force of public reputation and the threat of dishonor to those who failed to uphold their individual, family, and community obligations. Elsewhere, as other societies became more densely settled, anonymous, and bureaucratic, the strength of honor and shame necessarily faded, coincident with the declining importance of personal relationships.

In every slave society, the ruling caste relied on a steady campaign of physical abuse, torture, and terrorism to survive; masters needed to "make them stand in fear," as Kenneth Stampp phrased it. This requirement exaggerated the patriarchal values of nineteenth-century America and added a practical imperative that rewarded male brutality. From a young age, white southern boys were taught the functional value of violence and loyalty to one another. If the slaves rebelled, whites were all in it together; Nat Turner convinced them of that. During the anxious summer of 1835, when rumors of slave rebellion excited dozens of Mississippi communities, white men repeatedly called on each other to close ranks and protect the women and children—through wholesale murder if necessary. Periodic insurrection scares called out the white male community, testing every man's commitment to slavery and his neighbors—imperatives that were magnified in Mississippi, one of only two states with a slave majority in 1860. As one man who had moved from Kentucky via Ohio wrote his sister, "The discipline here is more rigid—necessarily so on plantations where the blacks so far outnumber the whites."[14] The possibility of slave revolt, however, only added to basic values instilled through the daily routines of racial control: aggressiveness and violence were important, even imperative, for white men to function effectively in antebellum Mississippi. Loyalty and dependability solidified one's value to the community and to fellow men, as neighbors, husbands, and fathers.

Of course, masculinity and honor were not static concepts, despite certain fundamental principles that persisted across class, geography, and time. The most obvious and fundamental change in New World honor was the valuation of personal reputation and accomplishments over family lineage. Spanish settlers to America distinguished between *honor*, which signified status from noble birth, and *honra*, meaning individual virtue. *Honor* depended largely on *limpieza de sangre* (purity of blood) and remained important to the European elites in Latin America's relatively fluid racial environment, especially among the poor.[15] In the United States, obsessed with repudiating Old World aristocracy and inherited privilege, *honra* prevailed over *limpieza de sangre* and became *honor*. This transformation made southerners' honor (like masculinity) even more competitive, based as it was on reputation earned and defended.

In Mississippi and the Old South, as in all societies, gender norms also evolved over time and varied among people of different classes. Wealth, of course, was indispensable as a sign of inner virtue and personal success, although America's egalitarian mythology of the self-made man could make inherited money a disadvantage. Yet, as society matured and life became less primitive, elite men especially added learning, hospitality, and gentility to the list of important manly qualities. No doubt an "aristocratic" planter like Jefferson Davis understood manliness and honor somewhat differently than did the poor farmers, herdsmen, and "wood choppers" who populated much of rural Mississippi. Davis probably recoiled at their language and manners every time they crossed paths at a neighborhood barbecue. On their side, Mississippi's dirt farmers, like the poor everywhere, envied Davis's wealth but also resented his "haughty" assumption of superiority.

Nonetheless, all men shared common ground. The gentry, like the poorest Piney Woods squatter, expressed a commitment to courage and loyalty to kin—witness the many duels, which helped the elite overcome the hint of effeminacy that came with too much education, piety, or family money. Mississippians of all classes agreed that a man's foremost duty was the defense of personal honor, home, and family reputation. Another shared element was the valuation of physical form, even comeliness. A man's stature, bearing, even his nose and his genitalia, reflected his inner manliness. Two drunken ruffians who attacked farmer Joshua Meacham in Monroe County left no doubt of what parts they considered crucial to a man's public image. After "cutting and disfiguring his face," they "nearly severed his penis from his body, and cut and slit his bag," finally depositing him naked on his front porch.[16]

Finally, society's definition of the male gender role gradually came to incorporate Christianity. Initially, secular honor and the paramount manly virtues conflicted, at least theoretically, with the renewed religious ethos that spread across the region after 1800. At first, when evangelical Methodist and Baptist preachers attacked worldly honor and a secular hierarchy based on wealth, they even questioned slavery. Their egalitarian message of conversion and a personal relationship with God challenged the cultural and moral authority the gentry claimed for material success and education. Evangelicals also made self-control and personal restraint central to their definition of morality, urging men to respect biblical condemnations of gambling, violence, and strong drink. In short, they proscribed most of southern male behavior.[17]

Ultimately, though, southern culture changed evangelicalism more thoroughly than evangelicals reformed southern men. First, church leaders faced the impossibility and self-destructiveness of emancipation and chose instead to christianize the institution of slavery. This meant converting slaves and telling them to accept their earthly fate, which helped ensure eternal salvation (and protected the white community from possible rebellion). And they urged masters to treat slaves humanely as fellow Christians. These tenets— whether successful or not—allowed evangelicals to defend slavery as a Christian institution that protected "inferior," "child-like" people and brought eternal salvation to "heathen" Africans. The evangelical blueprint for gender roles and proper behavior also came to reflect southern reality. It accepted southern male characteristics and used them to make men into public defenders of their society and of slavery, while picturing white women as the guardians of private morality and self-control. This accommodation allowed men to maintain, even to celebrate, their "ungodly" behavior because it served both to separate them from women and to elevate female virtue. Women's piety thus let them off the hook.

Evangelical Christianity also accommodated men's aggressiveness and preoccupation with public reputation, which they used to defend slavery and their status as good Christians against the charges of Yankee abolitionists. As spokesmen for the white community, ministers, planters, and politicians led the way. By the 1830s and 1840s this leadership had developed a full-scale defense of the South as a conservative and Christian, yet also democratic society founded on, and guaranteed by, slavery. When evangelicals admonished men to consider the public implications of private immorality, they also sanctioned the intimate, mutually dependent relationship between individual and community that characterized honor. Evangelicals' "watchful care" encompassed "both the private and public, personal and collective aspects of life," concludes one leading scholar of the movement. It was "a persistent concern with the social character of private acts in which community and individual each had a stake." Finally, when evangelicals acceded to slavery and honor, they also embraced a hierarchical worldview. Militant levelers in the Revolutionary era, evangelical Baptists and Methodists had become nineteenth-century defenders of inequality and the worldly status quo. Thus, although the Great Awakening initially challenged both slavery and secular concepts of masculinity, the ethic of honor and the imperatives of slavery ultimately absorbed and adapted Christianity into the regional definition of manhood. In the end, Mississippi's men could be good Christians and still celebrate their worldly virtues.[18]

Most of all, manliness was something earned, defended, and then reasserted over and over again. "Real men are made, not born," concludes one student of masculinity. The relationship to Mississippians' notion of honor is obvious: a man's individual honor, like that of his family and community, required constant reaffirmation and remained open to challenge. This entailed constant male rivalries as men measured themselves against each other. Of course, societies also understand masculinity as the opposite of femininity (i.e., men are men because they are not women, or children); but the decisive part of the equation for men themselves remained (and remains) male rivalry. As David Leverenz points out, the proposition that masculinity was (is) defined within patriarchy, at home, may be valid for men's private relations with women. But most men measure themselves at work or at play, in public rivalry with one another. "In large part, it's other men who are important to American men," Michael Kimmel concurs: they "define their masculinity, not as much in relation to women, but in relation to one another." Mississippi's white men assumed their basic superiority over all "inferiors," an opinion reinforced constantly by their Protestant ministers and their understanding of evangelical Christianity. But domination over women or children gave men no satisfaction and added nothing to their individual power or status. Therefore, the political culture, which men considered their exclusive public sphere, was defined by their understanding of aggressive, competitive masculinity.[19]

Though obsessed with male rivalry and demonstrating their superiority over one another, men also sought to reduce the inherent dangers of competition by creating a mythology of male bonding that included poker, hunting, and passing the jug. These sorts of activities were (and are) designed to dampen the ever-present contest for manliness and, theoretically, reduce the potential for violence. John Claiborne's description of a hunting party in Mississippi's Piney Woods captures the many functions of such occasions: "[C]heering each other with loud shouts and making the woods ring with the crack of their long whips," men galloped "thirty or forty miles a day and rendezvous[ed] at night at the *stomping ground*. Here they 'bivouac' in the open air," roast a young steer or buck killed during the day's adventures, and this, "with water from an adjoining branch, just touched perhaps with a little *'old corn*,' constitutes the repast." Claiborne may have underestimated the touch of old corn, but his description typifies other accounts of this ubiquitous occasion. A community ritual that confirmed everyone's good nature, it also offered a chance to demonstrate courage, ability, and trustworthiness in a competitive, but sociable, atmosphere. Finally, it can be argued that the necessity for bonding rituals is greatest in societies that are egalitarian and competitive. In nineteenth-century America, realistic expectations of upward mobility and a popular culture committed to "all [white] men are created equal" sharpened the competitive edge and heightened the potential for conflict.[20]

Lawyer and writer Joseph Baldwin understood this public system of male rivalry and obligations as well as anyone. The Mississippi he describes was governed by "the game of winning and losing played in public . . . there is no private occasion because there is no private space." Men scorned "private virtues" as "insufficient [to] constitute identity until openly challenged and tested"; personal integrity and honor only mattered after confirmation from the community at large. Baldwin's account of one bungling provincial, Paul Beechim, conveys the importance Mississippians placed on public image and reputation, and the gravity of shame. Beechim is humiliated in public by a companion, Phillip Cousins, who tricks him into drinking from the finger bowl after dinner. Mortified, Beechim stumbles from the restaurant but gathers himself and later "licked [Cousins] within an inch of his life with a hickory stick." At his trial for assault and battery, the whole story comes out and Beechim is acquitted on the grounds that his act was justified. The judge even commends the defendant for his self-control. "Most men would have seized their gun, or bowie, on such terrible aggravation, and taken the life of the culprit." His honor and the community agreed: such a public shaming demanded that Beechim try to recoup his reputation by giving the scoundrel Cousins a thoroughly "manly" thrashing.[21]

Baldwin's tale suggests the importance of public perceptions but also of status and power. Mastery over others, slave or free, demarcated relations of power between men and accentuated the hierarchical nature of society.

Honorable behavior included loyalty, even obedience, to those of greater status but also required a man to exercise his own power. Thus, as Bertram Wyatt-Brown points out, "the chief problem was the discrepancy between honor as obedience to superior rank and the contrary duty to achieve place for oneself and family." These requirements conflicted, but they also lent stability and mitigated the potentially unending rivalry between men. Besides rites of male bonding, the ancient code offered men of lesser status a way out: there was honor in respecting, even deferring to those of superior rank as long as it stopped short of obsequiousness or fawning. Thus, the conflicting, yet mitigating virtues of independence and deference expressed in the culture of manhood and honor offered a blueprint for southern male behavior.[22]

Slavery added to these hierarchical tendencies because it created white men accustomed to exercising power and receiving obedience in a society committed to the proposition that all men were *not* created equal. Mississippi's Horace Fulkerson remembered how "slavery had wrought its natural effect upon the characters of these [early] planters. Accustomed to implicit and unquestioning obedience, they could illy brook contradiction and opposition from their equals." Planters, he said, "were slow to regard any as their equals except those of their own class." As Mississippians elaborated their slave society, the repercussions of honor and the peculiar institution shaped ethics. "I speak of these things as being natural," concluded Fulkerson, "because they were the necessary consequences of the institution of slavery." Like the demands of honor, hierarchy and deference followed slavery.[23]

Yet, slavery also created a white man's democracy, for even the poorest white tenant was always a free man. Mississippi's frontier conditions also nurtured democratic, egalitarian tendencies. As hundreds of contemporaries testified, a boom-and-bust, speculative economy made some men rich overnight but brought sudden poverty to others. The region's exaggerated geographic and social mobility furthered the impulse to consider individual accomplishments before family lineage or "purity of blood." All of these factors helped set Mississippi and the Old Southwest apart from the southeastern seaboard. "The plainer classes in Virginia," claimed one Mississippi planter's daughter, "recognized the difference between themselves and the higher classes, and did not aspire to social equality." But "in Mississippi the tone was different. They resented anything like superiority in breeding." Many candidates sensed, and appealed to, these voters' shared values. "My wife slept on a shuck mattress, without sheets," claimed Albert Gallatin Brown during one campaign. In one of his first contests, he accused his opponent, Powhatan Ellis, of "effeminacy" and "dandyism," portraying them as the consequences of too much wealth and breeding.[24]

Even in the rough Southwest, though, society matured as the country became more settled. People built schools and churches, saloons and hotels; men joined the Masons and other organizations, including political parties.

And men and women got married. Relatives of spouses from farther east joined them in Mississippi, bringing with them even more extended kin. The transformation took time, but ultimately it magnified the pressure of family and community reputation and the importance of local networks. The change remained incomplete even in 1860, and it proceeded differently from place to place: Bolivar County in 1850 looked much like Warren County in the 1820s. Yet certain commonalities bound the counties together. By 1840 settlers in much of the state lived in familiar neighborhoods and benefitted from a maturing infrastructure that bespoke a more coherent society with class distinctions to sustain a myriad of local hierarchies.[25]

The conflict between egalitarian ideals — and, to some extent, reality — and the hierarchical tendencies of honor and slavery was mediated in the state's face-to-face political culture. Plain folk celebrated their privileged place as white men in a white man's democracy; politicos offered endless paeans to the wisdom, liberty, and sovereignty of the masses. On election day voters demonstrated personal power, loyalty to neighbors and kinsmen, and deference to powerful planters — all at the same time. Grounded in local neighborhoods, Mississippians developed a political culture infused with rituals that allowed men to validate the personal qualities they most admired. Manly independence and American egalitarianism coexisted with deference and hierarchy in Mississippi's hybrid, slave-based, antiparty political culture. There was no place for an institutional party structure that would replace direct, intimate relationships with impersonal bureaucracy, a routine, perfunctory patronage system, and untestable candidates. Thus, as the state's population expanded and neighborhoods matured, men adapted their political culture to the necessities of honor, slavery, and the popular virtues of communal manhood.

Mississippi's most dramatic population growth came after 1815, when treaties with several groups of native Americans opened the rest of the state for settlement. The cotton boom that followed the War of 1812 ensured that the remaining tribes would be forced to move west to accommodate commercial "progress." The Treaty of Doak's Stand, signed with the Choctaws in 1820, opened up a large area along the Mississippi, Pearl, and Yazoo rivers. This region developed quickly in the late 1820s. During Andrew Jackson's presidency the treaties of Dancing Rabbit Creek (1830) and Pontotoc (1832) completed the job of "Indian removal." Driven by avaricious fantasies, immigrants from the Atlantic states, poor and rich farmers and speculators in search of land and wealth, flocked to the fertile Southwest. In 1820 the white population stood at 42,176; ten years later it exceeded 70,000 and by 1840 reached nearly 200,000, a 400-percent increase in twenty years. Demographic growth was only slightly less impressive over the next two decades: the population reached 295,718 by 1850 and just over 350,000 on the eve of secession. The flood of slaves into the state proved even more spectacular: white Mississippians owned about 32,000 blacks in 1820; by 1840 there were almost 200,000 slaves, a 700-percent increase. Like that of the white population, the growth rate of the slave population slowed in the last decades before the war: they numbered about 300,000 in 1850 and 436,000 ten years later. Mississippi's population thus spiraled sharply upward in the two decades following the removal of Indian claims and continued to rise steadily, if less strikingly, between 1840 and 1860.[26]

Increasing population sparked growth of the social and economic infrastructure as men built homes and schools, churches and country stores. Rural neighborhoods that settlers identified as "home" offered one measure of their progress. "Joshua White and others of the neighborhood succeeded in getting a school," wrote Duncan McKenzie to his relatives in North Carolina; several years later he recounted that "John P. Stewart . . . is in this, or rather the adjoining neighborhood teaching school." When he arrived in 1835, Hugh Stewart described the location of his new home to family members as "75 [miles] North West from the neighborhood of D. McKenzie." This way of designating localities often developed because isolated farms and poor roads limited movement for most people to about five square miles. Farmers' demanding work routines, which left little time for traveling — even after better roads were established — further oriented their relations toward local neighbors. Even when clusters of farms blended together, "residents continued to refer to the places where they lived as neighborhoods." Relations with neighbors varied, of course, but whether congenial or belligerent, amicable or quarrelsome, neighborhoods provided the primary foundation for life in a lonely country.[27]

Settlement patterns often reinforced the definition of neighborhoods when friends and kin immigrated together, and many families worked to recreate old residence patterns in their new state. "You will see [my] Brother John," wrote Duncan McKenzie to an old family friend: "Tell him . . . whenever I settle I will try to select a convenient place for him near my own." McKenzie then reassured John himself that there would be friends and property available if he made the long trip to Mississippi. "Your late neighbors the McGils arrived in this settlement about 3 weeks since & rented a place." The correspondence between Duncan McKenzie, John and Hugh Stewart, and their relative Duncan McLaurin in North Carolina detail a web of extended kin and neighbors shared by two communities. Others moved to a particular neighborhood, apparently to stay near friends, and shopped for the right piece of land. Especially in places where speculators failed to gobble up the best land, family or clan migration seems to have been widespread. Along the Chickasawhay River, for instance, South Carolinian William Powe and his extended family recreated much of the community and social structure from which they came. Mary Welsh's father brought his daughter and family to Mississippi in 1834. "The previous year," she remembered, "he had sent by his brother Victor Welsh two hands and mules that he might get preemption and withal make some provision for our arrival." Group migrations such as the McLaurin, Welsh, and Powe families carried out reduced the loneliness and unfamiliarity of moving to the Southwest and fostered neighborhood development—all of which re-established the importance of public reputation.[28]

When strangers moved into their neighborhoods, Mississippians relied on numerous public events to introduce one another and foster a sense of community. Camp meetings, house and barn raisings, hunting parties, militia musters, and rumors of slave insurrection all brought men, and some-times women, together. Religious meetings, in particular, often became family events lasting several days. Quilting bees, corn-shucking contests and other communal events—what one early settler called "social functions in the woods"—all worked to promote sociability and neighborhood identity. Each of these occasions called on men to demonstrate their commitment to each other and to the community. They tested men's reliability and pro-moted a general spirit of cooperation and camaraderie, but also taught new-comers about the distribution of power and status in the local community. For men, competitive contests and demonstration of skill or strength were frequent. Like hunting parties, such occasions were never entirely social but, rather, mixed good cheer with displays of manliness.[29]

As in most American communities, these events were common in Mis-sissippi. Election day, however, was probably the most familiar all-male rit-ual. New residents immediately noticed the sheer number of elections and candidates: "Nearly all of our officers are elected by the people from Gover-nor to the Constable," wrote Jonathan Stewart. "There was an election for Magistrates & constable in this precinct or Captain's beat. There were 6 candidates for the former and 5 for the latter office." He later estimated that "we have [an election] about every three months from deaths [and] resignations." His brother, Allan Stewart, also marveled at the everpresent democratic process. "I have nothing more worth your attention," he wrote to North Carolinian Duncan McLaurin, "save the common news here of candidates & electioneering."[30] In the McLaurins's home state of North Car-olina, important county officials were appointed for life terms and suffrage was limited by property requirements. The same was true in Virginia, where the (nonelective) sheriff appointed his deputies and members of the county court chose their clerks. In Mississippi all these positions, and many more, were elective.[31]

The frequency and inclusiveness of elections became a fundamental part of the state's political culture. Regular and special elections often brought men to the polls several times each year, and on average about 10 percent of the eligible white men would be running for county or precinct office. In the 1843 Madison County general election, for instance, there were between 115 and 120 candidates out of approximately 1,100 eligible voters. In addition, there were election inspectors, clerks, and returning officers at each precinct, meaning that a third to a half of the adult white male population typically played some formal role in the election process beyond casting their vote. Thus, election day provided one of the most common rituals for all men, the chance for a public display of loyalty, sociability, or neighborhood solidarity. The tremendous number of offices on the ballot, usually with multiple candidates, and high voter turnout all contributed to the ritual power of election day. It lent stability to a mobile society, socialized and politicized newcomers, and helped unite the male community.

Mississippi's extraordinary commitment to white male democracy started early in the state's history. Even in the 1820s, compared to residents on the Atlantic seaboard, Mississippians enjoyed great power at the polls. The state's 1832 constitution, however, was one of the most egalitarian and democratic in the country and remained in force until Reconstruction. It swept aside the statutory foundations of aristocracy or privilege, removing property, tax, and militia qualifications for suffrage or office and shortening residency requirements for U.S. citizens to one year in the state and four months in the county or town. Almost all state offices — including secretary of state, treasurer, auditor, and attorney general — became elective rather than appointed.[32]

But what really distinguished the state's commitment to democracy was its extension to county and local offices. The constitution replaced county courts, which had been appointed by the state legislature, with elected boards of police; voters also chose justices of the peace and constables in each precinct. The decision to elect judges was more divisive. "Whole Hogs" wanted to elect all judges; "Half Hogs" agreed to most elections but favored appointment to the state supreme court; and "Aristocrats" opposed all judicial elections. The Whole Hogs, led by future governor Henry Stuart Foote, carried the day. Aristocrat leader John Quitman reportedly lost twenty pounds during the emotional battle but later admitted that the practice of popular election had merit. The controversy largely faded as voters elected mostly veteran, proven judges.[33]

These unusually democratic provisions make Mississippi an ideal place to study political culture and the interaction of democratic politics and social ethics. In particular, it offers a special chance to assess how one southern society solved the conflict between nineteenth-century egalitarian rhetoric and democratic reality and the hierarchical requirements of honor and slavery. Because voters had nearly unprecedented power in Mississippi, the political culture revealed their values and attitudes more completely than it did in most states. All white male adults could participate, and the great majority did. What they said and how they behaved present compelling testimony to the culture and values of the Deep South.

With a growing population and expanded suffrage, a more complete political system evolved in the 1830s. In the preceding decade, the state's social and cultural capital was Natchez, in the extreme southwest corner of the state. Settled during the colonial period, the old Natchez district was home to Mississippi's founding families and most of its wealth — as measured in land and slaves. Natchez planters often favored conservative political practices, including, for example, viva voce elections at the 1817 constitutional convention.[34] In the 1810s and 1820s, however, settlers in new counties to the north and east allied against the Natchez faction to block efforts to ease banking and credit restrictions. Indian removal also set Natchez against most other parts of the state because its leaders realized that their political clout was eroding as each new section was opened for settlement. The anti-Natchez forces displayed their new power in 1827 by choosing Wayne County's Powhatan Ellis as the first senator from the Piney Woods. But farmers exploiting the rich soil along the Pearl River soon realized their common interests with the Natchez planters. In particular — needing credit to buy more slaves, improve land, and fund improvements to facilitate cotton shipments — they reversed their contrariness toward banks. Eventually, they supported a branch of the Bank of the United States, which opened in Natchez in 1831. Territorial expansion and demographic changes, then, translated into a series of shifting political alliances during the state's first fifteen years.[35]

As in many other southern states, the presidency of Andrew Jackson helped generate the development of parties. The president's standing among Mississippians rested primarily on his military exploits and support for Indian removal, and he carried the state easily in all three presidential campaigns. While Jackson remained personally popular, however, opposition to some of his policies generated rival factions that coalesced around several disgruntled leaders. The Nullification Crisis and the president's threat of force against South Carolina, as elsewhere in the South, precipitated the first popular break with Old Hickory. Mississippi's Nullifiers, led by John Quitman, bolted the Jackson standard in 1833–1834 and joined with a smaller opposition group, then called National Republicans. The Nullifiers never gained a large following (although they were a significant minority) among Mississippi's voters; Jackson's personal popularity and support for Indian removal apparently seemed more important to most voters than some vague statement of principle. The other faction of what became Mississippi Whiggery resulted from Jackson's "war" on the Bank of the United States and his choice of New York's Martin Van Buren to replace Vice President John C. Calhoun. Although the three dissident factions came together in 1834, the Democrats carried the state for Van Buren in 1836. Yet the relative uncertainty of party politics had allowed the Whigs to elect one of two House representatives and the governor in 1835. Growth of party influence was even slower in state legislative elections. In Hinds County, for instance, because neither party could control the nomination process, eleven men ran for the legislature.[36]

Regional patterns of settlement created by immigration also affected these nascent party divisions. Federalists, and eventually Whigs, predominated in the older southwestern plantation belt centered in Natchez and the

lower Mississippi Delta. Those areas had been opened for American settlement during the nation's early years of Federalist ascendancy after Pinck-
ney's Treaty in 1795. East of the Natchez district, the Piney Woods opened
in 1805, and a solid majority of voters in the area favored Thomas Jefferson's
party. After the 1830 and 1832 treaties with the Choctaw and Chickasaw
tribes, white settlers swarmed into central, north, and east-central Mississippi, which soon became the most populous region in the state. By 1840,
notes one historian, "over one half of the white population resided in counties that had not even existed ten years earlier."[37] Farmers filled these new
counties at the height of Jackson's fame, fixing Democratic loyalty on a
generation of Mississippi voters and, usually, their children. This tide of
settlers, most of whom owed their new lands and expectant prosperity to his
harsh removal policy, flooded the Old Hero's party. Jackson's frontier warrior
image only added to his popularity among men who prized the same virtues.
Even the moniker Mississippi's Democrats gave themselves — the "Unterri-
fied" — reflected their admiration of manly physical courage.

As Whigs and Democrats evolved into these heterogenous factions, their
core activists struggled to create stable organizations and cement the loyalty
of voters. Persistent antipartyism, however, limited their success. Antiparty
fears drew on the nation's Revolutionary heritage and republican fear of
cliques and "unnatural combinations." Men who supported such organizations, republican critics preached, pandered to selfish individualism rather
than promoting the commonweal. Democrats in particular had to fight the
popular perception of Van Buren as the caucus candidate. "A tremendous
effort was made by the 'Van Burenites' to fix down the Caucus Yoke on this
State," wrote one Mississippi voter in 1835. Typical rhetoric condemned caucus nominations as "a system at once abhorrent and odious; one which
strikes at the very foundation of our free and happy institutions."[38]

Despite this antiparty tradition, most historians contend that Mississippi's parties achieved a high degree of stability and nearly fanatical loyalty by
the late 1830s. Rigid party organization — in particular the convention system
and the official nomination of candidates — purportedly replaced personal
relationships. In short, party loyalty superseded the haphazard arrangement
of factional or neighborhood interests. By 1837, concludes one recent
scholar, antipartyism was "obsolete." Between 1835 and 1839, voters developed strong loyalties and indicated their widespread acceptance of parties.
In the "new political climate," argues another study, "party endorsement was
a *sine qua non* for political advancement."[39] Democrats led the switch to
party organization, using county meetings and a state convention in 1834–
1835, although with mixed results. When they withdrew from the practice in
1837 and did poorly, party leaders blamed the result on the abandonment of
regular nominating procedures. In 1839, therefore, the party permanently
returned to nomination by conventions. The Whigs also adopted the convention system in 1839 "against some resistance and, although the party

structure was not as mature as the Democrats', it represented a significant and final break from the past."[40] Antiparty rhetoric, which was central to all politics in the 1840s and 1850s, did seem less evident in the late 1830s.

It is undoubtedly true that parties had enthusiastic supporters, and certain conditions did seem to facilitate organization. Many voters were forced to follow party labels in national and state elections because they could not know candidates personally. At the local level, parties seemed more effective when the uncertainty of new and rapid settlement made voters unsure of their neighbors. When frontier conditions remained most unsettled — before permanent churches and stores, before militia musters or regular court days — men were most unfamiliar with one another and parties apparently peaked. In 1845 Bolivar County, just a few years after its formation, returning officer William Harmon recorded votes in two columns headed "Democratic" and "Whig." Even for county posts, including the board of police, his returns suggested that voters drew party lines. In this county's first years, as it filled with newcomers, voters may have needed party labels to sort out candidates. Less than five years later, however, Bolivar's county contests showed no trace of party influence. By then the settlers had established neighborhoods and personal relationships and no longer needed parties. Elsewhere, in 1841 Canton, the Whig editor argued for party nominations for the board of police. In Pontotoc, that same year, a resident complained of "servile party sycophants" and "caucus dictation" in county and local contests: "From the Chief Executive to the most unimportant Beat Officer," he claimed, "hollow hearted demogogues" were "sent forth by the Caucus' to the people." Perhaps his protests were successful, because in a few years county returns from Pontotoc showed no evidence of partisan voting.[41] Parties also seemed more important in Mississippi's older and more populous counties, especially those, like Warren (Vicksburg) and Adams (Natchez), with towns and competing newspapers. These unusual characteristics placed them at the vanguard of socioeconomic development and diversity, which sometimes, although still only rarely, gave core activists a chance to push party organization.

Rather than demonstrating popular support for parties, however, evidence from the 1840s and 1850s suggests that the voters continued to reject parties whenever possible. Instead of stable organizations and voter loyalty, Mississippi politics in the decades prior to 1860 reflected the continuing power of antipartyism. Neither Democrats nor Whigs developed an organization strong enough to control nominations regularly; outside of party workers, newspaper editors, and state candidates themselves, few Mississippians apparently conceived of politics in partisan terms. Public rhetoric and the voters' behavior all suggested that the state's parties peaked in the late 1830s but declined after 1840–1841. The contours of this evolution ebbed and flowed to some extent, depending on a county's time of settlement and conditions; generally, parties seemed more successful during the frontier stage.

Party success was evidently a necessity, and not a choice, for the parties weakened after a short time. Their brief, limited success also suggests that their hold on voters was never intense, and virtually no one—even core activists—ever defended parties as a good idea in themselves.

In the vast majority of elections, those for county and local offices, voters did have a choice, and they largely chose to avoid parties in favor of personal politics. This attitude conformed to the values of communal manhood and honor that celebrated both personal independence and loyalty to other local men. Most voters preferred to rely on their neighbors and kinsmen, men they knew personally and felt more comfortable entrusting with the defense of the community. Thus notions of masculine loyalty combined with the nation's republican ideology to perpetuate an antiparty political culture. "We are called upon to say whether we will sanction the vile, slavish doctrines of *caucusism*," wrote one editor, mixing the classic images of republicanism and masculinity. "We know that you are possessed of moral and physical courage," he continued, "that you possess the unconquered spirits of *American freemen*" and the "hearts of *southern* men."[42] Rooted in the face-to-face relationships that sustained honor and defined masculinity, the state's antiparty, noninstitutional political system was fired in the savage 1820s, refined in the 1830s and 1840s, and matured in the 1850s, and resulted, ultimately, in secession and Civil War.

More than attitudes about manliness and honor, however, frontier conditions and the state's early history contributed to the weakness of parties. Poor roads in most areas affected men's ability to attend meetings and conventions as late as the 1850s. Furthermore, events at the state and national levels undermined party development. There were two especially divisive state issues in the early 1840s: the banking system in general and the fate of several million dollars worth of state-guaranteed bonds issued by banks that failed in the depression following the Panic of 1837. A mania of speculation had gripped Mississippi in the early 1830s; anyone with some resources borrowed more and invested them in new land and slaves. The emergence of "King Cotton" fostered the spirit of reckless optimism, materialistic rapacity, and human greed that Baldwin captures so vividly in *Flush Times*. "The people here are run mad with speculation," claimed one 1836 visitor to Mississippi. "They do business in . . . a kind of phrenzy. Money is scarce, but credit is plenty, and he who has no money can do as much business as he who has."[43]

Because of record public land sales, Mississippi's banks filled with deposits, which they loaned again, freely, to speculators and farmers. But in 1836 President Jackson's Specie Circular and the Deposit Act leveled the state's financial house of paper. The circular required settlers and speculators to purchase federal land with gold or silver, siphoning off virtually all the hard currency in circulation. The Deposit Act had even more calamitous effects; it required banks to distribute all money from federal land sales to the states in quarterly payments throughout 1837. Because so much public land had been sold in the state, Mississippi banks had collected a huge amount (over six million dollars), but they had loaned out much of it to finance further investments. Under the terms of the new law, however, Mississippi was entitled to keep only $500,000. Thus, in 1836 and 1837 the state was drained of federal money, prompting many banks to call in loans. When debtors could not pay, both settlers and the banks faced ruin. An 1837 investigation of banking in the state revealed that the ratio of coin to paper money in circulation was one to fifteen and that the banks had acquired less than half of their prescribed capital.[44]

The depression that followed this cycle of collapse rivaled some of the bleakest moments in American economic history. Residents moved west to Arkansas, Louisiana, and Texas, fleeing creditors and bad memories alike; plantations stood empty while the courts filled with petitioners seeking debt relief. Many faced public auction. Travelers such as John Claiborne and Jehu Orr remarked on the devastation. Claiborne noted the "memorials of the former wealth and prosperity of this [Wayne] county." The "palsying hand of time" had exposed "miserable tenements—the wrecks of better times!" Waxing poetic, Orr compared the abandoned plantations to "bits of wreckage and flotsam marking the unseen graves of those who have perished there." Another resident claimed that a "large number" of "planters, merchants and politicians are completely Bankrupt in fortune and some in reputation." In 1842, Jonathan Stewart recorded that land values were down 50 percent and "the price of Negroes is nominal." The severity of the crisis sobered Mississippians and forced a reassessment of their financial system. The bank issue suddenly dominated politics.[45]

Democrats exploited the growing antipathy toward banks with great success by denouncing them in general and supporting the independent treasury scheme. Distinguishing between good and bad banks, the Whigs pointed out that Democrats had controlled the state legislature in 1836 and 1837 when most of the failed banks were chartered. Democrats, however, did better with their all-out attack: in Canton, the *Independent Democrat* actually included the phrase "separation from banks" on its masthead. The most lasting political question to come out of the depression, however, was the fate of bonds issued by the Union Bank. State legislators hoped that this institution, which was chartered after the Panic had already begun, would stem the tide of failure by resuming specie payments and following more rigorous loan policies. Most importantly, the state legislature guaranteed the bank's bonds, which were issued in return for capital investment. When this bank failed, too, taxpayers suddenly found themselves on the hook for millions of dollars worth of bonds.[46]

Governor Alexander McNutt was the first to suggest officially that Mississippi repudiate the Union Bank bonds; in his annual message of January 1841, he claimed that "fraudulent" bond sales nullified the people's responsibility to honor the debt. Although he couched it in constitutional language, the governor recognized a plain truth: there was simply not enough money in the state to pay off the bonds. "Such an enormous tax can never be collected from the hard earnings of the people of this State," McNutt admitted. "They will not elect representatives who will impose it, or tax gatherers who will collect it." Yet despite these dire predictions, the Democratic-controlled legislature resolved to pay the bonds, hoping to protect the state's credit and honor. The bond issue took center stage in 1841, when Whigs generally supported paying the bonds and, in contrast to their usual apathy, ran an organized campaign to elect Methodist minister David Shattuck governor. A majority of Democratic voters supported repudiation and the party's nominee Tilghman Tucker. The Democrats won again, and the next legislature passed a resolution that effectively repudiated the bonds.[47]

Although Democrats generally supported repudiation and Whigs opposed it, the bond issue never divided Mississippians on strict partisan lines. A significant minority of bond-paying Democrats worked with Whigs throughout the antebellum period. In 1843 leading Whigs praised candidates on the "Democratic Bond-Paying Ticket for Congress" and throughout the decade supported Democrats who favored "fusion" on the bond question. During the same period, "independent" and bond-paying Democratic candidates ran for the state legislature, sometimes on the same ticket with Whigs. One exasperated resident resorted to the terms *anti-bond men* and *pseudo-Democrats* in an attempt to make sense of the bewildering party landscape.[48]

This powerful state issue also affected local politics. Duncan McKenzie claimed that "the State Bond question is agitated by the different candidates from the constable to the Governor." In 1839 Port Gibson's John Skinner proclaimed himself a candidate for constable and a stern opponent of the "Brandon and Grenada" banks: "I look upon them as barbarous wolves," he declared. One Whig editor urged his readers to support only bond-payers, even at the local level. "Heretofore we have voted a mixed ticket, but at this [county] election we shall vote for no repudiator." Like sectionalism in the next decade, the bond issue cut across party lines and — unlike the usual Whig-Democratic contests — excited voters enough to penetrate past the state level.[49]

Devoid of banks and starved for capital, the Mississippi economy limped through the early 1840s. But the soil was simply too rich and the population growing too fast for the economy to stagnate very long. When cotton prices rose in the mid-1840s, the boom returned and continued virtually uninterrupted until the war. After 1850 more and more of the state's farmers cultivated cotton and exploited the growing rail network to tap external markets. Productivity also improved. In 1849 the state ranked third nationally among cotton producers; but ten years later, with no increase in the percentage of Mississippians engaged in farming, it produced over one-fifth of the country's total crop. The economy, then, though not diversified in exports, grew through the last decade of the antebellum period.[50]

The banking and repudiation issues dominated state elections between 1839 and 1843; the bond-paying faction, which was strongest among Whigs, lost all of them. These repeated failures, followed by Henry Clay's surprising defeat in 1844, sapped Whig enthusiasm. Editor William Jacobs made a pathetic appeal to his town's Whigs in 1845, urging them to rally, although "we cannot expect to succeed in the coming election."[51] War with Mexico further disrupted the state's ineffective party system and united Mississippi's voters in support of a "southern war for slavery." The Compromise of 1850 realigned voters yet again, creating new organizations for the 1851 campaign that lingered into 1853. Thus state and national issues upset Mississippi's incipient parties during the period when they might have matured. The conditions and events of the 1840s bolstered the state's dominant antipartyism and destroyed effective party organizations.

The state's early settlers fought rugged, wild conditions. Men's pride in their physical conquest of such a savage land imbued their culture with reverence for personal independence and ferocity but also for loyalty to neighbors and kin. Living in rural neighborhoods and conducting their lives through a series of face-to-face encounters, Mississippians placed extraordinary value on public behavior and honor. As communities matured the force of family connections and reputation became even greater. At the same time, notions of manliness handed down from the frontier years and sustained by slavery endured. Men infused their political culture with the same cultural imperatives, eventually using manliness and regional honor as the lingua franca of the sectional crisis. Finally, the state's political culture demonstrated that most voters showed little confidence in parties or party activists. In fact, it needed to remain antiparty in order to function properly; face-to-face politics allowed voters to mediate between independence and democracy and the hierarchical tendencies in a culture founded on the conviction that all men were not created equal. Voters made most decisions based on individual relationships and public reputation and, in the process, invested all political conflict and rhetoric with a personal quality. In 1860 this way of thinking would combine, ominously, with their sense of manliness and honor.

Ten years earlier, however, the voters faced a similar sectional crisis. The events of 1849 to 1851 revealed the essential features of the state's political culture. The language of antipartyism, manliness, and honor never rang out more clearly.

2

EARLY AUTUMN

An Episode from Mississippi's Political Culture—
The Secession Debate of 1849–1851

Between 1849 and 1851 Mississippians wrestled with a number of sectional issues: the Wilmot Proviso, California's possible admission to the Union as a free state, and the Compromise of 1850. At first uniting men across party lines, these problems ultimately divided the state's voters into new factions supporting or opposing the compromise and culminated in a convention to consider secession. Throughout the long controversy, men's behavior and rhetoric exemplified the foremost qualities of Mississippi's antebellum political culture. First, it betrayed voters' feeble attachment to the Whig and Democratic parties as thousands of men discarded their former affiliations in favor of new ones. The 1851 contests at every level evinced an energy and intensity far greater than earlier contests between the two old parties. Second, the nearly two-year-long debate — really one uninterrupted political season — revealed a common discourse among Mississippi voters as they confronted northern "insults." Partisans on both sides employed the same vocabulary and invoked the same set of symbols rooted in powerful notions of manhood, honor, and Christianity, along with images of family and community. Finally, and most portentous of all, was the unanimity with which men reacted to northern rhetoric: they assessed and interpreted it on a personal level from within the framework of honor that linked every individual with his community.

When Pennsylvania's David Wilmot introduced his Free Soil proviso in the U.S. House of Representatives, he touched off a political protest that erased party lines throughout the Lower South. During 1849 Mississippians expressed their outrage in several mass meetings, at which many Whigs and Democrats spoke with one voice. One of the first indications of a new consensus was the Central Association meeting held in Jackson in October. The gathering was initially proposed by Democratic editors who were soon joined by many Whigs. The newspapers sparked public agitation as leading men from both parties, supported by local meetings across the state, endorsed the bipartisan October convention.[1] At their third-district convention, for example, Democrats resolved "to lay aside all party feeling" and make common defense against the "antislavery" North. Most county meetings were explicitly bipartisan and chose an equal number of Whig and Democratic delegates. Citizens in Carroll County expressed outrage at northern actions and resolved that "the chairman of this meeting is requested to appoint six delegates (three of each political party) to represent the county of Carroll in the Southern State Convention." In Coahoma County, Patrick W. Tompkins and J. J. Davenport, a Whig congressman and well-known Democrat, respectively, urged citizens to forget party differences on the all-important issues of slavery and southern rights. Even in county nominating conventions, Democrats from Holmes, Madison, and Rankin, for instance, all made explicit appeals to the Whigs.[2]

When the delegates met in October of 1849, they selected William L. Sharkey, Mississippi's leading Whig, and Democratic Governor Joseph W. Matthews as president and vice-president of the convention. In his address, President Sharkey urged delegates to "lay aside party predilections, and meet it [northern aggression], not as politicians, but as patriots—as statesmen." Unity was the essence of the convention. Since the initial call for the convention had come from several Democratic editors, selection of arch-Whig Sharkey sent a clear message of nonpartisanship. The meeting also endorsed the upcoming Nashville convention slated to discuss a cooperative response by all the southern states. In this initial phase, then—after the Wilmot Proviso but prior to the Compromise of 1850—Mississippians made a firm bipartisan response. The *Vicksburg Whig*'s editor published a typical condemnation of the hated proviso. He claimed that most northerners and southerners agreed that climate and other factors prohibited slavery in the new territory, so why pass the hated measure? It was, he concluded, only to "taunt and insult" the South; it would have grave consequences, because southern men would never endure such "oppression." Northern "aggression," it seemed, united voters across party lines.[3]

In the 1849 regular elections, moreover, Mississippi's Whigs and Democrats demonstrated a telling lack of partisanship. The Whigs in particular seemed ambivalent about mounting a challenge. When Democratic editors speculated about making General John Quitman their nominee, one Whig editor wrote that he "is a brave man and an honorable one, and if a member of that party is to fill the gubernatorial chair during the ensuing term, *we* would greatly prefer him to any other that we know of."[4] Quitman, a hero of the recent Mexican War and widely regarded as a military chieftain, was a former bond-payer and popular with many Whigs. Even in midsummer, partisans seemed unconcerned that there were no moves toward assembling a slate of Whig candidates. In Madison County local Whigs apparently preferred farming to politics. "We have conversed with many of our political friends from the country," the editor in Canton reported, "and they inform us that [with] late frosts, and the amount of work to be done at home, they are not anxious to open this year's political campaign" until the summer. As late as June, Whigs in Claiborne County wanted "no partisan action during the summer and fall."[5]

Even after the Whigs fixed a date for their state convention, some members remained diffident. In Port Gibson they admitted "no measures of State policy, on which parties are divided" and declared that "no good" could come of a Whig state convention. The local editor recommended that the party choose some candidates for Congress in the various district conventions and, if it was imperative "to nominate a Gubernatorial candidate in opposition to Gen. Quitman (with whose election we would be quite well satisfied), why let us take up Major Bradford, and vote for him." The editor finally admitted, however, that he would participate in the Whig convention if it was held. Vicksburg's editor decided in May that he was "in favor of running a candidate for Governor" but hoped the party could avoid a "divisive" and naturally "unpopular" convention.[6] Some Whigs finally met in the late summer heat of Jackson, although only sixteen of the state's fifty-nine counties sent delegates. After changing their name to the "Taylor Republican party," they nominated General Thomas Polk for governor. Polk was from Port Gibson, but even there he failed to spark interest among local Whigs. The citizens of his home town organized no rallies to convince the general to accept the nomination, which he eventually declined. In mid-August the party still had no candidate. Jackson attorney Luke Lea finally agreed to run as the Whig nominee for governor, but it took another month for the party to find a congressional candidate in the fourth district.[7]

This ineptitude and lack of commitment to the convention system characterized Whig campaigns throughout the 1840s. During the supposed height of the second party system, Mississippi's Whigs seemed unwilling or unable to muster much enthusiasm for party organization. In 1841 Whigs gathered delegates from thirty-five counties at their Jackson convention, although nearly half of them came from host Hinds County. Two years later they offered to endorse the Democrats' gubernatorial nominee if he was a bond-payer. Not surprisingly, Whig delegates from only thirty counties bothered to attend the convention that year. In 1845 the party nearly bottomed out with a "meeting" that represented about a dozen counties but declined to make formal nominations. The man "recommended" for governor decided not to run and the party had no candidate until October 10, less than three weeks before the election. In Madison and Yazoo counties, both traditionally Whiggish, voters never did get the message, because the local editor misidentified the party's candidate. On October 17 he announced that "Isaac N. Davis is now our candidate for Governor, than whom none is more trustworthy." Perhaps, but there was one big problem: the nominee was actually Colonel Thomas Coopwood. The error appeared three weeks before the election, and the party failed to correct it; voters in the two counties cast over a thousand votes for Davis and only one for Coopwood. That same year, the *Vicksburg Whig* repeatedly confused the names of its party's candidates. For Congress, the paper initially reported, the candidate was Walter Brooke, later corrected to Walker Brooke; for secretary of state George Torrey, but changed to John L. Torrey; for treasurer William Gray, but sometimes Joseph P. Gray; and for auditor, either Joseph Williams or John Williams. Such miserable communication barely qualified the Whigs as an organized party.[8]

The Whig experience in 1847 further disheartened party enthusiasts. They held no convention at all and by late September still had no candidates for state office. "[W]e have candidates for Congress in several districts," lamented one editor, "but as regards a State ticket, we are positively *nowhere!*" He suggested some possibilities for governor and urged the party to decide on one before any more time slipped by. Not until October 16, two weeks before the election, did the paper announce that General A. B. Bradford was the Whig candidate for governor. Democrats could scarcely fail to notice their opponents' ineptitude. Editor Benjamin Dill reminded John Quitman in September that "the Whigs offer no organised opposition to our slate of candidates."[9] Throughout the 1840s, the Whigs often failed to find state nominees on the first try and sometimes ran multiple candidates (as did the Democrats occasionally). One Whig editor summarized the attitude of many fellow partisans: "There is a growing dislike of the whole partizan convention system in this community, we have never seen any good result from them, they being ever controlled by a clique of wire workers, who totally disregard the wishes of the masses, and we are therefore not at present disposed to take any part or lot in such matters."[10] Thus, the party's history belies historians' claims that Mississippi's Whigs and Democrats were committed finally or irrevocably to the convention system.

Many Democrats also complained about a nominating system that favored candidates from the state capital. In 1849 Jasper County partisans argued that no one should be allowed on the convention floor who was not an accredited, voting delegate. "The distant counties are most generally represented by one or two gentlemen, and frequently by proxy," they explained, "while the counties contiguous to the capital appoint some twenty or thirty delegates . . . who exert undue influence upon the Convention by their presence." This was not simply a self-serving protest, for Jasper County was itself relatively close to the capital. Other critics objected that delegates from the other counties simply ratified the prearranged decisions of Jackson's party leaders. In 1849, typically, the editors of the state Democratic organ, the *Mississippian*, faced charges that their Jackson clique would "rig" the whole convention "as usual." They defended the convention system at length, arguing that it prevented the election of someone like Zachary Taylor, a man without any "established creed." The editors insisted that the actual nominee was unimportant as long as he was committed to the party's principles—a claim many in outlying counties found spurious at best. Clearly some Democrats in and around the capital liked conventions, but others remained skeptical. These regular complaints in rural newspapers underscored a smoldering resentment of conventions and "party dictation" that characterized many Democrats outside Jackson, where even active partisans commonly expressed doubts about the party system.[11]

Reuben Davis's "independent" candidacy in 1849 summarized some common complaints and suggested that many voters acquiesced in the convention system reluctantly. Something of a maverick, Davis announced his intention to run for Congress in the state's second district without a nomination from the Democratic state convention. He later explained his aborted campaign as one motivated by the voters' opposition to conventions. During the previous two elections, he maintained, the Whigs had taken advantage of the "caucus" issue; their most effective tactic was "the abandonment by them of party ties and party principles." The Whigs shrewdly condemned the convention system, Davis continued, because "they full well know a very extensive and very just opposition exists in the body of the party that resorts to its use."[12] Davis's phraseology not only intimated that contemporaries considered the Whigs an "antiparty party" but also suggested enmity toward conventions among Democratic voters.

In 1849 the Democrats did nominate General Quitman for governor. They mustered delegates from only thirty-nine of fifty-nine counties, although compared to their opponents they ran an organized campaign. Yet, with sectional tension mounting, the entire campaign seemed especially lackluster. The almost complete lack of partisanship showed in the district three race for Congress. "Taylor Republican" nominee Henry Gray vowed to vote against any new national bank, a higher tariff, internal improvements, or distribution of money from federal land sales (all traditionally advocated by the national Whig party). He further swore to denounce his own president if Taylor signed a bill that endorsed Free Soil. The only difference between Gray and his opponent, William McWillie, seemed to be the former's greater confidence in Taylor as a southerner and his belief that "Old Zack" would veto the Wilmot Proviso. One Democratic observer reported sardonically after a debate between the two candidates that he remained unsure as to which party each belonged.[13] Quitman won an easy victory, helped by his status as war hero and supporter of southern rights. Some voters probably associated the gubernatorial election with the southern movement and saw Quitman as a more vigorous and prestigious champion than the obscure Luke Lea. The November election, held only a few weeks after the statewide bipartisan October convention, showed Mississippians largely united in their opposition to northern "aggression."

The Compromise of 1850, however, broke up the unanimity among Mississippi's voters. Its provisions included admission of California as a free state, resolution of the Texas–New Mexico boundary dispute, and organization of the southwest territory gained from Mexico without restrictions on slavery. Although it abolished the slave trade in the District of Columbia, it upheld the institution there and supported a stringent fugitive slave law. As early as January 1850, men were dividing over whether to acquiesce in these congressional measures or resist them as unfair to southern interests. Mississippi's Democratic congressional delegation told their constituents that they considered the proposal to admit California an attempt to implement the hated Wilmot Proviso. Next, Henry Clay introduced his compromise which was designed to solve all outstanding difficulties between the sections. These key developments — California's constitution and Clay's adjustment measures — polarized southern public opinion.

In late February, men "friendly to the Union" and favoring Clay's compromise began meeting in Jackson and other towns. Although the Whigs initially dominated these meetings, Democrats soon joined them. Observers frequently commented on the cooperation between former Whigs and Democrats: "There was no bank question, or sub-treasury question, or tariff question raised," reported one Unionist, but simply "friends of the Union" standing "shoulder to shoulder." In several weeks, contemporaries noted, former rivals put aside their old loyalties. Throughout March and April men rallied for the Union; in May some Democratic newspapers began to defect from opposition to the compromise. The *Monroe Democrat* criticized the incapacity of the recent state legislature, which was controlled by its own party. The legislators, editor William D. Chapman wrote, agitated for disunion and resistance to northern aggression simply to curry favor with the voters; he concluded that "There never has been concentrated about our state capitol such an amount of bastard patriotism and unmitigated demagogueism as assembled there last winter."[14]

A new partisan order took shape as the compromise worked its way through Congress during the summer and fall of 1850. One of the central figures who piloted the adjustment bills through the Senate was Mississippi's Henry Stuart Foote. A political maverick in the 1830s dubbed Colonel Weathercock by his opponents, Foote had been a Democrat for several years. Although opposed to Free Soil, he supported the admission of California as part of an overall compromise package and worked with Illinois's Stephen Douglas to get the related measures through the upper house. Mississippi's other senator, Jefferson Davis, opposed the compromise, and public opinion back home coalesced around these two leaders. When the entire compromise finally passed both houses of Congress in late September, Governor Quitman added fuel to the political fire by calling a special legislative session to discuss the measures and Mississippi's possible response. The legislators recommended holding a convention to consider the state's options, including secession, and scheduled an election of delegates for September 1–2, 1851. This election quickly became a contest between the new Union and State-Rights parties.

Just as Whigs initially provided the core of Union Party supporters, Democrats at first led the emerging opposition to compromise. But, like its opponent, the State-Rights Party soon drew strength from both of the old organizations. As one contemporary wrote to a friend, "the Democratic and Whig parties here are cut into fragments and these fragments have formed Union and Disunion [State-Rights] parties." Some Whigs wrote their local newspapers, urging fellow partisans to oppose the compromise and join the new party. "A *Whig* presided over our County meeting," wrote the new party's central committeemen to one county secretary, "and Whigs were appointed among the delegates to the June convention." Another contemporary penned a series of articles for his local paper detailing the breakdown of old partisanship and the rise of new organizations. The editors of the *Mississippian* also explained to Whigs who joined the State-Rights Party that a convention — described as a Democratic tradition — was the best means to organize and ensure victory. Thus, while Democrats often led the State-Rights campaign, they recognized the presence and importance of their new Whig allies.[15]

Newspapers as well as voters reflected the breakdown of partisanship. In November of 1850 the Jackson *Southron* became *The Flag of the Union*, Whig Thomas Palmer and Democrat Dr. Edward Pickett presiding. Editor W. H. Jones of the Jacinto *Democrat*, in Tishomingo County, changed his masthead to the *North Mississippi Union* in January of 1851 when he deserted the State-Rights cause. Some newspapers formerly aligned with one party or the other were independent for a time, then became committed to one of the new parties. The *Ripley Advertiser* followed this pattern, finally coming out in support of the Unionists in July of 1851.[16] In Columbus William D. Chapman and J. R. Smith began a new paper, the *Southern Standard*, dedicated to the State-Rights cause. The editors vowed to support southern rights and states' rights independently of either new party, even beyond the current election and regardless of its outcome. "It will be the aim of the publishers," Chapman and Smith stated in classic antiparty language, "to elevate the Standard above party and the vituperating bitterness of grovelling party spirit and the degrading vocabulary of partisan demagogues." Chapman and Smith remained true to their antiparty principles, criticizing Whigs, Democrats, Unionists, and State-Righters alike. "It is now . . . our settled determination to rise above party," the editors concluded, "and merge these Southern issues into general issues." Nonetheless, in July, they endorsed the State-Rights ticket.[17]

The State-Rights party nominated Quitman, archsecessionist, for governor. His strident support for disunion went beyond his own party's more moderate platform, which preached resistance to the compromise and defense of southern rights but did not openly advocate secession.[18] Quitman set the tone for his party, however, despite its platform. Editors Chapman and Smith, for example, withheld their endorsement of Quitman until July precisely because they deprecated disunion. They wanted to form yet another new party—one committed to southern rights but opposed to disunion. The Union Party chose Senator Foote for governor and filled the state ticket with other Democrats, demonstrating to voters that they were not the Whigs "in disguise." Foote, an acclaimed stump speaker, bettered his opponent in a series of debates. He remembered Quitman as the "dullest and most prosy speaker I have ever known"; Reuben Davis declared Foote himself "the best stump speaker then living." The two candidates actually came to blows in Sledgeville, prompting cancellation of their joint speaking tour.[19]

The entire campaign, in fact, was unusually violent, causing dozens of duels and probably hundreds of fistfights. One local candidate recorded that "Jim Kelly killed Jim Simmons at Rocky Point on Saturday after we left" the debate. The previous week he had witnessed a confrontation between two men on opposite sides of the compromise measures; it resulted in part from a rumor that one had called the other a "damned abolitionist." Newspapers reported the threat of violence at nearly every rally, and candidates scheduled to speak carried "extra" weapons. One Mississippian observed to a friend in Virginia that "politics are running high. . . . There are so many shooting frolics among the people & candidates here that instead of inlisting the public's sympathy, as they do with you [in Virginia], they are more frequently turned into ridicule. We have a great set of Political Demagogues hunting office on the Hobby Union & Disunionism." Comparing Mississippi politics to those of the Old Dominion, this voter found his new home notable for tough, riotous characters and the constant threat of violence. One older resident, perhaps showing a deeper perspective than these young upstarts, declared that "there is more excitement than I have noticed since the embargo and late war [of 1812] with the english."[20]

In the September election for delegates the Union Party earned a majority, carrying forty-one out of fifty-nine counties. Quitman accurately viewed the outcome as a vote against secession and a personal defeat, and he immediately resigned his candidacy. State-Rights activists eagerly accepted his withdrawal and convinced Jefferson Davis to replace him. "By indiscretion & the want of judgement," wrote Powhatan Ellis, "I am apprehensive that the Democratic party is scattered to the four winds of Heaven. The late election for the State Conventions overwhelmed it. We are however making proper efforts to retrieve the fortunes of the day."[21] Davis and the party press worked hard to convince voters that secession was no longer an issue, although the opposition worked equally hard to remind voters that Davis's candidacy made no difference—it was still a choice between union and disunion. State-Rights leaders increasingly appealed to past partisanship, hoping to exploit the state's Democratic majority. Given another month Davis's personal popularity and more moderate approach might have succeeded, but Foote survived to win the governor's chair by a thousand votes.

The Union Party's victory depended in large measure on the destruction of old party loyalties. As the Whig Party, defeat was inevitable. Yet sectionalism was powerful enough to convince many voters to abandon their former loyalties and take up the banner of a new party. As one citizen concluded: "The whigs say it is immaterial to them, whether they are called whigs or democrats, if they are doing battle in the right cause; so says the democrats."[22] Both parties, in fact, relied on what spokesmen perceived as a widespread distrust of party organization and professional politicians. Editor F. G. Baldwin of the Unionist *Primitive Republican* considered his new party a temporary organization whose life should not continue after the current election: "We would consider its [the Union Party's] unnecessary and invidious continuance as the source of much evil." Baldwin, normally an independent editor, probably represented extreme antipartyism, but even partisan editors tapped that strain of the voters' hostility. "Party drill" seemed so essential to the State-Rights partisans, claimed another Unionist editor, that they cannot conceive of honest voters working independently of "spoils-hungry politicians." State-Rights spokesmen used the same logic in attacking the Unionists. *Union* was a good name for the party, they often said, because it was a "union of disaffected and disappointed politicians" bound together for one object: duping innocent voters to get themselves elected so they could feed at the public trough.[23] Thus, running throughout the rhetoric of 1850–1851 was a strong current of antipartyism expressed equally often by spokesmen of both parties. It reflected the reality of tenuous partisanship and a widely perceived lack of faith in professional, "huckster" politicians and the machinations of conventions and caucuses.

The speeches, editorials, and letters of Mississippians also explain why they had such different reactions to the compromise. The common rhetoric and symbols of honor and manliness were used by partisans on both sides, and all voters seemed to consider the problem from within the antiparty, noninstitutional political culture. But opinion divided and the battle lines hardened over whether or not the compromise denied southern equality and manhood. One young voter summarized how men in Mississippi assessed northern rhetoric and the threat of compromise: "Political feeling is now much as it has been. There is unity of feeling as regards that matter [sectionalism and the Compromise]," and disagreement "only in this particular[:] a portion appear to think that the aggressions are already sufficient to withhold resistance no longer, while others dreading consequences cast a happy thot [sic] to the time when matters of so much interest may be settled amicably." Both sides, in short, measured the crisis as an insult or a potential insult to their individual and collective reputation. Some believed the insult was already too great to ignore; others disagreed but were equally grounded in the language of honor and also drew on the apparently universal male perspective that considered political discourse a personal matter.[24]

Most Unionists seemed to respect northern motives and did not consider the compromise an "affront" or "insult" to southern honor. The measures, they conceded, perhaps gave too much to the North; though hardly ideal, they were not inequitable enough to threaten "manly independence" or community reputation. Their opponents saw things differently. State-Rights supporters believed that the antislavery implications of California's Free Soil statehood represented insults too gross for southerners to suffer. These compromise measures, they asserted, designated the South and her people as inferior to those of the free North. California's constitution, according to Representative Albert Gallatin Brown, made an "insulting discrimination . . . between southern and northern people." He reminded his constituents of the northern threat to impose the Wilmot Proviso if southerners rejected the compromise. "Let them pass it," Brown said, "it will not be more galling than this." One Democratic meeting lashed out at the "insulting audacity" of northerners who argued "the evils and the sin of slavery by defamatory harangues against slave owners . . . in which they are presented to the world as heartless tyrants . . . or pirates and robbers." Governor Quitman's fiery proclamation denounced the "unjust and insulting discriminations" that "subject us to the scorn and contempt of mankind." Should Mississippi's men "patiently and meekly submit to the wrongs which have been inflicted upon us, acknowledge our inferiority," or should they stand up as "freemen and equals" and "take steps to redress past wrongs?" Characteristically, these speakers took northern proposals as slurs to their individual and collective character, not simply as criticism of the institution itself. Accepting them would mean personal dishonor and humiliation. Thus, they counseled aggressive, even violent resistance.[25]

Resolutions from the delegates to one district convention summarized many State-Rights complaints. Their objections make clear that these Mississippians considered the stain of Free Soil a personal insult that questioned the moral character of individual southerners: "We have been abused and insulted by every form of expression deemed best adapted to that end," began one resolution. "Excited discussion of the evils and the sin of slavery by defamatory harangues against the slave owners of the South [have] denounced us" as an un-Christian stain on the national character. Mississippians should unite, it continued, regardless of former loyalties and in "bonded brotherhood" go forth to defend their sacred honor and constitutional rights. Finally, northern critics should not mistake the South's "gentle measures of remonstrance" for "pusillanimity, or as evidence of final submission." Another writer urged men to support resistance unless "you regard yourselves justly odious in the sight of God and man . . . and should be cast out from the Territories as so much *sin and pollution*." Northern insults, summarized one young man, "have implanted in the bosom of the southern people a

feeling of contempt and disgust which if not eradicated by generous sentiment and feeling, will terminate in strife and bloodshed." In short, Mississippi's men were insulted by northern criticism leveled against their social system, accusations that questioned their claim to be good Christians and men
of equality within the national heritage.[26]

State-Rights men habitually referred to their opponents as the "submissionist" party, or simply the "subs." This epithet succinctly conveyed their
opinion of anyone who supported the compromise: a weakling who spine-
lessly obeyed the northern majority and was not "man enough" to resist.
Another favorite term for Unionists was "dirt-eater," which was traditionally
a pejorative term for poor folks who ate clay. In this sectional context it also
played on the secessionist and duelist nickname "fire-eater" and implied
some who groveled in the lowest, most unmanly fashion and was willing to
submit to humiliation and disgrace. Unfailingly, State-Rights men used the
code words — humiliating, degrading, insulting. The question, they repeated,
was whether Mississippians would "submit" to the "oppression" of northern
insults and "bow their heads," bending "suppliant" knees to the "yoke" of
northern mastery and accepting a "prostrate South"; or would the State
"manfully vindicate" its rights under the Constitution as an equal partner of
the national covenant. Men from Holmes County asserted that Free Soil
was "grossly unjust to the South, and for Southern men tamely to submit
thereto, is to make themselves accesories to their own dishonor." Using the
classic images of Christianity, personal honor, and communal manhood,
one voter summed up the resistors' position: any man who "fears to defend
the sober promptings of his reason, because of [cowardly] prejudice or
dreaded calumny, is a coward in the eyes of God; untrue to himself, and
derelict in his duty to his fellow men." They filled the discourse of resistance
with symbols of power and manliness, potent images in a society that placed
physical courage, ferocity, and loyalty above all other male virtues.[27]

For Mississippians masculinity and male honor were intimately bound
up with the equality of states under the Constitution, usually referred to as
simply "states rights." When southerners spoke of constitutional equality for
themselves and their communities, they suggested much more than a legal
impartiality. If northerners treated Mississippi as unequal and unworthy of
brotherhood with other states, the insult referred to more than the abstract
concept of rights decreed by the founding fathers. The taint of inequality
reached into one's community and, ultimately, into one's home and family.
Jefferson Davis often blended these images of manliness, equality, and family. Their cause "was a right and holy one," Davis preached in the small
town of Fayette. Men must maintain it against all odds "to protect their
honor and their equality, that they might transmit to their descendants the
same heritage which had been given to themselves." Representative Jacob
Thompson agreed: "Will we leave to our children the task of resistance; a
task which we had not the manliness and courage to perform ourselves?"

Lafayette County representative James Brown admonished his listeners that this was "the time when every man who feels an interest in the future safety of himself, his family, and property" should rally to the defense of community rights and community honor.[28] Politics offered men the best chance to demonstrate fidelity to other men and to defend themselves and their families against the "outrageous insults" of northern "fanatics." The State-Rights name, therefore, conveyed flesh-and-blood convictions with implications that went beyond mere defense of a constitutional theory.

Opponents of the Compromise of 1850 openly questioned the Unionsts' masculinity. They ridiculed their opponents' "spirit of pusillanimity" and spoke of a "craven, contemptible fear" of resistance. Representative Albert Gallatin Brown hinted at cowardice: "Have we sunk so low that we dare not complain of wrongs like these, lest the cry of disunion shall be rung in our ears?" Jeff Davis called his critics cowards and claimed that "he was unable to find one of them who had ever lost a drop of blood in defence of his country." Davis even dared the voters to forsake him. He stated, one newspaper reported, that if defeated "he would say nothing, nor would he have aught to regret save their [the voters'] own unmanly courage and deep humiliation."[29] Editor Benjamin F. Dill accused the "craven submissionists" of having "livers white as milk" and embracing a "degrading and ruinous policy of mean-spirited submission." Finally, one writer suggested, if the compromisers discovered their "hearts still faint," then "let them exchange clothes with their mothers, wives, sisters and daughters, and send them out to support the honor of the South!" Another instance of gendered imagery was the often-used symbolism of rape. Southerners routinely referred to their region in the feminine, speaking, for example, of "her honor." And many opponents of the Compromise extended the metaphor, perhaps unconsciously. Among others, Jefferson Davis repeatedly used the phrase "to lie supinely on our backs" to describe what the Unionists asked them to do. In short, Unionists asked Mississippians to accept the humiliation and shame — in the masculine language of honor — of "complete helplessness."[30]

The Union press responded with the same set of images, confirming that the two sides relied on a shared culture and set of masculine imperatives, although they drew different conclusions from them. Unionists reiterated how much more "manly" their platform and position was compared to the "impotent petulance" and "bravado" of secessionists. They ridiculed State-Rights truculence about southern honor: "The truth is, we are too sensitive — too timid & touchy in relation to this institution of slavery," declared one Unionist.[31] The Unionists could not, as adherents of the same political culture, accept the label of submissionist or the proposition that the compromise degraded southern honor. They therefore denied that northern actions constituted an unreasonable insult. The Union newspaper of Port Gibson admitted that one could, in fact, argue that the compromise was inequitable, on paper; but its *intent*, the editor insisted, was "honorable and just." Northerners were trying to be fair and intended no insult. The compromise measures had not affronted southern honor, wrote one supporter, and he did not consider himself an "aggrieved party." But if that were the case, he agreed, then he would opt for immediate secession. Unionist Gibeon Gibson of Vicksburg took that same position, contending that southerners could remain in the Union without damage to "our honor, and with our manly dignified independence" intact. But if they accepted any "real" insults, then they would deserve "the appellation of submissionists, than which no epithet can be more odious, none more repugnant to the feelings, to the sensibilities, and to the manly pride of freemen." The Unionists of the Cayuga precinct in Hinds County summarized this argument: the compromise might not be everything the South wanted, "but we do believe that we can remain in the Union without in the slightest degree compromising our honor, diminishing our prosperity, or jeopardizing our safety."[32]

This strategy was not lost on the Unionists's opponents. "It is a singular fact[,] reader," declared one State-Rights editor, "that all the friends of the compromise measures, expend all their arguments in proving that the South has not actually been disgraced, and that she by acquiescing in them, does not dishonor herself." He denounced the Unionists' "craven, contemptible fear." "Is this the way to command respect either of friends of foes, in short, is it a method by which equality is maintained between equals?" It was this Unionist defense of southern honor that prompted all the long arguments about the legality of California's constitution and its admission to the Union. If the procedure was fair and legal, then southerners could not complain; they might not like it, but it was honorable. Therefore, according to the Union Party, the Compromise of 1850, including the admission of California as a free state, was equitable. State-Rights spokesmen, conversely, hammered away at the "shadowy circumstances" surrounding California's constitution — in particular the question of whether there were enough legal residents in the territory. Senator Brown called it the "so-called constitution . . . made by unauthorized persons — that among them were foreigners not speaking our language, knowing nothing of our laws."[33]

Other Unionist tactics demonstrated the pervasiveness of values associated with honor and manliness. Congressional candidate Benjamin D. Nabors argued that only the Unionists could stop Mississippi from "disgracing herself." State-Rights partisans, he claimed, made demands they knew the North would never accept, which would force Mississippi either to secede and be "ruined" or to back down and be disgraced. "A leading object with me from the commencement," Nabors recounted, "has been to save Mississippi from committing herself to any issue, from which the force of circumstances would oblige her to recede [and thus be disgraced]." This was exactly the position, he finished, in which South Carolina now found itself: "Supposing she now recedes, will she not lose to some extent, her own self respect and the confidence of her neighbors?" Thus, Nabors argued, only the Unionist strategy of calm deliberation and careful but manly remonstrance would uphold and satisfy the honor of southerners.[34]

The two sides' constant wrangling over which deserved the epithet *sub-missionist* further reveals the potency of these same masculine values within the political discourse. Unionists insisted that the term best applied to their opponents. "Who are the true submissionists?" asked countless writers. One editor quoted from Webster's definition of a *slink*, indicating a man who "creeps away meanly," to show the "natural identification" of the true slinks in this controversy: anyone who would abandon the republic and all the South's investment and heritage was truly a slinking submissionist. Another Unionist indicted his opponents with their own language when some State-Rights spokesmen denied that they advocated secession. They maintain that the compromise is morally wrong and insulting, he sneered, but say they will not secede? "Is this not submission in the opprobrious sense of the term? When were freemen known before to submit to wrongs, when they were in possession of a clear and 'essential' remedy?" "Who were the true slinks?" he concluded, men who "acquiesce in a compromise, which does not in their opinion aggress upon their rights," or those who "resolve not to submit to aggression, [then] confess to aggressions having been made, and then . . . repudiate the only alternative to submission!"[35] With similar arguments both sides worked to pin the accusation of "unmanly submission" on one another; if it stuck, there could be no worse indignity.

Public spokesmen's frequent references to religion and Christianity make it clear, however, that the insults of Free Soil attacked more than southern males' bravado or notions of physical courage. After the Great Awakening the claim to be a good Christian formed an increasingly important part of the code of honor. The noncompetitive virtues of Christian honor softened some of the region's aggressive ideals and refined the gentry's standards of masculinity. They helped the calm, cool behavior of dueling, for instance, to supplant brutal eye-gouging. By the 1830s most Mississippi men took pride in declaring their Christian virtues, and their reactions to northern criticism always included protestations against the insinuation of moral turpitude. The evangelical mutation after 1800 had turned southern men into Christian gentlemen, public advocates of an ostensibly more humane version of slavery and hierarchy and defenders of the region's Christian virtue. Yet men who showed too much piety risked being labeled "feminine"—churchgoing was still basically in the female sphere. The role of women, of course, only raised the stakes. The northerners' "insult" to southern Christianity not only impugned male honor, it was also a slur on family, including female, honor. Put another way, if the South was not a Christian community, then its wives and daughters were not good Christians.[36]

With their personal and family reputations thus at stake, men naturally lashed out. "The northern brethren, a people so pure, so christian, so sensitively holy," hissed one editor, have determined "that affiliation with brothers who hold slaves [has] darkened their path towards the gates of Paradise." The Hinds County delegation to the 1849 October convention declared that northerners had tried "to brand us with moral sin, and to deny us the privileges of christian fellowship with our brethren of the North." One Democratic convention expressed indignation at northern insults that "denounced [slavery and slaveowners] as a flagrant violation of the laws of God, or religion, and of humanity, and we are assured that this foul stain upon the National character shall not continue."[37]

Personal honor included the affirmation of moral behavior, and Free Soilers denied that the southern way of life was moral. William Sharkey informed his fellow Mississippians that northerners had declared slavery a political and a moral evil. "Let them eradicate moral evils from their own land; we can take care of our own morals," Sharkey said. "I must admonish my Methodist and my Baptist friends to be on their guard. . . . You may soon be told that your religion [itself] is a moral evil, and must be exterminated. . . . [This] moral evil, it seems, is exclusively in the South, and those who have determined it to be so, and wish to eradicate it, reside [only] in the North." Jefferson Davis likewise declared that "religion has been perverted from its mission of peace, good will, and brotherly love to sanctify this unprovoked hostile aggression, and the word of God offered as authority for the commission of half the crimes defined by the Decologue." Mississippians responded to the insults of Free Soil with one voice, as Sharkey, a Whig and Unionist, and Davis, a State-Rights Democrat, demonstrated. It was their interpretation of the Compromise of 1850 that drew the lines of partisanship.[38]

Mississippi's spokesmen invoked the language of honor and masculinity as the lingua franca of sectionalism. Drawing upon shared assumptions and code words, Unionists and Secessionists alike assessed Free Soil rhetoric from a common framework based on their collective understanding of political rhetoric as a personal exchange. Furthermore, they voiced the conviction of all Mississippians that individual and community honor were inseparable. The partisan cleavage of 1851 depended on whether or not the individual considered the compromise too insulting to accept. Secessionists saw it as degrading to their community and, therefore, to themselves; Unionists disagreed about the gravity of the insult but assessed the compromise in the same terms. This first sectional crisis also shows that in 1850 antiparty sentiments remained vital and that party lines were fluid. In statewide elections many Democrats and Whigs quickly renounced their previous affiliations and took up the banner of new organizations.

But antipartyism was a central feature in Mississippi's political culture even when there was no heated sectional controversy. Its ubiquity called into question the notion of widespread partisan loyalty and reflected the voters' deep distrust and resentment of parties and professional politicians, which helped turn all political rhetoric into a personal matter. Combined with the language and values of southern honor and faced with the suddenly dominant Republican party of 1860, this political culture fostered a powerful popular crusade to leave the Union. It is true that Republican language inflamed Mississippians because it violated their sense of honor; but it was so highly charged only because of the way they thought about and conducted their politics.

3

MORTAL STAKES

The Politics of Antipartyism

Mississippi's struggle over the Compromise of 1850 suggested the inherent weakness of its party system as many voters abandoned old loyalties and invoked a pervasive antiparty discourse. Throughout the history of Mississippi's two-party system, men expressed the same distrust of organization, declaring that anyone loyal to parties remained suspect. Common to all parties and spokesmen from the 1840s to secession, the politics of antipartyism helped define Mississippi's political culture. It was more than the disgruntled griping of frustrated office seekers; even pro-party extremists conceded in public and private that most rank-and-file voters disliked and avoided parties whenever possible. In particular, the antiparty tradition condemned the essence of party organization: the convention system and professional politicians, both of which, its adherents argued, promoted selfish, scheming candidates who wanted simply to feed at the public trough.

The institutional framework of parties created the basic problem by interfering with personal relationships. Most voters could never really trust a party candidate who remained unknown, not subject to the usual mechanism of personal and community evaluation. Of course, some Mississippians did become enthusiastic partisans, but even the most committed Whigs and Democrats respected the antiparty mainstream they sensed among voters. Partisan newspapers, in fact, were replete with antiparty editorials and speeches. Ironically, this meant party leaders often undermined their own effectiveness to assuage voters' fears. Yielding to the politics of antipartyism, editors and party boosters struggled to present their organizations as the least partylike, offering voters what they really wanted—antiparty parties.

The state's antiparty tradition is especially striking when compared to public rhetoric in the Upper South and the North where, by the mid-1840s, most voters expressed much less apprehension about conventions or politicians. In Virginia, a recent student concludes, the second party system was a "transformed political culture [which] came to accept, even revel in, the politics of conflict and an affirmation of party affiliation as an essential element of American democracy." No longer considering them a serious threat to manliness or personal independence, most Virginians embraced institutional politics. One detailed study of 1850s northern politics concludes that the revolutionary ideology of republicanism had been transformed and shorn of its inherent antipartyism: "Political parties were now deemed essential to the health of the Republic rather than its bane." Of course, antipartyism remained and was called upon by third parties in particular; but it defined politics only in the Lower South. Mississippians expressed a qualitative difference from voters farther north by refusing to grant parties any positive role beyond that of a grudging necessity in national and most state elections.[1]

The state's antiparty tradition included a number of standard charges. One of the foremost accused parties of denying voters independent thought, forcing "blind loyalty" to selfish party leaders who threatened the national commonwealth. This traditional complaint was hardly limited to Mississippi, where voters shared republican ideals that historians have found throughout antebellum America. "We are ever boasting of our independent spirit," wrote one Mississippian, "yet it is an undeniable fact that a majority of our citizens are laboring under the most galling political bondage." Another complained that "a majority of voters never look beyond the paragraphs of campaign journals or the crude effusions of party orators. Deriving their whole knowledge from this source, it must necessarily partake of the passion, prejudice, and error common to it." One Whig used typical language to attack the Democrats' electioneering tactics: "I fear Sandy has no mind of his own and is dictated to by others, such are the means by which that party gains their ends." In 1845 another writer claimed that the Democratic Party "takes from its followers all independence of thought and action," and "places them under the control of party leaders, who are to think for them, and whose bidding they are to do without a murmur."[2]

These antiparty sentiments found a special place among men obsessed with proving their own power and independence: to them, obedience to party always smacked of unmanliness. One writer echoed hundreds of editorials when he ridiculed the "honor" of serving as an "instructed or *commanded*" party delegate. "But when party sends forth its edict the promptings of self-respect must be crushed out," he claimed. "We do not envy the *honor* conferred upon [instructed] delegates." Editors routinely used the language of masculinity in their antiparty sermons. "Clandestine cliques" were not only unrepublican, argued Levi Robertson, but attracted nothing but "fawning sycophants who bow and submit to the[ir] unmanly and pernicious influence." Partyists "make themselves entire slaves to party." Men *"forced to vote"* for party nominees, preached one independent candidate, weakly make "a tame submission to the dictation of the Convention and [agree to] the humble performance of *their will*."[3] Are "we . . . ready to wear a servile yoke imposed upon us by self-appointed dictators . . . the iron shackles of tyranny?" asked another typical editorial. Others rebuked partisan editors as unfit for a "man's position": "Of all things in the world we do most despise a cringing parasite, clinging around the feet of his party god-heads without the spirit to cry [anything] else than hurrah!" A party hack, in short, scarcely qualified as a man.[4]

Slavery and southern culture hindered party development in other ways. Predisposed to favor planters, the southern legal system respected their mastery over rural, often isolated plantations. Both contemporaries and historians detail the weakness of southern institutions, usually focusing on extra legal forms of crime and punishment — the prevalence of lynching and charivari, for example. These social and legal patterns extended to a political philosophy that celebrated the personal, honor-bound connection between a representative and his constituency. Critics regularly assailed "scheming politicians" who employed trickery and falsehood, which was especially threatening to people who lived by reputation. "All demagogues are emphatically the same in principle," wrote one editor, and "have one common object, that of deception." In a social order founded on personal image and public presentation of the self, persistent and carefully planned deceits constituted a grave threat. Southerners also attached a stigma to patronage, the lifeblood of successful organizations. Doled out like weekly rations to a faithful servant, a "dull, plodding job" in the bureaucracy provided the officeholder no satisfaction and presented him with no chance to embellish his personal reputation. Not just unrepublican, in Mississippi party "dictation," even party loyalty, carried the taint of dependence, a hint of effeminacy, and offered few chances to display personal honor.[5]

This antiparty argument helped distinguish Mississippi (and probably much of the Lower South) from other states where antipartyism was based on classical republicanism, evangelical Protestantism, or, as one historian concludes, "secular frustration" with the "political and governmental context" of policies that lacked "a larger moral vision." While these strains of antipartyism, especially classical republicanism, were present, Mississippi's tradition was grounded foremost in men's notions of honor and masculinity, not in religion, political theory, or dissatisfaction with public policy.[6]

Any sort of obsequiousness stained a man's public reputation, and the politics of antipartyism condemned all professional party politicians as too malleable in their opinions, men always seeking the "popular breeze." John Quitman regularly vented his frustration over "scheming demagogues" who practiced political flexibility for the sake of electoral victory — behavior unworthy of true patriots and statesmen. "I am a Democrat," he avowed after the 1851 election, "because Democracy has heretofore sustained state rights, [but] when it shall cease to do so, the name will have no charm for me." In

1853 the former governor was incensed that supposed State-Rights men would cede principle merely to defeat the hated Governor Foote: "Foote is now assailed, not for his agency in robbing us of the public domain, and stigmatizing our institutions by odious discrimination," but for abandoning Democrats and leading the Union Party to victory. When many State-Rights men refused to discuss the compromise in the interest of "party harmony," Quitman concluded that "the hard blow of a defeat and exclusion from office makes them sensitive at the very idea of state rights." He lamented that "I can sustain my position against every thing but gold or office — these I fear constitute the democracy of many political managers." Like other public figures, Reverend William Winans announced his refusal to campaign in antiparty terms: "I cannot reconcile it to my sense of propriety to engage in an electioneering canvass, or to solicit suffrage for an office of honor."[7] Such stock rhetoric, of course, also came from disappointed office seekers and from candidates trying to clothe naked ambition in respectable language. Even delivered disingenuously, though, the language suggests that voters expected deference to mainstream antiparty opinion. To succeed, even demagogues had to respect the politics of antipartyism.

Distaste for professional politicians and selfish ambition made easy fodder on any public occasion. In a lecture before the Odd Fellows, educator Samuel M. Meek, a renowned speaker whose height allowed him to tower over the audience, attacked the "modern demagogue." "His greatest mental effort," Meek accused, is "paper politics — he squabbles over a County election as if the fate of the nation were involved — and his only contribution to social enjoyment & improvement" consists of whispering in the ears of ladies. Meek blamed politics for taking too much time away from the pursuit of literature and the arts and so retarding "social progress" and "refinement." But the damage went further, he argued. Obsession with political advancement and greed contributed to the South's lack of higher learning and, ultimately, to Yankee domination and southern cultural extinction.[8]

To others, demagogues represented the ultimate perversion of political liberty and statesmanship. "Fierce bands of demagogues who are sowing the seeds of dissension," complained one author, epitomized selfishness and grasping ambition, men who played on public emotions simply to get elected and satisfy their lust for "gold or office." True statesmen, "independent and honest politician[s]" thought only of the common good, not their own personal satisfaction. Of course, one critic recognized, party politicians "profess one thing and do another just as the whims of the moment and their view of interest and popularity may dictate to them, not for the first moment taking into consideration the good of their country." The companion to this accusation was the standard charge that virtue and statesmanship had declined since the revolutionary generation. By every measure, professional politicians and other party toadies exemplified the nadir of manliness and statesmanship.[9]

While these accusations of demagoguery filled the partisan press, men lamented it in private as well. One observer summed up his feelings with a timeless refrain: "Office seeking has become a professional business." Even an enthusiastic partisan like Democrat William R. Cannon disapproved of blatant jockeying for position. "So many hungry politicians desire place," he complained after one convention, "that no pains are spared to pull down all above them, in order to fall into the scramble, & they [party leaders] even go so far as to say, that they will vote for no man who will not *ask* for office."[10] Another potential candidate expressed "unmitigated contempt" for politicians interested only in personal advancement. He felt qualified to be secretary of state but refused to campaign for the nomination: "I could not reconcile it with a proper sense of delicacy to endeavor to obtain the nomination." He concluded that party leaders considered the office as simply a party reward. "There are so many party leaders[,] aspirants who are zealous of self agrandisement the emoluments of office &c. that this boasted republick cannot . . . stand." Party leaders, according to this observer, were all self-serving hacks: "God save the State and curse the demagogues."[11]

This widespread criticism of party politicians blended easily into open hostility for the caucuses and conventions that selected them as candidates. "The demagogue is a factious leader of the people," lamented hundreds of editorials and speeches but the demagogue himself was not solely, or even primarily, to blame. Instead, many observers indicted the apparatus that conspired to put these scheming men before the public: "Perhaps there could not be devised a more effectual means of perverting the true principles of democracy," ventured one writer, "than our present system of caucuses and conventions." Such means of selecting candidates alienated statesmen and effectively shut out the working classes. Farmers and mechanics had no access to these secret caucuses; even if chosen as a delegate to some faraway convention, they usually lacked the time or money to attend. "This false initiatory step [of conventions]," concluded this writer, "vitiates the whole process" of democracy. Committeemen and newspaper editors were a big part of the problem because the convention system limited participation to these privileged few who had the time, money, and interest (more outspoken critics said selfishness) to work at politics year-round. In a typical outburst, one editor lumped "unscrupulous politicians, stump orators and a degraded and hireling party press" into one foul basket. Conventions and nominations constituted the essence of party organization, and when antiparty spokesmen denounced them and active partisans they attacked the foundation and essence of institutional parties.[12]

The partisan press featured regular tirades against the convention system. Colonel James Herbert, candidate for state legislature in Monroe County, complained of the backroom deviousness that denied him a chance for the State-Rights nomination in 1851. Herbert protested that in the few months preceding the convention he had "not been as active as some have been, to fix up tricks, with which to control caucuses." Consequently, "a little squad" of party insiders "juggled" the nominations in a caucus held the morning of the county convention. Herbert then ridiculed the county chairman's later call for candidates during the afternoon session: "Why, he should have said that the nominations had been made — that the caucus had done that much for the people, and," he finished, "the present meeting had just been called in to ratify — to approve the *veritable* action of the caucus, which had just usurped the powers of the convention." With democracy thwarted by party hacks, Herbert vowed to continue as an independent candidate. Of course, his objections came at least partly from personal disappointment. Yet he evidently believed the public would sympathize with his complaint about caucus jugglers.[13]

Furthermore, accusations like Herbert's always had the ring of truth, as county conventions surely could be rigged in advance. In May 1845, Yazoo County's Whig editor called on local partisans to meet "Monday next . . . for the purpose of nominating a candidate to represent this district in the next [state] Senate." He then listed the three possibilities already "named for this station." In other words, "someone" had chosen three men in advance — one would get the state senate nomination, the other two probably went into the lower house. Other party insiders voiced similar concerns about controlling nominations. As the Democratic caucus debated whom to put forward as their choice for U.S. senator in 1853, Colin Tarpley warned Jefferson Davis that Governor Foote might try to exploit public opposition to secret nominations and campaign "over the head" of the party organization. Common school teacher, lawyer, and veteran politico Hiram Van Eaton confided to a friend that he feared nominating a candidate for district attorney in 1858 because "[o]ur county is averse to such things & I am afraid to meddle with it." Vicksburg's Whig editor approved of Henry Gray's unofficial nomination for Congress without a convention "because in some counties strong prejudice exists against caucuses and conventions; and a candidate thus nominated must consequently lose many votes which he would otherwise receive."[14]

Although leading Democrats, like other active partisans, evidently sensed the dominant antiparty mood among rank-and-file voters, the official party line endorsed conventions. "The Democratic party, always in the majority in the country, owes it continued success and ascendancy in the National Councils," resolved one meeting of delegates, "to the organization by means of the Convention and Caucus." This system, these activists argued, reserved to the majority within the party the right to name its popular candidates. In addition, caucuses and conventions ensured that only those men responsible and accountable to the public would receive party endorsement. Another Democratic editor similarly urged his readers to support the party's state convention: "We like the Convention system, and shall continue to advocate it until its uses are eclipsed by its abuses."[15]

Democratic activists often defended "party fidelity," painting it as a positive sense of loyalty to one's fellow partisans, as opposed to "party spirit," which implied "blind devotion" to factious leaders. "Fidelity" certainly sounded better than "unthinking devotion," given the notions of communal manhood. But even those who defended conventions quickly agreed that the system was "liable to abuse," and could be "subversive of democratic principles." As one voter insisted in 1843: "The convention system was only resorted to, in the first place, to prevent divisions . . . it was never justified except upon the ground of necessity." This sort of tepid enthusiasm characterized most editorials that endorsed conventions. One local meeting resolved that "we, a portion of the democracy of Lowndes co. are willing to *abide* the [convention] system until a better one is devised." These lukewarm partisans concluded that at the time it was the best way to organize politics. Partisan editors also carefully defended every convention and nomination, typically presenting them as "fairly got up and as fairly conducted as any that ever was held."[16]

Other Democrats, however, believed that conventions benefitted only a few activists and "wire-pulling lawyers" inclined to party scheming. James Phelan accused the "Jackson clique" of foul play when the state convention nominated William Barksdale for Congress instead of his friend Reuben Davis. "It is a bare faced usurpation, and makes the Convention system, *bad enough at best,* a mockery. If a caucus can be called to control the Convention," he speculated, "another caucus may be called to control the caucus, which controls the Convention, and so on indefinitely." Another voter claimed that people hated conventions so much that they refused to support any official nominee just to spite party organizers: "There are hundreds of men in this county who believe that such a thing as a fair nomination is impossible, and would therefore vote against the nominees — no matter how well qualified." In 1843 Democrats were forced to hold two state conventions when supporters in the northern counties balked at "Jackson clique dictation."[17]

While the Democratic Party officially supported conventions, the Whigs did not. Throughout the party's existence, antipartyism remained a central part of its platform. Whigs lampooned their opponents' "partisan zeal" when compared to their own "statesmanlike" attitudes. "The natural inability of the Whig party to make itself a unit at all sacrifice of principle for the mere sake of naked triumph," insisted one editor, "is one of the plainest marks which distinguish it from the present opposition." He continued, praising his own party's "remarkable and honorable characteristics" of disorganization, unlike Democrats, who pursued the "cohesive power of public plunder" at whatever cost.[18]

The claim was more than mere rhetoric; the Whigs actually were more disorganized than their opponents and sometimes failed to unite behind state nominees. Given the party's problems throughout the 1840s, its weak and pathetic effort in 1853 was unexceptional. Whig delegates chose Joseph McDowell of Rankin for state treasurer, but in their ratification meeting Yazoo County leaders "suggested" Daniel McLaurin of Covington. The local paper soon printed his name as the county's "official nominee." The editor expressed no concern when Whigs in nearby Madison County decided "to support a mixed ticket, not recognizing the recommendations of the late so called Whig Convention, as binding upon them." With party unity like that, no wonder the Whigs had trouble. Their problems often extended to the state legislature. For example, despite returning a majority for Henry Clay, Claiborne County Whigs could not find two men to run for the state legislature in 1845. The lone Whig candidate finished first among the four men running, but a Democrat claimed the second seat.[19]

Many members of the Whig Party and press also seemed to practice, in general, a more conciliatory style than the Democrats did. Leaders of both parties acknowledged the widespread distrust of party organization and vituperative rhetoric, and each side tried to avoid public censure on that account. Some Whig leaders, however, seemed to be more genuinely moderate. When William McWillie beat their candidate for third-district representative in 1849, the *Vicksburg Whig* responded with not uncommon magnanimity: "The Whigs did the rejoicing over the previous election in this District, and, we suppose, 'time about is fair play.'" The same newspaper often printed the Democratic state ticket as well as their own party's.[20] Another party editor commented that "I have not long time met a more pleasant gentleman than [Democratic] Governor [John J.] McRae, though my paper was sometimes hard on him during the last and preceding political canvasses." One Whig wrote to his local editor commending the Democratic legislature on its performance: "I believe everyone admits that there never has been a more attentive and hard-working set of members assembled in the Capitol than the members of the present session." Finally, in his review of the recent legislative session, one opposition editor declared that "the Senators and members with a very few honorable exceptions, who appeared to be actuated by a truly patriotic desire for the good of the State, were members of the Democratic party." Many Whig editors and partisans, apparently even less enthusiastic about organization than Democratic leaders, often failed to match their opponents' truculent outbursts.[21]

Democrats conceded the need to answer Whig charges about their fondness for caucuses and conventions; they responded by accusing their adversaries of the same "loathsome affliction." The Jackson correspondent for the *Port Gibson Reveille* reported on the 1853 Whig state convention in typical fashion. "The [Whig] delegates are holding darling little Caucuses all about town for the purpose, I opine, of presenting their . . . *no-caucus* candidates." He concluded with another warning: "The ticket which the Convention will probably present, may decline; but be assured, the ticket which opposes ours in the end, will have its conception and birth to-night and to-morrow — *and it will be the offspring of a CAUCUS!*" In 1847, the *Mississippian* made similar charges. "Nothing can be more hypocritical than the cant of the whigs about *caucus candidates, king caucus, and cliques, or the clique.* They pretend to oppose nominees of democratic conventions," the editor complained, "*because they are nominees* when it is well known that all over the Union wherever they have the strength to succeed, they are united in the support of *regular convention nominees.*" Even in Mississippi, he finished, in "almost every county where they have a majority, a caucus or a convention have brought out their candidates." At least some Whig outrage was, of course, hypocritical. As early as 1843 one of their most zealous editors suggested holding county and municipal nominations in Vicksburg because Whigs enjoyed a large majority there.[22]

Over and over, Democrats hammered Whigs as the party of "secret caucuses," something "even worse" than conventions because the former took place behind closed doors. Whig caucuses, claimed one editor, "are held in the back rooms of stores and offices . . . in them party leaders rule with absolute sway . . . and when they have compassed their ends in secret, they proceed to reward the 'lucky fellows' openly." Another partisan charged that "Whigs never hold any public meetings in this county. About five or six Whigs hereabouts, attend to all such matters, as appointing delegates for the party and nominating candidates for county offices." Hiram Van Eaton lampooned the Whigs in 1853 when they finally produced a slate of "independent" candidates: "Yet look again and there it is, just as pretty; plump and saucy looking a caucus bantling, as can be seen anywhere or manufactured by any clique or secret conclave under the sun." Another Democrat claimed that "the first convention I ever saw in the town of Oxford, was a convention of whigs, assembled for the purpose of nominating their candidates. And yet," he concluded, the Whigs "believe that the people are so dull and stupid, that they can induce them to believe that the convention system is dangerous and sinful . . . and that the pure and immaculate whigs have never been guilty of such sinning in all their lives, either by holding County or State conventions."[23]

The managers and activists of both parties, then, assumed that most voters distrusted and disliked the convention system. Whig criticism and public posturing forced the Democrats, in particular, to defend their organization constantly. They strove to convince the still-skeptical public of the 1840s and 1850s that parties were legitimate. Democratic strategy usually concentrated on the argument that conventions were more open and democratic than Whig caucuses; Whigs condemned both conventions and caucuses and claimed that they employed neither. Spokesmen for both parties assured voters that they offered the least-proscriptive organization, presenting their party as the antiparty alternative.

The Democrats worked hard to answer Whig accusations but had to work even harder against the successor American (or Know-Nothing) Party. In Mississippi and in the South in general the nativist Know-Nothings encountered a host of problems, including their ties to northern reform and antislavery activists.[24] But the new party made a potent appeal as the ideal antiparty party unconnected to existing organizations that were rotten with wire-pulling hacks. Untainted and "fresh from the voters," Know-Nothing candidates invoked the politics of antipartyism. "I do assure you most solemnly," wrote one early propagandist, "that there are among its members men of *all* former parties, and that by thousands upon thousands . . . and among them not only prominent politicians." "To the demagogue and party hack," pledged another, the Know-Nothing "is as terrible as an 'army with banners' . . . and expose[s] selfishness and partisan bigotry in all their deformity." Some candidates even implied that the Know-Nothings were not really a party. "Mr. Samuel Matthews, the American [Party] candidate for the Legislature was called to the stand," reported one editor and said he was a Democrat "and was proud that his democracy did not prevent his espousal of the great American doctrines."[25]

Know-Nothings consistently targeted demagogues and spoilsmen. "We do not weep to see the good people of the country repudiating the maxim that 'to the victors belong the spoils,'" preached one partisan. Rather, "we are glad to see they begin to be indignant that offices . . . should be conferred as the reward of electioneering services, without regard to the qualifications of the appointee." Other editors ridiculed the hollow partisanship typical among members of the old parties, and claimed that few could ever explain why they supported one side or the other.[26] Know-Nothings pledged to rescue honest patriots disgusted with degenerate, selfish party leaders, and their ability to stir antiparty feelings had an unsettling effect on the Democratic majority. In 1857, the Democrats' state organ apparently decided that it was better to join than to fight them: "We are pleased to see that this spirit [of antipartyism], to a great extent, is animating the masses of the people. They are sick and worn out with this senseless and insane cry of party, party, and nothing but party."[27]

Yet their own antiparty rhetoric eventually helped defeat the Know-Nothings. The secrecy that initially fascinated many men soon became a liability. Working within a political culture so hostile to caucuses, conventions, and any meeting that smelled the least bit clandestine, nativists had to come into the open. When the Know-Nothings were exposed as just another "typical" party by their opponents, many voters lost faith in their antiparty message. Still, the party's public relations nightmare offers further proof of the public's distrust of party managers and secret cliques.

While Democrats worried about their opponents' public criticisms, they were squabbling about the convention system among themselves; the quarrels betray a bitter intrastate rivalry that always lurked just below the veneer of statewide harmony and constantly threatened the party's fragile unity. The practice of meeting in Jackson gave nearby partisans an advantage at every state convention because they could send the most delegates and pack the assemblies to lobby for their own men.[28] The Jackson clique centered around the party's leading newspaper, the *Mississippian*, and typically controlled nominations. Distant counties naturally resented that control; their rancor was aggravated by the fact that the Democrats were strongest in the north and southeast, while Jackson itself lay in Whiggish Hinds County. Thus counties that typically provided the party's majority felt slighted when they saw men from the "opposition districts" claim most of the nominations. "Again has the Jackson Regency been triumphant," wrote one typically frustrated rural editor. "It seems strange indeed that a Cabal, not at all remarkable for numbers or talent, should rule the State of Mississippi, but nevertheless it appears that such is the fact." Although the most notorious sectional revolt happened in 1843, when the party decided to hold a second convention to mollify disaffected northern Democrats, virtually every campaign featured some dissatisfaction with unfair nominations and the undemocratic nature of conventions or party organization. In 1845, for instance, many northern editors opposed the gubernatorial nominee, A. G. Brown; the editor in Coffeeville essentially sat out the campaign, refusing to print Brown's name among the party's candidates and supporting only Stephen Adams, from nearby Monroe County, for Congress and the county's two nominees for the state legislature. Partisans from around the state repeatedly tried to move the state convention to Holly Springs, Columbus, or Paulding.[29]

Unhappy Democrats, including some of the most ardent champions of party organization, routinely used the politics of antipartyism to exploit the voters' suspicion. When Secretary of State Samuel Stamps died in the summer of 1850, the Democrats again degenerated into territorial factionalism. To replace Stamps, the *Mississippian* endorsed Joseph Bell, a resident of Jackson and the interim appointee, for the upcoming special election. Editors and partisans from around the state howled that just because the Jackson clique had decided upon a candidate, the whole party would not "supinely" concur. The *Vicksburg Sentinel* charged that the "whole affair has been 'cut and dried' at Jackson for weeks," while another editor charged Governor Quitman of conspiring for Bell. North Mississippi eventually backed Colonel John Wilcox; the *Sentinel* endorsed Robert Haynes; and many in the south and east supported Captain R. T. Daniel. Editor Benjamin F. Dill, normally an extreme party advocate and one of the only men from either party to advocate county-level nominations, lambasted the Jackson clique. "We repeat our objection to a nomination by a few wire-workers who may happen to be in attendance on the Federal Court at Jackson," he complained. "This gross abuse of the Convention system, is what has rendered it odious to many good and true democrats of Mississippi," Dill continued, "and if persisted in, it will, sooner or later bring the whole thing into utter contempt."[30]

Other Democratic leaders easily resorted to antipartyism when they wanted to appeal to rank-and-file voters. In 1843 Oxford's Democratic editor, E. Percy Howe, attacked the faction of his party cooperating with Whigs to pay the repudiated Union Bank bonds, focusing attention on several recent meetings of bond-paying Democrats. "But we ask the farmers — the hard working yeomanry of the land: Are you represented at these county court meetings?" Of course not, Howe answered, because they were controlled by lawyers and hack politicians. In 1857 Owen Van Vactor criticized Governor John McRae's use of pardons, in part to advance the claims of William McWillie, another hopeful Democrat angling for the gubernatorial nomination. He employed classic antiparty language, condemning earlier Democratic conventions for selecting "professional office holders — that contemptible class of whiffling and whining wire-workers . . . those self-seeking politicians of small mental and no moral caliber." It is no wonder that most voters remained skeptical, ambivalent, or hostile to parties when editors themselves attacked conventions and nominations as undemocratic, unmanly, and unrepublican whenever it suited them.[31]

A further measure of popular distrust and disinterest in party organization was the typically abysmal turnout at local, county, and state conventions. Democrat Wiley Harris acknowledged that "the system of conventions or caucus system very often exposes the fact that the people are indifferent." In party meetings, most voters failed to show. "What is the consequence of indifference and inaction upon the part of the masses of every government and country?" asked another Democratic partisan. "It is the usurpation of power by designing demagogues and ambitious men." Editors begged men to attend county conventions. In Hinds County, Whig activists had to meet several times "in consequence of the county not being fully represented (only four of the precincts having appointed delegates)." In 1845, one Whig leader urged the importance of a "full turn-out from each precinct." "A Convention, small in numbers, would, possibly do the cause more harm than good" since "every man has his personal preferences, [and] any thing having the slightest bearing towards caucus dictation, will certainly create heart-burnings and jealousies, and will inevitably draw some voters from our ranks." More than ten years later, another Mississippian agreed that primary meetings were still poorly attended, and any convention not "gotten up by a majority of the party would . . . do more harm than good." Of course, this widely acknowledged problem only encouraged critics who condemned the party system as unrepublican and unrepresentative. Thus, contemporaries conceded, antipartyism was both a cause and an effect of general distrust of party organization.[32]

The voters' suspicion of politicos and parties was also manifested in the widely sanctioned "Right of Instruction." This republican tradition gave to constituents the power to instruct a representative on policy, theoretically denying his freedom to act independently of their wishes. Historian Gordon Wood argues that the practice reflected the Revolutionary regard for community consensus and the strong current of antipartyism running through all republican thought: "The *legislature* are [merely] the *trustees* of the people and *accountable* to them," wrote Revolutionary William Paca of Maryland. He argued for a "trusteeship relation between constituents and representatives." By invoking the Right, voters were conceding, in effect, the improbability of electing real statesmen and choosing instead to monitor closely their "agents" of the popular will. Such concerns reflected antipartyism: as voters simply could not trust party politicians they did not know personally, they had to keep them on a short leash.[33] Elected officials "are merely agents," wrote one Mississippian: "These agents are becoming extremely delinquent in the discharge of their respective duties — particularly careful of their own interests and negligent of those of their principals [the sovereign voters]." The people, in short, needed to keep a close eye on selfish partisans, who should pay more attention to what the voters wanted. "Congress," concluded this writer, "should only be considered a National Convention of Delegates, to canvass and record the will of the people, the real law of the land."[34]

Jefferson Davis regularly toured the state after each congressional session, speaking to voters and "giving an account of my recent stewardship." In Raymond, after the heated discussion of the Compromise of 1850, Davis reiterated his opposition to the measures. But he refused to say he favored armed resistance at the moment and pledged that he would follow the "dictates of the people implicitly" whatever they decided. As Davis suggested, the Right of Instruction called on politicians to deny any impulse for autonomous power. Many such standard denials, of course, were simply ritualized expressions; but they demonstrated to voters that the representative was in accord with their concerns. Even in private, however, Davis acknowledged the power of instructions; reviewing his response to the compromise, he told a friend that "I opposed them because I thought them wrong and of a dangerous tendency, and also because of the people in every form, and the Legislature by resolutions of instruction required me to oppose them."[35]

Satisfying the Right of Instruction became a balancing act for candidates who needed to assert their independence in order to earn respect from the voters yet could not seem too powerful or independent, which could alienate the same constituents. A circular signed by Unionists and Whigs and opposing the call for a secession convention in 1851 summarized the dilemma. Mixing the metaphors of slavery, mastery, and masculinity, it asked voters if they would "permit your *servants* to arrogate to themselves the authority of *masters*, and to dictate terms to you." State legislative candidate William M. Smyth invoked the same imagery, claiming "the right of opinion, as a *free-man* . . . yet I shall be found at all times, *when acting as their representative . . . yielding obedience to the will of the majority*." The Right of Instruction, he averred, "constitutes the first duty of a Representative."[36]

Some Democrats tried to make the Right of Instruction a partisan issue. While they themselves upheld the Right, they argued, the Whigs preferred the "Federal doctrine that the representative should not be controlled by the will of the people."[37] Democrats who made that claim erred, however, for Whigs and Unionists also defended the Right of Instruction. In fact, Lawrence County Unionists condemned their state senator and representative for supporting the secession convention in 1851 against the expressed "will of the people" manifested in local meetings. Unionist editors Thomas Palmer and Edward Pickett declined to support anyone for governor until the county conventions had made recommendations. They urged that "delegates be instructed by their county delegations only," so as to avoid pressure from both the media and the party cliques seeking to control the process. One Whig from Bolivar County complained that elected officials enjoyed too much freedom. He suggested a complicated series of committees organized in each county or precinct to consolidate reports of public opinion and instruct representatives in Jackson and Washington about how to vote on certain issues.[38]

It is revealing that there was no discussion of applying the Right of Instruction to county officers, members of the board of police, or local magistrates and constables. Men clearly felt more comfortable trusting these fellow members of the community, and, if necessary, they knew where to find them. But a party politician who could not be assessed in person remained an unknown commodity and bore close watching. Voters only needed the Right, then, when the candidate was not a part of the face-to-face political culture. Because representatives were supposed to express the community will, party politicians needed guidance, while locals did not. Mississippi voters always placed loyalty to one another ahead of faith in institutions such as parties, the law, or government. A man's "community" was, foremost, his fellow men, those who confirmed his honor — it was not necessarily a geographical place. Popular support for the Right of Instruction, then, was one more indication that at midcentury most Mississippians still considered parties unnatural and contrary to the usual system of personal politics. Institutional parties violated the political culture, an arrangement designed to accommodate the demands of honor and masculinity and to mediate between personal independence and deference.

In both public and private, Mississippi's spokesmen condemned party organization. The politics of antipartyism found a hospitable climate in a male-centered public culture that valued manly independence so highly. Demagogues and party sycophants hardly qualified as men, for they had ceded their personal independence and become "commanded" delegates. Yet voters expected obedience to the community's wishes: fidelity to neighbors and kin, after earning their respect, was honorable and manly; truckling to party leaders to win office was not. State party organs, which were focused on national and state candidates and issues, emphasized organization and often gave the mistaken impression that parties were the sine qua non of politics. But those few enthusiastic supporters of parties — professional lawyer-politicians, editors, lifetime delegates — were forced to accommodate themselves to what ordinary voters wanted: antiparty parties. Whigs and Know-Nothings were founded on antipartyism; Democrats officially supported conventions, but remained touchy, defensive, and wary, pronouncing the necessary paeans to antipartyism to assuage voters' fears. On that unstable foundation even the pretense of a permanent, effective party foundered. Democrats, with their own regionalism and factionalism, matched the Whigs' dismal organization and just plain ineptitude. The Democrats were somewhat better organized, and more party activists advocated conventions and nominations, for there were simply more Democrats. But none of that changed the essential hostility to parties that dominated mainstream public opinion. Even in the late 1850s, the general public had not accepted party organization and many activists themselves seemed dubious. Divorced from an institutional context, politics remained what it was supposed to be — a personal affair conducted among individuals, ideally within their home community.

4

SMALL VICES

Voters, Elections, and the Myth of Party Dominance

"Elections before the war were simple affairs to what they have since become," recalled Mississippi's Frank Montgomery. "In the election of county officers, [party] politics was unknown; Whigs and Democrats ran as they pleased, and were voted for without regard to their politics. The same was true of judges, who were then elective. Only in the election of state officers, members of the legislature, congress and in presidential elections was the line drawn."[1] Both Montgomery's account and the pervasive antiparty rhetoric suggest that weak parties failed to cement voter loyalty. Of course, most people left no direct written evidence of their feelings. Election returns provide the only extensive record of their behavior, and, though incomplete and imperfect, they offer insight into the attitudes of otherwise inarticulate voters. In Mississippi the extraordinary number of elective offices and the consistently high voter turnout provide historians with uncommonly good evidence. The voters' behavior throughout the 1840s and 1850s supports Montgomery's description of a continuum of partisanship that ranged from national and state to county and precinct elections. Parties offered men reference points in national and state elections; unable to know candidates personally, most were resigned to following party symbols in these elections, although their loyalties shifted and they complained endlessly about the evils of party organization.

Parties were rarely involved in county elections, but turnout was invariably high, suggesting that factors other than organization brought men to the polls. Personal leadership and influence, family connections, and residence provided the guiding forces in this community network of voters. County and local contests are decisive for gauging voters' attitudes about parties; until voters embraced them in those elections—when they did not have to—we should consider their attitude to be antiparty. Unlike their counterparts in the Upper South and the North in the same period, Mississippi's Democrats and Whigs generally failed to extend their influence beyond state-level elections. Parties mattered to a small core of activists, but for all the bluster and scheming of editors, delegates, and state candidates, they possessed little of their supposed vigor among the mass of voters. Election returns confirm that parties, for most men, remained an unwelcome necessity. Instead, the vital and competitive local political culture that pervaded the vast majority of Mississippi's elections ensured that most voters, most of the time, did not consider or experience politics in institutional terms.

All elections brought Mississippians to the polls in great numbers. In the seventeen state and national contests between 1839 and 1860, voter participation exceeded 72 percent fourteen times (see table 4.1). The efforts of party activists obviously contributed to these impressive turnout figures. The hoopla and barbecues during campaign season attracted voters, women, and children to hear candidates and the "party message," although many accounts suggest they were more important as social occasions. Election day itself, a male event marked by drinking, gambling, and camaraderie, satisfied important social needs for men living rural, often isolated, lives. Perhaps the most obvious factor affecting turnout in these state and national elections was competition between the two major parties. Only late in the 1850s, when

TABLE 4.1. Estimated Voter Turnout in Mississippi Elections (All Counties), 1839–1860

Year	Office	Turnout (in percent)
1839	Governor	81
1840	President	80
1841	Governor	75
1843	Governor	74
1844	President	79
1845	Governor	72
1847	Governor	76
1848	President	78
1849	Governor	80
1851	Governor	77
1852	President	59
1853	Governor	73
1855	Governor	75
1856	President	73
1857	Governor	49
1859	Governor	51
1860	President	79

Source: The Tribune Almanac: For the Years 1838 to 1868, Inclusive: Comprehending the Politician's Register and the Whig Almanac, 2 vols. (New York, 1868); Mississippian, 1838–1860; U.S. Census, 1840, 1850, 1860.

the Democratic majority approached two-thirds, and in the Whigs's final and lackluster 1852 presidential race, did turnout drop to about 50 percent.

The general course of the voters' behavior in state and national elections can be traced by using the statistical technique of ecological regression, a methodology that estimates individual choices over time. Perhaps most important, its formula included nonvoters, making it possible to measure mobility into and out of the active electorate. While the results should be treated cautiously as estimates and not as precise figures, they do suggest certain trends.[2] First, the data indicate that a portion of the voting population remained fluid in its partisan loyalties. Some men changed their allegiance from year to year, responding, for a variety of reasons, to party propaganda, slogans, or simply personal whim. As the troubles over banks, bonds, and sectionalism imply, a powerful issue sometimes broke down party lines in just a few months. Later in the 1850s, the Know Nothing movement and possible secession demonstrated equal power to affect the voters' choices. The regression estimates also suggest that Democrats gained followers more consistently throughout the late 1850s, especially after 1856 when the Know Nothings disintegrated as a national party. Touting their organization as the only national, permanent party, Democratic activists recruited from the opposition and among young, first-time voters.[3] Based on these data, in the 1850s about one of every ten or twelve voters switched parties from one election to the next.

More important than switchers, however, was the apparent uncertainty created by a significant number of nonvoters and new voters, the result of mobility, death, and coming of age, as well as just staying at home. All parties relied on newcomers in every election. In 1855, for instance, Know-Nothing gubernatorial candidate Charles D. Fontaine gathered about half his votes from previous Democrats and nonvoters; the following year one-fifth of Millard Fillmore's Mississippi supporters had not voted in 1855. In 1860, John Bell's Constitutional Union Party drew significant support from former Democrats, Whigs, and Know Nothings, but over half its followers had not voted in the previous year's gubernatorial contest. The regression estimates suggest that between one-fourth and one-half of voters in any given election had not participated in the previous contest—most, probably, because they lived elsewhere, but some because they had chosen to stay home or been too young. Thus, in every election each party's support included 15 to 30 percent of new voters or converts.[4]

These regression estimates are supported by the observations of contemporary politicos. William Sharkey, one of the state's foremost anti-Democratic leaders, advised Know-Nothing gubernatorial candidate Charles D. Fontaine to campaign actively in 1855: "There [are] many people with whom a man's presence would have an influence, and if one party canvasses and the other does not," Sharkey cautioned, "you and I both know that the canvassing party would gather up hundreds of voters who are not governed by any firmly fixed principles." One Democrat relayed similar sentiments during the 1852 canvass: "Still, we have broken the enthusiasm of the Whigs, and you know, that much depends upon *enthusiasm*. It carries along the *floating vote*." Another experienced Democrat reminded his candidate that "you have been long enough amongst the people of that region [the piney woods] to know that they have no defined political principles."[5] These party regulars knew that hundreds of votes would be up for grabs each year. Their comments and the voting data indicate not a party system characterized by stable and committed partisans but rather a small group of devoted activists who worked to create enthusiasm among their core voters and to mobilize enough of the floating vote to win elections.[6]

The variability of election results shows up in the sometimes changing partisanship of individual counties. Amite County, for instance, was carried by the Whigs in 1847 and 1848, the Democrats in 1849, the State-Righters in 1851, the Whigs in 1852 and 1853, and the Know-Nothings in 1855, 1856, and 1857; the Democrats regained the majority in 1859. Claiborne County displayed particular inconstancy between 1847 and 1853, shifting from the Democratic to the Whig, Democratic, Unionist, Democratic, and Whig parties before supporting the Democrats for the rest of the decade. Although some counties remained consistently in one column or the other, the variability demonstrated by voters in Amite, Claiborne, and elsewhere illustrates why Mississippi's state and national elections so often produced partisan shifts. It was, of course, the fluidity created by mobility and nonvoters that prompted activists to hold all those barbecues, parades, and fish-frys; these staples of nineteenth-century politics helped socialize voters and get them to the polls. Voters accepted parties by stomping and hollering for Jackson or Clay, and they eagerly swilled liquor or ate barbecue; but that was not the same as considering parties a good idea or embracing a genuinely institutional political culture.

The impact of parties on district elections—where personal factors were accentuated—was even less. Offices chosen in districts included U.S. representative, circuit court judge, district attorney, and some high-ranking militia posts. District boundaries for these various contests were not necessarily contiguous but all encompassed several counties. (Some state-senate districts included two or even three counties, but they were unusual in this respect.) Only congressional elections consistently featured partisanship, although even then other factors often intervened. One Whig editor expressed a common fear when he admonished readers: "We hope the Whigs of Warren [County] will not be apathetic in regard to this [congressional] election merely because the candidate is not personally known to all of them." Henry Gray, the party's nominee, lived on the other side of the district. Democrat Hiram Van Eaton, discussing his party's choice for Congress with an acquaintance, voiced similar thoughts. He had hoped that his friend Stanhope

Posey, then a district judge, would pursue the nomination. But when he declined Van Eaton admitted that "I feel little interest in the matter beyond a desire for party harmony & the nomination of some good Democrat." In other words, he was willing to manipulate the party organization to advance his friend's interests, but when the election no longer involved a personal association he became indifferent.[7]

Charles D. Fontaine's 1853 campaign for seventh-district judge evinced the mixture of party and personal factors that characterized district politics. Something of a maverick, Fontaine was usually a Democrat, although he later ran for governor as a Know-Nothing. The three-way judgeship race included Phineas T. Scruggs, by reputation a Whig, and John W. Thompson, a recent Democratic convert. Several of Fontaine's correspondents also reported lingering effects of the 1851 confusion; the Unionists of Marshall County had sent Scruggs to the state convention while both Fontaine and Thompson lost as State-Rights candidates in Pontotoc and Tippah counties, respectively. "There are some Union Democrats that are gone for ever," warned one Fontaine supporter, "and are more dangerous than the most rabid Whig." Others related their attempts to paint Thompson with the brush of Whiggery so as to present Fontaine as the only "true Democrat" in this majority Democratic district.[8] Democrats from DeSoto and Tishomingo counties expressed their support as Democrats; the latter endorsed Fontaine's stance on the Bond question, "together with other issues," as consistent with the party in their county. Other letters recounted Fontaine's efforts to capture traditionally Whiggish voters who expressed concern about railroad development. These correspondents reported that they were working to convince Whigs that Fontaine did not oppose railroads, as Scruggs and Thompson had charged. Another Democrat underscored the potential value of party organization when he assured Fontaine that "your name is on our regular [Democratic] ticket and consequently will have a fair show."[9] National and state partisan issues, then, seemed important to some of Fontaine's supporters; but the confusion over party labels and voter loyalty — Whig, Democrat, Union, State-Rights — revealed the uncertainty common to Mississippi party politics.

Factors other than parties, however, evidently affected the contest. Fontaine's numerous correspondents, trying to convey the benefit gained in a personal appearance before the voters, repeatedly urged him to campaign more and to visit each region. One after another, they reminded Fontaine that it was imperative for voters to meet him and hear him speak in person: "You had better visit this County as soon as you can," warned one friend, echoing the pleas of many others. Some of Fontaine's men communicated the advantage gained from prestigious benefactors; one relayed the good news that "Dr. Dandridge is campaigning for you," and another reported that Dr. Morris and "all his friends" had come out for Fontaine: "They amount to at least 150 Whigs and the same number of Democrats."[10] Other informants hinted that party labels would not be decisive. One assured Fontaine that his concerns about religion were incorrect: "I think your impression in regard to Scruggs getting the Methodists is all wrong." The form of election tickets also varied from county to county. "According to the arrangement of the general ticket in this county," wrote one printer from Panola County, "the name of no candidates for judge was inserted." This meant that voters had to write in their choice of Fontaine, Scruggs, or Thompson; party candidates were usually printed on party ballots.[11]

The actual results of Fontaine's (unsuccessful) run for seventh-district judge suggest that partisanship had little impact. The total for Scruggs, the only acknowledged Whig, bore no relationship to the Whig vote for governor in those counties. Comparison to 1851 results likewise shows no logical pattern: Fontaine, the most prominent State-Rights man of the three, won his highest total in Tishomingo, which was the banner Union county just two years earlier. Scruggs and Thompson each dominated his home county, demonstrating the importance of residence. In short, some active partisans who wrote to Fontaine conceived of the election as a partisan contest and in terms of what they perceived as party issues, but others saw it as a matter of personal politics. The returns spoke to the voters' varied motives and perspectives, but the importance of party identification in this case was decidedly equivocal.

The election discussed by Fontaine and his supporters typified district races and especially judicial contests. Mississippi was a pioneer in the election of judges, a controversial provision of the 1832 Constitution. Most rhetoric held that magistrates should be "above mere party politics," and each side routinely accused its opponents of secretly uniting behind one candidate, thus perverting the "purity" of the process. Whig and independent journals more consistently supported a nonpartisan judiciary: Democrats complained less and several editors advocated party nominations as early as 1851, but the idea received little support. In 1858 Democratic party leaders at the *Mississippian* were still trying to convince voters that judicial nominations were a good and "progressive" idea. Election returns, however, fail to sustain the concern of antiparty spokesmen and indicate that judicial contests rarely hinged on partisanship. Although only sparse data are available below the county level and offer only a crude measurement, even a casual look indicates that vote totals simply do not correlate with those for governor or other state offices. Many races featured only one candidate, and even those with two or more tended to be lopsided. In sum, the state's dominant antiparty tendencies apparently overwhelmed those zealous editors and party operatives who were urging judicial nominations.[12]

If district races suggest some mixture of partisan and personal factors, the evidence from county elections reveals an even more negligible role for parties. Only for the office of county representative to the state legislature could party organizers hope to enforce nominations, although even that hold on power was tenuous. Spokesmen typically justified this party influence on grounds that the legislature dealt with questions touching on national or state issues that went beyond individual counties — for example, choosing U. S. senators and drawing congressional boundaries. Editors referred to representatives by party affiliation and the legislators sometimes cooperated. Yet considerable evidence demonstrates that voters did not automatically extend partisanship to the legislature. Independent candidates were common, and the parties' ability to control nominations was always dubious. Election returns also indicate no linear trend toward partisanship; in fact, legislative contests became much more unpredictable in the late 1850s.

Party editors frequently pleaded with voters to limit legislative candidates to just enough to fill the county slate. "It is very probable there will be four or five whig candidates for the Legislature," complained editor Milford N. Prewett, "but we will guarantee they [Democrats] do not have more than two." Democratic editor John Thompson bemoaned the fact that there were three candidates of his party for two legislative seats from Winston County, which allowed the lone Whig to be elected to one of them despite a solid Democratic majority. Local partisans, he complained, should have called a county convention to "harmonise the little personal bickerings that prevail."[13] Personal considerations — particularly friendship and kinship expressed in the persistence of residential voting — continued to undermine party effectiveness. The timeless partisan appeal to "principles, not men" was another expression of the same problem: how to replace personal with institutional loyalties.

In some cases just a few switching voters could upset party control. Yazoo County voters elected Democrat Harrison Barksdale and Whig John R. Burrus in 1853; the latter beat another Democrat by only sixteen votes despite the county's Democratic majority. In 1851 voters in Marshall County favored Jefferson Davis's party by a slim margin, 1380 to 1350 but sent two Union and two State-Rights men to the legislature. Lowndes County voters supported Davis for governor but returned three Unionists as representatives. The future president of the Confederacy polled 681 votes, but the top State-Rights legislative candidate garnered only 650. The three winners got 750, 723, and 660. Two years later the voters in Lowndes chose one Whig, one Union Democrat, and one State-Rights Democrat.

At other times the vote for state legislature was completely unrelated to party totals. The men from Harrison County, for instance, supported Democrat John J. McRae convincingly in 1855 (430 to 240), but for the legislature John Henley only squeaked past Robert Saffold (307 to 300). Sometimes sheer chaos reigned. In 1849 Tishomingo County produced thirteen competitive candidates for four seats in the legislature. The voters' usual Democratic majority held up for Governor John Quitman (1432 to 734) but no representative received more than 918 votes. In a majority of elections for the state legislature between 1840 and 1860, partisanship was probably the most important factor in deciding the outcome. But the data for many other cases reveal that even in these county contests assumed to be partisan, the weak organizations often failed to decide the outcome.

For county offices other than representative, Whig and Democratic activists failed to generate any consistent support for nominations — the most important measure of party organization. The voters' rejection signaled their persistent belief that personal relationships should always take precedence over institutional ones, whenever possible. Zealous editors who occasionally called for voters to place party ahead of neighborhood networks met with frustration and, ultimately, with failure.

Among those who favored nominations, Whig editor H. E. Van Winkle was perhaps the most persistent. From his headquarters in Jackson, in 1845 he urged the party to choose all candidates in Warren and Hinds counties, where Whigs typically enjoyed a majority. The editor of the Democratic *Mississippian* predictably declared that "all good men must deprecate the existence of that furious party spirit." Fellow Democrats in Whiggish Claiborne and Yazoo counties also attacked Van Winkle's plan: "Such a course serves to kindle afresh the spirit of party — and to add fuel to the flames of party animosity so destructive to the quietude and harmony of society." Port Gibson Democrat W. B. Tebo naturally invoked the politics of antipartyism. County nominations, he wrote, will "cause the most bitter political hatred among the people. God knows that that feeling already exists throughout the Union to a very alarming degree. Instead of feeding this dangerous flame, pregnant with discord, dissolution, proscription, anarchy, and all their attendant evils, it should be the duty of every good citizen to prevent its spread."[14]

As members of the minority party, self-interest naturally colored the reaction of these Democrats. But Van Winkle's own Hinds County Whigs also divided over the controversial plan. The county's other Whig editor, George W. Harper, criticized Van Winkle for his aggressive tactics and urged him to adopt a more liberal policy that accepted different viewpoints on state policy and on the idea of a county convention. "We would remind the ultra Conventionists," Harper lectured, "that the principle upon which was achieved the first whig victory in Hinds county, was the *Anti-Caucus* principle." "We think it, therefore, quite natural, that some of the old 'rank and file' should yet cherish the impressions made during the revolution [origins] of parties." Throughout July Harper criticized the upcoming convention and eventually reported that he was "unable" to attend, although Jackson was only sixteen miles away.[15]

Undeterred by the controversy, Van Winkle plunged ahead and hoisted a slate of Whig nominees for all Hinds County offices. Typically erratic election returns, though, demonstrate that for most voters residence and neighborhood identification remained more important than partisanship. Among state offices, the Whig nominees for auditor and treasurer carried the county, but Democrats won a majority for governor and secretary of state. Whig nominees for Congress and the state legislature did well, winning seven of eight contested seats. Yet most of Van Winkle's county candidates lost, including his "nominees" for sheriff, probate court clerk, tax assessor, and treasurer, the last finishing a distant third in a four-man race. Only for circuit court clerk (no opposition) and coroner (token opposition) could Van Winkle claim dubious success. The editor complained bitterly about Whig indifference: "Is there no reason why county offices in whig counties should not be filled by whigs, is there any reason why locofocos should have them all?" The answer, apparently, was that neighborhood loyalties were more important than parties. In the sheriff's race, for instance, Whig and Jackson resident John Oldham received two-thirds of the votes cast in his hometown but lost the election to Raymond's Daniel Thomas, a Democrat who won three-fourths of his neighbors' votes. In the coroner's contest the two candidates each won overwhelming majorities in and near his home precinct; winner Robert Brown outpolled his opponent 664 to 63 in those precincts nearest his residence. Most voters, in short, apparently thought county nominations a poor idea, and by the next election Van Winkle was gone and nobody suggested that Whigs try them again.[16]

Carroll County's Democratic editors also pushed unsuccessfully for county nominations in 1845. They argued — apparently with a straight face — that "the whigs are as well drilled as were the armies of Napoleon" and "never . . . [run] two of their men for the same office in the county." Others supported the call for "harmony and concord" but made no formal nominations. Yet returns showed a remarkable number of two-man races, possibly suggesting that some informal arrangements were made. But in Carroll County, as elsewhere, it only happened once.[17] In other counties, activists periodically pushed county-level organization. "Believing the necessity of a full and thorough organization of the democratic party," wrote "Many Voters" from Lowndes County, "we would respectfully suggest the policy and propriety of their bringing forward candidates for every office in the County." "Many Voters" was probably the editor himself, who had defended conventions in several previous issues. True to the politics of antipartyism, he accused Whigs of making county nominations in 1839, which therefore forced Democrats to do so simply to compete. As usual, county delegates in 1849 spurned the idea and nominated only candidates for state senator and representative.[18]

That same year, Democrats in Lafayette County tried nominating candidates for all county offices and for policemen. Benjamin F. Dill, editor of *The Organizer* in Oxford, led the move for better organization. Democratic activists in three of the five beats followed Dill's advice and recommended local favorites for each county office. The county convention chose the nominees for most county offices, although its initial choices for sheriff and circuit clerk both declined to run. Election returns show lukewarm support for the idea, or at least the candidates. Democrats carried five of the seven county offices but lost the prestigious races for sheriff and probate judge. For the board of police they claimed only one winner out of five. The reasons for voters' support or rejection of the nominees remain speculative, of course (particularly without detailed returns), but it is obvious that party "discipline" had faltered. Editor Dill could claim victory in obtaining the nominations, but their results offered little encouragement to those who hoped parties might overcome personal loyalties. Dill abandoned the idea of local nominations in 1851.[19] Tishomingo Democrats also tried county nominations in 1849 and eventually split the party into conventionists and anticonventionists. There, as everywhere, party activists made the mistake only once.[20]

The several earlier attempts at county nominations between 1841 and 1845 also reinforce the impression that Mississippi's parties peaked in the early 1840s, when many counties were still in their formative years. Having overcome some of the early opposition to caucuses and "secretive cliques," party organizers seemed to make progress between 1839 and 1843. Returns from early Pontotoc and Yazoo counties, for instance, suggest partisan contests for sheriff in those years, although other local races demonstrate no clear pattern. Newspapers contained less antiparty rhetoric and a few Whig editors even advocated nomination by convention. While defending voters' independence against "dictation," Holly Springs leader Thomas Falconer named conventions "among the 'things misnamed.'" He admitted the possibility of manipulation and "a widespread and deep set prejudice . . . against what is commonly termed conventions," which voters "associated with the idea of unfairness, juggling, and intrigue." Yet he declared it "absolutely necessary to success, that we run no more candidates, than we have representatives to elect." To neglect conventions, he concluded, was the "height of folly," especially when Democrats were using them more often. His words mostly fell on deaf ears, even in 1843; within just a few years positive comments like Falconer's would be unheard of.[21]

Apart from these rare attempts at nominations, most elections for county offices featured multiple, self-chosen candidates and gave no indication that parties made any impact. "It is folly to suffer party to interfere" with county politics, admitted one editor. Or, as a voter explained, neighborhood ties always sabotaged the likelihood of a nominating convention for local offices: "[D]o you not suppose that every man in this county has some particular man that he desires to support for some office."[22] Frequently seven, eight, or as many as ten men vied for positions in county government. In Marshall County, for example, eleven men ran for probate court clerk in 1858; that same year, sixteen candidates vied for Panola County assessor and eight for coroner. In Tishomingo, the situation was typically chaotic in 1853: there were five candidates for coroner, six for ranger, six for assessor, and four for treasurer. In 1849 Amite County voters could choose from among five candidates for assessor, five for treasurer, and six for tax collector. Lauderdale County's 1845 experience typified many general elections: there were six candidates for state representative — another failure of parties to nominate even for that office — three each for probate clerk and coroner, and five each for sheriff and assessor. In short, little evidence suggests any effective, or even tangible, party organization in county elections. Between 1848 and 1860 the surviving returns from 408 elections in ten sample counties record three or more candidates in 159 of them (39 percent) while 171 races (41.9 percent) had only two candidates. Offices in the remainder of the elections went uncontested.

Even when there were only two candidates, the results show little or no relation to state races. In 1853 Jasper County voters supported Democrat John J. McRae for governor, 551 to 310, but for sheriff and surveyor, the only contests with just two candidates, voters split 402 to 394 and 409 to 391, respectively. In Jefferson County the 1847 party vote, at 439 to 44, was overwhelmingly Democratic, but the two-man race for sheriff stayed close at 346 to 242. All the other contests had either just one or multiple candidates. The outcome in Lowndes County's 1849 elections typified local elections and parties. Voters sent one "Democrat," one "Taylor Democrat," and one "Whig" to the state legislature. They also elected a Democratic sheriff (748 to 656), a Whig for circuit court clerk (899 to 639), a Democrat for assessor (742 to 701), a Whig for treasurer (777 to 662), and the Democrats who ran unopposed for coroner, ranger, and surveyor. For the board of police, county voters chose three Democrats and two Whigs to represent the five districts. Elsewhere, men showed similar disregard for party affiliation. In Hinds County, where voters consistently opposed the Democrats with large majorities, they still elected Democratic leaders Benjamin F. Edwards as circuit court clerk in (1853, 1855, and 1860), T. F. Owen as coroner (1855), and Napoleon B. Ward as circuit court clerk (1849). In Carroll County, the voters supported Whig gubernatorial nominee Francis Rogers in 1853 but also returned Democratic state leader Andrew M. Nelson as probate clerk.

Precinct-level data often provides one final and very graphic indication that party loyalties did not determine county elections. The data shown in figures 4.1 through 4.3 pertain to county contests that, superficially, appeared to be partisan. Each of these elections involved two competitive candidates whose county totals corresponded closely to the votes cast for governor, suggesting that voters carried their party loyalty into the county races. But in these cases, county-level data are misleading. Each point on the graphs represents the percentage of votes cast for the winning candidate in each precinct. While the cumulative totals for the county candidates nearly match the county's gubernatorial vote, the precinct data reveal almost no relationship. Thus in 1849 Hinds County (figure 4.1) the Whig candidate for governor, Luke Lea, carried the county (with 54 percent of the vote); Jackson's John P. Oldham for sheriff (53 percent) and Utica's Napoleon Ward for

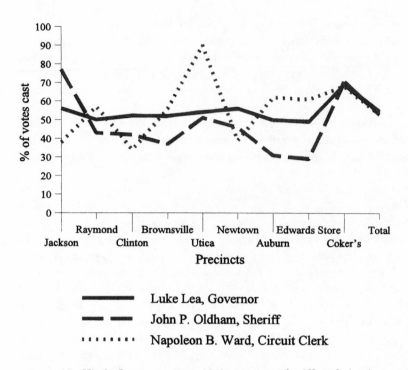

FIGURE 4.1. Hinds County contests, 1849: governor, sheriff, and circuit-court clerk. *Source*: Record Group 28, Volume 28a, Mississippi Department of Archives and History.

circuit court clerk (53 percent) also won the county, by nearly identical totals. But the precinct totals for the county candidates demonstrate almost no relationship to the partisan base line (Lea's totals) or to each other. If partisanship had decided these county elections, the lines would run parallel. Instead, wild fluctuations from precinct to precinct point out that despite very similar countywide totals — evidently a coincidence — most voters seemingly followed neighborhood loyalties. Thus even in these very rare instances when partisanship seemed to shape county politics, a more detailed look at voting data indicates once again that parties had failed.

More than antiparty ideology or natural family and neighborhood loyalties, however, procedural factors and legal changes sustained the antiparty political culture. The facility with which candidates could nominate themselves, the unlimited variability in the way ballots were printed, which showed little party influence below the state level, and legal requirements for separate, multiple ballot boxes and elections all contributed to, and reflected, party weakness.[23] Editors charged only modest fees for announcing a man's candidacy, usually five or ten dollars for state and district offices and between two and five dollars for the county or precinct. They also complained loudly about nonpayment. "We have established the rule that all persons announcing their names as candidates," wrote James H. R. Taylor, "shall pay the fee before the first insertion." He insisted that neither "favor nor affection will cause us to swerve from this regulation."[24]

Descriptions of tickets suggest almost unlimited variation and imply that parties exerted only minimal influence over the actual voting process. The law provided only that each ballot should be "a ticket or scroll of paper, on which shall be written or printed the names of the persons for whom [the voter] intends to vote."[25] On printed ballots, candidates needed to request, and pay for, inclusion of their names. Some descriptions were vague: "Candidates for this county wishing their names inserted in the tickets," wrote one editor without elaboration, "will please notify us." Another declared that it "has been a uniform practice . . . in the Southern section of the state to print the names of all candidates, whig and democrat, on the tickets . . . knowing it was just as easy to erase [cross through] as to write a name."[26] Elsewhere, it seemed, anything was possible: "There will be at the Creole Office . . . a large number of Election Tickets, for this and other counties. Candidates, or their friends, can have them struck off in any form desired."

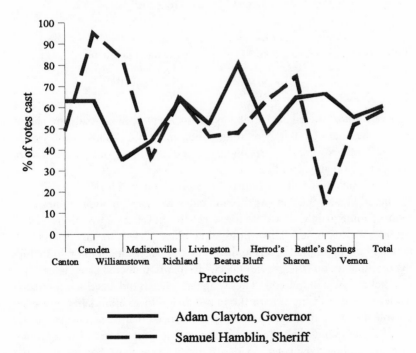

FIGURE 4.2. Madison County contests, 1843: governor and sheriff. *Source*: Record Group 28, Volume 28b, Mississippi Department of Archives and History.

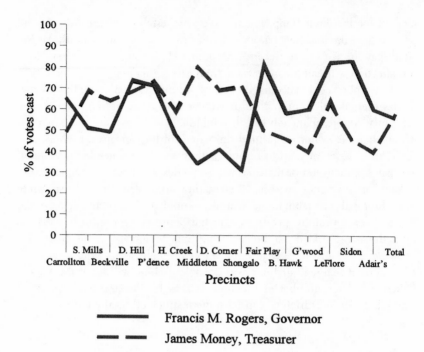

FIGURE 4.3. Carroll County contests, 1853: governor and treasurer. *Source*: Record Group 28, Volume 30b, Mississippi Department of Archives and History.

Another editor offered to "print tickets for every body and in any shape. This is the understanding here among the candidates. — Some want Tickets 'straight,' others want Tickets 'slightly mixed'. So make out your tickets to suit yourselves, and send them in."[27]

John Richardson of the *Prairie News* printed tickets for four counties in northeast Mississippi. He urged candidates to "send in their names [and money] immediately, as we desire to get the tickets to all portions of said counties in due time." This would allow office seekers to have friends stationed at the appropriate polls to distribute the tickets. In addition to including their names on "the general ticket," Richardson offered candidates "Special tickets, $1 a hundred." These, apparently, would have a candidate's name printed with the title of the appropriate office, eliminating the need for voters to write it in. Another editor announced that he received an order for three thousand blank tickets containing only the names of offices, presumably to allow each voter to write in his own selections; but, for $5.00 per thousand, a candidate could also have his own ballots printed with his name in the appropriate place. The cost of including a candidate's name usually depended on his office. Editor Prewett of the *Yazoo City Weekly Whig*, for instance, charged $5.00 for state and district candidates and $3.00 for those at the county or precinct. J. H. Leatherman at the *Woodville Republican* asked $5.00 and $2.50, respectively.[28]

State party candidates, too, bore much of the cost of printed ballots themselves. The Democrats' custom was that each nominee deposited $100 for printing expenses with a "Committee on Printing" or with some prominent party member. In the spirit of unity and loyalty, the party hoped, the ballots so produced would be true Democratic tickets. In 1849 party leaders appealed to printers: "It is scarcely necessary for us to add our expectation, that under no circumstances will the name of a *Whig* candidate for a district or county office be printed on the tickets distributed for our State nominees under this arrangement." They worried because of the past "abuse which has sometimes been made of Democratic Tickets to the detriment of worthy Democratic Candidates for District and County offices." In other words, Democratic nominees wanted editors to facilitate, or force, local partisanship by informally keeping non-Democrats off the party's official tickets. This meant that editors would be limited to accepting fees from fellow partisans.[29] Because party tickets were typically distinguished by color, shape, or symbols — allowing observers to identify voter choice — few nineteenth-century Americans enjoyed a secret ballot when parties controlled their distribution.

Surviving tickets, however, are suggestive of the weakness of party discipline and demonstrate, again, the inability of parties to move effectively beyond the state level. In Tippah County, Democratic tickets in 1849 included the names of their state candidates but no judges or district officers. For county races, only the names of Daniel Hunt (probate court clerk), John F. Ford (ranger), and Henry J. Bickerstaff (coroner) appeared on the ballot. Hunt was the only candidate for probate clerk, and Ford published the local Democratic newspaper, the *Ripley Advertiser*. For the remaining offices, including representative to the state legislature, other county officials, and the board of police, voters needed to write in their choices. Even worse for party leaders, in Leake County the so-called Democratic State Ticket included the name of almost every district, county, and board of police candidate. The editor even printed the names of Whig candidates for the state legislature. It is no wonder, perhaps, that by 1855 the Democratic state nominees virtually gave up the idea of a party ticket: "The conditions we desire to affix to this proposal is, that the name of *no other candidates for the same offices for which we are running* be placed on the tickets. We leave you, however, free to make any proper arrangement with District, County or Beat officers, of either party, who desire to have their names on the tickets." The nominees, of course, were conceding that editors and printers wanted the extra income they earned by including all paying candidates on the party's ticket. The candidates' emphatic plea about state offices clearly suggests that some editors even inserted Whig nominees for those positions. These Democratic candidates concluded with a pathetic request that tickets simply spell their names correctly, "as some papers have printed the *given names* of the candidates wrong."[30]

Activists from both parties also warned repeatedly of "fraudulent" tickets. "Our 'scrupulous' neighbors of the *Mississippian*," wrote Jackson's Whig editor, "are making a loud outcry against the probability of fraudulent or tricky tickets being printed by the *whigs*." He insisted, however, that "instead of being a *whig* fault the saddle, so far as we have observed has almost always been upon the other horse, all over the country." Furthermore, he claimed "one of the tricks of king caucus is to print the names so closely that an independent voter cannot change one of them so as to write another name in the place of one erased with any chance of rendering it legible." One Democratic editor warned all voters to beware of ballots printed with too many candidates for Congress: "Those who vote a Congressional Ticket with *five* names, will cast an illegal vote and all the candidates voted for will be thus defrauded." These complaints offer only fragmentary evidence about how widespread fake tickets actually were, although the warnings were standard practice before every election.[31]

The shadowy practice of "swapping votes" also remains difficult to gauge. Editors from both parties begged voters not to trade their votes for party nominees in order to gain support for friends running in local or county races. "Go for the ticket — go the whole ticket — and the whole ticket will be elected," preached one typical refrain. "If democrats endeavor to advance the interests, each of his particular friend, by swapping, partial, if not entire defeat will be the consequences." "You have a full democratic ticket for the county [representatives], composed of men every way capable and faithful," admonished another frustrated editor, "a ticket fairly got up, without caucusing or secret management." He pleaded with voters to support their party: "Your vote, in fact, is not your own to be determined by the whim of the moment *or the dictates of personal friendship*." "*Especially for political offices*," implored one Know-Nothing leader, "vote for *measures*, not for *men*." She urged voters not to accept Democratic offers "to vote for your friend for sheriff, for clerk, for probate judge." Holly Springs editor Thomas Falconer lectured his Whig readers after their candidates for legislature were defeated in 1843: "You have lost your ticket by not coming out to the polls, and by swapping off your own political candidates, for county officers." Thankfully, he concluded, the presidential election was always separate from county contests, or else local Whigs "would swap off Henry Clay for a constable." Like warnings of fraudulent tickets, reproaches against swapping were routine. If swapping was commonplace, of course, it underscores the weakness of party loyalty and identification relative to more personal ties of friendship or kinship.[32]

Finally, the timing of elections worked mightily against party enthusiasts. From 1833 (after the new constitution) through 1855, Mississippi held elections for all state, county, and local officials on the same days at the same polls and used one ballot box. In theory this practice should have facilitated partisanship in all contests—although it did not—because voters could deposit only one ballot that included every office from governor to constable. After 1855, however, a constitutional change separated county and local contests from state elections. The governor and state legislature still were elected in odd-numbered years, but voters chose local officials in 1858 and 1860. This change hurt partyists because rank-and-file voters would have to accept county conventions every year in order to nominate party candidates for all offices. Before 1856, at least voters were accustomed to having county conventions to nominate men for the legislature; and in several cases editors had convinced them to try nominations for other county offices as long as delegates were already gathered together. Another new provision implemented in 1858 called for separate ballot boxes—and therefore separate tickets—for precinct offices. Voters then needed one ticket for county candidates and another for the board of police, justice of the peace, and constable.[33] In 1860 voting became even more complicated: "Voters will remember that THREE boxes will be opened at each precinct," one for "the general county ticket," another "the military [militia] ticket," and a third "the beat ticket."[34] Separating state polls from other elections, therefore, undermined county nominations and straight-party voting, further weakening the parties' chances of penetrating local politics and replacing personal, neighborhood ties with partisan loyalties.

Although county elections did not involve parties, and the names of many local candidates apparently did not appear on any printed ticket, turnout remained very high. One way to measure participation in county contests is by the rate of *roll-off* from state offices. Roll-off simply measures the extent to which men voted for state, normally partisan, candidates but not for those farther down on the ballot. In other words, roll-off calculates what percentage of voters went to the polls but, for whatever reasons, chose not to vote for some offices. From the early 1840s to 1858 the rate of roll-off for the five principal county offices averaged between 1 and 2 percent (see table 4.2). Roll-off was 2 percent or less in nearly two-thirds of these contests and 5 percent or less in about nine out of ten. For sheriff and circuit court clerk, roll-off was less than 2 percent in seven out of ten contests and averaged less than 1 percent overall. Furthermore, these figures are calculated with data from all elections with two or more candidates, including some lopsided elections in which roll-off was greater than usual. If we limit the calculations to competitive races, roll-off becomes statistically insignificant. These figures are dramatically lower than those historians Paul Bourke and Donald DeBats discovered in 1850s Oregon, where roll-off averaged between 7 and 12 percent; the lowest rates among "competitive" races between partisan candidates (and most county contests were partisan in Oregon). In Mississippi roll-off almost never topped 3 or 4 percent, whether elections were competitive or not. Voter turnout for county and local elections during the longer

TABLE 4.2. Roll-Off in Sample Counties, 1841–1855

	Percent of all elections falling within each range					Average Roll-Off (%)	Total No. of Elections
Office	0% & negative	0.1% to 2%	3% to 5%	6% to 9%	10% & higher		
Sheriff	25	44	25	6	1	0.7	89
Treasurer	20	23	35	16	7	3.1	75
Assessor	21	27	31	15	6	2.3	86
Circuit clerk	31	38	26	6	0	0.9	72
Probate clerk	28	35	30	4	3	1.3	71
All five offices	25	33	29	9	3	1.6	393

Source: Election Data from Amite, Attala, Bolivar, Carroll, Chickasaw, Harrison, Hinds, Jasper, Jefferson, Lafayette, Lauderdale, Lowndes, Madison, Marshall, Tippah, Tishomingo, and Wilkinson counties.

period from the 1830s to 1860 remained very consistent, regardless of competitiveness.[35]

In about one in four contests voting for county offices equaled or exceeded that for state (i.e., party-controlled) elections (*negative roll-off*). In 1843, more Yazoo County men voted for sheriff and circuit court clerk than for governor. The same held true in Claiborne County in 1845: 791 votes were cast for governor, but 900 for county treasurer. The eight candidates for assessor in Marshall also outpolled the party candidates. Lowndes County's 1843 returns reveal that more votes were recorded in each of the five county races than for governor. The contests for treasurer (seven candidates) and assessor (fifteen) were especially warm. These cases of negative roll-off were repeated in the county's 1847, 1851, and 1853 elections.

These data are even more compelling when we consider the evidence that some, probably a majority, of county candidates' names were not printed on ballots but had to be written in by voters or election clerks. The Mississippi experience contradicts the findings of scholars who argue that strip ballots prepared by the parties reduced roll-off. Perhaps that happened in other states, but in Mississippi voters apparently participated in local contests in equal or greater numbers despite the inconvenience of open or blank ballots. The numerous cases of zero or negative roll-off undermine the popular argument that parties alone generated the high rates of voter participation in the nineteenth century. Instead, these startling figures underscore voters' concern for county government and passion for local politics despite, or perhaps because of, the absence of parties.[36]

Another measure of how compelling most voters found county politics was the persistent competitiveness and high turnout of county elections in the late 1850s, after state (party) races had become hopelessly one-sided. Democrats carried the state easily, with majorities of nearly two-thirds, in both 1857 and 1859, as public enthusiasm lagged and turnout fell to about 50 percent (see table 4.1). In 1857, Hinds County editor George W. Harper judged that "this has certainly been the mildest political canvass that we have ever witnessed. So far as all this region in concerned, no interest whatever has been shown by either party." In Panola County the situation was repeated: "The usual interest manifested in State Elections has, at the present time, almost totally vanished."[37]

But county politics in 1858 and 1860—now separated from state elections—remained hotly contested and turnout often topped 80 percent. Results from Carroll County demonstrate statewide trends with unusual clarity. In 1857 turnout fell to an all-time low of 31 percent and in 1859 remained less than 50 percent. In both elections the Democratic candidate garnered nearly 70 percent of the votes cast. In the 1858 county elections, however, more than eight out of ten eligible voters participated, and competition remained fierce. In the race for sheriff, Frank Pleasants beat J. C. McKenzie 857 to 834, and there were close contests for all other county offices except treasurer. Two years later turnout neared 90 percent and competition was fierce. Elsewhere, the Democrats carried Harrison County 508 to 30 in 1859, while in the next year's county election for sheriff and treasurer, candidates won by 262 to 259 and 219 to 208 to 75, respectively. In Lowndes County, Democrats won the gubernatorial elections of 1857 and 1859 by huge margins (908 to 83 and 1,004 to 35), but county races remained close. Other counties showed similar results. In 1858 editor Harper commented that "the vote polled [in Hinds County] was nearly a full one" and larger than "for some years past."[38] A summary of turnout data from the sample counties appears in table 4.3.

These high rates of participation indicate that county politics remained business as usual and again suggest they were perhaps the chief reason why voters went to the polls. The incidence of negligible or no roll-off before 1858 and higher turnouts late in the decade makes it clear that county and local elections drew voters in equal, if not greater, numbers than did state and national contests. Important county races sometimes even pushed state and national concerns completely out of the press, especially in papers that were not state party organs. Local taxes, public improvements, education, and convict labor were just a few of the issues that animated elections for county representative or board of police. These voting trends bolster the judgment of historians who argue for the preeminent importance of nineteenth-century county government. For most people it was the only legal authority they encountered and was paramount for many who were only marginally connected to the regional or national economies. National, and even state, officials seemed remote, but most men dealt regularly with the county tax assessor, sheriff, or member of the board of police; and each of these officials made decisions that were more important to their daily lives than those made by representatives in Jackson, much less Washington.[39]

What emerges from the election data is a local political culture operating independently of party organizations or party issues, one that shaped the

TABLE 4.3. Estimated Voter Turnout in Sample Counties, 1857–1860

County	Office, Year, and Turnout (in percent)				
	Governor 1857	Sheriff 1858	Governor 1859	Sheriff 1860	President 1860
Amite	67	73	65	74	75
Bolivar	62	80	47	85	93
Carroll	31	83	48	88	97
Chickasaw	—	87	53	87	90
Claiborne	60	61	49	—	72
Harrison	48	—	53	52	55
Hinds	52	65	61	58	82
Jasper	69	75	70	75	74
Lowndes	52	72	53	63	85
Madison	71	72	72	67	68
Marshall	50	69	55	67	79
Tippah	40	75	44	69	69
Tishomingo	—	73	55	75	76

Source: Record Group 28, Mississippi Department of Archives and History; *House Journal*, 1859; *Mississippian*, 1857–1860; *Weekly Panola Star*, Oct. 13, 1858, Oct. 12, 1859; *Daily Southern Reveille*, Nov. 7, 1858; *Commonwealth*, Oct. 9, 1858; U.S. Census, 1850, 1860.

vast majority of Mississippi's elections and its voters' behavior. County and local elections generated enthusiasm and competition that ensured a high turnout even when party contests at the state level held little attraction. When politics mattered most, it seems, parties were least important.

One final indication that typical Whig-Democrat contests failed to inspire many voters was the partisanship evident in some county and local elections in 1851 as the Union and State-Rights parties battled over the Compromise of 1850. Although most voters found typical party battles muddled or personally meaningless, the intertwined issues of slavery, honor, and secession generated sudden excitement and presented an imperative that extended their significance into some county contests. In Hinds County, the disunion crisis even affected the race for probate court clerk. Several voters wrote to the *Mississippian* to ask about the stand of each candidate running for that office. "It having been laid down as a rule to carry the [current] party question into every election," they declared, "we desire respectfully to propound to you the following questions." Their inquiries dealt solely with the compromise and sectional issues. Incumbent probate court clerk William H. Hampton replied in the subsequent issue that he was a Unionist and intended to vote for Henry Foote. "While I deprecate the system of making political opinions a test of qualification of ministerial office, I yet accord to my fellow-citizens the right to demand of candidates for public favor their opinions on any political questions that may agitate the country."

Hampton asserted that he had always remained nonpartisan while in office and that if reelected would "leave the discussion of political questions to politicians." The other three candidates made similar replies. During a debate at Edward's Depot one local man announced his candidacy for clerk of the chancery court. Someone in the crowd asked if he intended to vote for Quitman or Foote, to which the candidate replied, "Quitman."[40] Finally, in Holmes County the Unionists from Botter's Store precinct resolved that the current crisis was "of such vital importance to freemen, and to struggling liberty . . . as to make it the duty of the Union men to support the candidates of the Union party, for the political offices of both State and County." Although they realized it was a departure from custom, they argued that Unionists ought to vote a "straight party ticket . . . regardless of former party distinctions or personal considerations." Possible secession, then, seemed important enough to override the usual bases of local voting.[41]

In these cases the acute partisanship also reflected, to some extent, the peculiarities of Hinds County. Jackson hosted the conventions of both parties and, unlike most areas, had two or more regular, opposing partisan newspapers. More than the usual number of rallies, conventions, and meetings in the city that year heightened the competitive tension. In short, Hinds was somewhat atypical in its potential for partisanship. Nearby Carroll County showed some of the same excitement in 1851. Like Hinds, it had a large town (by 1850s Mississippi standards) with two party newspapers. It usually provided the second greatest number of delegates to the parties' state conventions. In 1851 the precinct returns for probate clerk, circuit court clerk, and assessor were somewhat similar to those for state offices. Although the totals varied slightly, as did some of the precinct returns, there was a definite congruency. Furthermore, longtime probate clerk Andrew M. Nelson lost his only election; he was a high-profile State-Rights partisan in a county that supported the Unionists. Yet even here the impact of this crisis was limited; the races for sheriff (five candidates) and treasurer (three) conformed to the traditional pattern. The varied returns from most counties give no indication that the new parties had a meaningful impact on county politics, in only a few instances did the voters demand that local candidates reveal their party loyalty.

Nonpartisanship normally extended to local contests for board of police, justice of the peace, and constable. As one indication, party activists were often elected in districts where the opposition was strong. Amite County voters in Thickwoods and at Toler's box, for example, supported the Opposition candidates for governor in 1857 and 1859 (45 to 9 and 63 to 20) but elected Democrats Henry G. Street and C. C. Lea for justice of the peace in 1858 and 1859, respectively. In Carroll's district three, carried by Know-Nothing Charles Fontaine in 1855, voters chose Democratic state delegate Patrick H. Brown as their board of police member. Democrat Henry Matthews triumphed as justice of the peace in the Whiggish Duck Hill precinct in 1849. Returns for municipal elections reveal similar cases. The residents of anti-Democratic Carrollton returned prominent Democrats William W. Hart and William Cothran to the town council year after year.

Voters in Hinds County showed a similar disregard for party politics when choosing their local officials. In 1849 Raymond precinct voters supported Whig Luke Lea but elected longtime Democrat Drury J. Brown justice of the peace; Democrat William H. Dean won the race for that office in Newtown, another Whig precinct. Democratic constable John A. Gallman won reelection in the Raymond-Coker's Store precinct in successive elections between 1849 and 1853 despite the area's consistent Whig majority. Even in the heated contest of 1851, State-Rights delegate A. K. Barlow won election unopposed in the Edward's Depot precinct, which voted for Governor Foote 63 to 40. Jackson's voters, who gave the Unionists a two-hundred vote majority, chose as their justice of the peace Henry J. Shackleford, chairman of the State-Rights committee of arrangements. Democrats in Clinton chose Whig James W. White for the same office in 1859 even though nearly 65 percent of the town's voters marked their ballots for Democrat John Pettus for governor.

Overwhelmed by the antiparty tradition, Mississippi's parties failed to capture the loyalty of most voters, who apparently remained more satisfied with their face-to-face political culture and the luxury of backing men they knew personally. While they relied on the Right of Instruction to keep party hacks in line, they could trust—or believed they could trust—their friends, neighbors, and kinfolk. They were only too happy to dispense with parties whenever possible. "The question among us should be," summarized one writer, "is the aspirant for the office of Sheriff, Clerk, &c. capable, faithful and honest?" This question could only be answered, wrote another, when "a majority of the voters have form[ed] some [personal] acquaintance with him. . . . This can only be done by the candidate canvassing the county. Can a man afford to do this before a nomination, without knowing whether he will be the nominee of his party or not [?] Of course he cannot. Therefore, I say a majority of the voters cannot act intelligibly in the primary meetings." This, he concluded, "is the greatest objection I ever had to Conventions." These opinions reiterated the basic problem, for voters, of an institutional party structure: it interfered with personal relationships and the usual mechanism for testing a man's reputation, honor, and fitness for leadership.[42]

A comparison to other states underscores the feebleness of Mississippi's parties and the enduring strength of the state's antiparty political culture. In the North and the Upper South effective party organizations controlled most county elections by the 1840s or 1850s. The prevalence of nominations and a declining number of lopsided precinct returns signaled the end of a consensual political culture and the triumph of partisan organization. Slavery, population density, and diversity explain part of the regional differences.

Slavery undermined other institutions and muted white class conflict; small, lightly settled rural precincts facilitated personal, face-to-face campaigns; and the homogeneity of the state's Evangelical WASP community prevented meaningful ethnic or religious conflict. Voters elsewhere relied more on party labels when they could not know candidates personally, as even Mississippians did in some counties' early years. In many other parts of the country dense settlement created local precincts so large that candidates could not make the same personal connections, and the ethnic and religious diversity absent in antebellum Mississippi created natural, identifiable divisions within the electorate. In New England especially, where the transformation came earliest, parties were effective at the local level by the 1830s. And one recent study concludes that voters in New York and Pennsylvania had already begun to move away from family-based oligarchies and toward parties during the colonial period, even in local contests for sheriff.[43]

But socioeconomic change and demography cannot account for all the discrepancy. Kentucky was hardly Boston or New York City, yet Bluegrass Whigs and Democrats took control of county elections in just a few years. In 1851 a new constitution reformed county government and made most offices elective. Following a short period of nonpartisanship, county elections became "largely partisan by 1858 because each party was suspicious of the other's intentions and because party leaders and spokesmen believed that party activity at the local level would assist the party effort at the state and national levels." For the good of their parties, Kentucky men apparently embraced an institutional political culture. Their loyalty sometimes extended to holding primaries to choose sheriff's candidates and even deputies. In North Carolina, candidates for sheriff appeared on printed party ballots. Mississippi parties' failure to control sheriffs' elections in particular demonstrated their weakness and the voters' disdain, for, as the county's chief returning officer, the sheriff could influence the actual counting of ballots and disqualification of suspicious tickets. When he suggested party nomination for sheriff in 1858, one Mississippi voter seemed amazed to recognize suddenly that sheriffs "can wield a considerable political influence." Even so, there is only sporadic evidence of partisanship in their selection — perhaps just slightly more than for other county officers. Partisan conflict or victory, the voters seemed to say, were just not important enough to override personal factors.[44]

Like Kentucky voters, Virginians made a quick transition to local partisanship. The Old Dominion inaugurated a new constitution in 1851, too, replacing appointed justices of the peace with an elected county court. Local elites tried to resist party influence but lost the fight in just a few years. By 1856, one study concludes, in local elections "partisanship became significant." That year, "a spirited race for sheriff" featured two partisan candidates. In addition, "no longer could the selection of the county court be isolated from partisanship. In every magisterial district, voters heeded party labels in choosing justices of the peace." William Shade, Virginia's most recent historian, concludes that antipartyism was "futile" after the mid-1830s and argues that local politics were partisan even before the democratic revisions of 1851.[45] In both Virginia and Kentucky, county politics became partisan in only four or five years, whereas Mississippi's party leaders failed to gain control in thirty years of local elections. In North Carolina, Maryland, Tennessee, Missouri, and Arkansas as well, parties had extended their influence to county politics by the 1850s. In Maryland, according to one study, county officeholders even paid bribes to the dominant local party to stay in office.[46]

The two most interesting comparisons with Mississippi may be frontier Illinois and Oregon. Though they had to fight a strong antiparty tradition, Illinois Democrats began to gain control of county and municipal contests in the mid-1830s. Party advocates there succeeded only by presenting their organizations as — the supreme irony — defenders of republican, antiparty politics. Ultimately they thrived. Especially in the northern counties, where few southerners settled, a recent student concludes that "straight party voting was suddenly the dominant mode of political expression in 1840." Two interesting factors stand out in Illinois' slow transition to a partisan political culture. First, the southern counties remained antiparty the longest, suggesting that migrants from Kentucky and Virginia resisted parties more strongly than New Englanders did. Second, county elections that coincided with presidential balloting allowed party activists to extend conventions and nominations more naturally (the 1840 election seems to have been pivotal to party development in Illinois), even though most voters also knew local candidates personally.[47] In Mississippi staggered elections meant that county and local contests never coincided with national, presidential politics; and after 1855 they were even separated from state elections. This allowed the local, neighborhood political culture to operate without party interference, which even Mississippians grudgingly accepted when they could not know candidates personally.

Oregon voters accepted party control of county contests in the 1850s, despite rural settlement patterns similar to those of Mississippi. Party activists led some voters to the polls in rank order, a practice we have no evidence of in Mississippi. As in Illinois, the Upper South background of Oregonians from Dixie — most came from Missouri, Kentucky, and North Carolina — was perhaps telling. Apparently they brought to the West a partisan political culture that influenced voting forms, deference, and the structure of local government. Despite a similar low population density, and little ethnic or religious diversity, Oregon voters' easy embrace of parties provides another stark contrast to Mississippi's antiparty political culture. Studies of Texas and several states of the Old Northwest likewise posit that migrants carried with them an Upper South political culture different from that of the Lower South or, of course, states in the Northeast. By the same token, most Mississippians — who came from South Carolina, Georgia, and Alabama — apparently brought some of their antipartyism with them.[48]

A combination of factors, of course, contributed to Mississippi's ineffective parties. Southern honor and masculinity, the demands of policing a slave society, the republican antiparty heritage, and the state's enduring ruralism all played a part. Their cumulative effect was a political culture that labeled parties a necessary evil, a last resort. One voter recorded his sense of the disparate political cultures of Mississippi and the Upper South. "I spent about a month last summer in Tennessee and Kentucky," wrote Jonathan Stewart, "and was present at the Whig convention in Nashville. . . . The contest was very warm in those states — I could hear of nothing but politics and political meetings wherever I went. I call myself a pretty strong Whig but I must acknowledge that I was tired of a good thing and glad to get where there was less [party] excitement."[49] To him, parties and politics were much different in Mississippi.

There, among ordinary voters party loyalty remained uncommonly weak. In Mississippi's state and national elections, the words *instability* and *fluidity* aptly characterize the electorate and the party system. A small minority of activists maintained their devotion to the party and worked for its success. Many of these unusual partisans — probably no more than 5 to 10 percent of voters — apparently maintained loyalty to a Whig or Democratic ideology. In county elections the parties had virtually no impact, although turnout remained high, often higher than in state contests during the 1840s and 1850s. The frequency and intensity of local contests also suggest that county government remained most significant to many Mississippians, a mutually sustaining relationship that kept voter participation high. A largely ineffective partisan subculture operated within a dominant mood of ambivalence or hostility to party institutions. By nearly every measure, voters favored personal loyalties. Throughout the antebellum period the bottom line remained the same: whenever possible, most voters avoided parties.

5

PLAYMATES

Voting and Governing in the Neighborhood

On election day 1860 state geologist, traveler, and diarist Benjamin L. C. Wailes noted his vote for Constitutional Union nominees John Bell and Edward Everett and carefully prepared a small table in his journal to tally the returns. A successful planter and historian, he had recently returned from a long trip that included Philadelphia and Washington. If anyone in antebellum Mississippi could qualify as cosmopolitan, it would be Wailes. Yet his outlook on the presidential election was inevitably local: "At this precinct," he wrote, "Bell & Everitt received [blank space] votes." Like his less sophisticated neighbors, Wailes's perspective on politics began in his home precinct within a neighborhood community that sustained the state's antiparty political culture. Election returns betrayed the emptiness of partisan rhetoric and the lack of commitment of many Mississippi Whigs and Democrats. Instead of a stable party system driven by issue-oriented partisans and voters divided by ideology, the state's politics were an amalgam of contending local interests and issues. In the great majority of contests, voters supported men who lived nearby—out of kinship, friendship, or duty to a patron-client relationship. And they did so because most local issues also created geographic alliances. For most voters, party politics, too, seemed defined by neighborhoods, and communities often maintained a consistent partisan identity over time, regardless of migration or changing socioeconomic characteristics. Moreover, lawmakers in Jackson and on the boards of police made use of the neighborhood as an organizational unit and gave local gentry the responsibility for supervising elections, taking care of the poor, and administering public funds. Like hunting parties and other male rituals, politics remained a neighborhood exercise that reflected Mississippians' confidence in personal rather than institutional relationships.[1]

97

The changing nature of American communities has been the subject of an insightful and ongoing debate among historians in recent decades. In the 1970s and 1980s, dialogue focused on the colonial era, particularly in New England. Most studies argue that rural communities broke down in the eighteenth century as cooperation and shared purpose gave way to an open, mobile, and increasingly voluntaristic social order.[2] Studies of nineteenth-century communities usually begin with the assumption of widespread mobility and lack of face-to-face relationships; they focus on Americans' attempts to build a community out of the seeming chaos of dizzying demographic change.[3] Other scholars argue that communities retained a distinctive character and cohesiveness despite a moving population because underlying cultural values remained constant, or because the social and economic elite tended to stay behind. The latter's residential persistence allowed them, as an entrenched cadre with privileged access to resources and government, to maintain a community into which a moving column of population naturally fitted itself.[4] Local leaders thus formed and reformed the networks of friends, neighbors, and dependents that helped preserve political stability and continuity over time.[5]

Neighborhood communities in rural Mississippi often retained their cohesiveness and solidarity despite demographic turnover. Most Mississippians participated in a local network of exchanges, conducting business through personal relationships in a day-to-day world lived on a small scale; that world was intimate and often — although certainly not always — cooperative. And although conflict among whites could be bitter, lasting, and of course violent, it occurred within a set of shared values. Moreover, Mississippi's large slave population made white unity and local stability more imperative than it was in other parts of the country, including the Upper South. The interaction between every community and mobile individuals also demonstrates the evolving character and socializing power of the community itself. Stable residents were the foundation of the traditions and individual identity that each rural neighborhood preserved over time. When newcomers formed relationships of cooperation or conflict, they did so within a shared and continuing set of mediated relationships that matured within a collective history.[6]

For male Mississippians allegiance to neighborhoods also reflected individual commitments to one another — to those who confirmed honor and policed slavery — rather than to state or other institutions. One group of men, for instance, writing to the governor to obtain his help in apprehending two local criminals referred to "this community, *who* are greatly outraged." The local political culture reflected and reinforced the conditions and attitudes that lent stability to the neighborhood and helped overcome the disruptive effects of mobility. Electoral behavior, county issues and governance, and the ritual act of voting all bespoke the neighborhood as the sine qua non of Mississippi politics.[7]

Explaining how or why men voted has often preoccupied political historians. In studies of nineteenth-century America, these questions are complicated because the chief suspects — class, religion, ethnicity, residence, and family history — overlap and disguise one another. This makes inference from aggregate data a tricky problem; in the absence of individual polling data, deductions about the determinants of party choice, or any other voting behavior, remain necessarily tentative.[8]

Progressive historians in the early and mid-twentieth century emphasized class differences between the two parties, portraying them as poor, egalitarian Democrats and wealthy, aristocratic Whigs. It is true that class-conscious rhetoric infused antebellum politics. Albert Gallatin Brown's Democratic supporters invariably praised him as "entirely a self-made man . . . unaided by *wealth* and *royal blood*." But all parties made similar appeals; no Whig ever forgot the homespun lessons of Log Cabin, Hard Cider, and "Old Tip." In local races, too, the language of class worked both ways. In 1857 Oktibbeha County, for instance, the Whigs chose yeoman farmer Samuel H. Daniel to oppose incumbent Democrat and planter Robert Muldrow for county representative. Daniel's background allowed Whigs to attack Muldrow's wealth. Thomas Carroll describes "a cartoon [that] represented the candidates as contestants in a race; Daniel was mounted on a mule, and Muldrow was seated in a two-horse buggy, a slave driving." Portrayed as the champion of poor farmers, Daniel eked out a close victory, even though Democrats traditionally won the county by a large margin. Democrats probably used class language most consistently, but other partisans did so as well. One study of active partisans found no difference in the value of real property they owned: Whigs averaged $4,203, Democrats $4,202.[9]

The most popular variant of the Progressive argument links partisanship to competing versions of political economy. Southern Whigs, these historians maintain, prevailed in towns, the plantation belt, and among farmers connected to the market or adhering to a "progressive" vision of the future. Southern Democrats favored a "negative state" and predominated among subsistence farmers. "Alternate visions of the future," concludes one influential study, "made some people receptive to [socioeconomic] change while others found it alarming."[10] Those party ideologies probably distinguished a majority of core activists. The state party organs, private correspondence between state and national politicians, and other evidence from party insiders suggest that ideology or the party's program were important to many leaders. Most historians also posit, or at least imply, a direct link between national leaders and ordinary voters by using phrases like "Whigs thought . . . " or "Democrats believed. . . ."[11] On the other hand, nearly every study focusing on actual voting behavior concludes that residence was the paramount influence on most voters' choices.

Contrary to the Progressive or neo-Progressive interpretations, economic issues or competing visions of the future seemed unimportant to Mississippi's parties or voters. National Whig support for economic development probably reinforced some southwestern planters' Whiggery; but almost all Mississippi farmers produced for the market, and virtually no one opposed internal improvements. Voters consistently approved taxes to fund railroad construction; disputes hinged not on their desirability but on what route the rail lines would take. Democrats as well as Whigs touted progressive projects to improve travel and trade. One typical controversy involved the Memphis and Charleston Railroad, which was slated to run through northeast Mississippi. When the state legislature altered the proposed route in 1852, taking it through Holly Springs instead of Tishomingo County, residents of the latter howled in protest. Though it was an area with almost no slaves, Tishomingo's poor, yeomen farmers still yearned for access to the railroad. They even threatened to withhold state tax money and "secede" from Mississippi if the legislature did not approve the rail line through their county. In the same year voters in nearby Lafayette County voted 475 to 53 to increase their own taxes so they might attract the railroad. After the depression of the late-1830s and bond repudiation, neither party offered much support for banks, which were discredited by the wild speculation and mismanagement of the previous decade. In short, the state's parties generally agreed about many economic issues that supposedly divided national Whigs and Democrats.[12]

Any attempt to link grassroots behavior to party ideology or to national issues is dubious and prone to frustration — not least because most nineteenth-century Americans did not take a national or even state perspective on most issues. Partisan positions clearly mattered to some voters at some times, and most party leaders probably operated within some kind of belief system. But the great bulk of voters apparently did not (and do not), as countless studies by historians and political scientists confirm. The instability in Mississippi's state and national contests — in which each election included 15 to 30 percent of new voters, further complicates any discussion of why or how men voted. Yet, despite all the turnover resulting from coming of age, death, residential mobility, and party switching, the Democrats kept winning and the Whig, Know-Nothing, and Opposition parties kept losing. With few exceptions, the Democratic majority ranged between 52 and 57 percent. How could the outcome look so similar year after year? Precinct-level data that reveal more consistent behavior suggest a possible answer.

Individual precincts, or beats, often maintained partisan continuity despite turnover within the electorate. In Amite County, for instance, none of the eight voting districts changed from Democrat to opposition or vice versa between 1855 and 1859. Although the gross numbers changed dramatically over the four years, individual precincts maintained partisan continuity. Democrats carried Zion Hill (38 to 23 in 1855, 46 to 18 in 1859) and Talbert's (99 to 47 and 76 to 25), while the opposition won Thickwoods (50 to 13 and 26 to 13) and Toler's (22 to 1 and 37 to 7). Carroll County showed similar trends; between 1853 and 1859 Democratic precincts included Middleton

(93 to 48 and 58 to 8) and Shongalo (119 to 53 and 102 to 14), and the opposition carried LeFlore (28 to 6 and 11 to 7), Sidon (33 to 7 and 25 to 9), and Adair's (29 to 19 and 19 to 12). Other Whig strongholds in Carroll — Black Hawk, Greenwood, and LeFlore — remained stalwart throughout both decades. Lowndes County voters at Lowndesville and Swearingen's registered consistent support for the Democrats between 1843 and 1853. In Hinds County the Democrats carried Utica precinct in successive state elections between 1853 and 1859 by nearly identical totals: 80 to 69, 80 to 63, 80 to 67, and 71 to 62. The voters at Cayuga registered their loyalty to the opposition throughout the same period: 47 to 27, 49 to 23, 22 to 16, and 31 to 8. The county's most rural precinct, Sturges's Store, backed Whig candidates between 1844 and 1853 with remarkable stability: 51 to 9, 51 to 17, 40 to 10, 42 to 19, and 76 to 29. In Madison County the Whigs won Sharon, Battle Spring, and Beatie's Bluff by nearly identical margins between 1845 and 1849. The Democrats won Madisonville, 28 to 22 and 29 to 21 over the same period. Willow Spring's voters, in Claiborne County's smallest precinct, favored the Democrats from 1843 to 1853: 30 to 14, 30 to 10, 18 to 7, 21 to 17, and 14 to 9.

Of course, some precincts showed more volatility. Towns such as Jackson (Hinds County), Liberty (Amite), Columbus (Lowndes), Port Gibson and Grand Gulf (Claiborne), and Carrollton (Carroll) typically recorded more change than smaller, rural areas. Larger beats that combined several neighborhoods or that mixed town and rural voters often lost their distinctiveness and held more competitive elections. The returns from other precincts reflected the Democrats' steadily increasing dominance throughout the 1850s as the opposition and competitiveness waned. Still, it is safe to conclude that there was limited partisan stability at the local level: there were Democratic precincts and opposition precincts. Apparently the job of maintaining continuity over time fell to longtime elite residents who set a tone for the community and used the open balloting tradition that made it easier for leaders to influence the votes of newcomers.[13] Seemingly, as new men moved into an area, teenagers came of age, and those previously inactive became voters, their choice of party often depended on divisions that already existed in each neighborhood.

The origin of local partisanship often lay in early county issues or in patterns of settlement. When the parties organized state and national contests, voters carried traditional, precinct-level rivalries into the new arena. In Warren County location of the courthouse engendered a north-south enmity between Milldale and Warrenton, a division that persisted in the 1840s as Democrats and Whigs split the county along similar lines. Partisanship, in this case, depended largely on a local issue and on residence patterns established years earlier and showed little relation to a Whig or Democratic ideology.[14] When a local politician succeeded from local to state or national politics, some voters probably faced a conflict between his party affiliation and their own history. The customary strong support given party candidates in their home precincts suggests that many voters remained loyal to neighbors even when that support conflicted with their party identification.

Neighborhood voting also started (and was reinforced) because polling precincts were typically established in early settlements. It was logical for a new county's board of police, meeting for the first time, to draw precinct boundaries that conformed to existing communities. Harrison County's first board of police, for instance, designated the courthouse and homes of four prominent settlers as polling places. Throughout the antebellum period, plantations, churches, and crossroads stores served as sites for most of Mississippi's polls. In Bolivar County, the policemen referenced their first districts to individual plantations: "[t]he fourth district extends from Orrin Kingsley's down the river to the line between Dr. Dodd's and Colonel Field's, including all back settlements." In Oktibbeha County, the earliest precinct boundaries "probably ran to fit the population; the residence of the first members of the board of police . . . who were supposed to live in their prospective beats, indicates this." Some early residents of Panola County complained to the governor when their first board of police election returned four members living on one side of the Tallahatchie River and only one on the other. They naturally wanted an equal division of the county into precincts that accommodated settlement patterns and would prevent a "scism amongst our people." As each county's population expanded and needed more beats, the board usually added them to conform to new or evolving neighborhoods. Most boards created new polls liberally, both to accommodate voters who found travel difficult and to offer policemen more patronage. With elections thus geared toward neighborhoods, consistent and often consensual voting was hardly surprising.[15]

Many young men remembered following community and family tradition when casting their first ballots. Politician Wiley P. Harris recalled that "I found myself a democrat without being able to explain why I was of that party. My uncle was a staunch Jackson man and I adopted his preferences without examination." National issues or party ideology were unimportant: "I began therefore as a follower of Jackson knowing nothing of the Force Bill, regarding "nullification" as a heresy without knowing what it meant." Whig Horace Fulkerson likewise admitted no knowledge of banking or the repudiation of bonds, but "I was a Whig and thought that any measure supported by the Democrats generally, must be wrong!" Another Mississippi voter remembered the influence of his unusually memorable college professor.[16] During the 1852 presidential campaign a letter from one of Lowndes County's local squires suggests how community context might influence new voters. After several requests, former state representative John Gilmer sent a public letter to his local newspaper. "I have been so often asked how I intended to vote . . . that there seems to be no mistake that many, who

have not had the pleasure of seeing, would like to know where I stand."
Many locals apparently considered Gilmer's opinion worthwhile; after all,
his family had settled in the county in the 1830s, prospered, and been prominent in northeast Mississippi for more than a decade.[17]

The importance of community and family tradition, rather than ideology, also helps explain the enduring regionalism handed down from the
1820s and 1830s. Whigs predominated in the Mississippi River delta, having
settled there before Andrew Jackson's and the Democrats' rise to power,
while Democrats carried most counties to the east and north. The timing of
settlement, in short, greatly favored the Democrats because their frontier
hero ruled the political nation while most of Mississippi was being occupied
by whites. The new regions became Democratic counties and neighborhoods, and few changed their allegiance over the next thirty years.

Ideological parties and residential voting are not mutually exclusive, of
course, and voters surely responded to party symbols, slogans, and rhetoric,
at least at times. Parties could work like other voluntary associations — the
Masons or church membership, for instance — becoming part of a man's
network of friends and neighbors. Undoubtedly some Mississippi voters considered whether a man was "also a good Democrat" when weighing local
choices for office. Furthermore, as party organization advanced to the local
level, rank-and-file voters became more likely to absorb a sense of their party's agenda. In the North and Upper South during the three decades before
secession, the linkage between national or state issues and leaders and grassroots behavior probably solidified because parties more effectively fixed the
allegiance of voters in local contests.[18] What stands out in the rhetoric and
behavior of most Mississippi voters, however, was the weakness of their identification with the party institutions. Rather than allegiance to a party or its
message, most voters seemed to place personal ties foremost, and their whole
political culture was designed to accommodate the public, personal requirements of honor and communal manhood. By implication at least, evidence
of how men actually voted casts serious doubt on the importance of ideology
to individual men, especially in the absence of effective parties.

Among Mississippi voters, ideology apparently motivated only core party
activists. One editor bemoaned the "melancholy fact that near four-fifths of
our freeborn sovereigns . . . have not the most remote idea" about the "measures of national policy which constitute the articles of faith of the two prominent parties. . . . Their comprehension of the meaning of . . . Whig or Democrat . . . is natural rather than acquired." Most men continued to follow
neighborhood voting patterns that showed little consistent relationship to
parties' platforms or stands on national issues. Often laid down years before
and founded in obscure, long-settled local disputes, these patterns persisted
throughout the 1840s and 1850s. The continued relative isolation of many
rural neighborhoods encouraged little interaction with more distant areas

among residents who found travel difficult and mostly unnecessary. Rural newspapers often recorded only the vote of its home precinct and ignored state or even countywide totals.[19]

Historic patterns endured because of family and community tradition, the work of some party activists who held barbecues and dances, and the influence of local elites. Activists, of course, often were the local elite, and they tended to move less often, giving them the added benefit of unequal access to local power. These advantages positioned them to convince, or coerce, new residents into adopting the community's prevailing partisan identity. Since many voters demonstrated little institutional loyalty or ideological consistency, they might presumably follow the orientation of local leaders with little anguish. Besides, why not please the local planters and lawyers with whom one would probably do business or socialize?

Finally, slavery, southern honor, and the values of communal manhood accentuated the importance of local solidarity. Slavery made white unity imperative to the social order; communal manhood emphasized loyalty to other men, and the public pressure and demands of honor heightened men's awareness of such community rituals as voting. As a public display, every voter could demonstrate his willingness to stand shoulder to shoulder with neighbors. In the Upper South these regional peculiarities were muted: the white population was more diverse and densely settled, and there was less danger from slaves who constituted a shrinking minority of the population. Thus, examining how Mississippi's political culture operated in the context of men's day-to-day lives and reality highlights differences with the Upper South and demonstrates that politics in Mississippi remained much less partisan, ideological, and democratic than is often presumed.

That ideology was peripheral for most voters is also suggested by the accounts of most party events. Party activists typically began each campaign with local meetings to select delegates and shape a local "platform," but the notoriously dismal attendance at these gatherings evinced the voters' ambivalence. More important than these small meetings of core activists, however, were community functions that often brought out the whole family. Organizers invariably appealed to the "ladies," and women and children formed a large part of any crowd at barbecues and debates.[20] The focus, as always, was on the neighborhood. "The Barbecues at Auburn, Utica and Cayuga were highly creditable to the citizens of those neighborhoods," wrote one editor. "The attendance was large at each place — particularly on the part of the ladies." The residents of Spring Ridge invited local candidates to a barbecue during the 1851 campaign. "Ample arrangements," they assured residents, "will be made by the neighborhood to supply a good dinner to all who may be pleased to attend." Other events were "Basket Meetings," to which "every body carries his own dinner."[21]

Including the entire white community offered the allure of women; with them party leaders hoped to entice potential voters to hear their message. This tactic was aimed mostly at young men, who were more likely to be unmarried, first-time voters, or politically uncommitted. Party leaders hoped to convert voters, although accounts suggest that many young men had other ideas. One resident described the "Bran Dance at Quitman Springs" for his local newspaper: "At the usual hour, a very large crowd," he said, composed of "candidates for office *and* candidates for matrimony, were congregated under the spacious arbor, anxiously awaiting the first notes of the soul-stirring violin." One politician remembered these neighborhood events as scenes of "great social enjoyment and festivity" when "lads and lasses came out to enjoy the frolic, and even children were brought to see the great men of the day." In semi-isolated rural areas, rallies to instruct the faithful became, equally or more importantly, a chance to mingle with the opposite sex or visit family friends.[22] These large community events often drew crowds of several thousand, compared to the dozen or so activists who typically attended local nominating conventions—a disparity that reiterated the ambivalence of most voters, who showed little interest in the party's ideology but were more than happy. to eat barbecue or dance with the local ladies.

The emphasis on dinner and entertainment, of course, underlines the social nature of these events. Mississippi satirist Joseph B. Cobb lampooned party "debates" in his account of "A Campaign Barbecue in the Southwest." At his fictional meeting, only 3 of the 199 eligible voters were not already committed to one party; uncommitted voters, he claimed, avoided rallies to escape pushy activists and worthless blather. Thus, the meeting was an exercise in enthusiasm, drinking, and eating: "Calm, dispassionate argument, sound reason, and a candid exposition of the principles which separated the two parties, were, it was distinctly understood, to be totally expurgated and eschewed." After some meaningless speeches, "a general dash was instantly made for the tables." After the ladies began, "each voter . . . fell greedily to work. Roasted beef, and mutton saddles, and greasy, barbecued shoats, and venison haunches, and whole armies of minor victims were indiscriminately assaulted and unceremoniously dispatched." The "smack of lips and more appalling crash of teeth" could be heard throughout the picnic grounds.[23]

Canton's Whig editor, anticipating sarcastic jeers from his Democratic counterpart, explained a small party rally held in his hometown: "The meeting, then, demonstrated clearly the fact that no large assemblage of the People can be obtained, without a *Barbecue*—without some preparations to satisfy the cravings of the 'inner man'. The people will not come to partake of a 'feast of reason,' without a feast of roast meats, also! This is well known by every man in Madison [County], of every party."[24] While more esoteric questions motivated a small number of party leaders, neighborhood barbecues threw into clear relief the nonideological, issueless party politics familiar to most Mississippians.

Hinds County planter Jefferson J. Birdsong captured many of the neighborhood features and social functions of politics in his diary. Born in Sussex

County, Virginia in 1810, Birdsong settled in Mississippi in his early twenties and actively followed politics, serving on the board of police and attending several county conventions as a Whig and Know-Nothing delegate. His personal commentary almost never mentions national or state issues, but records each barbecue or bran dance as another event in his busy social life that included the Masons, several Baptist churches, and regular hunting and fishing trips with a variety of male Birdsong relatives — including his twin brother Joe and close friends like Dr. Sam Brown and farmer Sam Parsons. Like his poorer neighbors, Birdsong rarely traveled outside the immediate area. A former slave trader turned cotton planter, he paid the second highest tax bill in Hinds County. It is perhaps no wonder that his account of election day in 1856 shows more interest in Henry M. White's election to the board of police than to the presidential contest. That Millard Fillmore carried Hinds County, or even that James Buchanan would be president of the United States, apparently held little interest for him. He recorded in his diary only that "Brownsville [his home precinct] have given Filmore 56 majority."[25]

If the varied individual motives that shaped partisanship in state and national politics remain murky, returns from nonpartisan county and local elections clearly demonstrate residence as the decisive factor. Each candidate typically enjoyed and depended on overwhelming support from the voters near his home. In Marshall County's 1858 elections, for instance, five men ran for tax assessor. Winner Thomas H. Smith received 68 of the 77 votes cast in adjacent precincts Tallaloosa and Red Bank. Similarly, 152 of the 164 voters in Cornersville and Belldazzle, the southeast corner of the county, supported local resident B. R. Long. The other three candidates failed to register such impressive support from banner precincts, although each received his highest total near home. The three-way race for surveyor proved just as telling: victorious William J. B. Rudery gathered 112 of 115 votes at Snow Creek, 31 of 37 at Hudsonville, 162 of 183 at Waterford, 117 of 118 at Cornersville, and all 86 votes tallied in Belldazzle. He also earned a large majority in Holly Springs, the county seat and largest town. In short, he swept every precinct in eastern Marshall County. J. C. Babb, who finished second, dominated the northwest corner of the county, winning 149 of 160 votes at Byhalia and 63 of 65 at Oak Grove. Finally, J. G. Wilson, who finished a distant third with 268 votes, nevertheless received over 80 percent of the votes in his home of Chullahoma — the largest precinct in southwest Marshall. The three candidates, in other words, divided the county into three unequal geographic regions.

Some counties suffered a town-and-country split or enmity between competing towns or neighborhoods. A prolonged antagonism between the towns of Jackson and Raymond generated chiefly by Raymond's monopoly over county jurisprudence upset any attempt to classify party alignments in

Hinds County throughout the 1840s and 1850s. Elections for county officers often set Jacksonians against men from the county, and newspapers typically referred to county candidates by their home neighborhoods. In 1845, Raymond editor George W. Harper announced the Whig candidates for representative as "D. S. Jennings of Jackson; A. R. Green of Newtown; Henry S. Pope of Raymond; and Charles S. Spann of Brownsville." As a promoter of party unity and harmony, he recognized the potential for dissatisfaction if each neighborhood was not represented. In 1848, Jacksonians tried to claim the county seat, prompting a dispute involving plans for a new county that would take territory from southern Hinds and neighboring Claiborne and Copiah counties. The question returned in 1853, when David Williams ran for county representative on the issue of "removing" the courthouse. Since only the state legislature could authorize relocation of a county seat, control of the county's delegation became paramount.[26]

The decade of hostility between the two towns culminated in the Hinds County elections of 1859. At issue was a state measure that made the circuit court "ambulatory" for citizens of Jackson, allowing them to conduct their business without traveling the sixteen miles to Raymond. Men formed tickets dedicated to "Repeal" or "Anti-Repeal," and voters followed their natural loyalties. "When it was proposed to build a new Court House at Raymond, the people of Jackson opposed it," wrote editor George Harper, leader of Raymond's opposition. "*Their* member of the Board of Police, acting under instructions, opposed every step for the erection of a new building."[27] Thus, rather than state, much less national, issues affecting county elections, the reverse was often true. The 1860 contest for probate court clerk underscored the lasting antagonism between Jackson and the rest of Hinds County. Samuel Donnell, who finished last with 453 votes, received 364 of 444 in Jackson itself. Yet, he received only 10 out of 288 votes in Raymond and none at all in Brownsville, Cayuga, or Burnett's Wells. Merchant B. F. Edwards and eventual winner Samuel Thigpen split the Raymond vote, but Thigpen won big majorities in the southeast precincts of Byram and Terry and a large share in nearby Auburn. Although Edwards had consistent support throughout the county, a disappointing 46.7 percent plurality at his home precinct—actually designated "Edwards' Store"—cost him the election by just six votes.

These cases offer clear testimony to the importance of residence, but voting patterns are not always so obvious. A complex network of relatives and friends contributed to any candidate's success: an unlikely victory might stem from an influential uncle or a fellow church member. Mississippian Reuben Davis described the decisive advantage of friends and neighbors. In his first campaign for public office, Davis faced a tough opponent in long-time resident Thomas J. Word. As one local told young Davis, his opponent was "a good fellow, tells a capital story, and plays the fiddle." In addition to these seemingly unbeatable qualities, he was handsome and a polished speaker. But Davis soon found allies of his own. He met an old family friend, Colonel William L. Duncan, who pledged his friends and family from throughout Tippah County. Davis, the son of a Baptist preacher, similarly impressed a local Methodist minister, who appreciated Davis's religious up-bringing and particularly favored Mrs. Davis, a "most devoted Methodist." "The next morning there was a large crowd at [the] tavern," Davis remembered, "most of them members of his church." The reverend "introduced me to them, dwelling upon the fact that I had married an enthusiastic Methodist." Davis wisely befriended the tavern keeper, who afterwards "worked for me manfully until the election." After another speech, one listener ascertained that he had known Davis's father and immediately pledged the votes of his family and as many fellow church members as he could muster. Davis concluded: "[i]t seemed that I was to learn on that occasion how large a part family friendship can play in such cases."[28]

Local politicians like Davis stayed alert for any chance to meet voters. Duncan McKenzie described his gin-house raising in September 1843, just six weeks before the general election. Among the "15 of our white & black neighbors" who helped with the "heavy and hot" work, he counted "one Justice of the Peace, one Judge of Probate, and a member of the board of County Police. Consequently you would suppose that we had a pretty decent raising, especially when you add to our company a member of the late called Session of the legislature & a candidate for reelection." Candidates, it seemed, roughly equaled potential voters. Helping to raise the new gin house let politicos show their loyalty to neighbors and express their sociability among men who valued the same qualities.[29]

Residence and personal reputation determined precinct elections even more clearly than they did in county races. In each police district Mississippi voters elected a policeman and at least two justices of the peace and two constables. Justices had legal authority over small civil cases and served to "keep the peace"; constables lacked judicial power but helped the sheriff when needed. Unlike most states, Mississippi elected all these officers, providing us an almost-unparalleled look at men's priorities and attitudes in the most intimate setting of local politics. Voting data frequently includes precinct totals but rarely subprecinct returns. However, in precincts with more than one poll box, and when the returning officer took the time to record separate totals, the preeminence of neighborhood associations is conclusive.

In Amite County, police district 4 included Smith's and Spurlock's boxes—individual polls within the fourth precinct. The voters chose farmer Eli S. Westbrook and teacher Reiley Corcoran over incumbent John C. Wilson for justice of the peace in 1855. Westbrook and Corcoran received all of the votes at Smith's box; Wilson got all of the twenty-six tallies at Spurlock's box. In the election for constable, A. W. Westbrook bested three rivals, thanks to twenty-seven votes in Smith's box. Mark Tarver lost, despite receiving all nineteen votes cast at Spurlock's box (see table 5.1). Police

TABLE 5.1. Police District 4, Amite County, 1855: Votes for Justice of the Peace and Constable

Candidates	Votes at Smith's Box	Votes at Spurlock's Box	Total votes for each candidate
For Justice of the Peace			
Eli S. Westbrook	34	0	34
Reiley Corcoran	33	0	33
John C. Wilson	0	26	26
For Constable			
A. W. Westbrook	27	0	27
Samuel Tarver	6	0	6
S. T. Wilkinson	23	0	23
Mark Tarver	0	19	19

Source: Record Group 28, vol. 31c, Mississippi Department of Archives and History.

district 2 repeated the scenario: voters at Thickwoods and Toler's box supported only their neighbors. Candidate for the local board of police Moses Jackson defeated L. G. Gayle, thirty-seven to twenty-nine. Gayle carried Thickwoods, but Jackson got all eighteen votes at Toler's box, which put him over the top. For justice of the peace, Francis H. Hitchcock beat a trio of opponents, receiving all of his nineteen votes at Thickwoods. One of the defeated, Archibald Cain, got every vote cast at Toler's.

Voters in Carroll County's first district demonstrated similar loyalty to their neighbors. Local planter William McD Martin won election to the board of police by receiving 113 of 120 votes in Black Hawk and 80 percent at Sidon. His opponent, Patrick H. Brown, lost but enjoyed unanimous support in Greenwood. John W. McRae and Simon T. Lane, who were both from Black Hawk, were chosen justices thanks to overwhelming support at their home precinct and in adjacent Sidon. Greenwood merchant Jesse C. Wood received nearly unanimous support from his customers but no votes at all in Sidon or Black Hawk. For constable, voters around Greenwood decided not to participate since both candidates lived in the Black Hawk beat. Results from district 2 — composed of Smith's Mills, Point LeFlore, and Jefferson — were the same: as all three candidates for constable lived in the Smith's Mills beat, no one from Point LeFlore or Jefferson bothered to vote. Similar outcomes from Hinds County are shown in table 5.2.

Such detailed returns from the subprecinct level do not exist for party elections. One suspects, though, that they would show the power of community context even more clearly than precinct data, which often lump several neighborhoods together. The smallest precincts, which may have encompassed only one neighborhood, usually recorded dramatically uneven totals. In Amite County, the 1843 vote was typical: Thickwoods and Toler's precincts divided 67 to 5 and 39 to 5 for the Whigs, and Spurlock's went 23 to

TABLE 5.2. Raymond Box & McManus' Store Beat, Hinds County, 1855: Votes for Justice of the Peace and Constable

Candidates	Votes at Raymond Box	Votes at McManus's Store	Total votes for each candidate
For Justice of the Peace			
Lemuel Hudson	0	23	23
B. F. Trimble	150	0	150
Joseph Gray	125	0	125
William G. Moore	116	0	116
For Constable			
Joseph Martin	0	14	14
Mr. Dunn	0	13	13
A. J. Willis	190	0	190
John A. Gallman	165	0	165

Source: Record Group 28, vol. 31c, Mississippi Department of Archives and History.

6 for Democrat Albert Gallatin Brown. They were the three least-populous polls in the county.[30]

Precinct elections protested to the governor also testify to neighborhood loyalties. When Alexander Stringer was defeated for a seat on the Hancock County Board of Police, he complained that the election was improperly advertised "in our beet." He claimed, phonetically, "that it was dun for the purpus of [moving] the Cort [county seat] back to Shealsburough and by keeping me out they could do so." Residents of Washington, in Adams County, appealed to Governor McNutt against the Natchez-controlled board of police, which, they claimed, unfairly joined several precincts in order to control local elections. This left "the whole of the eastern part [of Adams County] . . . destitute of a single Justice of the Peace or constable."[31]

Election returns from the late 1850s also suggest the power of community and neighborhood loyalties remained potent up to secession. In Bolivar County, the 1860 race for county treasurer typified the enduring strength of neighborhood cohesiveness. James McCracken, who lived near the polling precinct at Concordia, won a majority there, and 48 of 50 votes at nearby Australia (northern Bolivar). William L. Stewart received no votes in Australia and less than 10 percent of Concordia's votes. Stewart, who ran a hotel in Prentiss, did receive 38 of 43 votes in his hometown and a large majority in nearby Bolivar (the town). Third-place finisher William W. Arnold, also from Concordia, did best at home, but failed to carry any precinct decisively. The three men split the votes at Beulah, which lay in between their home neighborhoods. Despite years of economic and demographic change, voters in Bolivar County, like others across Mississippi, rallied to support their neighborhood candidates just as they had for the preceding twenty years.

These and other cases reveal the overwhelming power residence wielded in all elections. Often, unanimous support from neighbors carried local candidates, and anyone who failed to sweep his home precinct could expect to lose. When Hugh Stewart lost a bid for circuit court clerk, by just 80 votes out of 1,800 cast, he correctly attributed his defeat to another candidate from "the town in which I live," which cost him "200 votes which I am almost certain I would have got had he not run."[32] According to surviving election returns and contemporary comments, partisanship among the rank-and-file turned primarily on residence and on family or community tradition rather than on any set of shared principles or party ideology, which probably shaped the perspective of the few party insiders.

Instead, it was neighborhood loyalties and contentious county issues that produced the rich diversity of local politics. National issues, which dominated the pages of state party organs and private correspondence among party politicians, often took a back seat in regional newspapers. Allegiance to Whig or Democrat meant little to most voters when the state legislature moved the county seat or when the board of police voted $20,000 in additional taxes to build a bridge at the other end of the county. A complex interplay of local issues and personal relationships defined county politics, with neighborhood loyalty providing the guiding force. Recognizing the importance and divisiveness of these concerns underscores the difficulty of trying to link national parties and issues to grass roots political behavior.

One editorial captured the primacy of neighborhoods and local issues, recapping the problem for party organizers who wanted to make their institutions paramount. "All county and local interests," began editor A. C. Baine in 1847, "whether a man shall travel five miles or twenty-five miles to court all his life . . . whether the produce of the farmers shall be forwarded to market by good turnpikes or through nearly impassable bottoms, &c., using up his horses, oxen, wagons, &c. — are all . . . *neighborhood* questions," and should always take precedence over party matters. Baine's outburst was prompted by a call from the editors of the state party organ to put aside county issues in favor of "higher considerations." "It will be regarded as something new, certainly," Baine sarcastically concluded, "that the *chief* object of members of the legislature is *not* to attend to the interests of their neighborhoods or counties." He articulated a basic truth: neighborhood matters would always predominate among men whose perspective rarely extended beyond the bounds of their voting precinct.[33]

Boards of police, which were in charge of raising and spending county funds, often attracted the attention of voters and local editors. Men registered their concern for these local offices with election-day turnouts that typically surpassed 60 percent. Roll-off in board of police elections probably ranged between 7 and 10 percent, which exceeded that for county offices. However, the less-competitive races and changing police board election rules and boundaries complicate interpretation of the data and make calculations difficult and somewhat unreliable.[34] Membership on the board was a position of status, power, and influence and attracted the counties' wealthiest residents. Local editors also commented on the boards' activities. George W. Harper of the *Hinds County Gazette* expressed a general sense of confidence in the newly elected board of 1853, although he had one complaint. Because people felt that board proceedings were too secretive, he urged new members to make its actions public: "We do not see the propriety or policy of the Board suppressing its proceedings," he concluded. As annual county tax rates usually exceeded state levies, citizens were understandably curious about what the boards did with their money. Many newspapers included notices from the board announcing when they would fix future tax rates, allowing county residents to attend the meeting and offer their opinions and, one suspects, their objections.[35] Editors and private citizens often supported board projects and stirred up enthusiasm among fellow taxpayers. Harper, for instance, urged the Hinds County board to invest $100,000 of tax money to finance the Jackson and New Orleans Railroad, a new courthouse, and a bridge over the Big Black River. He further suggested that they combine the measures into one big bill with "something for everyone."[36]

One series of letters to Jefferson County newspapers demonstrates the weight given to local issues and the overriding intracounty regionalism that shaped political conflict. The controversy began when the board of police contracted to build a new bridge over Cole's Creek at Dobyn's Ford. Critics complained that the board lacked authority to make such an agreement without approval from the voters, provoking a debate over the nature of county government and the mutual responsibilities of citizen and representative. A correspondent of the *Fayette Watch-Tower* defended the court, noting that policemen had every legal right to do what they thought best for the county.[37] Unsatisfied with this argument, bridge opponents incited regionalism and resentment over the increased taxes each citizen would pay for an expensive structure ($28,000) most of them would never use. Letters from "Humble Citizen" and "Public Spirit," though, defended the board's plan and noted that Jefferson's tax burden was lighter than that of surrounding counties. Furthermore, they noted, planners had sited the bridge within a mail route, which would benefit all county residents.[38]

The first critic, however, continued to attack the bridge as the pet project of one district. Board members, he charged, voted for it merely out of local considerations and ignored the good of the county. Two respondents claimed that their representatives did rise above district loyalties and again urged citizens to take pride in their county's public works. By February of 1858 the debate had turned to a discussion of county improvements in general, prompting a series of acrimonious letters from residents of the various precincts. The complaints had little to do with taxes or opposition to internal improvements; rather, residents of northeast Jefferson simply resented the localism of precincts that had previously benefitted from county projects but now failed to act fairly toward other neighborhoods.[39]

Finally, "Public Spirit" tried to inspire residents of Jefferson County to overcome the regionalism that divided them. Those "so grounded in selfish motives [and] sectional prejudices, that they can see no public good in anything except that which contributes to their own personal benefit" reflected only a lack of training and education in civic virtue. A product of Mississippi's political culture, this writer invoked the state's universal language of politics in an attempt to unite his county, labeling his opponents "demagogues, contemptible wise-acres of the land, who corrupt the genial flow of patriotism."[40] The Jefferson bridge debate underscores the power of regionalism that was inherent in Mississippi's county politics. As they did when voting for county officers, Mississippians looked to their neighborhoods in times of conflict.

Like this discussion of local improvements, county politics rarely involved parties. The only exceptions came in contests for the state legislature, in which Whigs and Democrats typically made formal nominations. Yet local questions constantly intrude on any neat classification of county partisanship or connections to national issues or ideology. As we have seen, county issues that typically divided voters regionally by neighborhoods blurred party identity and connections to national institutions. These instances underscore again the complex and diverse nature of politics in Mississippi, where neither ideology nor national issues — other than sectionalism — seem to have had little lasting impact.

In 1857 the confusion in Calhoun and Yallobusha counties (which composed one senatorial district) showed the danger of attaching national party labels to local politicians. The Democrats nominated Judge Brashear, but a party faction in Calhoun rebelled and chose A. M. Reasons, citing the "undemocratic" rules and regulations adopted in an "illegal caucus" at the first convention. The controversy also involved a question about the location of the courthouse, further splintering the party. Finally, a third Democratic faction objected to the lack of banking facilities in the county, even though the state party had opposed chartering any bank since the late 1830s. Thus, there were at least three potent local issues dividing Democrats in Calhoun and Yallobusha, and each of them affected the election of state representatives.[41]

Another courthouse dispute, this one in Jasper County, summarizes the interplay of personal and neighborhood loyalties within a local issue that made party labels meaningless. The county seat, Paulding, was about five miles east of Jasper's geographic center. Disgruntled western farmers hoped to erect a new building on some open land they owned that was closer to the county's geographic center. Citizens of Paulding, led by powerful Democratic editor Simeon Roe Adams, opposed the measure as extravagant and unnecessary (and undoubtedly bad for his business). The confrontation began in 1857 when one Democratic faction repudiated its party's nominee for the state legislature because he opposed the removal. During the next two years the debate became increasingly hostile and also split the county's Know-Nothing Party. Arguments for and against removal included a bewildering array of charges and countercharges that involved "needless" taxation, a disputed election, interpretation of an earlier state law, and an argument over just exactly where the "geographic center" of Jasper County was. Organizers on both sides resolved to make removal the only issue in electing a county representative in 1859 and to "utterly discard the question of party politics." "[U]ntil this matter is finally settled, we will recognize no other issue in elections for members of the Legislature, but that of 'removal or no removal.'" Despite this organizational momentum, neither side managed to nominate a candidate for county representative. Editor Adams cited spring flooding, which prevented many of his antiremoval supporters from attending the Paulding meeting, as the reason. Besides, he pointed out, the general election was still six months away.[42]

Several correspondents, however, soon related a different and more compelling reason to forego nominations. The voters, they argued, could not separate the courthouse issue from "personal" motivations. One regular contributor claimed that the majority of those who resisted nominations believed that the "personal influence of the opposing candidates would be brought to bear" and would be decisive.[43] In other words, regardless of how compelling the courthouse issue seemed, and no matter how much the voters disliked taxes, they would still vote out of loyalty to friends, neighbors, and kin. This imperative, he maintained, made nominations for the legislature based on "removal or no removal" pointless. Leaders from both sides pondered their options and sought advice from local citizens. Lazarus J. Jones was one who offered his opinion. A planter who owned twenty slaves, former state representative, and longtime resident of the county, Jones agreed with earlier assessments. He advised that running candidates for the legislature on the courthouse issue "would never work" because the losers would always regard the winner's "personal popularity" as the cause of their demise. Instead, to gauge "true sentiment" they should hold a referendum on the "naked" question of removal or no removal. The race became even more chaotic when George Ryan entered as an independent candidate. He agreed with Jones on the courthouse issue, favoring resubmission to the electorate; but he also took a stand against reopening the slave trade. This view conflicted with the opinion of many Democratic state leaders but coincided with editor Adams's. After stirring up the slave trade issue for sometime, Ryan resigned the canvass. That left two candidates: Peter Loper and Absalom F. Dantzler. The former put his faith in Circuit Judge Jared Watts, who was scheduled to rule on the legality of the initial, disputed election several years earlier. Dantzler favored holding a new referendum. He won, 549 to 500.[44]

The race for senator from the combined district of Jasper, Clarke, and Wayne counties proved even more chaotic. It involved several candidates, the slave trade issue, the courthouse issue (for Jasper voters), a Democratic railroad tax resolution, a controversy surrounding a candidate who was a minister (the subject of churchmen running for political office was persistently debated in Mississippi), and a candidate who advocated free public schools but later quit the canvass. (The school issue spilled over into the Smith County contest, which also featured the slave trade, "unrepublican" caucuses and nominations, the Gulf and Ship Island Railroad, annexation of Cuba, and the upcoming presidential election.) In the end there was one "official" Democratic nominee, another Democrat who received more votes, and an independent who attacked the caucus system in general.[45]

While not every election for state legislature became this complicated, voters in Jasper and elsewhere had ample reason to fall back on the clarity of neighborhood and kinship ties. Given the limitations of voting data and without personal letters describing the operation of neighborhood networks, one can only infer their motivations. But the Jasper courthouse jumble underscores yet again the fragility of party labels and loyalties and manifests the danger of imputing any solid connection between Whig, Democrat, or Know-Nothing ideologies and events at the local level. The partisan culture in Mississippi was extremely shallow and often failed to command party loyalty in races for state legislature, much less county or local elections. Moreover, in Jasper, as in Hinds County and elsewhere, a *local* question became the deciding factor in an election usually assumed to be partisan. The flow of issues progressed not smoothly from national to state to local levels but more haphazardly. Any model that fails to recognize the diversity and potency of local concerns gives an unrealistic impression of politics, issues, and the voters — one that mistakenly suggests that parties and national events were the sole driving forces of politics.

State and county legislators, of course, recognized the power of neighborhoods and designed legislation to accommodate them. Their actions not only acknowledged but also facilitated the local orientation of political life, priorities manifest in the method of electing policemen. Amendment 2 of the 1832 state constitution specified that each county's voters would choose five members of the board of police, "one from each district." The legislature originally interpreted this to mean countywide voting for all candidates, with one resident serving from each district. Thus, if the two most popular candidates happened to live in the same district, only one of them could take office. This system could have encouraged a certain amount of partisanship (although there is no evidence that it did), as it would be difficult for all voters to know all candidates personally. In 1852, however, the legislature reinterpreted the measure, and thereafter a separate election was held in each district, allowing voters to use the same neighborhood networks they relied on for other local elections. This change, like the one separating state from county elections after 1855, should caution us further against linear thinking: nineteenth-century political culture did not move from prepartisan to partisan in a straight line but rather ebbed and flowed. Moreover, not only antiparty attitudes, but also legal or structural changes affected the evolution of political culture. In this case, reinterpretation of the voting procedure thwarted the potential for county partisanship and facilitated neighborhood voting.[46]

By reinterpreting the law on board elections to accommodate neighborhoods, legislators also acknowledged the way policemen did business. Because each county included five districts and members represented their home neighborhoods (even before the law was reinterpreted), duties naturally revolved around those divisions. One of the boards' chief responsibilities, for instance, was county roads, which depended on the work of local citizens designated as "road overseers." Each board member customarily made assignments for his own district, dividing certain roads into sections, naming one man as overseer and apportioning "hands" to work on the road as needed. Each policeman's duty was implicit, although several counties made specific stipulations about carrying it out. For example, Claiborne County's board resolved in December of 1853 that "hereafter it shall be the burden duty of each member of this Board, to find out all work that is absolutely necessary to be done on Roads & Bridges in his district and have the same done at the Cost of the County." Although the position of road overseer was unpaid, it provided an "honorable" service to fellow citizens and so carried a certain amount of prestige.[47]

Other board appointments did bring financial rewards. Perhaps the most regular patronage board members could give faithful supporters were the fees for serving as election officials. For each precinct the law required three inspectors, three clerks, and one returning officer. Customary payment was $2.00 a day, enough to satisfy the yearly tax bill of many nonslaveholding farmers. While most inspectors came from the ranks of slaveholders — even large planters — yeomen farmers often served as clerks. These positions helped create a network of clients and friends loyal to their respective board member.[48] Another source of patronage came from appointment to road juries. When any group of citizens petitioned the county to create a public road, the board commissioned a jury of "disinterested" citizens to survey the proposed route and decide on its feasibility. Typical compensation was $1.00 a day. Each policeman, naturally, selected men from his own neighborhood. Some counties had more exceptional opportunities for rewards. Claiborne County, a land of rolling hills and streams near the Mississippi River, had a number of toll bridges. Each year its board of police appointed several persons to serve as toll bridge keepers at an annual salary of between $300 and $400. In November of 1853 millionaire planter James J. Person represented

district 5 on the board, which included Toll Bridge Number 2. He secured
the position of bridge keeper for Port Gibson barkeeper Edward J. Rickhaw.
Rickhaw was a perfect "city man" for country resident Person — single, a
barkeeper, and a former town constable, he had a wide circle of friends in
Port Gibson.[49]

Election supervisors, road jurymen and bridge keepers were only some
of the most obvious recipients of patronage. Board members exercised other
equally important, and more subtle, forms of influence, included the granting of licenses to sell liquor or operate a ferry service. Everything the boards
supervised revolved around the five police districts and, within them, the
polling precincts. Local politics naturally coalesced around these neighborhood relationships in the form of favors and obligations among planters and
yeomen. These patronage positions also gave local government a prepartisan,
patron-client quality. In its reliance on the local population, particularly
slaveowners, Mississippi's administration often resembled a colonial regime.
In Latin America, for instance, the Spanish and Portuguese crowns, unable
and unwilling to provide enough royal officials, depended on wealthy white
settlers to run the government, ceding local authority in the interest of social
control and stability.[50] In the same way, the structure of local authority and
administration oriented Mississippi's political culture toward personal, face-
to-face relationships and away from more distant, anonymous bureaucracies.

The boards of police also used local planters to supervise the poor fund
and the public schools. In 1849 in Claiborne County, where commissioners
of the poor included some of the area's wealthiest men, the board appointed
Milford Hunter, a successful planter who would soon become a policeman
himself; Andrew J. McGill, another slaveowner; Henry F. Shaifer, part of a
wealthy family that included his brothers, George W. H. and S. P. Shaifer;
and James J. Person, another future board member and the owner of 150
slaves. In 1858, the situation was similar. All seven commissioners were slaveowners, including two members of the powerful Humphreys family led by
George Washington Humphreys, who held 199 slaves. Other commissioners
were Henry G. J. Powers, who registered 97 slaves in 1860, and Dr. Thomas
B. Magruder, who had over 50. Magruder was a former state senator who
owned two plantations ("Cabinwood" and "Oaken Grove") at which he held
open house for the neighborhood. William Sillers and William Holloway,
both longtime residents and board members themselves, also served as commissioners. In Carroll County, overseers of the poor for 1858 were Pearson
Money, member of a large and influential family that included his brother
James, one of the county's largest slaveowners; Stephen B. Arnold, another
planter with more than 50 slaves; and Albert F. McNeill, who owned 35
slaves and $50,000 worth of property.[51]

In addition to serving regularly as judges and inspectors, board members
called on men of property and influence to conduct special elections. Carroll County's policemen authorized T. C. Harris, G. G. Gordin, and Samuel

T. Lockhart "to advertise according to law and hold an election for Justice of the Peace in the Shongalo Beat occasioned by the resignation of W. T. Cain, Esqr." The same body "ordered that Wiley Kelley & T. B. Kennedy be appointed commissioners to advertise according to law and hold an election for five [school] trustees of the 16th Section in Township 17, Range 5."[52] These appointments, repeated in counties across the state, suggest that patronage and administration reinforced rural, neighborhood networks of men cultivated by county policemen, who relied on their supporters and rewarded them with valuable favors. County government especially required the support and prestige of local planters—a circle of fellow "gentlemen" who collectively managed local affairs.

Neighborhoods were such a recognized feature of political life that state and county legislators even codified them into law. The boards of police typically appointed slave patrols by neighborhood. When Carroll County's policemen assigned patrol leaders for 1860, they "Ordered that W. D. F. Threadgill, Calvin J. Coleman, Wm. Hobbs, [and] James Flowers, be appointed Captains or Leaders of Patrol in their respective neighborhoods."[53] Control of the subordinate population always remained a community-based exercise that conformed to the values and imperatives of communal manhood.

Efforts to control strong drink and develop public schools similarly reflected faith in neighborhood stability. The law to regulate inns and taverns required boards of police to grant licenses only after a petition from "respectable freeholders, or house keepers, of the town, village or neighborhood, in which such inn or tavern is proposed to be kept . . . [who] shall certify that the person recommended is of good repute for honesty and temperance." As their language indicates, lawmakers treated neighborhoods as rural towns; and, like local candidates, prospective innkeepers relied on neighbors to affirm their reputation. Another proposal to prohibit liquor sales in amounts of less than a gallon similarly recommended that licenses be granted only when the applicant presented "a petition to the board of Selectmen of said town, signed by a majority of the head of families residing therein, recommending the person . . . as [one] of good moral character."[54] The eventual law incorporated these sentiments and extended them to rural areas. Any hopeful liquor dealer needed a petition, "signed by a majority of the legal voters in the police district," that attested to his "good reputation." After the petition was given to the board of police, anyone opposed to it had one month to present an appeal, which, again, had to be signed by a majority of household heads. Schools were organized in the same way: "Any neighborhood, organizing itself into a school district" that provided a schoolhouse and a minimum number of pupils "should be entitled to the services of a competent teacher for ten months in the year at the expense of the county." Once again, state legislators relied on the ability of rural communities to run basic government operations, much as boards of police relied on the local gentry.[55]

The preponderance of evidence indicates that the neighborhood defined most politics in antebellum Mississippi. Successful candidates relied on community sanction and solid support from a personal network of local friends and kinsmen. Legislators enshrined the neighborhood in county and state law, helping to maintain Mississippi's prepartisan political culture up to the secession era. This localized system of face-to-face relationships rested on a stratified social structure: mutual obligations and friendships between some men and subordinate relationships between others bound the community together. The neighborhood context of elections, officeholding, and patronage conformed to the hierarchical set of social relations in which it operated and which it in turn helped maintain. The gentry's supervision of the voting process allowed planters to shape local politics and establish and maintain deferential class relations. Together, neighborhood politics comprised a statewide system that perpetuated an antiparty political culture relying on personal rather than institutional relationships.

6

CEREMONY

The Ritual Power of Politics

If neighborhoods were the sine qua non of Mississippi politics, then election day was its defining moment. When considered from a ritualistic perspective, the acts of voting and running for office take on deeper significance as social and cultural events. Besides a way to settle the issue of winners and losers, elections were frequent and inclusive ceremonies that submitted a man's personal reputation to the approval of his peers. The context of honor and communal manhood made them especially charged events in which candidates sought validation and the public support of friends and neighbors. To voters, this open, only semi-secret, process offered the chance to demonstrate friendship, loyalty, or gratitude; and its rituals incorporated the understanding of honor, fidelity, and duty that always mitigated American egalitarianism and masculine competitiveness. Of course, elections were only one of many public occasions that brought men together and — like court day or the militia muster — helped unify the ruling caste, test the loyalty of newcomers, and reaffirm camaraderie among old friends.[1]

More than these other events, however, elections were public and competitive affairs laden with implications of class and power. Judging the political culture as a series of rituals, then, reveals its mediating role between the ideal of white male democracy and the hierarchical realities of wealth, honor, and slavery. Elections validated a sense of egalitarianism because the franchise marked all white men as personally independent and sovereign. The gentry depended on yeoman votes to stay in office and craved the verification of their status that political success offered. In turn, politics allowed poorer folks to mingle with the wealthy and to certify their commitment to the shared promises of communal manhood. Elections were, in effect, a slightly less rough-and-ready hunting party (but were perhaps soaked in just as much old corn). Still, despite the egalitarian atmosphere, planters almost always won, and when they lost it was to men of the same rank. Thus, more than any other male ritual, elections shaped the local power structure and set the boundaries of class and honor. Moreover, elite supervision of the balloting process helps explain the political continuity evident in many rural neighborhoods. Positioned to influence voter behavior, election-day officials were often the same men year after year; inspectors drawn from the highest elites (men often wealthier than the candidates themselves) kept a close eye on the democratic process and worked to transfer family status and position to the next generation.

Yet, while elections often confirmed the existing contours of Mississippi's social, cultural, and economic hierarchy, they also redistributed power among men who might not know one another. Not simply static hegemonic rituals, elections were ways to negotiate class relations and accommodate geographic and social mobility, both of which were exaggerated — according to most historians — in the Old Southwest, at least until the 1850s. That was the real genius of the state's antiparty political culture: its ability to reconcile nineteenth-century democracy and mobility with the South's peculiar white male hierarchy based on slavery and honor.[2]

Students and observers of southern history from Daniel Hundley and Frederick Law Olmsted to Wilbur Cash and Eugene Genovese have debated the intriguing subject of white class relations in a slave society. As it is in most societies, wealth was distributed very unequally. But, like other nineteenth-century Americans, southerners paid daily homage to the mythic god of white male democracy and equality. Poor farmers jealously guarded their liberty and independence and the political power that entitled them to a certain degree of consideration from wealthier men. Mary Boykin Chesnut's famous lament over the fawning treatment her husband-politician James gave to the "squalid" well-digger MacDonald — who had mud between his toes — underscores politicians' respectful manner with poor folks, at least at election time. One Mississippi legislator similarly described the conduct of candidates among poor voters as "perfectly disgusting with bowing & shaking hands as intimate as if they considered themselves among their equals, when in fact they think very differently."[3]

The behavior of planters like James Chesnut or Mississippi's James J. Person (owner of more than two hundred slaves) as they mingled and talked with poor voters, offering them a handshake and a drink, is suggestive of *consensual governance*, a political model in which elites exercise formal power through an unspoken agreement ratified by the masses. As community leaders they steer public policy through "moments of consensus," which requires no real manipulation since planter-politicians were typically long-term residents, landowners and farmers, husbands and fathers, and fellow church members. In short, they were understood to have the community's interests at heart and to know what their less-wealthy neighbors wanted. In the context of American democracy this model is a good one, especially in antebellum Mississippi where voters chose almost all public officials, from governor to town recorder. The related *patron-client model*, on the other hand, emphasizes hierarchy and elite domination and argues that planters used their economic and cultural power to gain and maintain hegemonic control. In this model, rather than leading through consensus, patrons rule by manipulating their clients' dependent status—although they do owe certain reciprocal obligations to poor folks. Even in a hegemonic model, however, elite domination is most effective when legitimated by the masses; that is, when the latter believe in the value system championed by the wealthy. Furthermore, both paradigms underscore the importance of public rituals affirming masculine fitness for leadership and the institutional weakness that reserves political authority for local chieftains.

Considered within a continuum of world societies, the Old South can be characterized by either model. Southern yeoman farmers certainly exercised more independent power than peasants did in Brazil or Sicily; yet the impact of slavery and an extensive monoculture also created an exaggerated patriarchy that gave inordinate power to white, male, slaveowning heads of household. Mediterranean, Latin American, and some Southeast Asian societies represented more pure versions of the patron-client paradigm, but the Old South as well contained many of its central features: a commitment to hierarchy and values of honor, an extractive and expansive (rather than intensive) economy, an oligarchic landowning class that coopted other sectors of the economy, weak civil institutions, ritual exchanges of goods and hospitality, and the primacy of horizontal rather than vertical relationships, especially kinship ties. Of course, elite political power ultimately rested on some combination of hegemonic power and genuine ties between the classes.[4]

Numerous studies of southern communities detail a complex web of social, financial, and religious bonds between planters and yeomen, ties of kinship and economic interdependence that fostered a sense of mutuality, what Wilbur Cash called "class bondings." Shared virtues such as honor and masculinity, sanctioned by the community, also reinforced the face-to-face relationships between kin and neighbors. And slavery, of course, always encouraged whites to unify against the next Nat Turner. Historians are divided about the role of evangelical religion: many, probably the majority, emphasize its hierarchical qualities, while others underscore its egalitarian message. Virtually all agree, however, that southerners' spiritual homogeneity mitigated class conflict. Mitchell Snay concludes that southern religion "validated a hierarchical and organic vision of society and a particularist and egalitarian approach to social relations," satisfying both planters and yeomen and the demands for both deference and democracy.[5]

The antiparty political culture likewise balanced those contrasting beliefs, but it also met the public needs of honor and masculinity. For men, therefore, elections surpassed other elements of class bondings, including economics and religion, which typically lacked the necessary elements of public competitiveness or display. This hybrid model of class relations and community, then, suggests a local world of interpersonal ties between individuals driven by mutual obligations and exchanges—both economic and cultural—that produced a relatively stable society lacking open class conflict. Several studies, however, contend that these economic and social ligaments weakened during the 1850s as market relations and a more complex infrastructure slowly undermined local exchange and mutuality, changes that would have heightened the unifying importance of politics (and religion).

A central problem with the class-bondings model, however, is the issue of geographic mobility. If a large portion of the population migrated from most communities every five or six years, then how did such transient neighbors develop relationships of dependency or mutuality? Most estimates suggest that more than half of the heads of household moved each decade. Such a high demographic turnover, critics maintain, rendered honor, community opinion, and interpersonal ties irrelevant. According to their view, Southerners, like other Americans, were obsessed with a mad scramble for new land and material wealth, and cared little about the opinion of others and scoffed at the notion of inherited status. Not stability but mobility, not hierarchy and deference but an all-consuming egalitarian ethos defined the southern value system. Are the two interpretations irreconcilable?[6]

Mississippi's experience suggests that the structure of local politics—in particular, voting and running for office—provided a critical bridge between mobility and hierarchy. As one of the most inclusive and frequent rituals among southern men elections fostered stability and hierarchy, helping to negotiate status among men preoccupied with public reputation and their place in the local pecking order. "It was partly their unremitting concern with social ranking that made elections so important to most of the participants, whether patrons or clients," argues one student of ritual politics in Brazil. "Satisfying an almost unconscious need, elections worked to solidify among a mobile population the clearly ranked hierarchical order."[7]

In Mississippi too the framework of elections helped the gentry reestablish the prevailing distribution of power in the constant presence of demographic and social change. By serving as election inspectors, local squires displayed their economic and cultural power; they even schooled their sons and nephews to take over as the next generation of leaders. Since elites maintained stable residence at a higher rate than poor folks, the wealthy always had an advantage when men "interpreted" or "negotiated" community rituals (and, in turn, power relationships). In short, history favored the gentry, who were more likely to stay in one place, and tipped the balance toward politics reflecting current social relations rather than reconfiguring them. Yet, yeomen and other men could still assert their independence and virtue simply by participating in the election ritual. Moreover, some candidates moved up the ladder of public offices over time, indicating that the rituals of politics offered chances to renegotiate a man's place in the hierarchy. As always, the legacy of American political democracy in the context of slavery and honor was ambiguous. Running for local office and voting, like dueling, gambling, or hospitality, were rituals that reaffirmed shared values and established men's understanding of power and status.

The act of voting was itself the most ritualistic part of the political culture, an important chance for everyone who took part to make a public gesture. The way the process was structured allowed men of varying backgrounds and classes to assume different roles. The distribution of election-day duties especially suggests Mississippians's faith in an organic, deferential society and reveals the gentry's influence in a supposedly democratic, free process. Each precinct had a set of election officials — three inspectors, one returning officer, and three clerks — who were assigned to their positions by the board of police. Inspectors, with their broad discretionary powers over ballots and voters, carried the most authority. The "inspectors shall take care that the election is conducted fairly and agreeably to law," intoned the 1857 codebook, and "they shall be judges of the qualification of voters, and may examine any person offering to vote." They could commit unruly voters to jail or fine them up to $500. The returning officer guarded the ballot box and helped inspectors count the tickets at day's end. He also found replacements for any absent inspectors, "with the approbation of two respectable freeholders of the county." Yet, several passages in the law imply that he was subservient to the inspectors: "The returning officer at every precinct is hereby invested with full power, under the direction or with the concurrence of the inspectors, to preserve order in and about the house where the election may be held." Another summary stated that "every person entitled to vote shall deliver to the returning officer, in presence of the inspectors," a ballot, "which ticket the returning officer shall, in presence of the inspectors, put into the ballot-box, and at the same time the clerks shall take down on separate lists the name of every person voting." In this account, the returning officer was little more than a glorified clerk who carried ballots to the box while inspectors watched over his shoulder. Beneath these officials served the clerks, who assisted the inspectors and recorded the names of all legal voters. After the polls closed, they matched their lists with the ballots to make sure that there were no extra tickets.[8]

Policemen appointed only the wealthiest, most prominent men in each precinct as inspectors, and their names were usually announced in the local newspaper.[9] Returning officers were slightly younger and poorer, while clerks came from the ranks of small farmers and sons of the gentry; it was not uncommon for father and son to serve as inspector and clerk at the same precinct. The arrangement catered to basically elitist and deferential class relations and demonstrated the imperatives of family and honor. In a world of personal rather than institutional relationships the elite were commissioned to monitor the cherished democratic privilege. As each individual voter marched to the poll and handed his not-too-secret ballot to the returning officer, the local gentry stood in judgment, monitoring the grand event.

That was the legal ideal, of course; eyewitness accounts often sketch less genteel and occasionally underhanded scenes. "Drunkenness, swearing, fighting, and bravado were the ruling ills that marred the day," wrote one editor, "making the town appear as though wild beasts, instead of civilized men, dwelt within its limits." Besides the usual male frolicking, there was more-purposeful corruption—illegal voters, tampering with ballot boxes, and unlawful supervisors. Protested results offer vivid testimony that while elections were public rituals, and can be usefully analyzed as such, they were also contests for public office and money that sometimes brought out the worst in ambitious men vying for every advantage. One typical complaint, for instance, was that proper notice of an election was not given: "It was not known when or for what the election was to take place, except by a vague rumor" wrote one losing candidate.[10]

Probably the most common complaints about procedural dirty tricks involved improperly sworn election supervisors or officials who also were candidates. The latter was not specifically prohibited in the legal code—only the sheriff was barred from fulfilling his election duties as county returning officer when he was running for office—but was apparently proscribed by tradition and extended to "others personally interested." At least as frequent were protests that ballot boxes were inadequate or improperly secured. Each county sheriff was responsible for providing "a sufficient number of ballot-boxes . . . secured by good and substantial locks." The returning officer at each precinct kept the ballot box, while the keys were held by one of the inspectors until it was time to open it and count the ballots. Protests detailed the numerous chances for a breach of security. "Instead of having good Boxes with Locks some of them [polls] had nothing but an old hat," claimed two disappointed candidates from Chickasaw County. "Instead of opening the box in the presence of all the Inspectors they [returning officers] picked there [sic] opportunity and commenced counting out when some of the Inspectors were absent and also raised a row and blew out the Candles and ran off with the Ballot Box and the clerks were scattered all over town with their tallies." Finally, the two men accused, the miscreants "examined the votes and made them to suit themselves and Friends."[11]

These and similarly entertaining passages breathe life into the dry, formal statutes, but few elections were actually contested. Between 1835 and 1860 fewer than a dozen out of several thousand elections for state representative or senator were appealed to the legislature. Virtually every one of them involved county border disputes or the creation of new counties or the timing of special elections rather than procedural illegalities. Protests to the governor's office about county and local elections were equally scarce, and most were equally prosaic. The vast majority hinged on questions about precinct or county lines or tenure of office; only one solitary protest mentioned partisanship as a factor in electoral skullduggery. Instead, disputes turned on neighborhood or personal loyalties. Although there was undoubtedly a good deal of drinking, fighting, and gambling, to judge by the protests filed in Jackson the election-day inspectors evidently kept a close, and apparently effective, watch on the democratic process.

By every measure, appointment as inspector defined success: the wealthiest, most residentially stable, and most prominent and respected citizens served in that office. Election inspectors were more stable and wealthier than policemen and nearly twice as likely as all candidates for public office to be permanent residents. And while the very wealthiest men rarely ran for state or national office, they regularly served as election inspectors. Judging from the behavior of Mississippi's greatest planters, supervising elections outranked running for office; apparently they recognized both the real and symbolic power of guarding the cherished right to vote.

In Claiborne County, inspectors for 1853 included Thomas Freeland Jr., a young planter who owned seventy slaves and $50,000 worth of cotton land. Freeland helped found Oakland College and was a leader in the local Presbyterian church. Other inspectors were D. J. Dohan, a former policeman and master of seventy-five slaves, and Daniel Willis and James H. Hedrick, both planters. Less-wealthy inspectors often boasted of powerful kinsmen. William McLatham, hardly a poor man with his ten slaves and several thousand dollars in farmland, was part of a prominent family that included his brother Thomas, a planter who possessed over thirty slaves. Inspectors in Port Gibson came from the municipal elite and included merchant A. W. Hodge and master carpenter Amariah Rollins. A resident for over twenty-five years, Rollins recorded $10,000 worth of property and the ownership of several slaves. In 1858 the Claiborne County Board of Police designated the usual eighteen inspectors for its six precincts. Nearly three-fourths of the appointees appear in both the 1850 and 1860 censuses, indicating their uncommon stability. The roll included three men who owned over a hundred slaves and six others with more than twenty. All inspectors owned at least several bondsmen, and all but one of the eighteen were over forty-two years old. The only nonfarmers appointed—merchant R. C. Hume, watchmaker Stephen C. Keyes, and twenty-eight-year-old lawyer James S. Morris—lived in Port Gibson or Grand Gulf. Others who served there during the 1850s included some of the wealthiest men in the United States. Virginia native Richard T. Archer, a graduate of William and Mary, recorded 221 slaves and listed nearly $250,000 in additional property with the Claiborne census taker in 1860; William Briscoe and Smith C. Daniel owned "only" 130 slaves each.[12] Harrison County's inspectors also came from its social elite. In 1858 they included Jacob Elmer, a successful merchant and county pioneer who served as inspector for nearly twenty years, and John Huddleston, policeman, millowner, and part-time planter. Also stationed at the ballot box were Francis Peronsett, a Swiss-born merchant with several slaves and thousands of dollars in merchandise, and F. B. Spence, a planter with sixteen slaves and $5,700 worth of farmland — a fortune that made him one of the dozen richest men in this poor county. Of the thirty men appointed inspectors in 1858, all but three appear in either the 1850 or 1860 census and nearly half stayed in Harrison throughout the decade.

The overseers appointed for Bolivar County's 1855 elections exemplified the social and economic status of both inspectors and clerks. Many of the county's initial settlers and wealthiest planters served as inspectors. At the third precinct stood Joseph McGuire, Christopher G. Coffee, and John V. Newman, the last a four-time member of the board of police. Each man owned about 50 slaves and thousands of acres of prime cotton land along the great river. At William Vick's precinct the "poorest" inspector was physician and planter John J. Ross, who owned 36 slaves and $76,000 worth of property. William Vick himself recorded nearly 150 slaves on his Bolivar plantations alone. The average age of the county's inspectors was nearly fifty years old.

By contrast, of the eleven clerks located in the census records, ten were still in their twenties and, perhaps most interesting, many were sons of Bolivar's gentry and would some day serve as inspectors, policemen, and representatives. The clerkship was probably their first official duty. One of them, Robert E. Starke, was the twenty-year-old son of longtime state representative Peter B. Starke — who owned about $200,000 worth of slaves and land. Others were Isaac Bankston, son of original settler Ignatius Bankston; James Ross, son of planter John J. Ross; and nineteen-year-old Joseph W. Elliott Jr., Elliott Sr. had settled Concordia Island in the county's first years. Another clerk in 1855 was Frank Montgomery, a future policeman and son-in-law to Charles Clarke, currently the county's state representative. Montgomery, a rising young planter with political prospects, had recently moved to Bolivar; serving as clerk offered him the chance to meet the local community as one of its future leaders. By 1860 he was on the board of police and serving as an inspector.

The appointment of men such as Montgomery, Robert Starke, and Joseph Elliott Jr. to clerks' duties is suggestive; they clearly represented the future generation of leadership, often the heirs apparent of the neighborhood gentry. As local farmers and new residents trooped to the polls, they were supervised, approved of, or disapproved of by the local elite; then the next generation of leaders recorded their names and introduced themselves to their future patrons or clients. After the election clerks tallied the votes and compared them with the number of voters on their registration lists. Whereas the disposition of candidates for office established and reinforced the existing hierarchy — helping men learn where they belonged — the vot-

ing process was pivotal in transferring established relationships from generation to generation among a shifting population.

Consider the scene in 1855 at Bolivar's fourth precinct, William Vick's
"Nitta Yuma" plantation. Vick had provided the land for Bolivar's first
county seat, Bolivar's Landing, in 1836. The first board of police meeting
took place in his house, which was also the site of all county business and
elections in the early years. Known for his hospitality, the "old bachelor"
entertained numerous relatives, and "his home was the gathering place for
the young people of the county."[13] Naturally, the board chose Squire Vick
and fellow planters Christopher Field and Dr. John J. Ross as election-day
inspectors. Neighbors since the county's early days, all three men lived along
the river near Bolivar's Landing. This triumvirate sat in judgment on prospective voters, allowing or challenging their rights to democratic privileges.
No matter how often the inspectors exercised their authority, the symbolic
effect of the setting must have remained impressive. As they walked through
the gate and approached Vick's front veranda, some voters surely understood
the realities of wealth and power displayed there. Casting their ballots under the nose, even the watchful eyes, of the county's greatest patrons, young
farmers and new residents like A. H. Brice, who had recently arrived from
Louisiana with his wife and little else, quickly learned who mattered in the
neighborhood. One imagines Squire Vick offering him a friendly greeting
or a handshake to reduce the tension—after all, he might someday need
Brice's vote himself or one of his cohorts. And certainly Vick, the celebrated
host, would have treated the locals to drinks and food.

Once authorized to vote, each man handed his ballot to William E.
Starke Jr., the returning officer. Then only twenty-two, William Starke already owned thousands of dollars worth of cotton land and over thirty slaves.
He was also Peter B. Starke's nephew. The elder Starke, who moved up to
the state senate in 1855, was an old acquaintance of William Vick, as both
had settled the area around Lake Bolivar and Bolivar's Landing. Moving
down the line, each voter gave his name to one of the clerks seated nearby:
Robert E. Starke, Peter's son, or Dr. Ross's son John Jr. The implications of
such an arrangement could scarcely have escaped most voters, or those
seated as inspectors and clerks. For a man unfamiliar with the local power
structure, casting his ballot on Vick's porch with the next generation of leadership on hand to learn the routine effectively showed him his place.

Of course, these suggestive images also speak to the political continuity
of rural neighborhoods. Inspectors like Vick were positioned to influence
local farmers, who often depended on his harvest-time generosity or small
loans. Voters used printed ballots in all local, county, and state elections,
but the process was far from secret. Party tickets usually differed in size and
often color, making it easy to recognize a voter's choice. County and local
candidates often failed to appear on printed ballots, meaning that voters
needed to write in their selection. How many decided that it was easier

simply to announce their choices and let one of the clerks record the candidates' names? Illiterate voters had few options. According to census figures, which almost certainly underreport it, the rate of illiteracy was about 10 percent of adult white men. By a modern definition of functional illiteracy, the rate probably exceeded 25 percent.

All of these considerations betray the importance of the voting process as a public ritual, and underscore its many-layered meanings and implications. Especially in small rural neighborhoods, planter-inspectors potentially held vast power. Not everyone voted alike, but most did — some out of genuine class bonding or a shared masculine perspective but others because they felt pressured by elites like Squire Vick and his friends. Tenants, the most disadvantaged voters of all, probably faced the most direct pressure from their landlords; and, as landless workers also moved more often than other voters, they were frequently ineligible to vote and so relegated to the fringes of electoral politics. Certainly the record implies numerous limitations on freedom of choice and demonstrates that deference and intimidation survived the movement to printed ballots and mass democracy. At the very least, scenes like those on Vick's veranda discredit notions of frontier democracy or the rampant egalitarianism that supposedly made elite hegemony or inherited hierarchy untenable in the Old Southwest.[14]

Mississippi's elections were probably no less free or democratic than those in many other places. Voters in New York City faced polls located in the back rooms of ethnic saloons; some even had to know a secret knock to be admitted. In the Upper South, according to studies of North Carolina and Virginia, deference and elite power in local politics continued even after most offices were made elective in the 1850s. The critical distinction, of course, was that in other states parties mediated between the gentry and voters, maintaining undemocratic nominations and using patronage to perpetuate elite continuity. In New York the Democratic Party provided the means to control ethnic saloons with their backroom ballot boxes. In 1841 Ohio, William Tyler remembered approaching the poll to cast his first ballot, only to hear one of the inspectors yell "shut down the window, there are more whigs coming." He and other Whigs doubted that it was closing time but, because the inspectors were Democrats, they could not vote. Ohio's "election officials were usually diehard partisans," summarizes one historian, "who knew the politics of every voter in their bailiwicks long before they rode up to the polling place." Buckeye voters typically elected each precinct's judges before the actual balloting — a process obviously fraught with partisanship, susceptible to trickery, and hazardous for some unsuspecting voters like young Tyler.[15]

Mississippi's antiparty political culture positioned the gentry, who were already in control of the boards of police, to manage the democratic process as well. Moreover, there is virtually no evidence that parties organized to monitor the process. Newspapers never discussed the appointments of inspectors, and the boards of police did not debate the choice of election supervisors — or at least there is no record that they did. As social and cultural trendsetters, consensual mouthpieces for the white male community — or because of their personal scrutiny and intimidation — planter-patriarchs like William Vick could influence, if not entirely control, local politics.

For men who actively sought public office, the ritual significance of elections was greater than it was for voters or election-day supervisors. In a public and exposed forum, elections submitted office seekers' personal honor and reputation to the hands, or ballots, of other men. They were also contests for income, of course, and candidates sought the economic, as well as symbolic, rewards of public office. Ambitious men used to their advantage both the money and status that came with political victory. Mississippi voters demonstrated a sensitive understanding of the subtle distinctions in status among candidates, a ranking that both reflected and helped establish, or reestablish, the social and cultural hierarchy.

Mississippi conformed to American patterns of nineteenth-century mobility that show recent arrivals outnumbering older residents in any three- or four-year period. Those who stayed, including candidates and officeholders, were often from the social and political elite. Candidates for office and election-day supervisors typically lived in the area about ten years, although many of them remained even longer.[16] The socioeconomic profile varied; the cream of society in Jasper County, for instance, would barely have qualified as middle class in a long-settled cotton county like Claiborne. But the hierarchy always prevailed, and voters and candidates of all classes used elections to negotiate their place in it.

Some men who stayed in one place moved up the ladder of local offices as they advanced economically and socially. It was a hierarchical social structure but was not fixed, and self-made men successfully adopted the political trappings of the gentry. One reason for all the duels, of course, was that the southern definition of elite status remained more fluid than in most honor-bound societies. The American environment privileged *honra* over inherited status, making personal success paramount. The various factors that contributed to status — principally wealth, age, reputation, and length of residence — were interrelated. A longtime resident might compensate for relative poverty with extended friendships formed over many years or with a certain reverence often granted to men of advancing age. The cumulative effect of family history or honorable service included respect for some men's roles as county pioneers, leaders during settlement and early politics. More often, young men used fortune or family connections to overcome their youthfulness. Wealth remained the best indication of class, and slaves were the greatest part of any family's riches. Bondsmen also provided the most culturally significant mark of honor; mastery over other human beings always gave a man greater power than mere money. Thus slaves not only represented a capital reinvestment, they were also the ultimate form of display.[17] Finally, candidates relied on their personal reputation and manliness, qualities that largely defy quantitative measurement. The circular argument that election-day victories are evidence of an honorable public life is uncomfortable to make, but not without merit. Confirmation from the ballots of his neighbors did signify a man's standing in the community, and political accomplishments were unquestionably marks of status that simultaneously reflected and added to other criteria.

As men came of age or moved into a new neighborhood, running for local office helped confirm or establish their place in society. The state's unusual commitment to democracy meant that there were at least thirty-five or forty spots on the ballot in each county, including precinct offices. "Just returned from the election," wrote one Mississippi voter, and "there were 21 names on my ticket [at this precinct]"; he guessed "there are not less than some 40 candidates before the people" in the entire county. He was waiting up late into the night for his son Kenneth, who was "confined as one of the clerks at our precinct. . . . You know it must take some time to count out the vote on some 80 or 90 of those long tickets."[18] The "long ticket" meant that in many counties a significant proportion of eligible men were seeking office. In Amite County in 1850, for instance, the census reported that there were 764 white men over twenty-one years of age. The following year there were seventy-one candidates in the county—nearly 10 percent of the eligible voters. In 1849 in tiny Bolivar County *one-third* of the adult white men were running for office.

These figures include only county or precinct candidates and exclude those running in municipal and militia elections, which often pushed the figure to one-third or one-half of all men. Militia posts, in particular, attracted the gentry and its sons; impressionistic evidence suggests that, as explicitly hierarchical positions bestowing honor but no financial gain, they, too, reflected class distinctions. (Because the militia system was woefully unorganized until the late 1850s, very little evidence about officer selection survives from before the 1858 and 1860 elections.)[19] Including election judges and other appointees in the count raises the participation rate in many counties above one-half. With three inspectors, three clerks, and a returning officer at each precinct, and multiple polls in each of five police districts, most counties averaged between 75 and 125 election-day officials in any given year. Added to candidates, this means that in smaller counties nearly two-thirds of the eligible men were typically involved in the elections in some capacity. Even in the most populous regions, at least one in eight or nine men played some formal role beyond voting.

The profile of candidates for office in each county parallels that of male household heads (see Appendix).[20] Property owners were not overrepresented, and slaveowners predominated only slightly: 64 percent of candidates owned slaves, higher than the state's estimated average of 50 percent. Overall, these figures suggest that while slaveholders, especially large planters, dominated national, state, and the most prestigious county offices, men of more modest wealth held their share of other county and precinct offices. The profile of candidates for all offices nearly matches a model sampling of the white male population. In Amite County, for example, 72 percent of candidates owned slaves, precisely the same figure as in the county at large in 1850. In Bolivar and Hinds, slaveowners were actually underrepresented. Men without any property also acted as candidates in about the same proportion as their representation in the overall population. Of all the candidates located in either the 1850 or the 1860 census, nearly nine out of ten owned some property. This figure corresponds to estimates for the entire state, which indicate that while about 20 percent of all male household heads owned neither land nor slaves in 1860, many of them had other property. In short, the spectrum of candidates offered a representative sample of Mississippi's white male population; nearly all men had the chance to run for office and, rich and poor alike, entered the fray.[21]

Candidates for state representative and policeman were drawn from the elite, some of the wealthiest and most longtime residents of their communities. In the sample counties, 305 men ran for the two offices, and 277 of them appeared in either the 1850 or 1860 census. About two-thirds of legislative candidates appeared in both the 1850 and 1860 censuses, indicating a residential persistence rate well above the statewide average. About half of the policemen — though their rate was slightly lower — also appeared in both reports. Invariably slaveowners, the candidates for these offices exemplified their county's elite. On average, the stature of representatives surpassed that of board candidates, although some men moved back and forth between the two offices. Voters in Carroll County elected John M. Hamilton to the board in 1858 and to the state legislature the following year. A planter born in South Carolina, Hamilton owned forty-five slaves and had lived in Mississippi since the late 1840s. Joseph Regan, owner of more than fifty slaves, served Claiborne County in the legislature until 1855 and was on the board of police in 1860. William F. Dillon ran for one or both offices in Hinds County every year between 1849 and 1860. A resident since the 1830s, Dillon held over twenty-five slaves and valuable farmland outside Raymond. Jasper County voters returned Duncan McLaurin to the board in 1853 and to the legislature in 1858. Duncan resided in the area in the midst of dozens of his family for more than twenty years and owned several slaves. In Amite County another perennial candidate, planter Jehu Wall, won election to both offices during the 1850s.

Standing at the apex of Mississippi's political culture, state representatives and policemen symbolized the combined effects of wealth, age, and residence on elective office. Their ranks included some of the premier slaveholders in the entire South: Charles Clarke in Bolivar, Cowles Vaiden in Carroll, and John Murdoch and James J. Person in Claiborne, each of whom owned well over a hundred slaves. More modest wealth could be offset by family connections or public service. Frank Montgomery, only twenty-eight years old and a small (by local standards) but rising planter, won election to Bolivar's board of police in 1858, just three years after coming to the county. In addition to these modest assets, however, he had the advantage of being married to a niece of Charles Clarke, state representative and future Confederate governor. On his plantation, "Beulah," Montgomery enjoyed close ties with his powerful in-law. He also catered to the community by holding Methodist services there in the late 1850s.[22]

Other candidates relied on their status as local pioneers who had taken a formative role in their county's settlement. In Harrison County, farmer Daniel Walker seemed an unlikely policeman; he owned no slaves and little property, but his longtime residence apparently overcame these shortcomings. At the county's first board meeting in 1841, the members selected his house on Red Creek as the polling place for district 5. Walker stayed in Harrison throughout the 1840s and 1850s and held elections on his front lawn. In Bolivar County, Orren Kingsley faced no opposition to his election to the board in 1849 and 1851. Although more successful later, he owned just a few slaves in 1850; but Kingsley had been present at the county's first board meeting in 1836 and was among the first ten original land grantees in 1831. No absentee landlord, Kingsley settled permanently in the wilds of early Bolivar and took an active part in its development.[23]

Voters usually taught candidates who transgressed established boundaries a quick lesson. Men who tried to step up to a prestigious office, such as policeman, to which they did not belong, failed universally. In Carroll County blacksmith Henry Huffman, who owned no property, was defeated in his run for the board of police in 1853. Voters there likewise rebuked Julius Harbin and Thomas Harper, small farmers with little property. In Bolivar they rejected Nelson Blanchard. Although he had been a successful candidate for other offices, Blanchard lost to Isaac Hudson, an early settler and leading planter. John Woodhouse, a farmer with more than ten slaves, failed to win election to Claiborne's board of police despite being unanimously elected to three consecutive terms as the local justice of the peace. In 1855, trying to move up to policeman, he ran against Richard Valentine, who owned nearly two hundred slaves and $50,000 worth of cotton land. Predictably, Valentine managed an easy victory. Woodhouse, although evidently liked by his neighbors, was apparently outclassed by his opponent's wealth, connections, and status.

Apparently, one strategy to undermine an opponent's candidacy was to hint that he might not measure up to the job. In Madison County's 1855 contest for representative, for example one Democratic editor referred to the Know-Nothings' candidate as "Dr." Thomas Anderson. Nativist Owen Van

Vactor quickly jumped in to defend his party's nominee: "Though he has resided about ten years in the same neighborhood with Thos. S. Anderson, Esq., yet this stuck-up piece of vanity and self-conceit [the editor], speaks of him as 'Dr.' . . . The object of this small trick," Van Vactor concluded, was "to insinuate that our candidate was so obscure, that his neighbors could mistake his profession."[24] Anderson's opponents, in other words, were implying that he scarcely qualified as a proper county representative if the voters had to be reminded who he was.

Candidates for other county offices also formed a pecking order, although one somewhat distinct from the offices elected in precincts. Even more than policemen or representatives, many candidates sought county offices from financial as well as honorific motives. Income from fees could be substantial; the coroner, for instance, received ten dollars for each inquest on a dead body (of which Mississippi had plenty). The clerk of the circuit court collected money for twenty-seven different tasks, ranging from five cents for swearing in a witness to a dollar for recording each court judgment.[25] The majority of these candidates fell into three broad categories of approximately equal wealth but different occupational and family experience. First, young professionals and sons of planters gravitated toward the three "clerical" posts of assessor and circuit court and probate court clerk. Second, skilled craftsmen and middle-aged farmers favored the offices of ranger, coroner, and, to a lesser extent, surveyor. These two groups most clearly epitomized what James Oakes termed "dual-career" slaveowners, ambitious men with enough family or local connections to get elected. They combined farming, teaching, or the law with a public career that generated cash to pay taxes, buy slaves, or withstand a bad harvest. Consistent income provided them with a greater opportunity for social mobility and helped young officeholders move up in the ranks if they stayed in one place long enough.[26] Finally, candidates for sheriff and treasurer, the most prestigious county jobs, came from local gentry, although they were men lower in status than policemen, representatives, or election inspectors.

Sheriffs and treasurers, like policemen at the precinct level, were among the wealthiest and most well connected of county candidates. The position of sheriff offered financial opportunities, although it entailed a considerable amount of work. In addition to keeping the peace, each sheriff attended the regular meetings of the board of police and acted as general returning officer for all elections. The office of treasurer offered fewer chances to make money, at least legally, although holding it was a sign of responsibility and the voters' trust. Holders of both offices were required to post the largest bonds for surety in the county, reflecting their relative importance among other administrators.[27] The significance voters, too, attached to these jobs is reflected in the consistently high turnouts on election day. Roll-off for both sheriff and treasurer rarely exceeded 1 or 2 percent, and in about a fourth of these races the turnout was higher than in the gubernatorial election (table

4.2). In short, lawmakers and voters alike considered the jobs of sheriff and treasurer the most important ones in the county.

In Jasper County, the typical candidate for these offices owned only a few slaves and several thousand dollars worth of property but was a longtime resident. Washington Cundiff, a merchant and candidate for treasurer who lived in Paulding, was typical: he registered two slaves in 1850 and recorded $3,000 in property ten years later. William B. Ferrell, a merchant-farmer and candidate for sheriff, held four slaves and $8,640 in property in 1860. Lemuel Lassiter, sheriff and merchant, owned six slaves on the eve of secession; and Seth Travis, a merchant-farmer and would-be sheriff, was master of five slaves. The socioeconomic profile of Amite County was higher, and it took more wealth to aspire to be sheriff or treasurer there. Enoch George Wicker, elected sheriff in 1851, owned eight slaves and had lived in the county for at least thirteen years. For others, the path to political success and respectability followed economic advancement. Peter Ratliff was born and raised in Amite County but waited until 1860 to seek office. By then he had acquired seven slaves and over $20,000 in property. An active member of Galilee Baptist Church, Ratliff had "made it" by the time voters chose him as their sheriff.[28]

Carroll County's treasurers included the appropriately named James P. Money. Born in 1778 and a longtime resident, Money owned seven slaves and considerable acreage when he was elected in 1849, 1851, and 1853. Three-term sheriff John O. Young was a tanner, farmer, slaveowner, and had been a resident since the early 1840s. In Harrison County, where poor land and largely subsistence farming produced few wealthy planters, candidates for choice positions were often top artisans or merchants. They included R. C. Corvan, treasurer and merchant, William M. Jordan, candidate for sheriff and master carpenter, Samuel Staples, sawmill owner and hopeful sheriff, and Calvin Taylor, would-be treasurer and miller. As they did with policemen and representatives, voters usually rebuffed men who overstepped their place. Neither Samuel M. Phelps, a carpenter, nor D. A. Cully, a mechanic who owned one slave, received much attention when they ran for treasurer in Hinds County: Phelps finished a distant third in 1853, and Cully ran fifth in an 1859 special election. Aspiring sheriffs and treasurers generally ranked just below representatives and policemen; as men of property and standing, they showed residential stability and personal success.

The remaining county posts offered neither the status nor the attraction of sheriff's or treasurer's jobs, but they did appeal to certain well-defined segments of society. Candidates' overall patterns of wealth and slaveholding proved similar among the two categories (see Appendix) but were differentiated by age, family roots, and prospects. Young professionals and sons of the elite dominated the offices of circuit court and probate court clerk and assessor. Because of their youth, many of these candidates moved more often than others. One typical clerk was Marshall P. Bates, who was elected in Amite County in 1853. Bates was just twenty-four years old and the son of local planter Richard Bates. In 1850 he lived at home, but by 1860 he had acquired eight slaves and $25,000 in property, most of which he probably inherited from his father. Similarly, Christopher Caine was twenty-four when he ran for circuit court clerk in 1849. Born in Amite County, Caine was a new father with three slaves and a few hundred dollars' worth of merchandise. Like many young men, he moved away during the 1850s. Russell Davis McDowell, circuit clerk in Amite for most of the decade, lived at home when he first ran for the job at only twenty-two. Although he lost that race, he won it for the next four regular terms. By 1860, still just thirty years old, he had inherited eleven slaves and over $10,000 in property from his father, Thomas. In 1860 D. L. Duke ran for probate clerk of Jasper County, where he lived with his wealthy, widowed mother; he was just twenty-two-years old. Paulding merchant Thomas W. Grayson was thirty when the voters chose him circuit clerk in 1855. His modest wealth was typical of many clerkship candidates: he owned four slaves and about $5,000 in merchandise. Carroll County's clerks included young lawyers James K. Lea and Andrew M. Nelson. Later elected to three terms, Nelson lost his first bid for probate clerk in 1851 when he was barely old enough to vote for himself. Rufus Shoemaker was twenty-three and living at home when he tried unsuccessfully for the circuit court clerkship of Claiborne County. A student and later a newspaper editor, young Shoemaker had a father who owned several slaves.

These young men epitomized Mississippi's candidates for assessor and court clerks. Some were planters' sons living at home and probably needed something to do. Others were beginning merchants or teachers — literate men accustomed to paperwork — who needed money. Jasper County teachers Duncan McInnis and Thomas C. Moffatt ran for assessor and circuit clerk, respectively. Moffatt was twenty-three when he first tried for office and still living with his father, James. Young Jonathan Stewart served as Hinds County's clerk of the probate court for several years, a job he preferred to the "irksome" task of teaching school. He hoped to use "the acquaintances I have formed" in office to make more money in business or politics. He later declined an opportunity to run for the state legislature because he would have had "to resign all the offices I now hold and I am not high enough in the world to live without some of my own exertions." For Stewart income from his county jobs was crucial. Jonathan's relative and neighbor, Hugh Stewart, ruefully noted his own close defeat for clerk of the circuit court, an office he thought was "worth $2,500 per year."[29] These men were young and better educated than their peers. Not yet established, and often having only modest family connections, they could not expect to become policemen or sheriffs. But a clerkship reflected their education or above-average background, either of which bespoke a considerable future, most often as a slaveholding professional. Negative or low rates of roll-off, rarely reaching 2 percent, again signal voters' attention to these posts.

The remaining county offices — ranger, coroner, and surveyor — fell primarily to small farmers and artisans. For skilled workers with flexible schedules these positions offered extra income with few demands. Candidates were men of modest wealth chiefly differentiated from clerks and assessors by their age and occupations. In Claiborne County they included Rane C. Hutchinson, coroner and livery stable owner, age twenty-nine, and Charles Johnson, assessor and grocer, age thirty-four. William McKeever, who ran unsuccessfully for ranger in 1855, was a thirty-year-old carriage painter. James Smith, elected coroner the same year, was a shingle and brick maker. Jasper County candidates for ranger and coroner included printer Miller W. Ellis, hotel keeper Josiah Jones, and mechanic Amos J. Reid. Jones and Reid were both thirty-seven when elected; Ellis was twenty-five. Voters in Amite County chose thirty-five-year old C. C. Vannorman as surveyor in 1860. A tanner, Vannorman's household included nine other boarders, all of them skilled, single men; among them were a teamster, dentist, and master carpenter. In Hinds County, thirty-three-year-old John W. Hand, a tailor, was elected ranger in 1855. The aspiring coroners and rangers from Harrison County represented a wide range of skilled or semi-skilled workers: carpenter, seaman, woodcutter, merchant's clerk, and mariner.

Candidates for county offices, then, fell into distinct categories. For many, financial motives seemed paramount. Men often ran several times, sometimes for different offices, and incumbents tended to win reelection again and again. Income from catching a few strays or helping at an inquest might make the difference for a farmer with middling soil struggling to buy, or keep, a slave or two. Candidates for assessors and clerks were younger and more mobile than older farmers and artisans, who gravitated to the other county posts. The former, who were often on their way up the social ladder, were likely to become professionals and, even, planters. The latter frequently stayed in Mississippi and used their modest incomes from public office to clear a few more acres or purchase a few more slaves.

Unlike these county candidates, most men who sought precinct office ran only once. Income was apparently a secondary consideration, although policeman had access to county tax funds, licenses and permits, and patronage. Given the wealth of most policemen, their *per diem* and travel expense money was probably insignificant when compared to the importance of cultivating clients and helping friends with county favors. Above all, their tendency to seek office only once as well as a considerable number of uncontested or lopsided elections suggest that the ritual power of the office was its main attraction. Planters, particularly young ones, apparently considered the board of police as validation of their status — an accurate perception, it seems, judging by the behavior of Mississippi's voters.

Justices and constables received minor fees which were typically lower than those paid to county officers. Justices, for instance, received a dollar for each marriage performed and forty cents for each warrant served in a criminal case. Constables earned twenty-five cents for summoning a witness and a dollar for whipping a slave when ordered by the justice. They were also eligible for the sheriff's fees if they performed any of these duties on the latter's behalf. Like county officers, then, justices and constables could earn income to supplement farming or trades. Aggrieved constable John Blalock protested to Governor Joseph Mathews that William Peden was unfairly bonded as a constable in his beat and now competed with Blalock for "all the emoluments of said Office." After his election, Blalock complained, he "gave Bond and went into business," only to face "great injury" when the local judge allowed Peden to set up his own shop. For this small farmer the extra income was clearly important.[30]

Numerous precinct offices provided ample opportunities to make a public statement or earn public money. Each county had five policemen and between eight and twenty justices and constables. Announcing oneself as a candidate in the local newspaper, as editors urged a candidate to do, cost two or three dollars. This, wrote one editor, would cause "people [to] form a more favorable opinion of him." Sometimes friends announced a man's candidacy for him. Of course, many candidates had no local newspaper, and others dispensed with announcements in print, preferring to spread the news by word of mouth. As these candidates rarely appeared on printed ballots, they also avoided printers' fees, although some ordered special tickets listing only their name and office or paid to be included on the regular ticket. Using a ticket was easier than writing in a man's name, especially for illiterate voters, who would either need to have ballots filled out in advance or simply state their choices publicly. In short, although running for a precinct office required little more than the desire to do so, the more one spent on announcements and tickets the better. They seemed to give candidates with some resources an important, often decisive, advantage. This was especially true in counties or precincts served by newspapers; candidates in remote areas could more safely rely on word of mouth and open ballots. One editor chided candidates about the importance and benefits of ordering tickets: "If a man has not three or five dollars, and has *not the credit to borrow it, he is not fit for any office of trust.*"[31]

The number of positions available also accentuated the nuances within each local hierarchy. Subtle differences between constable and justice of the peace suggest how sensitive candidates had to be and how carefully most men gauged what was possible. Running for policeman, justice, or constable also meant putting one's reputation on the line before friends and neighbors.

Precinct elections took place within single neighborhoods among men best qualified to judge personal reputations. When legislators reinterpreted the election law in 1852, they made these contests even more of a neighborhood exercise by encouraging greater deference toward the local planters who dominated the board of police. The wealth and position of policemen far outdistanced other county candidates, placing them on a par with legislators. In many counties their profile surpassed that of state officers, including governors and even U.S. congressmen. Thus, when the very elite members of the planter class ran for office, it was typically the county government—not the state or national—that drew their attention. Few men from the middle and lower ranks ran for policeman, and voters rejected those who tried, whereas justices and constables included men from all social classes.

Legislators designated the office of justice of the peace a position of authority and respect. With their jurisdiction over civil disputes involving less than fifty dollars, justices resolved local debts, disputes over work and wages, and myriad transactions in the rural exchange economy. For most Mississippi farmers fifty dollars was a lot of money. The typical annual tax burden, for example, was under $10—for both state and county taxes. In Harrison, Jasper, and other nonplantation areas, it could be considerably less than that.[32] According to several estimates, justices settled about 80 percent of all civil suits. The state *Manual of Forms* summed up this officer as "warden of Peace and good behavior within his county, and particularly within his precinct [and a man] . . . of the conservative circle." "In him," the handbook's author continued, "the court leet is essentially transmitted, bringing justice home to the door." He also reminded citizens that Washington, on retiring as president, became a justice of the peace, "an admonition to the People to cast the care on the wisest and best of the beat!" Mississippians commonly dignified justices with the title "squire."[33] Constables could not, apparently, claim any former presidents among their ranks; lacking the legal power of justices, they simply helped the sheriff maintain peace. Constables reported to the justice in their precinct and turned over to him all money and chattel seized.[34] Acting as a sort of subjustice, constables made up the lowest level of precinct officials.

As it did for policemen, a mixture of wealth and personal history determined the place and success of these candidates. Justices were older and wealthier than constables but, of course, younger and poorer than policemen. (See the Appendix and profile of the precinct candidates in three of the sample counties, presented in figures 6.1 through 6.3.) Jasper County, where the typical justice had about twice the property and slaves as an average constable, demonstrates the usual hierarchy among precinct candidates. An unexceptional justice, Robert Donald was elected three times, first in 1856 at the age of thirty-six. A farmer with three slaves and some land, he had lived in the county for more than ten years. Another representative justice was Michael O'Brien, a house carpenter and part-time farmer.

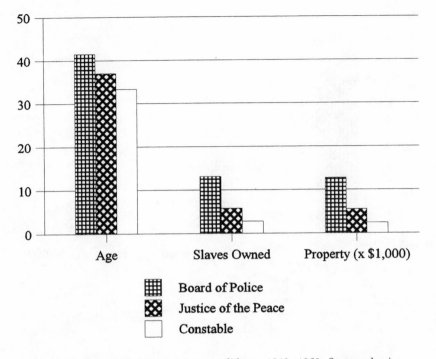

FIGURE 6.1. Carroll County, precinct candidates, 1849–1860. *Source*: election data.

Elected in 1849 at thirty-six-years old, he owned three slaves and $1,000 in land and tools. Addison Bounds, a small farmer with no slaves and but $500 in land, seemed an unusually poor justice of the peace. Bounds, however, was fifty years old when elected in 1855 and had been a resident of the state for at least twenty-five years. The experience of another justice, farmer John Harris, characterized for many the social gap between justice of the peace and policeman. Harris, who was born in 1825 was elected as a justice in 1853, at the age of 28. A longtime resident, he owned one or two slaves and about $500 in land. In 1858 he decided to run for policeman and finished third in a three-man race. The winner, Coleman Copeland, was older, a more substantial slaveholder, and owned nearly $10,000 worth of land, according to the 1860 census. Spencer Wade, who finished second, had nearly identical assets. Copeland and Wade, in fact, each received sixty-one votes, and the former was chosen by lots, as was the custom in a tie. Men of the same social position, they typified Jasper's policemen whereas Harris, though evidently popular with his neighbors, simply did not belong to the same class. Jasper's constables, in turn, ranked below justices such as Harris. Archibald Lovett, a young doctor, became constable in 1851. He owned no slaves and had no other property, but he was a longtime resident of the county.

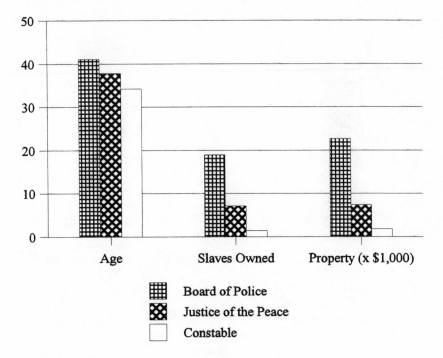

FIGURE 6.2. Hinds County, precinct candidates, 1849–1860. *Source*: election data.

William Sanders, who had lived there since the late 1830s, won election as constable in 1858. He owned two slaves and a small farm.

Across Mississippi, men showed a similar regard for the subtleties of rank. In Carroll County, precinct candidates flawlessly mirrored the usual hierarchy based on economic and cultural distinctions. Jesse and Caswell Pitman, candidates for policeman and justice, respectively, reveal the imperative differences between qualifications for the offices. Born fifteen years apart, the familial relationship between them is unclear. Both men ran for office in 1855. Jesse, who was fifty-nine years old, qualified as a planter (owning about twenty slaves) and recorded an impressive $36,000 worth of land in 1860. Caswell, only forty-four, ran unopposed for justice of the peace. The owner of ten slaves, he reported holding just $6,000 in land. Thus, while both men were slaveowners and successful farmers, they represented different segments of society.

Carroll voters validated similar distinctions between justices and constables. Justice Samuel Pickens and constable George Harvey epitomized some of the variables that helped determine a man's rightful place. Pickens was thirty-five when the voters of the Shongalo beat chose him as their justice. Born in Mississippi, Pickens had resided locally for more than ten years and

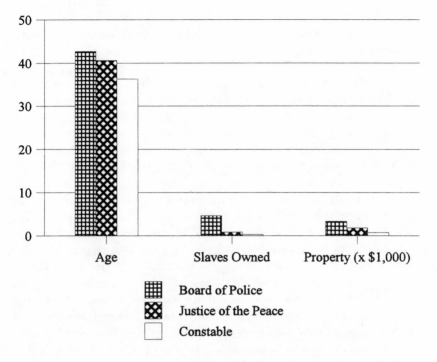

FIGURE 6.3. Harrison County, precinct candidates, 1849–1860. *Source*: election
data.

farmed his own property with the help of five slaves. Harvey won election
as constable of district 6 in 1849 at the age of twenty-nine. Also born in
Mississippi, Harvey recorded owning two slaves and land worth $300 in 1850.
He emigrated from the area ten years later. The older and wealthier Pickens
fit perfectly the profile of a Carroll County justice of the peace; Harvey was
younger, less established, and not a permanent resident. Many candidates,
of course, may have failed to consider such subtle differences consciously.
Yet the combined effects of reputation, wealth, age, and residence remained
consistent in each county; whether consciously or unconsciously, most men
in Mississippi seemed to recognize where they belonged. Of course, positions could change over time, which allowed elections to register social mobility as well as to reconcile the effects of geographic mobility.

Precinct elections also reiterated the importance of family. It was not
only that powerful relatives could help sons and in-laws get elected, but also
that certain positions were almost hereditary, being frequently passed down
from father to son. In wealthy Amite County planter John B. Easly served
the residents of district 5 as justice from 1849 to 1857. He had lived there
since 1837, owned sixteen slaves, and held over $10,000 worth of cotton land
in 1860. When Easly's eldest son, Harold, turned twenty-one, their neighbors

chose him to succeed his father. Between 1849 and 1860, Josiah Foster and his son Joel alternated as constable of district 5. Small farmers, the Fosters claimed no slaves in 1850, but by the time of secession they owned two bondsmen and over $1,000 worth of farmland. Robert Neal, Sr. and Jr., alternated as policeman of the wealthy Duck Hill precinct in Carroll County between 1853 and 1860. Born just seven years apart, the Neals were perhaps cousins, and both were successful planters. They actually ran against one another in 1855, with Robert Sr. winning a close contest.

Wealthy planters' sons also relied on the power of family connections, and voters often supported not only the local gentry but also the heirs apparent. The citizens of Newson precinct in Jasper County favored James M. Kennedy for justice three consecutive times during the 1850s. Although he farmed a small piece of land and owned no slaves, his father and neighbor was a successful planter. Andrew Richmond was a slaveowner and prosperous farmer when his neighbors in Beckville precinct supported his eldest son, Matthew, for constable in 1853. In the Duck Hill precinct of Carroll County, voters chose Daniel and Henry Salley as constables in 1853 and 1855, respectively. Neither man appears in either the 1850 or the 1860 census, apparently because they were on the move. In 1855, Daniel registered only a dueling pistol with the county assessor; Henry owned a similar weapon and two slaves. Their father, however, was John H. Salley, one of the neighborhood's leading citizens; the elder Salley managed nearly thirty slaves on his plantation and rode to social functions in a new horse-drawn carriage.[35] Family honor and position seemed to fall from father to son with little difficulty. Voters recognized the social hierarchy when choosing their representatives and often extended that respect to the next generation.

Voters' attitudes toward candidates who "stepped down" to constable or justice when their community position entitled them to be policemen or state representatives offer further testimony that Mississippians identified with a hierarchical social and political structure. Whenever this happened, nearly every candidate won election with the highest individual total, or, more typically, enjoyed no opposition at all. In Hinds County, planters A. K. Barlow, John J. Parsons, and William L. Taber, who each owned about twenty slaves, ran unopposed for justice of the peace during the 1850s. Archibald Clark Jr., son of a local planter, likewise faced no opposition in his election for constable in 1860. Claiborne County's unopposed justices included large slaveowners Edwin McCaleb and future governor Charles Clarke. It probably surprised no one that planter James G. Railey, master of nearly two hundred slaves, ran unopposed in 1851. Ormond Kimbrough, a planter with twenty-five slaves and $40,000 worth of Carroll County farmland, went unopposed in his two bids for justice. In Jasper County, no one opposed the elections of Robert Carson, John Crosby, Seaborne Jones, and Garret Longmire. Men of affluence positioned to run for policeman or even county representative, they instead chose easy election as justices. Such deference was not limited to justices and constables. When the very cream of society entered politics — a fairly uncommon occurrence — their candidacies often went untested. Jasper's John J. Harry, Claiborne's James Person, and Amite's Jehu Wall, for instance, each represented the very elite of his county and each enjoyed no (or only token) opposition in their elections to the board of police. When a member of the elite did lose, his opponent almost invariably came from a similar social position. Virtually never could a candidate claim victory over an opponent from a higher class. (It happened about once in each county in each decade.)

Many men who ran unopposed for justice or constable later moved up to their "natural" position as policeman or state representative. John Huddleston, a wealthy miller in Harrison County, won two unanimous terms as justice in district 3. In 1859, when nearly seventy years old, he moved up to policeman. Dudley Bonds, minister of Liberty Methodist Church in Amite County, won easy election as justice in 1849. Well acquainted in the county, Reverend Bonds owned over twenty slaves and later served consecutive terms on the board of police.[36] This process worked in reverse as well. William Oneal struggled to win election as a policeman in Harrison County. But when his term expired in 1853, he ran unopposed for local justice of the peace. Others who moved up in stature, and correspondingly in public office, included James W. S. Merrill, surveyor and later representative from Carroll County. In 1850 Merrill reported owning just two slaves and $500 worth of farmland. A resident of Mississippi for only the past five years, he lacked the wealth or accomplishments for higher office. By 1857, when the voters chose him as one of their representatives in Jackson, Merrill owned more than a dozen slaves, held many thousands of dollars' worth of land, and qualified as a stable resident. When the census taker returned in 1860, Merrill proudly reported his occupation as "planter," instead of "surveyor," as he had ten years earlier.

This hierarchy of candidates ranged from some of the wealthiest men in the South to some of the poorest in Mississippi. Slaveowners and property owners were only slightly overrepresented, and in some counties they served less frequently than chance provided. Most importantly, the status of each county and local office corresponded to a particular segment of the county's population. Wealth, age, and length of residence figured most prominently in fixing a man's position. When he chose to run for policeman, justice of the peace or constable, the choice reflected a social and cultural hierarchy that already existed, but it also served to establish or confirm his place. Particularly for new residents or young men, politics offered the most important way to assert oneself before the male community. The right office permanently conferred on a man the community's affirmation of status and honor; successful precinct candidates, in particular, often ran only once.

The ritual power of politics also manifested itself in special elections to replace deceased, resigned, or disqualified officeholders and in some munic-

ipal elections. Many elections to fill partial terms featured only one candidate, and surviving poll lists matched with manuscript census returns
indicate that neighbors and friends invariably turned out to show their support—in these cases, purely as a ritual gesture. A typical "contest" of this
sort was the election for constable in the Shongalo beat, Carroll County in
January of 1860. Young farmer Yancey McClung, thirty-one and still living
in his father's house, ran unopposed; yet sixteen of his friends and neighbors
voted in nearby Vaiden, including his brother Morgan, who lived on the
next farm with his wife and two children. Among the other voters were seven
young men about his age who were also living at home; like Yancey, almost
all of them had lived in the neighborhood for at least ten years. Also showing
their loyalty were the Gordin brothers, led by the wealthy planter, George.
He and Yancey's father, William, were about the same age and had lived a
few miles apart in Carroll County for at least a decade.

Several municipal elections also demonstrated the ritual potency of politics, which was accentuated by the apparent survival of viva voce voting
(although that was contrary to the 1832 state constitution). Returns from contests for mayor in Carrollton and Brandon suggest that the opposing candidates voted for each other. A public gesture of magnanimity, the act showed
respect for one's opponent and enhanced one's own personal reputation. The
viva voce custom also upheld community pressure—for either deference or
dependence—as a legitimate political instrument. Given that printed ballots
were often colored, oddly shaped, or sometimes specially ordered by individual candidates, the difference between using them and viva voce balloting
should not be overstated.[37]

Candidates for public office and election-day officials represented a nearly
complete picture of Mississippi's social and cultural hierarchy. The boards
of police appointed only the local elite to supervise and pass judgment on
potential voters. Operating in much the same manner as the commissioners
of the poor and school trustees mentioned in chapter 5, local planters func-
tioned as a quasi-official local government; county leaders, naturally, relied
on these most stable, successful members of society to carry out important
responsibilities. Meanwhile, the next generation of leaders was familiarizing
itself with "the people" by serving as court and election clerks. Thus, despite
demographic turnover, Mississippians maintained a social system based on
recognizable and acknowledged differences among men. When voters chose
their elected officials, they did so within a sensitive, subtle ranking of prospective candidates.

Although society's wealthiest men often declined to run for office themselves, their place was more firmly established and less open to question
than other men's. When they did enter the fray, usually for the boards of
police, voters typically deferred to them and offered little or no opposition.
Moreover, their role as inspectors evinced their powerful presence in the

community and suggested that they could manage politics without becoming candidates. Thus, it can be argued that contests for precinct officers and the process of voting combined to make neighborhood politics a ritualized expression of deference to, and confidence in, the local gentry. Mississippi's political culture, infused with the values of communal manhood, reconciled American egalitarianism with a hierarchical social system. It allowed white men to assert their privileged independence and power, their loyalty to neighbors, and their bonds of clientage or kinship with the elite. For planters, local elections validated their community power and reputation while giving them the chance to socialize with poorer neighbors. The political culture perfectly suited men's social and cultural imperatives, but only as long as it remained a personal exercise.

As the state and nation moved toward destruction, Mississippi voters continued to treat politics as a personal matter. By nearly every measure, institutional parties had failed. Neither Whigs nor Democrats ever convinced the general public to embrace their organizations, except out of necessity. To make political rhetoric less personal and more anonymous, and to defuse the potent language of manliness and honor that defined sectionalism, Mississippians would need real parties. Suddenly, in 1855, a new organization made a dramatic challenge to the state's dominant antipartyism. It nearly achieved a revolution in political culture.

7

CHANCE

Know-Nothings and the Political Culture

The intense competition and emotions he sensed in 1855 shocked Raymond's editor George W. Harper. The veteran campaigner declared that "political excitement, asperity and bitterness, run higher at this time in Hinds county, than, possibly at any former period. . . . During the last twelve years, certainly, we have witnessed nothing like it." The voters' enthusiasm resulted from the new American Party, an outgrowth of a secret nativist organization that started in New York City. The "Know-Nothings," as they were usually called, attracted Protestants who resented the growing political power of Catholics and immigrants. Like the Masons, they maintained secrecy with cryptic handshakes and code words.[1] The Know-Nothings entered politics as the American Party and stormed through several northern states in 1854 and 1855, sweeping aside many old leaders in a string of shocking electoral victories. In Mississippi Congressman Reuben Davis also remembered the new organization's stunning success: "Men who were not even [known to be] candidates were elected to office against popular candidates whose race was expected to be a walk-over."[2]

Davis's insight was more profound than he probably realized. For one or two years the Know-Nothings presented a fundamental challenge to the state's antiparty political culture. For the first time partisanship extended to many county and local elections and, in numerous cases, resulted in party nominations for offices "from governor to constable." With many voters casting straight party ballots, the returns from the 1855 election were unlike any in the state's antebellum history. Mississippi's face-to-face, antiparty political culture suddenly stumbled. Placing party ahead of personal and neighborhood loyalties, voters seemed poised to embrace a truly institutional political culture.

149

Thus, the exceptional feature of Know-Nothingism in Mississippi was not its nativist, anti-Catholic rhetoric but, rather, its ability to generate intense partisanship among so many voters. Public and private comments from astounded, longtime residents, as well as the voting record of ordinary Mississippians, all testified to the peculiar nature of the Know-Nothing movement. Long-time Democrat Wiley Harris recognized the new party's revolutionary approach: "Never before has the individual voter been approached in such a manner; never before has the individual voter been so completely penetrated with the purely partizan spirit. This spirit pervades the breast of every Know Nothing."[3] Other state and national issues had realigned voters, but never had parties reached below state-level contests to organize county and even municipal elections. These few years offered Mississippians a chance to change their whole approach to politics: a chance to defuse the rhetoric of personal politics by embracing a bureaucratic, institutionalized party structure and, perhaps, a chance to moderate their individual and collective response to northern "insults."

Why the Know-Nothing Party created such enthusiasm in Mississippi remains problematic. Few immigrants or Catholics settled in the state, although nativists warned that the greatest danger was to the national government, which stemmed from the supposedly antirepublican and antidemocratic tendencies of Europeans and Catholics and the extranational loyalties Irish and German Catholics owed to the pope, a foreign "potentate." The party's exaggerated patriotism appealed to some Mississippians who, like other Americans, treasured what they considered the country's defining heritage: republican government and Protestantism. Know-Nothing propaganda also attracted Whigs from all parts of the country who resented immigrants, support of the Democratic Party.

In the southern states, some historians argue, the new party also appealed to Unionists, who were more and more isolated by the Democrats' increasingly hostile stance toward the North. The Mississippi experience, however, suggests otherwise. The American Party's greatest success came in 1855, when its ticket was led by gubernatorial candidate Charles D. Fontaine, a former Democrat, supporter of states' rights, and ardent secessionist. Ecological regression estimates indicate that nearly a quarter of Fontaine's support came from former Democrats, perhaps another quarter from nonvoters, and only about one-half from former Whigs or Unionists. Millard Fillmore's nomination the following year drove men like Fontaine out of the Know-Nothing movement—they would not accept a candidate who had signed the hated Compromise of 1850 into law. Thus, not until 1856 was Unionism a part of Know-Nothing propaganda; in that election Fillmore lost over a quarter of the voters who had supported Fontaine back to the Democrats. Southern nativists also tried to pin abolitionism onto immigrants, but that strategy bore little fruit and eventually backfired.[4]

Probably the nativists' most effective strategy appealed to the voters' traditional antipartyism. They seized the chance to present themselves as a new organization uncorrupted by spoils-seeking demagogues. As hundreds of editorials and speeches claimed, Know-Nothing leaders came "fresh from the people," untainted by the venal avarice of snouts-in-the-trough huckster politicians. One Mississippi Know-Nothing used typical language to condemn the "worn-out" parties: "One knows he is a Whig, the other that he is a Democrat; when that is said it is impossible for him to say *why* he is either." Of course, the Know-Nothings initially had a big advantage because they actually were a new party. "When I first exercised the right of voting, I did so as a Whig . . . [and] then voted as a Union Whig," wrote one Mississippi voter to his relative in North Carolina. "From present appearances, it seems I may drop both, as the *Knowing Ones* consider the existence of such parties no longer necessary."[5] Democrat Wiley Harris also found the strategy effective. The Know-Nothings, he claimed, "enlist[ed men] in a crusade against parties." Many voters were "determined in spite of parties, to rectify abuses, and they are lead naturally and easily to refer to their own feelings," which convinced them that "it is a spontaneous movement of the people, in opposition to parties. The attacks of our speakers upon KN.ism are felt by each individual member of the order as aimed at him & he easily achieves the connection that the attack is prompted by party spirit, or self interest." Harris's insightful language not only suggested that antipartyism was widespread but also acknowledged the "abuses" that needed reform. Furthermore, it seems, men merely needed to tap their "own natural and easy feelings" in "opposition to parties." Harris admitted that when Democrats tried to refute Know-Nothing criticism, voters complained that their arguments were simply instances of partisanship and not an honest defense of the political system.[6]

Like other fraternal organizations, the Know-Nothings also offered fellowship and camaraderie. Secret rituals, code words, and private handshakes intrigued men who needed a break from routine farm life. One Mississippian observed that the Know-Nothings' "scheme is a cunningly devised one. Enshroud any thing with mystery and secrecy and the attention of the multitude will be drawn. Curiosity governs the majority."[7] As a community organization, then, Know-Nothing lodges satisfied persistent social needs, much as the older political parties did.

Within the state's antiparty political culture, however, the nativists' most radical innovation was their "Second-Degree" pledge. This sworn oath committed Know-Nothings to support only fellow members for all public offices — a logical extension of their predisposition for secrecy and unity. Affirming the Second Degree, each new recruit swore to "support in all political matters, for *all* political offices, members of this order in preference to other persons."[8] This fundamental departure attempted to place party loyalty on a par with family and community relationships, which were always paramount for men bound by honor or communal manhood. "To be sure," writes historian Bertram Wyatt-Brown, "fealty to family was the first law of honor. Close kin needed no oath-takings to seal mutual loyalties" whereas "the oath was meant to surmount the dangers of nonfamilial relationships." Thus, in a political context the Know-Nothings' oath attempted to accommodate partisanship, which necessarily ranged beyond kinship. In theory its use would place an institutional bond ahead of personal ones, although Know-Nothing lodges were organized locally among rural neighbors. In practice, the Second-Degree pledge made its most profound impact on county politics, where, instead of following the usual personal networks, Know-Nothings swore to vote a party ticket even for local offices.[9]

In Mississippi the new party made some formal nominations in 1855, but its covert organization and the impact of the Second Degree proved equally disruptive. The consternation of confused Democrats, who no longer knew whom to trust, testified both to the reality of Mississippi's face-to-face political culture and to the American Party's potential impact. Some voters who withdrew from the movement complained that the Second Degree conflicted with their customary partisanship, the antiparty tradition, or both. The history of the Know-Nothing years also underlines the indifference most voters felt toward Whig-Democratic contests and demonstrates the archetypal exception that proves the rule—in this case, the rule of antiparty parties.

Yet their success was short-lived. The demise of the nativists' national organization seemed to sap the new partisan zeal of many Mississippi Know-Nothings, more and more of whom—like gubernatorial candidate Charles Fontaine—came to emphasize southern unity against northern "aggression." The party split first at its 1855 national convention, where a minority of northern delegates walked out over the party's "twelfth section," a pro-southern resolution calling for congressional noninterference in the territories. One year later the party suffered a nearly complete sectional break when most northern delegates refused to accept Fillmore, whom they considered a friend of slavery, and bolted the party in favor of Republican John C. Fremont. This final schism destroyed Fillmore's chances of returning to the White House and convinced many Mississippi voters that the Know-Nothings were doomed as a national party.[10]

Despite the national meltdown, some Mississippi nativists tried to sustain their dying party. In 1857, however, the anti-Democratic choice for governor ran as the "Opposition" candidate and received only a third of the vote, the worst showing of any party candidate since the new constitution. Their growing majority prompted some zealous Democrats to advocate organizing at the local level beginning in 1858 to take advantage of the new law separating state and local elections. By making more frequent nominations and controlling local politics, some Democrats believed, they could create real loyalty among voters for the first time. Almost all of these efforts failed, however, and the 1858 and 1860 elections conformed to the pre-1855 pattern. The state's party period had ended—because the national American Party had disintegrated, because once the Know-Nothings became "just another political party" they could no longer claim the mantle of antipartyism, and because Democrats skillfully exploited the obvious affinity between northern abolitionists and Know-Nothings. And it ended because Mississippians increasingly spoke with one voice, united against "Black Republicanism" and northern "insults."

From the outset, American Party spokesmen emphasized antipartyism even more pointedly than their predecessors did. When the team of Levi S. Robertson and T. R. Stayman inaugurated their anti-Democratic newspaper, *The Fort Adams Item*, they began with a customary invective against party loyalty and professional politicians: "The pages of the Item shall not be polluted by the blackguard ribaldry, and offensive "buncome" of Whigs or Democrats, but will faithfully and fearlessly expose corruption, of any description in either." T. C. Jones of the *Tri-Weekly Mercury* also extolled his party's "destructive" potential and the fear it generated among "mere politicians" and spoilsmen, the "evil" consequences of parties that "have long existed and have led a most extensive influence in demoralizing the community, threatening the total extinction of public virtue and patriotism. We do not therefore sympathize with those who dread the Know Nothings, as likely to break up the party organizations which have so long ruled our country, absolutely and most tyrannically."[11]

As the politics of antipartyism demanded, Democrats responded in kind. Know-Nothings, they charged, permitted members to hear only their own propaganda, which shackled men to one party's opinions and violated republican traditions of a well-informed citizenry. "There is something wrong in those politicians who shun discussion, and permit their followers to hear only one side of any political question," accused one editor. He claimed that "Know-Nothing documents alone, and Know-Nothing 10 o'clock and midnight speeches are all that are permitted to reach the minds of the members of their Fillmore Clubs." Another Democratic newspaper included a cartoon of the "K. N. Council in Session, Initiating an Outsider!" (see cover) This comic image portrayed the Know-Nothing leader as half man and half fox, a sly, hybrid creature practiced in the art of deception. As he administered the oath to one new recruit, other members gazed on with blank faces and dumb smiles. The message was classic antipartyism: blind, slavish devotion to the Americans was simply uninformed, unmanly support of wily political hacks who duped unsophisticated voters to line their own pockets.[12] Democratic politicians also targeted Know-Nothing secrecy, "undemocratic caucuses," and the Second-Degree pledge. One Democrat characterized Know-Nothings as "the most thorough caucus system ever known in America," a "secret oath-bound order" of "wire-workers and office hunters." "The Know-Nothings do not avow their party associations," protested Senator Albert Gallatin Brown, "and enter into no defence of their principles in the newspapers, on the stump, or elsewhere." Mississippi's Know-Nothing leaders expressed grateful relief when the national organization allowed its state parties to go public with their platform and nominations in June of 1855.[13]

Another Democratic accusation labeled the nativists as simply the Whig Party under a new name. This time-honored strategy lost some sting, though, when the Know-Nothings nominated Fontaine, a former State-Rights Democrat, and American Party leaders urged their man to emphasize his partisan heritage at every opportunity. Powerful spokesman William Sharkey counseled Fontaine to "be a states right democrat, and an anti bonder, and avow your opinions boldly whenever occasion may require it." The new party, in fact, tried to nominate former Democrats whenever possible: "The *people* must be *satisfied* that there is no *Whig trick* in this matter or we will be defeated," warned another veteran campaigner.[14] Despite these fears, election returns indicate that the Know-Nothings captured about a quarter of Democrat Franklin Pierce's Mississippi supporters. Thus, although Fontaine lost by a margin typical of Whig-Democratic contests, the source of his support differed.[15]

That Fontaine attracted hundreds of former Democrats owed something to his former partisanship, but also something to the American Party's nativist message. The extent of nativist and anti-Catholic rhetoric varied — emphasized by some editors and virtually ignored by others.[16] Yazoo City editor Harriet N. Prewett had articulated her fear and hatred of Catholics for years; the new party simply made the attacks more regular and concentrated. In 1856 she emphasized with equal vigor Millard Fillmore's twin virtues of Unionism and opposition to foreign influence. After his defeat, she rationalized that "foreignism and disunionism [were] too much." Wherever the population included an unusual number of Catholics or foreigners, Know-Nothings achieved greater success. On the Mississippi Gulf coast, the presence of many French and Catholic families from Louisiana and of immigrant sailors from Italy and Spain prompted one Democrat to claim that "Protestant prejudices against the [local] Catholics" induced many men to join the order.[17] Finally, in the state's long-settled southwest corner, a Federalist and Whig stronghold, nativism was vigorous. Among other papers, The *Fort Adams Item* (Wilkinson County) tiraded against "Catholic despotism" and the unrepublican forces of popery.[18]

The new party's style and tactics were both traditional and innovative. By nominating former Democrats and appealing to the same nativist prejudices that motivated many of their northern counterparts, Know-Nothings captured more Democratic voters at the state level than Whigs ever could. Still, most of their rhetoric, particularly antipartyism and proslavery bombast, remained strictly within the state's bipartisan traditions. Their approach to party organization, and especially the use of nominations, however, were a radical departure from Mississippi's customary practices. Nothing short of revolutionary, the new party's county-level activism prevailed upon men to think differently about politics. It nearly produced a fundamental reconfiguration of the political culture.

In 1855 newspapers indicated that both Americans and Democrats nominated for every county office in Attala, Marshall, Tippah, Wilkinson, Lauderdale, Choctaw, Noxubee, and Yazoo counties, among others. Subsequent comments confirmed that the Know-Nothings had sparked the change.[19] But even among the supposedly ultrapartisan Democrats, such a departure from tradition aroused controversy; when rank-and-file voters seemed ambivalent, Democratic leaders defended their actions. They claimed that Know-Nothings had provoked county nominations by making secret agreements to support only fellow members and, later, the formal nominees of the American Party. "Whenever they have been in the majority," explained one editor, Know-Nothings, by making nominations for every county office, "have acted up to the strict letter of the maxim that 'to the victor belongs the spoils.'" Now, he continued, nativists were complaining that the Democrats had responded with their own nominations—"the application of *their* principles of action to themselves, where they are in a minority." The same editor recounted a similar story from Choctaw County, where Know-Nothings, erroneously believing they had a majority, "nominated for every county office, down to Ranger. They must not complain now if, to use a homely expression, Democrats feed them out of their own spoon."[20] The Americans, not the Democrats, had upset the rules of the game; the latter had simply followed suit in order to survive. Clinging to their affirmation as an antiparty party, the majority Democrats worked to fix the heinous label of "party enthusiasts" on their new opponents.

Newspapers offered some of the most obvious indications that politics had changed, including expanded coverage of local debates. With the coming of "Sam" (another Know-Nothing nickname), county issues increasingly surfaced as party disputes. In Tippah County, the *Ripley Advertiser*'s editor warned that Know-Nothings had vowed to capture the county treasury and board of police "to get control of the school fund for their own pecuniary convenience." In a subsequent issue Democratic nominee John F. Ford attacked his Know-Nothing opponent, E. A. Cox. Apparently Cox campaigned as a former Democrat and sought votes on that basis. An enraged Ford charged that Cox was never a Democrat, having "cast but one vote in his life; and that was this last summer [1855] for the *nominees of the Know Nothing's* of the town of Ripley." Invoking typical antiparty rhetoric, Ford criticized the machinations of his opponent who "sought the nomination of a party" while at the same time he "decries party spirit."[21]

In Lauderdale and Yazoo counties similar conflicts thrust county politics into the newspapers. Longtime Democrat Charles Wesley Henderson joined the Know-Nothings but later withdrew from the order and published an attack on its "secret oaths" and proscriptive policy. Democrats induced him to run as their candidate; editor Con Rea of the *Lauderdale Republican* printed a cartoon of "Wolf" Henderson devouring a hapless "Sam" and devoted nearly an entire issue to the contest for circuit court clerk. Rea also demonstrated the new partisan spirit in announcing other candidates: "Capt. Daniels," who was running for probate judge, was termed "an uncompromising democrat," and Mr. Bishop, candidate for coroner, was "well known as a good democrat." Finally, Mr. Rushing, "the present able and efficient county treasurer . . . is an anti-Know-Nothing of the strictest sect."[22] In Yazoo County R. B. Mayes, the "political editor" of The *Weekly American Banner*, was also a candidate for probate judge. Several Know-Nothings encouraged voters to support him out of party loyalty because he was so publicly identified with their cause. "In my humble opinion," wrote one man, "the American party should support Mr. Mayes to a man — they owe him . . . and his AMERICAN friends ought to support him." This frank request to consider party above personal friendship contrasted sharply with county politics before 1855; and although Mayes faced longtime, respected incumbent George B. Wilkinson, he won by a comfortable margin. Precinct returns for this contest reveal an almost perfect correlation with the county vote for governor, indicating that partisanship overcame Judge Wilkinson's personal popularity. Partisanship still drove county politics the following summer. In June of 1856, Know-Nothing editor Harriet Prewett gloated over the party's victory in a special election for coroner — never the focus of partisan interest before 1855. As usual, she accused the Democrats of forcing partisanship into the contest: "The Democrats were determined to make this election a party test, and we hope they feel satisfied — we do, most certainly."[23]

With or without formal nominations, the Democrats' confusion revealed the importance of Know-Nothing secrecy and its power to upset the traditional political culture. Secret associations created doubt, uncertainty, and undermined neighborhood solidarity. Writing to editor James H. R. Taylor, one Marshall County Democrat summed up the feelings of many in his party. If this new political culture prevailed, "every man would be jealous of his neighbor. Who does not feel even now a distrust of his neighbor? You cannot tell who is a Know Nothing." He continued, expressing a deep-seated fear among men of honor: "The fact is, to use a common expression, there is no telling who is who, and what men are." Nothing could be more upsetting for men who trusted the power of public reputation and feared those who wore a "false face."[24] Longtime Democrat J. F. H. Claiborne had similar trouble coping with the new realities. He believed his local sheriff of Hancock County was a Know-Nothing, possibly a mulatto, and "unsound" on the slavery issue. Claiborne also became convinced that Know-Nothings had infiltrated the ranks of election inspectors, unlawfully disqualified Democratic voters, and accepted illegal ballots from foreigners.

Finally, he worried that Know-Nothings controlled the mail. "We are afraid to mail any letters at any office in this county except Pearlington [his home]." He claimed that they thus "have it in their power to suppress . . . our papers and documents." Perhaps Claiborne's fears reflected more than partisan paranoia: Hancock County went from 80 percent Democratic in 1853 to a Know-Nothing majority two years later.[25]

Know-Nothings relished the doubtful expressions of their puzzled opponents. They acknowledged secrecy and ritual as not only a powerful charm but also a potential weapon. Nativist D. W. Owen cheerfully reported the Democrats' beat meeting in his town of Fulton. The gathering was small, he claimed, and the chairman "expressed an opinion after their adjournment *that their chief speaker 'was a Know Nothing'* — They distrust each other & are low down in spirits generally. They are very much puzzled to make out a ticket & they are very fearful that they will nominate K.N.s." Owen's letter also expressed the Know-Nothings' typical antipartyism: "The great American movement [is] now shaking the throne of Demagoguism & causing Placemen & Spoils-seekers to *tremble*." At least one Democrat noted with satisfaction that the new party could be caught in its own trap. "The Know Nothings find themselves in the same situation [now] in which they placed us at the outset," wrote Wiley Harris. "They don't know who to rely upon."[26]

Know-Nothing editors emphasized their organization's mysteriousness by planting doubts whenever possible. In Wilkinson County, American Party editor Levi Robertson described Woodville's Democratic meeting as pervaded by a "spirit of luke-warmness." "We are not positive," Robertson commented disingenuously, "that 'Sam' was looking on with complacency. But from the easy spirit of don't-care-a-centativeness manifested, by persons present, we should say that it was a 'mightily mixed' crowd." Robertson wanted Democrats to think there were Know-Nothings lurking everywhere, whether they were or not. Another editor reported the Democratic meeting in Holmes County. Its president, she said, expressed his fear that some delegates appointed to the state convention might be Know-Nothings: "The very thought made him desperate, and he cried out 'if there are any among you Know Nothings, for Heaven sake stand up and let it be known.' None rose, and so he don't know 'em yet." True or not, it was best to let the Democrats stew over it. One stanza of a Know-Nothing poem emphasized both the party's enigmatic reputation and its commitment to local partisanship: "If there are any 'Know Nothings,' pray tell me dear sir/ If they in our cities, have made all this stir/ About elections for Mayor and Magistrates, sir? I don't know."[27]

A great deal of Democrats' uncertainty and confusion resulted from local elections held in late 1854 and early 1855. In several towns the Know-Nothings swept into office by making secret agreements to support fellow members. One editor claimed (mistakenly) that Vicksburg's spring 1855 municipal election was the first in Mississippi to involve Know-Nothings. Democrats charged that successful candidates were all members of "a new club" and triumphed by larger margins than usual. The winning mayoral candidate, incumbent Robert Byrne, responded that the "Anti-Know Nothing, Anti-Tolerance, and Anti-Proscriptive" party initiated the unusual activity by campaigning against him for the first time. Predictably, neither side wanted to be branded with the label of partisan. Election returns show a nearly flawless party vote from mayor to hospital physician, market master, and even city sexton. Only the wharf and harbor master, D. C. Gay, escaped the partisan battle.[28] Canton's Democratic editor, Owen Van Vactor, suggested that Know-Nothings controlled the December 1854 election for selectmen. When reporting the results in 1855 (including his own success), he sneeringly referred to "Sam's surprising victory" the year before. Two years later, even as the American Party's power and organization dwindled, it still managed to retake Canton's town government. "A hundred Democrats have been [ignominiously] defeated," griped the editor, "by some fifty Knownothings."[29]

The effect of Know-Nothing tactics was particularly evident in Yazoo City, where "new men" elected in April of 1855 controlled both the town council and the school board. Anti-Democratic leader Harriet Prewett admitted that the "startling results of the late Municipal election" had evoked complaints of "midnight conspirators" from the party of Andrew Jackson. When the new town council selected her as official city printer, she accepted in typical Know-Nothing fashion: "We have called on some of the new Board," Mrs. Prewett said, "but they don't *Know Nothing* about it." The town's new school board similarly surprised many residents. Defeated incumbent Commissioner M. D. Haynes wondered how the "old citizens, gentlemen who have resided here always" could be "cast aside" for "a new set of men — men little identified with the school and its prosperity."[30] The two parties continued squabbling in 1856. In March the American Party held a city convention and made open nominations for mayor and selectmen in each ward. Responding to criticism from local townsmen, editor Prewett defended the efficacy of nominations: "It is useless for the luke warm to say that it is not a political election." The Democrats, she claimed, "are making a party question of it. They say that if they carry the election in Yazoo City, the County is lost to the Americans." But the Know-Nothing vote carried J. H. Lawrence into the mayor's chair, captured all four council seats in the first ward and three out of four in the second. Mrs. Prewett was again named city printer.[31] It is perhaps most intriguing of all that the previous council, with a majority of men known to be Democrats, had also chosen her as city printer — though a Democratic editor was available. The actions of the new council, therefore, offer proof that Know-Nothings furthered municipal partisanship by including patronage.

Like those from Canton and Yazoo City, the 1855 general election returns from numerous counties indicate that voters, for the first time, placed
party loyalty ahead of neighborhood ties. This startling development was
most evident in contests for county officers. Not only did both parties make
nominations in many areas — thereby diminishing the traditionally chaotic
array of candidates — but voters clearly responded to these choices. Marshall
County's returning officer signaled a new order when he arranged vote totals
for each office in two opposing columns. In Yazoo County each party designated a committee of four men to challenge illegal voters, in the interest of
"preserving peace and good order at the polls." This practice, which de-
parted from the Whig-Democratic tradition, may have resulted from the
Know-Nothings' reputation for violence. Reports of partisan trickery with the
ballot boxes from several polls also distinguished this contest from earlier
county elections.[32]

The races for circuit court clerk and treasurer in Carroll County typified
the impact of Know-Nothing organization. Both the countywide and the
precinct totals for the two offices match almost exactly, both to each other
and to the votes cast for governor (the party baseline).[33] Thus, unlike earlier
elections in which similar county totals give a mistaken impression of party
influence (as in figures 4.1, 4.2, and 4.3), in 1855 the almost perfectly
matched precinct totals reflect partisan continuity at the local level (see
figure 7.1). In short, voters extended party identification to county races
rather than favoring neighborhood candidates. In Yazoo County, the contests for probate and circuit court clerk, and probate judge show the same
results. County-level roll-off also remained low in 1855. Many counties recorded rates of less than 1 or 2 percent, while others show "negative" roll-off
(i.e., more votes cast for county offices than for governor), turnout figures
that underscore the close connection between competitiveness and turnout.

The effect of Know-Nothing strategy varied, of course. Successful efforts
toward party organization in several populous counties may have reflected the
impact of natural demographic and socioeconomic evolution. Where — as in
modern society — it was difficult to know every candidate personally, voters
accepted partisanship out of desperation, or necessity, to bring order to
county politics. Yet, the nonpartisan tradition of a number of counties
showed little change. In Hinds, one the state's largest and most diverse counties, only the contest for sheriff appeared to turn on partisan loyalty — although, in itself that was a sharp departure from earlier votes. The lack of
precinct-level data from most counties and the inconsistent returns in some
of those with detailed evidence caution us that our conclusions about statewide trends must remain tentative. Furthermore, in virtually every county
the parties failed to control subsequent elections, undermining the notion
that socioeconomic complexity was primarily responsible for party development. Rates of roll-off, perhaps slightly reduced in 1855, had typically been

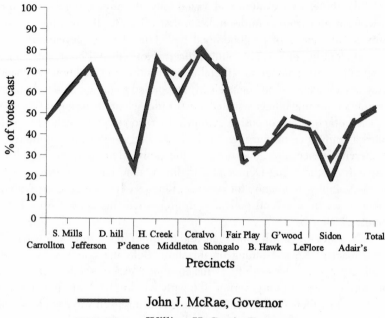

FIGURE 7.1. Carroll County contests, 1855: governor and treasurer. *Source*: Record Group 28, Volume 31c, Mississippi Department of Archives and History.

about 2 percent anyway; in 1858 and 1860, turnout remained high even without local nominations.

Despite those reservations, however, it is clear that voters responded differently to the Know-Nothings than to either the Whigs or the Democrats. Both newspapers and election returns testify to the new party's major impact on county and local politics. Local nominations and the Second Degree violated customary patterns and made networks of friends and neighbors much less important. In that sense, the Know-Nothings were Mississippi's first real party. Whether or not the nascent institutional culture they initiated would survive was problematic.

The 1856 presidential campaign energized Mississippi Know-Nothings, like their brethren across the South, to support Millard Fillmore. The former president remained popular among some southerners for his support of the Compromise of 1850. In the North, however, most Know-Nothings broke with the national organization and supported Republican Free Soiler John C. Fremont. Fillmore ran fairly well in much of the South, including Mississippi, where he captured over 40 percent of the vote. But the disintegration of the national organization under the stress of sectional issues had a deleterious effect on the party in Mississippi. Enthusiasm slackened, many voters drifted back to their customary networks, and the experiment with a real partisan culture seemed in jeopardy.

The state elections in 1857 registered further falling support for the American Party. Gubernatorial candidate William Yerger fared worse than any anti-Democratic candidate ever had. State legislators were chosen in 1857, and the Know-Nothings had trouble fielding candidates in every county; some ran simply as Independents. This poor showing further sapped the partisan fervor displayed by Know Nothings in 1855. Another indication of partisan decline was the disposition of American Party newspapers. In Okolona, The *Prairie News* changed its masthead from "An American Newspaper" to "A Weekly Newspaper" in July of 1858.[34]

The new state law separating judicial and county balloting from state elections took effect in 1858. As the new campaign geared up, many local activists tried to revive the partisanship of 1855. Democrats in particular, led by the editors of the state organ in Jackson, urged that the party nominate candidates for all district and county offices. Editors and activists sensed the opportunity to create a real partisan culture, hoping to build on the Know-Nothing departure of 1855 and supersede local networks with their own organizations. The ensuing debate demonstrates again that the Know-Nothings had instigated the changed political culture of 1855. The lukewarm response to nominations in 1858 also signaled a decline in the temporary spirit of partisanship. The organizational impulse survived in a few counties where party activists promoted formal nominations, but only a small minority of voters responded.

As early as February of 1858, the editors of the *Mississippian*, echoing fellow Democratic leaders from other areas, lobbied for regular nominations. In March they warned fellow partisans against their opponents's seeming apathy; it was simply a feint, they claimed, for a secret Know-Nothing plan to exploit the typical disorganization of county politics. If several Democrats ran for each post, their minority opponents would seize the victory; nominations would be a panacea ensuring that the majority party won its rightful share of all offices. At least one Opposition newspaper reacted with predictable concern and denounced the call for "proscriptive" nominations. The whole plan, said John Richardson, "looks to us like a small way of doing things, or rather a large way of doing small things."[35]

Protests such as those from editor Richardson provoked an outcry from angry Democrats. Noxubee County Democrats submitted nominations for each local office — although some delegates objected — and responded vigorously to the complaints of local Know-Nothings who saw nominations as a proscriptive policy designed to shut them out. William S. Barry averred that it "was not for the opposition to complain" since Know-Nothings themselves had nominated "clear down to constable" in 1855. "It was not for them to reject the chalice of their own preparation." The delegates then proceeded to nominate candidates for sheriff, treasurer, assessor, and probate court clerk. Another Democrat similarly scolded Know-Nothings who claimed to want no partisanship in the upcoming elections. Three years before, he claimed, the American Party had enjoyed a majority and brought parties into every election. Now, "our Knownothing friends . . . are . . . preaching what they do not practice under circumstances favorable to the election of their own partizans." According to the *Mississippian*, Democrats in Harrison, Tishomingo, and Lafayette also nominated men for some county offices, although none, apparently, included precinct officers (as some Know-Nothings had in 1855).[36]

The experience of Madison County demonstrates that the newfound rivalry of Democrat versus Know-Nothing lingered in some places. In November of 1857, the local Democratic editor urged his flock to support William M. C. Jones for the board of police in a special election. "Let no Democrat stay at home on Monday next, if he is anxious for the ascendancy of his party in the county," he warned. "A defeat in this District will be hailed as the resurrection of Know-Nothingism." This seat, he warned, represented the only Democratic spot on the current board, and although his party had won the recent gubernatorial election, the editor still feared Know-Nothing intrigues. When Jones easily defeated William C. Love, Democrats hailed it as a party triumph. The board of police remained the focus of Democratic leaders in 1858. They accused the "Know-Nothing Board" of mismanaging courthouse renovations, general malfeasance, and "foul favoritism" toward political cronies. Disputes over board politics had raged for years, of course, but the partisanship was new. Another Democratic candidate, for probate judge, used classic antiparty language to assail the Know-Nothings: "a party, too, that subsists upon the offal of county offices, 'the cohesive attraction of public plunder,' is its only bond of union."[37]

Throughout the 1858 campaign, editor Owen Van Vactor hammered at the Know-Nothing-controlled board led by President Nathan B. Whitehead, focusing on the board's tax program and its "grandiose" schemes for county improvements. "Were we to dive into the records of the Police Court, and expose acts reeking with corruption and manifold instances of foul favoritism," the editor speculated, "we would soon have a nest of hornets about our head." When the board contracted to redesign the courthouse, adding a $5,000 dome that threatened to collapse the building, taxpayers had to cough up another $800 to repair the damage. Van Vactor lampooned the Board's project, while Canton's Know-Nothing newspaper, the *American Citizen*, supported Whitehead, the board, and the courthouse dome. In the 1858 county elections Van Vactor supported John T. Semmes for the District 4 board seat: "Let such men as Semmes be put in office and we predict a wholesome revolution." Van Vactor finally attacked the board's attempt to gerrymander its districts to benefit President Whitehead, an attempt that evidently failed, for Whitehead lost in 1858 after serving several successive terms.[38]

Some Madison County Democrats called for county nominations as early as January of 1858 to forestall the possibility of another Know-Nothing triumph. The Americans, claimed one Democrat, will certainly complain about "proscriptive policies," but at the same time "sneak to some midnight meeting in a culvert and nominate for all offices from Congress to constable." Editor Van Vactor added that making county nominations was "fighting the devil with fire," as their opponents would surely make secret agreements as they had in 1855. In early February the Democrats nominated men for several offices but failed to agree on others, including the prestigious posts of sheriff and treasurer.[39] Other Democrats objected to any county nominations, and in early March local partisans agreed to hold a "ratification meeting" to decide whether to use them. "We are all, without exception, the more inclined to this course" (i.e., reconsidering the question), admitted one delegate, "as some considerable division existed in the last meeting in regard [to] the propriety of making nominations at all." Van Vactor concurred: he would rather scrap nominations than divide the party.[40] The editor did not mention the March 8 ratification meeting in the paper and made few comments regarding county offices throughout the campaign. As late as October 2, one candidate for probate judge claimed that "no meeting, called for the purpose of making nominations, was at all likely to represent the views of the party."[41]

Election returns for 1858 reflect the indecision of Madison County's voters. Although most races had only two candidates, hinting at party influence, the vote totals show little relationship to one another. Only the contests for sheriff and circuit court clerk produced results at all consistent with partisan voting. By 1860 the totals indicated a more-complete return to neighborhood politics, including the presence of multiple candidates who dominated individual precincts.[42] The returns from Madison County between 1855 and 1860 reflect the dramatic, if short-lived, impact of Know-Nothingism (see figures 7.2 and 7.3).

The chain of events in Tippah County likewise summarizes the upheaval caused by the Know-Nothings, as well as their ultimate failure to effect lasting change in the political culture. The 1853 elections produced a typically chaotic situation at the county level, there were multiple candidates for probate clerk, treasurer, and assessor (nine men), and the two-man contests for ranger and coroner ended in lopsided victories.[43] Two years later both the Democrats and the Know-Nothings made nominations for every county office and the board of police. Precinct-level returns show a nearly perfect party vote for every office and no roll-off in the races for sheriff, assessor, treasurer, or circuit court clerk.[44] Before the next elections in 1858, the fate of county politics hung in the balance. Sparked by suggestions for a Democratic convention to nominate a candidate for sheriff, several locals debated the issue in the *Ripley Advertiser*. All the writers agreed that as only a small minority of party members attended primary meetings, they always

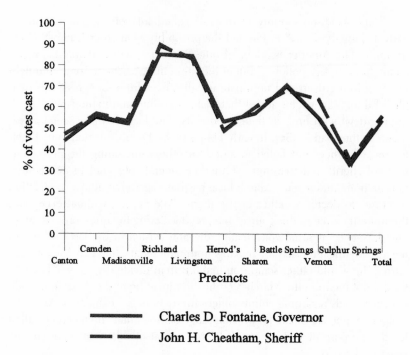

FIGURE 7.2. Madison County contests, 1855: governor and sheriff. *Source: Commonwealth*, November 17, 1855.

conveyed a feeling of inequity and of being dominated by "wire-pulling" caucus managers. Despite this persistent problem, "Anti-Mulligrubs" favored county nominations to ensure victory for the majority Democrats. The others, however, preferred the customary practice of supporting men known to them and thus known to be "capable, faithful and honest." One correspondent, "Tippah," explained further that conventions remained unpopular among county voters and that Democrats could "be induced to support the nominees at all, only for political positions." Insisting on county nominations, he argued, would alienate too many members of the rank and file and undermine their fragile loyalty.[45]

Another writer testified to the unusual situation in 1855. "I have been a voter since 1841, never failed to vote in my life, never gave for political offices any but a democratic vote," he averred, "but once have I been called on by my party to vote for a nominee for Sheriff . . . and that was in 1855, and you well remember the peculiar circumstances which forced the party to nominate that year." He suggested that a convention would disrupt the party for no good purpose, destroying its chances in upcoming state elections. Instead, party leaders should allow voters to support their friends and neighbors as they had always preferred. In short, Know-Nothings forced Democrats to

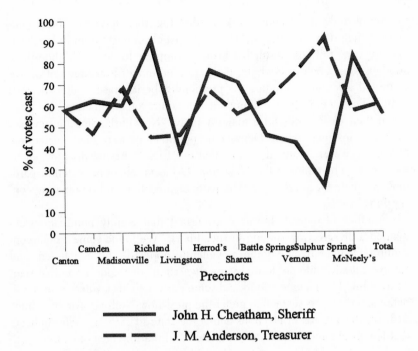

FIGURE 7.3. Madison County contests, 1858: sheriff and treasurer. *Source: Commonwealth*, October 9, 1858.

extend partisanship, against their custom; but as the crisis had passed, it was time to reestablish the politics of the neighborhood and the priority of personal relationships over institutional ones.[46]

Finally, several of the letters hinted at the growing sectional discord; the coming crisis between North and South suggested a more pressing need for regional unity. "I ask what good would a convention do? Would it tend to unite us as one people? Would it give us more confidence in Southern institutions?" The same writer continued: "For the time is coming when we must be one so far as it regards our institutions. If that is so, why should we keep up strife about civil offices?" Another resident agreed: "It matters little whether the Sheriff be a whig or democrat, or know nothing or know something, provided he is a true southern man." The growing importance of sectional issues, therefore, also undermined the fledgling organizations. The elections of 1858 resembled Tippah's pre-1855 experience: there were five candidates each for probate court clerk, treasurer, and surveyor; four for sheriff; six for ranger; and a whopping eighteen for assessor.[47]

Elsewhere, Democrats made nominations but enjoyed little success. Men in Harrison County, who supported the Democratic nominee for governor in 1857 by a stunning 450 to 88 margin, spurned the party's choices for sheriff and circuit court clerk. Predictably, the Opposition press lampooned such dubious success: "They put up a clean ticket from Judge down to Surveyor," but "the result has been a complete fizzle." In Tishomingo, another Democratic stronghold, the party's nominees lost three out of five contested elections, including the prestigious sheriff's race.[48] After the 1858 results, Democratic leaders admitted the failure of nominations but reasserted their basic utility for a majority party: "Notwithstanding the reverses in several instances where Democratic nominations were made for county officers . . . we are gratified to note that our friends are not discouraged by the result." The editor of the *Mississippi Democrat* encouraged fellow partisans to agitate for a more complete party organization and nominating conventions in 1860.[49]

Another Democrat, however, confessed that county nominations remained a divisive issue among his neighbors. "We found some ardent convention Democrats, and some as violently opposed," he concluded, and "thought it advisable not to make any suggestion" of a convention that year. Thus, while Democratic editors and some party activists favored local nominations, most voters seemed to prefer the pre-Know-Nothing style of politics. At least, the records of elections across the state in 1858 and 1860 indicate that few local candidates were nominated and that the idea of county partisanship received little support among either Democrats or their opponents. In 1860, although the *Mississippian* reported several Democratic successes with county nominations, the election returns, even in those few counties, were equivocal.[50] Rather than moving toward permanent, more effectual institutions, the behavior and testimony of most men reconfirmed the enduring strength of the state's dominant, antiparty political culture. The Know-Nothing Party was torn apart by slavery, and Mississippi voters apparently lost interest in its program; clearly, part of the nativists' growing unpopularity included a reaction against the attempt to place party ahead of personal loyalties.

The advent of Know-Nothing secret organization produced a temporary revolution in Mississippi's antiparty political culture. In 1855, for the first and only time, many voters followed the dictates of party in preference to their personal loyalties. Had it been allowed to develop, this new enthusiasm could have produced an institutional party system that might have defused political rhetoric. But when sectional issues broke up the national party, Mississippi Know-Nothings lost momentum, and many voters abandoned their cause. As a result, the organization withered. The state's dominant antiparty tradition also reasserted itself when Know-Nothings no longer seemed like a radical departure from business as usual and looked more like a "real" political party — in fact, the state's first genuine organization — than the ideal antiparty party. Finally, the new legislation separating state from county elections made it much more difficult for party activists to extend the nomination process to the local level. Rather than allowing them to push for a strengthened party structure while voters were meeting to nominate legislature candidates—as they did successfully in 1855—the new law gave the antiparty mainstream a chance to undermine the institutional momentum. By 1858 Republican Free Soil rhetoric had also begun to unite Mississippians behind their sacred institution and cherished ethics. In sum, the unfortunate coincidence of several developments in 1856 destroyed the chance for a lasting partisan culture: Republican popularity and renewed sectionalism, Mississippi's new election schedule, and the success of the American Party, which, ironically, undermined its claims to be an antiparty party.

As the sectional crisis worsened, southern men challenged each other to stand up "as men" and defend their communities. In a political world still defined by neighborhood loyalties and face-to-face relationships, the language of honor and manliness was a combination ultimately fatal to the Union.

8

VALEDICTION

The Political Culture of Secession

After 1855 the nascent institutional parties spawned by the Know-Nothings' oaths and organization withered. Voters reaffirmed their primary commitment to personal relationships, ensuring that Mississippi's antiparty tradition would continue to define its political culture. At least one perceptive editor recognized the potential consequences of this antiparty "flaw": "So long as the Convention [or party] system is [accepted], the candidate loses sight of himself and becomes the mere representative or exponent of a class of principles." If one loses, it is with the "honors of party" and "there is nothing personal in his defeat or triumph." But, the editor concluded, when candidates are separated from the institutional context of parties, "all is personal, nothing but personal, and it is a miracle if it terminates otherwise than in hostilities."[1]

It was from within this political culture that men of the Deep South measured the developing sectional conflict and, especially, the Republican party's Free Soil, antisouthern agenda. When Mississippi's community leaders called on the passionate language of manliness and honor to articulate their interpretation of these northern "insults," the volatile combination of personal politics and honor proved fateful. Once the voters defined Republicanism as an insult to individual and community honor, they had to seek satisfaction. By contrast, in the Upper South and the border states a different political culture helped delay or prevent secession. The voters' perspective allowed Unionists to resist the quick, visceral reaction that resulted in immediate secession. Men in Virginia and Kentucky assessed Republican rhetoric more calmly, within a framework of institutionalized politics that allowed most of them to separate their personal and political selves. Kentucky-born Abraham Lincoln, who came of political age in southern Illinois, a region largely settled by people from northern Dixie, was nearly forced into a duel with James Shields over a caustic public letter that Lincoln wrote in 1838. The future president avoided the encounter by convincing Shields that his commentary was intended "wholly for political effect" and should not be construed as a "personal" attack. Mississippians would never have understood.[2]

For men bound by honor and raised in the antiparty tradition, political insults challenged both individual and collective reputations for manliness because the opinion of a man's peers confirmed his honor. When Republicans questioned the moral turpitude of the entire region, they also maligned the individuals who lived there: if the community was not honorable, then one's sanctioned claim was suspect. Republicanism, therefore, presented a challenge that linked each individual with his greater community — especially friends and family. Mississippi's Benjamin Grubb Humphreys considered secession hasty and unwise, but he could never renounce his state: "Beneath her soil my ancestors and my children slept in death. All I held dear on earth, family, friends and property welded me to that soil by the strongest cement of nature. Her God was my God; her people were my people." As they had ten years before, Mississippians complained of the moral insult of Free Soil that denigrated them to the status of second-class citizens; but the difference in 1860 was the Republican party and its rapid ascendancy in the North. The vast majority of Mississippi's men now believed that northern criticism demanded satisfaction for the sake of family and community honor. They responded with anger and, eventually and predictably, with violence.[3]

Throughout the antebellum period, Mississippi politics reflected the culture of honor and male violence in which it operated. The state's reputation for killing was legendary. In 1854, for instance, one resident calculated that "more men died violently in Mississippi than in all six New England states combined, although they had five times the population." In one typical year, the *Mississippian* reported about twenty shootings and stabbings just in and around Hinds County — most of them fatal. "Mr. Jessey R. Miller was killed last week in Madison county. He was sleeping in the porch of his house, when some one [sic] discharged the contents of a double-barreled gun into his side." In Yallobusha County two men confronted each other after a "previous difficulty"; some words passed between them, and "May pulled out a pistol and shot Gillespie." State geologist and traveler Benjamin L. C. Wailes heard about Mississippi violence while on vacation in Philadelphia: "I saw in a Philadelphia paper an account of the killing of Doct. Selser & W. D. Griffen at Warrenton Mississippi by a Doct. Bell which appears to have been a brutal assassination." The next day he recorded another multiple homicide among husband, wife, and in-laws. "The character of Mississippi and Warren County," he ruefully noted, "is likely to have an infamous notoriety." Solely in his own county, politician and lawyer Jason Niles counted more than half a dozen shootings and stabbings in a period of about nine months. One night he sat with a guest "at Presley's, a gun was fired, and some of the shot struck Presley's house." When his visitor expressed surprise and concern, Niles admitted that "it was a very common thing in our town [Kosciusko] — [Parson] Davis came in, and said Tom Herring was shot by Dick White — we went to Browning's, and there was Tom lying in the back room on the floor, his face, mouth, neck, and eyes filled full of shot, and covered with blood." True to southern form, the community gathered to seek justice: "A good many were running about with guns, and mounting horses, and trying to get some dogs to follow his trail."[4]

Historians and sociologists, too, have detailed the abnormal level of violence in the southern states, agreeing with many contemporaries that Mississippi in the 1840s and 1850s was an especially dangerous place to live. In 1880 Horace Redfield's calculation of homicide rates in the antebellum and postbellum North and South found murder to be ten times as likely in Dixie. (His figures did not include assaults against slaves, only incidents between whites.) Redfield blamed an exaggerated sense of honor that prompted men to seek violent redress for seemingly trivial insults, the availability of weapons — especially in the "frontierlike" Southwest — weak institutional controls (including law enforcement), and a general lack of regard for human life. Using United States census data, historian Dickson Bruce found that "the South's 1850 murder rate . . . was over seven times that of the North's." The gap had narrowed by 1860, but southerners still killed each other at a much greater rate. Other historians also cite southerners' fondness for weapons and martial tradition, a frontier lifestyle (the combination of many young, single men, guns, and liquor), Celtic ancestry, and the ancient code of honor.[5]

The Reverend James A. Lyon of Columbus, Mississippi, expressed his distaste for such routine killings: "The reckless manner in which the sixth commandment, which forbids murder, is disregarded in this community, is truly alarming." But the real problem, Lyon argued, was how calmly residents accepted the violence, mainly because the social elite committed much of it themselves. If "these murders were committed by vagabonds and the scum of society . . . [the] moral effect would not be so injurious to society," the minister preached. "But . . . men of fair standing in society, received and regarded as gentlemen, are the perpetrators of the butcheries." Like Rev. Lyon, historian Dickson Bruce regards southerners' willingness to accept such high levels of violence, rather than the actual number of deaths, as most significant: "People there saw violence as unavoidable, as an essential fact of human life somehow built in, profoundly, to human relationships."[6] Vivid descriptions of murder and violent death also suggest a certain numbness on the part of southerners: "Mr. Wesley King," reads a typical newspaper account, "was literally torn to pieces [caught in a sawmill] — every bone in his body broken — and particles of him scattered in every direction!"[7]

Finally, the pervasive effects of slavery critically shaped the regional tendency for violence, just as it warped all aspects of southern culture. Slavery inured southerners to violence and made it a part of everyday life. Watching men and women beaten, tortured, and abused on a regular basis necessarily affected how people regarded all human life. More directly, the institution taught white men to be violent and that violence and aggression kept society intact. It should be no surprise that white men then used violence against each other to resolve personal disputes or to mediate other human relationships. To expect them to confine the use of functional aggression and violence within slavery or against black people was unrealistic. White Mississippians felt the corrosive effects of their peculiar institution as much or more than other southerners; living in the midst of a slave majority and constantly fearing rebellion made them all the more determined to ensure social stability at any cost. Of course, many factors contributed to the regional bloodletting, but slavery and honor always emerged as paramount and decisive.[8]

Whatever the underlying causes, perceived insults or slights to manhood sparked most of the white male violence. Living in small communities, men were highly conscious of their public reputation, and most reacted quickly to any threat of shame; conditioned by a cult of aggressive masculinity, their response was usually violent. Most confrontations were not "random" acts but served a specific, public purpose. Men used several types of stylized contests — dueling was only the most obvious — to resolve conflicts and defend their honor and manliness. The common theme in all of these encounters was their public quality. As Mississippi's Seargent S. Prentiss explained, ritualized violence was unfortunate, but "when a man is placed in a situation where if he does not fight, life will be rendered valueless to him, both in his eyes and *those of the community*." Another resident explained that men were "driven" to duel "by the irresistable tide of public opinion." The duel's public, community function was sometimes reflected in large crowds of onlookers. When Isaac Caldwell dueled Samuel Gwin outside Clinton ("because Gwin had 'hissed' at Caldwell"), an estimated four hundred people watched. Other engagements drew spectators who even wagered on the outcome. Thus, what appeared to be a personal contest between individuals was actually a public ritual that linked the individual with his male community.[9]

The significance of duels to those other than participants and witnesses (or gamblers) was enhanced by newspaper accounts and word of mouth. One chief reason for witnesses, in fact, was to make sure that someone could confirm or deny the principals' honorable behavior, especially if they managed to kill each other. A clear expression of the duel's public character was the exchange of notes, which were often submitted for publication by participants (or their seconds). These accounts explained the origins of the dispute and the steps taken to resolve it, evidence intended to establish the correctness of a man's behavior. Strict adherence to the *code duello* required, for example, that gentlemen restrain from leveling pistols at each other until all attempts at mediation had failed. In 1853 Samuel Gholson published the correspondence from his conflict with gubernatorial candidate Francis Rogers. Gholson wanted to refute rumors that he had "challenged [Rogers] and afterwards permitted the matter to be adjusted without [satisfaction]." One correspondent reported an account of the 1854 duel between editor Con Rea and William Evans because "inquiry is rife." The two men "drank champaign [sic] amicably together, just before taking their positions," and then opened fire "with rifles, at seventy yards. . . . At the fourth round, Rea was shot in both thighs," while Evans was "cut by a ball near both his knees."[10] Many encounters, of course, were settled before guns were fired, and most never made it to the pages of local newspapers. While those involving national figures received widespread publicity, one suspects that stories of most duels between editors or local politicians were recited at the crossroads store or tavern. In any case, every ritual encounter involved more than two aggrieved individuals.

Dueling among gentlemen was the most punctilious encounter within the code of honor, but men of all classes used ritual violence. Many poorer folks preferred "rough-and-tumble" fighting, a combination of wrestling and grisly eye-gouging. These public battles "grew out of challenges to men's honor — to their status in patriarchal, kin-based, small-scale communities — and were woven into the very fabric of daily life." Some local politicians, candidates for constable or justice of the peace, wrestled and gouged their way to prominence, thus demonstrating their physical courage and manliness. Although rarely chronicled in newspapers, such matches often drew large crowds and lasted several hours; they helped men assert and defend their reputations before the local community. "Eye gouging was the poor and middling whites' own version of a historical southern tendency to consider personal violence socially useful — indeed, ethically essential."[11]

Rough-and-tumble, or street brawling, often degenerated into a more deadly confrontation, blurring the line between gouging and dueling and testifying to the wide range of public encounters. In one editor's account of a typical altercation in Yazoo City, "a man by the name of Head and Mr. S. V. Stewart, Coroner and Deputy Sheriff, met on the street by appointment both armed with double-barreled guns. They advanced within a few feet of each other and both fired, and Stewart received several balls in his heart, which killed him almost instantly." His assailant escaped. This brief narrative by editor Harriet Prewett suggests a number of points. First, of the two men involved, Head was evidently not a gentleman or member of the social elite, since the editor could not even provide his full name. Second, the encounter violated the *code duello*, because Head and Stewart "advanced" toward one another before firing — even though they had met by appointment, which suggests planning or negotiation. Finally, the editor implied that there were political grounds for the fight by noting Stewart's position as constable and coroner.[12] Regardless of its cause, this type of incident testifies that it is misleading to draw a sharp distinction between street fighting and dueling.

Whether gouging or dueling, ritual violence pervaded male culture and confirmed the most important masculine qualities, especially courage and loyalty. The threat of death was crucial. It helped unite rich and poor as men who prized physical courage above other manly traits and valued a man's willingness to die for his principles. Dueling, although not as gruesome or as tied to sheer physical strength as street brawling, still confirmed that despite his learning or piety, a gentleman was still a man. Risking death demonstrated courage and reliability, proving that a man could be trusted to defend the community if necessary. Many ritual encounters also demonstrated loyalty and dependability because they began over insults to family members or friends.

Among all duelists, politicians probably appeared most often. Celebrated cases involving Henry Clay, John Randolph, Thomas Hart Benton and, of course, Andrew Jackson testified to the potential for violence among southern politicians. In Mississippi duels between editors, fistfights, and even gunplay at barbecues and rallies were commonplace. The potential for violent confrontation always lurked near the surface of seemingly benign political encounters. Reuben Davis remembered local politics as a succession of "wild days of feasting, speech-making, music, dancing, and drinking, with, perhaps, rough words now and then, and an honest hand-to-hand fight when debate was angry and the blood hot."[13]

Like the one between Robert Saffold and Roderick Seal discussed in the introduction, these frequent fights imply that political rhetoric was assessed as part of the face-to-face, personal culture of honor. Within the ancient code, nameless, faceless insults could be ignored as cowardly or unmanly. The crucial factor that linked words with honor and violence and drove men to seek satisfaction was their personal implication. According to this distinction, partisan rhetoric should not have provoked such violent reactions. As the product of an unseen, unknown candidate or a faceless editorial writer, accusations, insults, and all the inflammatory bombast of antebellum politics would have annoyed men of honor but scarcely sent them to the dueling ground. If Mississippians had embraced parties as the natural order of politics, ordinary party rhetoric would not have sent politicians and editors to the *code duello*.

Printed or spoken, words were decisive, and certain terms—*coward, liar, puppy, poltroon, scoundrel*—carried the greatest offense. The deeper implication of these ritual words was that they questioned manhood and masculinity, which, for politicos, cast doubt on their ability as leaders. Among gentlemen, the printed word often superseded the spoken insult, but Mississippi and the rest of the rural South remained largely an oral culture, which preserved a preliterate attitude toward words that blurred the boundary between talk and action. Within the context of honor and in a rural society, words were powerful weapons not used lightly.[14] Historian Kristen Neuschel notes that "to persons whose principal experience of language is oral, words are irretrievable sounds rather than objects; they exist only at the moment of expression." Mississippi's legal system also recognized the power of words: "All words which, from their usual construction and common acceptation, are considered as insults . . . shall hereafter be actionable." More to the point: "in all trials . . . for assault and battery . . . the defendant may give in evidence, in course or extenuation, any insulting words used by the person on whom such assault . . . was committed." Using repetitive, formulaic expressions — such as those prescribed by the *code duello* and southern political oratory — reduced the inherent risks of verbal jousting by limiting the possibility of careless, offensive language.[15]

This type of reaction to political language, and especially dueling among politicos, always characterizes an institutionally weak political culture. According to one recent scholar, in nineteenth-century France a "man's political opinions were only as good as his willingness to defend them, by force if it came to that." Scrutinized by his peers, a man demonstrated "courage or cowardice, self-mastery or fear, qualities that reflected significantly on [his] reputation as a leader, and, by extension, on the worthiness of his cause." These manly qualities evolved from the nobility, whose "unique feature . . . as a political institution [was] the nobles' claim to political power by virtue of their personal identity." Other studies of dueling and honor in Germany, Ireland, and Italy also describe political cultures that failed to separate the personal from the political self. For this reason, dueling declined when institutions, including political parties, came to replace personal relationships.[16] As more complex structures and rules governing behavior replaced community sanction, there were corresponding changes in how people thought and behaved as "psychological entities." In other words, in an institutional culture men thought differently.[17]

As the most public forum in any community, politics also raised the stakes for any insult or threat to reputation; whether in person or in print, political words carried even greater significance than most. Accentuating the personal implications of political rhetoric was the Mississippi tradition of elections as a neighborhood ritual that put men on display before friends, neighbors, and blood relatives — providing additional pressure that ultimately made the sectional discourse of honor and manliness more demanding. To back down would mean not only failure as a man — psychologically damaging even in an "anonymous" world — but also humiliation and shame before one's own community, the very people who affirmed one's honor and manliness. Contemporaries acknowledged the special urgency of campaigning in the neighborhood: "Unless he [the candidate] can stand up before the assembled majesty of the people," wrote one Mississippian, "and there manfully and earnestly plead his cause, he can never rise to political distinction."

Every candidate, in other words, needed to survive the test of public scrutiny in this hothouse atmosphere if he hoped to receive an endorsement from the community. One Democrat expressed similar thoughts after attending his county convention. "We called upon [J. A. P.] Campbell of Attala to make a speech, in order to test his calibre, as he is extremely anxious to receive the nomination for Congress whenever he can get it. We tried him and I can honestly say that we found him wanting. He is no orator," concluded Samuel Meek, "having little ability and is, in fact a very *small gun*."[18]

Echoing thousands of similar comments, one public letter summarized why derogatory comments so often led to armed conflict, or at least the threat of violence: "To most [candidates], reputation is dearer than life itself," he lectured, "and ruthless attempts to tarnish or injure it, must necessarily endanger the peace and well being of society." Honor, in short, demanded satisfaction. This was especially true in Mississippi, the editor concluded, because of everyone's "familiarity with the personal history of candidates." Therefore, "partisan presses should [not] be encouraged in the indulgence of the most wanton and violent vituperation and personal abuse of the candidates presented to the people for their suffrages." It is no wonder, then, that editorial judgments drove politicians and their accusers to risk death.[19]

When they used the *code duello* to settle differences of opinion caused by rancorous articles and comments, politicians and editors also staked a personal claim for power and loyalty. It was a drama played out before one's admirers, or potential admirers, confirming physical courage, manliness, and devotion to principle. Locked in a culture that defined men by their public reputation and having little patronage to dispense, editors and politicians acknowledged that personal loyalty cemented a network of close supporters. To demonstrate their fitness for leadership, politicians and editors, even more than other southerners, depended on public affirmations of reliability and physical courage, including their willingness to risk death for the sake of principle. For Natchez editor Lorenzo Besancon, these demands of honor and the political culture were apparently too much. After leading the local antidueling society for more than two years, he finally accepted a challenge and promptly killed his opponent. Elsewhere, with the advent of effective, institutionalized parties, allegiance became less personal and more institutional; leaders founded loyalty on networks of patronage. In the northern states, of course, dueling faded soon after Alexander Hamilton's death, an event that coincided with the advent of effective parties. But well into the nineteenth century, men from South Carolina, Mississippi, Louisiana, and Alabama — where parties most clearly failed — were considered the most notorious duelists.[20]

Newspapers often reported duels among Mississippi's editorial fraternity. "A duel was fought opposite Vicksburg on the 22d inst.," reported John P. Richardson in the *Prairie News*, "between Maj. McCardle, editor of the

True Southron, and Col. Partridge, editor of the Vicksburg Whig. Partridge was wounded in the ankle." A few months later Richardson also described an aborted duel in which one of the participants was arrested on his way to the field and missed the scheduled time. His opponent refused further hostilities, as provided under the code. The detained editor then "became belligerent," called the other a "cowardly poltroon," and demanded satisfaction; but "the affair terminated without a fight. Each side published cards in the papers, and so it ended — honorably, perhaps, to both." Editor Richardson himself maintained a running battle throughout 1858–1859 with his nearby competitor, Benjamin Owen of the *Houston Petrel*. Although they never traded fire (Owen refused to duel), their exchanges reveal the urgency of honor, masculinity, and personal leadership among politicos. Perhaps the most tragicomic part of the dispute was Richardson's claim that he spat in Owen's face. Owen vehemently denied suffering such a gross humiliation and gathered and published sworn testimony from witnesses about the final resting place of Richardson's saliva. With deadly seriousness, Richardson defended his ability: "I, of course, cannot say whether Mr. B[arton] [one deposed witness] saw the spittle lodge, but I'm sure I can spit, and hit an object the size of the side of a man's face, at a distance of three feet." On average, a nonsalivary duel between Mississippi editors or politicians that reached the field of honor appears to have occurred monthly, if not more frequently. Many more difficulties, perhaps hundreds during each campaign, were resolved without gunfire but still according to the *code duello*.[21]

Among the state's editors, Mississippians recognized Irish-born Dr. James Hagan of the *Vicksburg Sentinel* as the foremost duelist, although he engaged in street fights as well. He reportedly fought at least half a dozen duels during his raucous tenure as editor; he was eventually slain on a Vicksburg street in 1843 by Daniel Adams, whose father, Judge George Adams, Hagan had disparaged in print. The *Sentinel*, in fact, had perhaps the most violent history of any partisan sheet in Mississippi. The local president of Vicksburg's Railroad Bank wounded reporter James Fall after an uncomplimentary story appeared. Several years later J. M. Downes shot editor T. E. Robins (Hagan's successor) in a duel, followed by a similar encounter between Downes's second and Robins's replacement, Walter Hickey. Hickey fared better than his predecessors, killing his challenger outright. In 1848 editor John Jenkins was shot down by Henry Crabb after he stabbed Crabb on a Vicksburg street. This incident followed "a difficulty" at a "political meeting" and an article in the *Sentinel* describing the disagreement. Another editor reported that Crabb was "mortally wounded" and noted that Jenkins was the third editor of the paper to be murdered in five years. In the 1850s the violence continued when *Sentinel* editor James Ryan was killed by the publisher of the competing *Vicksburg Whig*. Then Hickey, who was still writing for the paper, proved less successful in his second duel and was shot, although he later recovered and moved to Texas, only to be killed there.

While not every newspaper had such a bloody history, all editors expected frequent challenges, if not actual gunplay.[22]

Caustic editorials precipitated most of these conflicts between editors and their readers. In 1859 editor Owen Van Vactor was shot down by one of the state's candidates for Congress. "An editorial article was the cause of the difficulty," reported another member of the press. "Mr. V.'s wound is severe, though not necessarily fatal." That duel took place just two weeks after congressional candidate Franklin Smith had attacked Van Vactor in the street, inflicting the proverbial "flesh wound" in the hip. Another editorial had provoked this assault. During the same campaign, the *Vicksburg Whig*'s editor exchanged shots with Mr. McGarr, a candidate for city representative.[23]

Some features of this political culture were also evident in the career of Harriet N. Prewett, Mississippi's only "editress" (as her colleagues referred to her). When her editor husband Milford died in 1849, she took over the *Yazoo City Weekly Whig* (later the *Weekly American Banner*) and remained in charge until 1859. More than a figurehead, Mrs. Prewett actively pursued her craft. She backed local candidates for statewide office, penned editorials, and discussed strategy with fellow Whigs, although, of course, she could not serve as a delegate or vote. She also could not duel, which, it seems, presented a dilemma for herself, her supporters, and her opponents. After serving as editor for several years — during which she had some bitter exchanges with her rivals at the *Yazoo Democrat* — the local Know-Nothings engaged R. B. Mayes and John T. Smith as "political editors" for the *Banner* during the 1855 and 1856 campaigns, respectively. These men both fought duels that stemmed from political commentary.[24]

Why, after five years, Mrs. Prewett's newspaper suddenly needed a male editor was unclear. Perhaps the Know-Nothings were anxious about her ambiguous position relative to the secret nativist lodges, which she tried but failed to join; perhaps they wanted a member of the order as their local leader. It is more likely, however, that local opponents resented her ability to write with impunity. When Smith joined the *Banner* in 1856, Mrs. Prewett reprinted reports of his five previous duels, all supposedly fatal to his opponent. In the next issue Smith, now dubbed "the fighting editor," announced, with slightly tongue-in-cheek sarcasm, that he would "accept all challenges" on behalf of the editor. These notices came one month after she wrote a scathing editorial disparaging a local politician, calling him a "low and petty malice of a *man* that don't know the first throb of a manly heart." Later, she labeled rival editor William Roy a "cowardly defamer" and invoked her status as "lady and matron" by appealing to Democratic men as "husbands and fathers" to cleanse themselves of "such a pestiferous depot of corruption." One can imagine the frustration of men obsessed with honor and public insults who knew the "editress" was safe from their reprisals. Mutual friends finally intervened between her and Roy, but not before she fired a shot at Roy's wife, something else a male editor could not, or would not, have tried.

Finally, the appointments of Mayes and Smith perhaps came because local Whigs and Know-Nothings decided they needed someone to defend their party on the field of honor. When political editor Mayes dueled in 1855, the *Banner* noted, it was "in defence of true American principles." All of these possibilities underline the personal basis of politics within antiparty parties. It is clear that Mrs. Prewett earned the respect of many fellow editors—ample evidence confirms that—but there were requirements of public, personal leadership inherent in the office of party editor that she could not satisfy.[25]

Mississippians preserved this violent, honor-bound political culture throughout the antebellum period. Unable to separate personal from political insults, they faced the sectional crisis and increasingly interpreted the events of the 1850s as proof that northerners no longer respected them as equal Americans, white men, and Christians. Each new sectional controversy contributed to hundreds of individual decisions to support secession. Later, several writers remembered particular episodes as decisive. For Bolivar County planter Frank Montgomery it was John Brown's raid, until which "I had never for a moment lost my loyalty to the union, but after that I became a secessionist." "The manner in which his death was received in the north, for he was looked upon as a martyr to the cause of freedom . . . convinced me as it did thousands of other union men in the state, that if our liberties were to be preserved . . . we must endeavor to defend them out of and not in the Union." When the secession delegates justified secession, they too remembered Brown's legacy, noting that northerners had honored "the wretch whose purpose was to apply flames to our dwellings and the weapons of destruction to our lives." Northern personal liberty laws, which "nullified the Fugitive Slave Law in almost every free state," also appeared prominently among southerners' reasons for disunion.[26]

Within the history of sectionalism, however, the decade's critical development, the one that dwarfed all others in importance, was the formation and rapid success of the antisouthern Republican Party. Free Soil presented numerous possible calamities: rebellion and racial warfare if the growing slave population could not be diffused geographically; declining prosperity on land worn out by cotton; and social and economic polarization if poorer whites were denied access to new land or the dream of attaining planter status. Most Mississippians considered Free Soil equivalent to abolition, and emancipation always underlay their fear of Republicanism. William Seward's "Higher-Law" doctrine and Lincoln's affirmation that America could not endure "half slave and half free" convinced most Mississippi voters that slavery ultimately would perish under such a "heretical" government. Widespread prosperity in the 1850s allowed many farmers to become slaveowners, raising their awareness of Free Soil's long-range threat. Mississippi also had a higher percentage of slaveowning households than most Deep South states—according to several calculations, about half in 1860. In the late 1850s speakers at several commercial conventions emphasized "that the Union was an economic liability to the South" and urged regional independence to ensure continued prosperity and growth. The sectional tension that threatened the expansion of slavery provided a crucial underlying motive for men to consider, if only subconsciously, the need for disunion. The various resolutions on secession focused on all of these complaints and condemned the Republican-led assaults against slavery, which threatened internal revolution or slow strangulation through economic or political pressure. Many southerners emphasized both the political danger and the insult that Lincoln's election signified: the South's impotence within the federal system.[27]

But the common thread of sectionalism in Mississippi, what tied all these events and idiosyncratic motives together, was the way its men reacted to them and to the mere existence of the Republican Party. Representative Lucius Q. C. Lamar echoed other spokesmen when he complained about the North's insulting language and the threat to slavery: "It is a unanimous sentiment in the South that the existence of this Republican organization is a standing menace to her peace and security, and a standing insult to her character." In 1856 Mississippi's state legislators agreed unanimously that resolutions from Republican-controlled Maine and Vermont be returned because of their "insulting" language, "the ebulitions [sic] of malignant slander" that cast "premeditated insolence and insult upon her [Mississippi's] citizens." They rejected northern meddling, "either by any form of active hostility, or by pharisarical [sic] lectures upon the abstract wisdom or morality of the established relation of master and servant." Mississippians repeated endlessly these perceived threats to their reputation and the imputation of un-Christian immorality that branded them as personally and collectively unequal.[28]

Contemporaries and historians alike have emphasized the "sense of crisis" that existed among Mississippi voters in the late 1850s. Nearly everyone agreed that a Republican presidential victory, for many personal and particular reasons, was unacceptable. But it constituted such a grave threat to "manly equality" because of the state's antiparty political culture. The personal and community implications of Republicanism within the context of honor — men's interpretation of those sectional insults — made political secession possible, even imperative. As Mississippi spokesmen always concluded, Republican ascendancy forced them to choose between honor and equality or submission and shame — no choice at all. Within that consensus, of course, there was disagreement, and immediate, separate-state secessionists set to work to promote their solution rather than one of several cooperationist proposals. Still, men's collective judgment that the "humiliation" of Republicanism called for an appropriately manly response, limited the alternatives, and meant that secession ultimately would prevail.

Mississippians, in effect, bound up a series of issues and code words — states rights, white liberty, slavery, political parity with the North — under the rubric *equality*.[29] Equality was really the essence of their outrage, and it struck directly at the heart of manliness and honor. If northerners insulted their manly equality, then they were obligated to respond. Men challenged one another to stand up "as men" and defend themselves, their communities, and finally their regional way of life, to exonerate themselves as good men and good Christians. Of course, both slavery and continued white liberty were vital; southerners repeated endless paeans to both. Without slavery there would have been no secession and war, and southerners always linked their individual and collective "honor and safety" to the maintenance of their peculiar institution. But slavery and liberty came together in the emotionally charged question of equality, which, ultimately, challenged the bases of white manhood and could not be separated from southerners' understanding of community, honor, and civilization. The notions of honor and masculinity, in short, played the crucial role in forcing Mississippians to choose secession because it focused attention on public insults and called for an open, aggressive, and appropriately manly response before their peers. Sectional insults, therefore, engaged the voters where they defined their manhood — in public — and joined manliness and honor to electoral politics, which was the ultimate mechanism for disunion.

It was the political culture, however, that forced Mississippians into a direct confrontation, because it compelled them to interpret Republican Party rhetoric as a personal insult. Had Mississippians embraced a viable partisan culture in the antebellum years, they might have behaved differently. In the Upper South, men did. Most voters in Virginia, North Carolina, Tennessee, and elsewhere — southern men who also wanted to protect their beloved slavery — did not reply to Republicanism in the same manner. In those states an institutional party system helped to depersonalize political conflict. Regular competition was important because it helped establish a tradition of partisanship and a different way of thinking that voters incorporated into their political culture. But it was more than a moderating party platform that distinguished the Upper South from Mississippi. In this regard, the case of Arkansas is instructive. Controlled by a family and party dynasty throughout the antebellum years, the state had little or no party competition. Yet, "unlike much of the Deep South," concludes the state's most recent historian, "the people and press of Arkansas did not react shrilly to the news of Lincoln's election." The press advised caution and reminded voters of southern Democrats' power in Congress and the Supreme Court; Arkansas politicians articulated faith in party organizations and party security. When a faction led by Mississippi native Thomas Hindman invoked the discourse of shame and imperiled masculinity, it fell mostly on deaf ears. Lincoln's election, in short, was not enough to induce panic; most Arkansas voters remained calm.[30] Voters in the Magnolia State, however, interpreted Republican language from a different, antiparty perspective, a distinctive political culture.

After 1855 Mississippi spokesmen increasingly invoked the concepts of honor and equality because Republicans targeted southern behavior and southern political power so often. The popular idea of a "Slave Power Conspiracy" to control the national government and deny northern farmers good land in the West satisfied all the new party's guiding principles: nativism, racism, and antislavery. According to Republican propaganda, immigrant voters helped sustain the prosouthern Democratic Party; Free Soil would leave the West free of "arrogant" planters and despised free blacks alike, and—for those few Republican abolitionists—would provide a first step toward emancipation. Charges of the South's "bullying arrogance" and "aristocratic haughtiness" contributed to a dominant Republican critique that presented the region "as a backward, degraded, barbaric society built on brutality and depravity." This imagery became especially prominent during the 1856 campaign, particularly after Preston Brooks's notorious assault on abolitionist Senator Charles Sumner. A principal tactic, admitted one Republican, was "to prove that the South is, upon the whole, the poorest, meanest, least productive and most miserable part of creation, and therefore ought to be continually teased and taunted and reproached and reviled." The Republican assault was aimed primarily at wealthy planters, although party spokesmen often failed to distinguish among white southerners and indicted the whole region. Republicans' willingness to use state power made them doubly threatening; southerners saw them as the incarnation of "New England cultural imperialism" who were trying to "force their harsh and uncongenital puritanical creed down the throats of other men." Republicans embodied for southerners the meddling, holier-than-thou Yankee stereotype, a declaration of cultural superiority that southerners could not leave unchallenged.[31]

Republican popularity shocked Mississippians and forced many to reconsider their equal status within the nation. They repeated the discourse of 1850–1851, when they had confronted only the pitiful Free Soil Party. By the late 1850s, however, a majority of northern voters was endorsing the "raving insults" of Republican antisouthern propaganda. "Hitherto the South have little regarded the malicious and seditious ravings of the mad-capped fanatics," wrote editor Henry Baker of the *Fayette Watchtower* in 1857, but "the reptile [of "higher lawism and negrophilism"] contemptible in its insignificance, has enlarged its proportions, and disseminated its poisonous effluvia, with little exception, through the whole Northern and North-Western portion of the confederacy." Senator Albert Gallatin Brown voiced the same concern: "Twenty years ago," he told a large audience of Mississippians in 1858, "this [antisouthern] sentiment was confined to a few fanatics; now it pervades all classes, ages, and sexes of society."[32]

Familiar appeals to honor, manliness, and Christianity defined political discourse in the late 1850s. Over and over, men used the same words: *humiliating, degrading, insulting*. Republican propaganda labeled southerners and their way of life as inferior, morally degenerate, and unworthy of the national experience. "To deny us the right and privilege [of slavery in the territories] would be to deny our equality in the Union," summarized one local gathering, "and would be a wrong and degradation to which a high spirited people should not submit."[33] These objections were not just public rhetoric. Senator Brown wrote to his friend, J. F. H. Claiborne, lamenting the Republicans' growing strength among northern voters. Their platform, he said, represented a galling insult, "meant to break the spirit, destroy the institutions, and ultimately disgrace and ruin the Southern people." Republicanism meant much more than a threat to slavery. It was a humiliating disgrace to southern pride in general, and for men in particular an intolerable slap in the face. As one Mississippi voter summed it up: "The distinction sought to be made between the South and north cannot be tolerated by honorable men." By 1860 a Republican victory ensured secession; Lincoln's election decided Mississippi's fate because its sons would not accept the public insult it represented.[34]

More than simply a matter of male ego, Mississippians' response to the Republican critique interpreted it as an aspersion on their standing as good Christians. "The black republicans have proven themselves to be a set of black heathen infidels," fumed Powhatan Ellis to his son, "denying the Bible [and] God. What faith can we place in such a set of *Devils?*" Mississippians voiced righteous fury at Yankees who preached the sin of slavery. Most men believed themselves to be good Christians and saw no incongruity between their faith and slavery, drawing on widely circulated and respected proslavery arguments that used biblical justifications to ease southern consciences and answer charges of moral depravity. Reconciling slavery with Christianity absolved the individuals who maintained the peculiar institution. Most southerners probably concurred in Senator Brown's solemn belief that "slavery is a good thing *per se;* I believe it to be a great moral, social, and political blessing—a blessing to the master and a blessing to the slave . . . [and] it is of Divine origin. . . . What God has ordained, cannot be wrong."[35]

The northern attack, therefore, dealt a double blow to men's reputation, challenging their status as both "real" men and "true" Christians. Governor John Jones Pettus lectured his constituents that Republicans had "attempted to *degrade us* . . . by denouncing us as barbarians, pirates, and robbers, unfit associates for Christian or civilized men." Representative Lamar hammered his northern opponents with scripture and verse, arguing that there were no religious or moral reasons to attack slavery. The early Christian church, he reported, "itself was a slaveholder, and Christian kings and princes followed its example." Neither slavery nor white southerners violated the laws of God. This defense of southern Christianity related especially to the reputation of wives and daughters, who were increasingly praised as primary guardians of the region's morality and religious virtue. If slavery was unchristian, then southern women, as well as men, had failed. Republican rhetoric, therefore, also challenged southern men to defend their families and women against the accusation of immorality.[36]

In the late 1850s Christian virtue took center stage in debates over the international slave trade, which had been closed for fifty years. A minority of southerners were advocating its revival: if slavery was part of God's plan to bring Christianity to heathen Africans, why not reopen the Atlantic trade? Although most southern leaders opposed resumption, they still voiced outrage at northerners' critique of the trade. Senator Brown condemned public discussion of the slave trade, which, he argued, only divided southerners when they needed unity. Moreover, he acknowledged the power of Congress to make laws respecting the international trade. Even so, he declared that lawmakers had gone "out of their way to denounce the traffic as piracy. This was a gratuitous affront to the South. It implied that the trade was inherently wrong, and involved the highest degree of moral turpitude." That it was, legally, piracy he conceded, but "there is in it no inherent moral guilt." It was the suggestion of moral turpitude that Brown and many others objected to, not closing the trade. John Quitman also fumed over a Republican resolution that declared the slave trade "shocking to the moral sentiment" of "enlightened mankind" and a "horrid and inhumane" act worthy of the "reproach and execration of all civilized and Christian people throughout the world." Quitman and others — who did not dispute the illegality of the trade or want it reopened — offered the following response, admitting "that it [the trade] is inexpedient, unwise, and contrary to the settled policy of the United States to repeal the laws prohibiting the African slave-trade."[37] What outraged these southerners was the implication of moral depravity; it was not the trade they were defending but their status as Christian people.

Another link in the sectional chain, the debate over the Kansas proslavery constitution, typified Mississippians' reactions to Republicanism and revealed alternative viewpoints within a common political culture. Through the lens of personal politics and honor, men debated whether this latest Yankee "outrage" constituted an insult too gross to ignore. Some admitted that the state's admission with slavery was purely "a matter of *principle*, for there is abundance of territory south of her latitude where slave labor is needed and would be more productive." Still, those who favored taking immediate action if Congress rejected the slave constitution, argued that "*the South has but one course to pursue — a choice between hopeless shame and manly resistance.*" The *Port Gibson Herald* included a clear, typical statement of their position: "For one, we ask to be considered ready to meet the issue and its consequences, boldly, manly and defiantly, and should the wrong be enacted, we are ready for RESISTANCE." When some Democrats argued that forcing the issue of Kansas slavery threatened cooperation with the party's northern wing, they faced withering criticism from most colleagues. "We love our party," wrote the *Yazoo Sun's* editor, but could never endorse such a "slavish and unmanly" position or "yield to the dictations of the free soil rabble." Many editors and writers also reminded voters who had supported the Union Party in 1851 that their platform had endorsed secession if Congress refused to admit a slave state, as Republicans now threatened to do.[38]

Others, however, argued that this case did not merit disunion — repeating the Unionists' position in 1851. Yet men who voiced this reservation always reminded their audience that if, in fact, any insult threatened their honor, then secession would be proper. Editor John Richardson lampooned the notion that Mississippi should secede over "so trivial a pretext" as the nonadmission of Kansas, a state "palpably Northern in sentiment." "If we had to choose between disgrace and dishonor, or disunion and destruction," he summarized, "we would certainly choose disunion and destruction, but there is no need of a choice." Although the Kansas question did not seem worthy of secession, Richardson agreed that when "we are debarred the right of equally participating in the liberties dispensed from the Senate Hall . . . we say dissolve; absolve the ties that make us one people." When "we can no longer remain in the Union as equals — as freemen, enjoying the same liberties as Northerners, we are for a separate confederacy." Mississippi's Milford Woodruff declared no need for redress as late as February, 1859: "I am for our Union, out and out" he proclaimed, but if the Republicans "keep up their officious, unchristian, unconstitutional interference, I go in, with might and main, for a Glorious Southern Confederacy."[39] Few men denied that shameful insults to personal and community honor would require secession and possibly civil war, although some insisted that the Republican insults did not yet threaten their manly equality.

The course of editor Richardson's Prairie News suggested the slow transformation that some voters underwent in the late 1850s as they reacted to Republicanism and the growing sectional conflict. At first, Richardson evinced a deep hatred for all Democrats, and thought the Kansas issue a "humbug" stirred up by "fire-eating demagogues." Throughout the spring and summer of 1858, he defended the Union and ridiculed "Kansas secessionists." Much more important and insulting, he argued, was the fate of southern filibusters in Central America, especially the "gallant" William Walker. Richardson attacked a shadowy conspiracy of British and northern abolitionists and Republicans that was bent on humiliating southern "patriots" and denying them access to new slave territory. On July 1, 1858, he praised Walker's call to arms "for the honor of our Sunny South" and called for southern unity without "partyism." At the same time, Richardson moderated his position on sectional agitators. Earlier he had blamed northern and southern "demagogues" equally, but now he wondered how long southerners would "submit to any insult any impudent Abolitionist may see proper to cast" or "tamely submit to be kicked out of Congress as spiritless negro drivers. . . . We are no advocate of agitation, if it could be stopped on both sides," he concluded, "but the Northerners commenced the system, and we say let them be the first to abolish it. Let them establish a precedent which we could with honor follow."[40]

In early August Richardson still wondered "what is the use of harping on Kansas! Kansas!! If the cry was Nicaragua! Cuba!! there would be some sense in it, and we'd whirl our hat and shout hurrah." Two weeks later he defended William Yancey and the Southern League, blaming "the turbulent waves of northern fanaticism" for starting and continuing sectional discord. He admitted "with fear and trembling" that "in a few years" the "grand and mighty structure" of the Constitution and the Union "must fall." "As yet, there has been committed no act of hostility sufficient to justify extreme measures; but we know not how soon the prejudices of Northerners may prompt them to acts of direct hostility." By late September Richardson thought Albert Gallatin Brown, "an ultra fire-eater," was the best choice for president "as yet suggested" and offered to support him in 1860. Thus, in about six months Richardson moved from unequivocal support for the national American Party and Union to embrace many of the positions taken by Yancey and Brown. He stopped short of secession, at that point, but counseled readiness for the inevitable "Yankee outrage" that would demand "bold, manly" action. For Richardson, the question of slave territory in Central America seemed paramount, and, like all Mississippians, he articulated this and other issues in terms of honor and equality, the lingua franca of sectionalism. How many voters reacted to these issues in the same way is, of course, difficult to gauge. But Richardson surely absorbed and sensed the culture and attitudes of the community in which he lived and worked, and his transformation surely reflected, if even subconsciously, the same struggles of his readers.[41]

The sectional issues that arose between 1855 and 1859 were, of course, simply preliminaries to the presidential battle in 1860. Regarding a Republican victory as unacceptable, virtually all Mississippians were committed to some form of resistance if that dreaded catastrophe actually happened. Democratic victories in the state in 1859 suggested popular support for immediate secession, a position most of the party's county conventions advocated in the event of a Republican victory in 1860. Lowndes County Democrats declared that southern "honor and safety" was at stake: election of a Republican government "hostile to the political equality and security of the Southern States" was "an act so offensive and aggressive as to justify" secession. The more moderate state platform labeled Republican victory "a declaration of hostility" that would require Mississippi "to co-operate with her sister States of the South, in whatever measures she may deem necessary." John Pettus, the party's nominee for governor, generally ignored the platform and urged immediate, separate-state secession if a Republican won the White House. The fourth-district congressional race between Otho R. Singleton, an immediatist, and Franklin Smith, a champion of Stephen Douglas and Unionism, offers some measure of popular sentiment. Both men were Democrats. Singleton and secession swamped Smith and the Union, 8,040 (77 percent) to 2,376. Pettus won the same majority statewide.[42]

In the following year's climactic campaign, most supporters of John Breckinridge, like Governor Pettus, argued for immediate, separate-state secession if Lincoln triumphed. They believed that Republican victory embodied an intolerable affront to honor and manly equality and a direct threat to southern survival. Moreover, their plan presented voters with the boldest, most aggressive option and appealed to masculine virtues long held sacred. And, like dueling, the threat of death secession offered was an important part of confirming manliness. Breckinridge men repeated the sentiments of Congressman Reuben Davis, who predicted that if secession failed "it will be because the South is deluged with blood, and made desolate with fire." At Herbert's precinct in Neshoba County, a banner on election day evinced the importance of physical courage and the requisite danger implied by secession: "Death rather than submission to a Black Republican government."[43]

Lincoln's victory, of course, pushed the rhetoric of manliness and resistance to new levels. "The Insulting and Defiant Language of the Black Republicans," claimed one secession advocate, called southern masculinity into question. This author quoted from a New Hampshire newspaper predicting that the South would ultimately submit. Southerners, the northern editor wrote, "will not provoke a conflict which can promise to them only disaster, disgrace, and probably a halter." Since the election, wrote another Mississippian, "the entire Abolition press [has] sent hisses into the Southern ear, words of bitterness, hate and defiance." Over and over, Mississippians voiced outrage at the "insolent" Republicans who asked them to "eat dirt." Another writer asked Mississippi's men if they intended "to be whipped into submission — aye, whipped and cowed like *slaves*, by . . . a hireling army lead on and directed by abolitionists."[44]

Advocates of immediate secession often blended images of family with appeals to individual honor and manliness. One of the most common metaphors summoned men to defend their women and children from Yankee insults or marauding slaves freed by abolitionist Republicans. This call was an obligation for all men as head of household that tested, rather than reflected, their status as real men. Any man who would not risk his life to defend women and children — especially his own — failed the most basic test of manhood. When possible secession raised the risk of war and death, one editor scoffed at the notion that Mississippi's men even would consider the consequences: "Southern men have always readily [made contributions of] blood or money when the expenditure of both was necessary to the maintenance of their rights and the vindication of their honor. . . . How much more readily will they now be made, if need be, for the protection of their homes and firesides from invasion?" "Men of Mississippi, Do Your Duty!" began yet another statement of masculine responsibility to one's family, even across generations. "Decide for yourselves, whether you will be freemen or slaves . . . for yourselves and your children, whether you will give up that freedom, independence and equality, which our almost god-like ancestors won upon near a hundred blood-stained battle fields." Immediate secession — "one firm resolve, one bold and manly move" — would rescue honor and equality for the future. Under a Republican government, southern birth would represent a "stigma," "the brand of inferiority, deeper than Cain's, written upon his brow."[45] These images raised the specter of a northern "invasion" led by another John Brown, emancipation, and wholesale rape and murder. It was a racist fear of racial warfare, yes, but the metaphor presented a direct challenge to masculine responsibilities.

Of course, neither side advocated disunion simply for the sake of doing it, and Breckinridge men as well as moderate followers of John Bell also appealed to hopes for continuation of the Union. The latter presented their candidate as the only national hope; the former reasoned that if Breckinridge did not win, then Lincoln would, in which case Mississippi should and would secede. Opposition leader William Sharkey, a radical Unionist, warned voters that secession was "no remedy; it is an impracticable idea." Disunion could never be peaceful, he predicted: "If a State goes out of the Union she must prepare to wade through blood." Perhaps, replied Breckinridge spokesmen, but better that than "dishonor" and "degradation" under Republicanism. Reuben Davis preached "resistance even to bloodshed" to voters in northern Mississippi. His audience, the local newspaper reported, "hailed it with fierce delight — such as the war horse feels when he sniffs the scent of battle afar off." Unionists also appealed to traditional antipartyism, branding Southern Democrats "unscrupulous, dishonest, and unprincipled demagogues" who forced secession and stirred up voters simply to stay in power.[46]

The minority opponents of immediate secession in particular testified to the pervasiveness of honor, manliness, and Christianity as the lingua franca of sectionalism when they invoked the same images and the same perspective. Like their opponents, they assessed Republicanism — from within the same political culture — as a personal insult. Though they articulated another, more moderate and deliberative thread of public opinion, they still demanded satisfaction. Almost all agreed that they could not "meekly" submit to a Lincoln victory and offered a collection of "cooperative" proposals: some advocated working within the Union as long as possible while others called for a cooperative slave-state movement for secession. By the late 1850s few men openly confessed to "unconditional" unionism. To rule out secession and the possibility of death in defense of individual and community honor was too cowardly. Too many Republican insults threatened their sacred institution, their conception of white liberty, and, ultimately, the fabric of personal and collective southern manhood. Anyone who eschewed the most militant form of "redress" needed to account for his "timidity" or face the charges of "base submission" and "cowardice."

One Cooperationist argument turned the accusation of cowardice on the fire-eaters. "Who are the 'Submissionists' and 'Cowards'?" asked countless editorials. Real men who wanted to stay in the Union as long as possible and fight for the southern share of public buildings, the army and navy, and the Capitol itself were no cowards. The real submissionists, these men concluded, were hot-headed disunionists willing to "slink away" into the night and abandon seventy-five years of investment and heritage. Still, these lukewarm Unionists never failed to pledge their willingness for secession once the possibility of adequate "redress" within the Union seemed hopeless. As one editor concluded, "let us fight for our rights in the Union, and if we are overpowered, then let us all go together, and demand a fair division of all property belonging to the Union." Like the punctilious *code duello*, this position required a "true man of honor" to exhaust all calm, peaceful means — in this case, by negotiating within the Union — before turning, properly, to more drastic measures.[47]

In a similar fashion, some Bell supporters called on "restrained" manliness to defy "the vehement gesticulations and the indignation that almost consumes the Breckinridge orators," who "weep over the direful calamities [?] into which the South is being submerged [?] by the submissive spirit of her people." They urged Mississippi voters to act like men and not rush into war. "Will you yield, basely yield, . . . and lick the foot [of Breckinridge leaders] that kicks [and insults] you? Would you cringe and fawn to those enemies who would butcher your wives, fire your dwellings and . . . throw your children to the flames, or will you, like men of true Southern hearts, contend for the protection of your rights?" This writer appealed to "consciousness and reason," not to "the general panic." Real men would not, he argued, make unreasonable, worthless demands — referring to a proposed congressional slave code for the territories — instead of trusting in the existing, appropriate process to secure their rights, equality, and honor. Still, even this man, a nearly unqualified Unionist, made his appeal, in the cause of southern unity, to confront "the hellish clamor of the North" that threatened their rights, property, and "the conflagration of our cities, the desolation of our fertile fields, and the slaughter of Southern citizens."[48]

Hinds County's Fulton Anderson questioned the efficacy of separate-state secession, preferring instead a cooperative disunion movement. He, too, couched his proposal in the imagery and language of honor and communal manhood. He acknowledged that the "unrelenting hatred" most northerners showed toward the South and "her sacred institutions" constituted a "declaration of war." Southern men, Anderson continued, should resist for the moment this "contemptuously declared" war and meet in convention to seek "common redress." To act independently would signal a lack of faith in "our fellow southern men," bound together as they were "by every tie of honor and of friendship." Separate-state secession, he argued, called into question the manhood of other southerners. If Mississippians acted alone, what could Georgia's and Alabama's men think but that their neighbors felt unsure of their resolve and their very courage as men? On the other hand, uniting as southern men in defense of the greater community would demonstrate willful courage and mutual confidence in one another's manliness. A southern confederacy, Anderson concluded, "will not be [accomplished] by a few States taking the irrevocable step which declares to a majority of their Southern brethren that they are not to be trusted with the vindication of their honor."[49]

The opponents of separate-state secession, then, called on the same values of manliness as their hastier counterparts. Recognizing the need to defend their manhood and fearful for their honor and reputation, men like Anderson presented themselves as the "truly manful" defenders of the South. Of course, his proposed solution also underscored the basic unanimity of Mississippians. He did not rule out secession; in fact he endorsed it, but only in cooperation with other slaveholding states. Other "Unionists" also believed that Republicanism was an insult too gross to ignore; they simply wanted satisfaction within the Union if possible, but outside it if necessary. Supporters of Breckinridge and Bell—the "immediatists" and the "cooperationists"—accounted for more than 95 percent of Mississippi's voters. Both favored resistance. The former, nearly 60 percent of the state's voters, endorsed a party that favored immediate secession if the Republicans won. That possibility became more likely—and their position more evident—after Lincoln carried Pennsylvania, Ohio, and Indiana in October, which virtually assured his election. Some Breckinridge supporters organized "harmony meetings" to unite all advocates of secession behind their candidates, fixing the connection between themselves and secession. Mississippi voters who chose Breckinridge in November thus sent a clear message in support of immediate disunion.[50]

The Bell supporters, a less unified group, wanted either cooperative secession or cooperative resistance within the Union, but most agreed that disunion might be necessary. Walker Brooke, a former Whig from Warren County, embodied the position taken by many cooperationists: "I was elected by a large majority, as what is known as a co-operationist—which means, as I understand it, one who was in favor of united Southern action for the purpose of demanding further guarantees from the North, or, failing in that, the formation of a Southern Confederacy." Even the most rabid immediate secession journal, the *Mississippi Free Trader*, reminded voters that other Deep South states would secede if Lincoln triumphed, blurring the line between separate-state action and cooperation. In short, between Breckinridge's immediatists and the cooperative seceders who supported John Bell, a reasonable, perhaps conservative estimate is that four-fifths of Mississippi's voters considered secession the proper response to Lincoln's election; or at least they voted for representatives who embraced that position. Frank Montgomery remembered that Lincoln's election "in the minds of most people in the south, settled the question that safety could no longer be found in the union, and all began to prepare for secession."[51] The difference in short-term strategy should not obscure the essential harmony among most Mississippi voters: they interpreted Republicanism as a personal and collective affront that required bold action to salvage public honor and masculinity and to protect their slave-based way of life.

Two earlier students of Mississippi secession, Percy Rainwater and William Barney, also noted the voters' spontaneous reaction to Lincoln's victory: Even "conditional Unionists" and "Conservatives" labeled it unacceptable. Cooperationists from Rankin County typified the attitude of many. They thought secession an act of "cowardice" destined to inaugurate "civil war and internal strife"; but they also resolved to secure their rights "in the Union if it be possible to obtain them with honor; but if we cannot . . . we are determined to have them out of it." They concluded that "we are agreed upon the main question, that the South should ACT; yet we think it no cause of offence that we differ as to the mode of adjusting the matter in dispute and providing for our future peace and safety." Lincoln's election was "insulting to the slaveholding states" and unacceptable. They preferred resistance within the Union, then, if need be, cooperative secession, but clearly resistance of some kind. Only two newspapers suggested waiting for tangible evidence of Republican tyranny, and the *Vicksburg Whig* alone demonstrated its isolation from the popular mood by taking the radical position that "it is treason to secede."[52]

Many historians of secession imply that party activists played a leading role in creating public opinion; although disunion ultimately had strong popular support, it was control of the Democratic Party machinery that provided the decisive forum for secessionists. Of course, secession did have a basis in party conflict: it resulted, after all, from the outcome of a national election in which Mississippians had, as always, taken their cues from parties. Moreover, Democratic editors were the most supportive of immediate secession, although virtually everyone agreed that disunion might be necessary. The Democrats were also slightly better organized than other parties and had a few more newspapers and more voters who usually supported Democratic candidates. Nonetheless, the evidence suggests that editors and politicians articulated, rather than created, public sentiment and emotion, just as they always had—whether the issue was the politics of antipartyism, the politics of slavery, or the anger of voters insulted by the Republican victory.[53]

Rather than something manufactured by editors or politicians, the spontaneous sense of crisis was a product of the state's political culture and men's understanding of honor, masculinity, and Christian virtue. If local leaders, as Rainwater rightly concludes, voiced "the language of feeling and emo-

tion" when they discussed secession, it was because that was how voters
interpreted Republicanism. And, even though fire-eaters "rode the crest of
prosecession sentiment," as Barney makes clear, it was the voters' natural,
visceral response that created that wave.[54] Finally, the thesis that partisan
loyalty primarily decided Mississippi's fate in 1860 neglects the 1851 crisis—
when thousands of Democrats broke ranks to defeat secession. It ignores as
well much of the state's antebellum political history. Weak and mostly ineffective as organizations throughout the period, the major parties clearly failed to
establish widespread loyalty among skeptical, often disinterested and independent, voters.

After Lincoln's victory, secessionists of all stripes—the vast majority of
Mississippians—undoubtedly pressured doubters and intimidated dissidents.
The resulting atmosphere of popular, community-based violence also conformed to Mississippi tradition. Barney's description of the voters' response
to Republican victory details the force of community sanction and popular
enthusiasm for disunion. Vigilance committees, Minute Men clubs, committees of public safety, and volunteer militia units rallied and shouted for
secession, overwhelming Unionists and driving even moderate cooperationists underground. Planter Thomas Dabney described his own transformation
after the election: "I find myself drifting from my old moorings without the
ability to stop or conjecture as to the position I may find myself in on the
morrow." When Unionists organized a mass meeting in Vicksburg on November 29, Dabney's name appeared in support. But he characterized himself as not "a Union man in the sense in which the North is Union." Rumors
of abolitionist plots swept the state, and angry mobs threatened community
outsiders and unlucky northern travelers in a "quasi-ritualistic" fervor.[55]

The extent to which intimidation helped the secessionist surge remains
difficult to gauge. The election process that evolved throughout the antebellum years certainly presented opportunities for local elites to pressure voters.
Some scattered testimony records direct threats and fear among Unionists.[56]
But the 1851 Unionist victory, the tepid support for immediate secession in
1860 among most wealthy planters, and the evidence that Unionists had
many opportunities to rally support all militate against the idea that there
was widespread, systematic intimidation. If it had existed, a Unionist wave
in 1860, like the one ten years earlier, would have had wealthy, powerful
leaders and numerous forums from which to arouse the voters. The Opposition Party was disorganized in the late 1850s but was not significantly weaker
than the Whigs had been ten years earlier, and Unionists had built upon
that pathetic organization to halt secession in 1851. Most evidence suggests
that in 1860 there were simply too few Unionists left for men like Judge
Sharkey or Henry Foote to organize. Of course, intimidation is, to some
extent, also a matter of perspective and definition. Was questioning your
neighbor's manhood and courage an act of intimidation or a consensual,
visceral expression of personal and community outrage? Taking a broad per-

spective that considers the history of the state's political culture and men's professed values and behavior between 1830 and 1860 suggests that secession was much more populist than manipulated, more instinctive than coerced.

Immediatists remained "confident and aggressive," aware that almost two-thirds of the voters had endorsed their position. They benefitted from the qualities of their proposed remedy: "a quick, direct, and positive solution to the terrible threat that everyone agreed faced the South."[57] Immediate secession appealed to men raised in a slave society and to the tradition of aggressive physical courage and loyalty to neighbors and family. Most of all, it offered men the chance to stand up and defend their communities and homes as they were supposed to do. Governor Pettus summarized these feelings when he convened the legislature in special session after Lincoln's victory. "Can we hesitate! when one bold resolve, bravely executed, makes powerless the aggressor, and one united effort makes safe our homes? May the God of our fathers put it into the hearts of the people to make it." Cooperationists still argued that a unified southern movement more completely satisfied feelings of communal manhood by including fellow southerners, but that option represented only a variation on the same themes of personal and community vindication and the appropriately manly response to ensure it.[58]

One month after the presidential election, Mississippi voters chose delegates to a special convention to decide the state's formal withdrawal. This relatively spiritless canvass, taking place so soon after the heated, decisive presidential campaign, featured a murky mixture of "cooperation" and "coalition" tickets; in nearly a third of the counties, there was only one slate, usually a coalition package. Most candidates were not pledged to a specific position but were chosen out of respect by voters who entrusted them with the state's future. The elections resembled, in fact, those of many county contests in the previous two decades: they were expressions of faith and confidence in the local gentry. The turnout was only about 50 percent.

Overall the election was a much poorer gauge of popular sentiment than the presidential contest. In Hinds County, however, an unusually clear race and the memories of one candidate offer suggestive evidence of the outrage many voters felt towards Lincoln's victory. Hinds, a traditionally Whig county, had backed John Bell and cooperation over Breckinridge by a slim margin and seemed "a stronghold of Union sentiment." One convention candidate, Wiley P. Harris, although he was considered a separate-state secessionist, remembered he "was not put on a platform, nor was any plan of operation prescribed to me." The canvass and the debates between himself and the cooperationist candidates convinced Harris of "the uncertain attitude in which men stood towards an unmanageable difficulty." Yet, all candidates "professed to be united on secession as the ultimate remedy." Harris believed that waiting for cooperation would "fail of any result, through dilatory measures, conventions, conferences, debates and resolutions, all ending in no decisive act and that we would be covered with disgrace by it. That if there was in the present attitude of the free States cause for secession at all it was cause for it now." Separate-state secession won the county with about 60 percent of the vote. Of course, Harris's recollections reiterated the voters' basic, unanimous belief that resistance, and probably secession, was the proper response to Republican ascendancy. In a similar way, Lowndes County cooperationists argued that "wrongs of which we have a right to complain should be remedied"; they were "opposed to separate state secession at this time" and wanted to exhaust "all constitutional means for securing our rights in the Union before secession." They lost, overwhelmingly, to the immediatist ticket.[59]

Immediatist delegates held a majority of about four-fifths of the seats in the convention. Judging by the behavior of ordinary Mississippians in 1860, that division accurately reflected public sentiment. Opponents of separate secession tried several amendments to delay the action and wait for a cooperative movement, but all of them failed by about the same margin (78 to 20, 73 to 25, 70 to 29). The first proposal advocated cooperative resistance within the Union; the second wanted to wait for the Deep South to secede as a unit; and the last urged that the question be referred to another popular referendum. Conservative James Alcorn supported cooperation as long as possible but could not face the voters' condemnation of "coward and submissionist [which] will be everywhere applied" if he did not support disunion; finally, he endorsed separate-state action. Undoubtedly, many voters, too, would have supported, or even preferred, cooperative secession, though most endorsed the convention's decision. Representative Reuben Davis recalled he was "scarcely out of the sound of cannon all the way" from Congress to his home in Aberdeen.[60]

Advocates for immediate secession may have sped up secession by effecting it individually rather than cooperatively, but, judging by the behavior of other Deep South voters, it would have happened anyway. Contemporaries agreed. Cotton merchant Horace Fulkerson adjudged Unionism "insignificant" and predicted that "the large majority in the Convention" approximated that "amongst the people." Conservative Alcorn conceded that "the popular dogma" of immediatism among most delegates reflected public opinion and outrage. Governor Pettus articulated it clearly: "They have attempted to *degrade us* . . . by denouncing us as barbarians, pirates, and robbers, unfit associates for Christian or civilized men."[61] Although this unrestrained support for secession and bloody satisfaction did not survive four years of war, it reflected most men's attitude in 1861.

Mississippi's secession resulted primarily from the perceived affront to southern honor and men's visceral anger, both inflamed by the state's antiparty, community-based political culture. The movement tapped men's natural urge to vindicate personal, family, community, and ultimately regional

honor against the "egregious insults" of Yankee abolitionists. The threat of
Free Soil touched men's conception of themselves and their group and,
therefore, their personal claim to equality as men and as good Christians.
Mississippians did not need to be prompted by fire-eating editors or politicians. Instead, their public spokesmen articulated the voters' outrage and
expressed the moral indignation of men who dreaded the public humiliation
and shame they saw as inherent in Republicanism. In the tradition of communal manhood, they challenged each other to stand up as men and to
demonstrate loyalty to neighbors, friends, and kin. The ultimate responsibility for disunion, then, cannot be traced to any particular group of secessionists or to the dynamics of state and national party politics — although they
surely affected the course adopted in each state. Rather, secession is best
explained as the result of imperatives in southern male culture — shaped by
slavery — and particularly the implication of those demands within the region's different political cultures. This takes account of secession as a political event, but one driven by forces deeply rooted in men's understanding of
their public duties; and it explains why men in the Upper South reacted
differently to Lincoln's election, despite their equal devotion to honor and
slavery and their fear of abolition or slave rebellion. In Mississippi the political culture conditioned men's assessment of Republican rhetoric; southern
honor and the virtues of communal manhood determined their ultimate
response.

Only a tentative argument can be made that the same forces operated
in other Deep South states. Studies of Georgia and South Carolina also note
antipartyism, weak organizations, and many voters' spontaneous reaction to
Lincoln's election. Like numerous contemporaries, one southern moderate
sensed "a wild & somewhat hysterical excitement in all the Southern States
and especially in the tier of States from South Carolina west, to the Mississippi."[62] In Mississippi thousands of voters provided overwhelming popular
support for secession out of varied individual motives; but it was the fateful
combination of a noninstitutional political culture, and a personality structure based on honor with a particular understanding of masculinity that
created the atmosphere demanding a defiant, bold, and potentially deadly
response to the "galling insult" of Republicanism. Immediate secession offered men the most satisfying political action that linked communal manhood and individual, family, and community honor.

Appendix: Methodological Notes and Study Data

Election Returns

Statewide election data were collected from the *Tribune Almanac*, various newspapers, particularly the *Mississippian*, and manuscript returns in the Secretary of State Records, Mississippi Department of Archives and History (MDAH) (see bibliography for a detailed reference list). Most county and local returns were gathered from the manuscript collection in the MDAH and supplemented by newspaper accounts. To gauge the extent, or depth, of partisans voting, I designated the vote for governor as a partisan "base line" for comparison with returns for county and precinct offices. Estimates of voter turnout and ecological regression use data from all counties.

Census Underenumeration and Turnout

Historians have long debated the issue of how many people were missed by nineteenth-century census takers. Among political historians, this controversy has focused on estimating the number of eligible voters, which then determines turnout. To make my calculations comparable to other studies, I adjusted census figures upward by 10 percent (probably the most common figure used) when calculating eligible voters. I am unconvinced that this is a necessary adjustment. Numerous studies demonstrate that nonvoters were overwhelmingly the poorest Americans who moved the most often; longtime residents voted and ran for office more often and dominated local politics. For these reasons, official census figures may actually be more historically meaningful (for political, though not for social history) than adjusted totals that may or may not be more "accurate." Underenumeration was also more common among immigrants, free blacks (both groups were a minor factor in antebellum Mississippi), and people who moved most often—none of whom were eligible voters, at least by statute. I believe, therefore, that the historically significant voter turnout in Mississippi was probably over 80 percent in most elections, considerably higher than the figures shown in tables 4.1 and 4.3.[1]

Sample Counties

The great majority of county and local returns came from seventeen counties in the primary sample: Amite, Attala, Bolivar, Carroll, Chickasaw, Claiborne, Harrison, Hinds, Jasper, Lafayette, Lowndes, Madison, Marshall, Panola, Tippah, Tishomingo, and Wilkinson. These counties were selected for several reasons: (1) geographic distribution throughout the state; (2) range of socioeconomic patterns, from mostly plantation and cotton (Bolivar, Claiborne), to mixed agriculture (Hinds, Madison), to upcountry subsistence (Tishomingo), to piney woods (Harrison, Jasper); (3) age of settlement, from old (Claiborne, Amite) to young (Bolivar); (4) stage of development, from expanding (Bolivar, Jasper, Tishomingo), to "stagnant" (Harrison, Carroll), to losing population (Wilkinson, Marshall, Chickasaw); (5) total population (i.e. density of settlement); (6) presence or absence of newspapers or two competing party papers (Carroll, Claiborne, Hinds, Lowndes, Marshall, Lafayette); and (7) quality of surviving election returns. I included other counties in some instances (Warren, Adams, Rankin, Jefferson) to demonstrate particular trends or to accommodate special elections, unusual surviving records, or data from the two largest towns (Natchez and Vicksburg). I excluded Adams and Warren counties from the primary sample (despite excellent records) because of their early maturation and unusually large towns, both of which made them more cosmopolitan and socioeconomically advanced than most of the state. However, by including Jackson, Carrollton, Holly Springs, Columbus, Paulding, Port Gibson, and other medium-sized towns, I avoided unfairly neglecting "urban" areas. If anything, the record underrepresents rural counties, as it usually does, because their election returns were less likely to be published or to survive.

Elections and Offices

I excluded, from most calculations, including roll-off, contests for magistrates, militia officers, and town officials. These elections were most consistently nonpartisan, both from tradition (especially magistrates and militia officers) and circumstances. It seemed unreasonable to include them, given the argument for antipartyism I make here; moreover, these elections were often nonpartisan in other parts of the country as well. (Their inclusion, of course, would greatly strengthen the case for Mississippi's antiparty political culture.) Surviving returns for these offices were often inconsistent or incompletely reported (especially municipal and militia elections). In addition, district boundaries and rules for militia elections changed often enough to make such comparisons over time extremely difficult. Finally, these offices were most often uncontested.

Roll-off

The calculations for roll-off are based on aggregate totals, not individual voting data from poll books. They compare the number of votes cast for governor and for five county offices at the same polls on the same days (and are, therefore, unaffected by the underenumeration/turnout controversy). The counties included (see table 4.2) presented the most consistent surviving returns for the period between 1841 and 1855 among the primary sample of counties. I included returns from all elections with two or more candidates, regardless of how competitive they were. Thus the sample includes numerous contests in which one man was the overwhelming choice, which reduced turnout for those offices. These figures, therefore, exaggerate the roll-off in competitive contests, many of which had higher turnouts than elections for state-level positions.

County and Local Candidates

The principal basis of chapter 6 was a catalog of data on 1,425 candidates for county and local offices collected from seven of the sample counties (Amite, Bolivar, Carroll, Claiborne, Harrison, Hinds, and Jasper) and drawn from the surviving records of all regular and special elections held between 1849 and 1860. I included the following offices: representative, sheriff, treasurer, circuit court clerk, probate court clerk, assessor, coroner, ranger, surveyor (all chosen at the county level) and policeman, justice of the peace, and constable (elected in precincts). The total number of contests in the seven sample counties, counting six regular and several hundred special elections, was approximately two thousand. I located as many of the candidates as possible in the 1850 and 1860 manuscript schedules of the federal census and others in county tax records and other sources, including county histories. In all, 1,191 men appeared in at least one census, and numerous others were found in county tax rolls. These records provided biographical data on about 90 percent of all candidates.

The summaries of candidates for each office within five of the sample counties appear in tables A.1–A.16. Similar data from additional sample counties is in Olsen, "Community, Honor, and Secession," 336–50.

Categories and Calculations

Average Residency. I assigned fifteen years of residency to candidates appearing in both censuses and five and a half years to those listed in only one.

TABLE A.1. Total Sample of County and Precinct Candidates, 1849–1860

All Candidates	1,425
% in 1850 or 1860 census	84
% in 1850 and 1860 censuses	35
% Slaveowners	64
% Property owners	89
Average years of residency	9.5
% Slaveowners among male heads of household in all sample counties, 1850	59
% Slaveowners among male heads of household in all sample counties, 1860	59

Source: Record Group 28, Mississippi Department of Archives and History; U.S. Census, 1850 and 1860, Population and Slave Schedules, Amite, Bolivar, Carroll, Claiborne, Harrison, Hinds, and Jasper counties.

Note: Percentage calculations, of course, are based on candidates actually located in one or both censuses, not on the total number of candidates. Of the 1,425 candidates 1,191 (84 percent) appear in either the 1850 or 1860 census or in both. Of those 1,191 men, 768 (64 percent) owned slaves and 1,065 (89 percent) owned property of some kind. These categories were calculated in the same way for each county.

Most men who appeared in both censuses were permanent residents and lived twenty years or more in the same location. Some of those listed in only one census appear in the one most distant in time from their candidacy (e.g., a man who ran for office in 1851 but appears only in the 1860 census clearly lived at least nine years in the area). Finally, some portion of those who appeared only in the 1850 census were absent in 1860 because of death and not migration. Thus, the figure of nine and a half years of average residency for all candidates probably errs on the low side.

Overall Rates of Slaveholding and Property Ownership. In each county, I tallied the number of male owners in the slave schedules. I divided that figure by the total number of households in each county and multiplied by 0.95 to compensate for those headed by women. This produced an estimated percentage of adult male heads of household who owned slaves. I used these figures for all residents for comparisons with those for men who became

TABLE A.2. Amite County: All County and Precinct Candidates, 1849–1860

Total Candidates	197
% in 1850 or 1860 census	84
% in 1850 and 1860 censuses	37
% Slaveowners	72
% Property owners	95
Average years of residency	9.7
% Slaveowners among male heads of household in entire county, 1850	72
% Slaveowners among male heads of household in entire county, 1860	74

Source: Record Group 28, Mississippi Department of Archives and History; U.S. Census, 1850 and 1860, Population and Slave Schedules, Amite County.

TABLE A.3. Amite County: County Candidates by Office, 1849–1860

	Representative	Sheriff & Treasurer	Clerks & Assessor	Ranger, Coroner & Surveyor
Total Candidates	13	13	27	11
% in 1850 or 1860 census	100	92	96	82
% in 1850 and 1860 censuses	61	61	38	64
% Slaveowners	100	83	85	89
% Property owners	100	92	100	100
Average age	37.9	36.7	29.4	35.9
Average no. of slaves	30.9	12.0	3.6	5.8
Average value of property ($)	24,653	13,350	4,453	4,782

Source: Record Group 28, Mississippi Department of Archives and History; U.S. Census, 1850 and 1860, Population and Slave Schedules, Amite County.

Note: The averages shown, of course, are based on the candidates located in one or both censuses, not on the total number of candidates. For example, twelve of the thirteen candidates for sheriff or treasurer (92 percent) were found in either the 1850 or 1860 census or in both. Of those twelve men, ten (83 percent) owned slaves, and eleven (92 percent) owned property of some kind. The average age of those twelve men when they ran for office was 36.7 years; they averaged ownership of twelve slaves and $13,350 worth of property. These categories were calculated in the same way for all precinct and county candidates in each county.

TABLE A.4. Amite County: Precinct Candidates by Office, 1849–1860

	Board of Police	Justice of the Peace	Constable
Total Candidates	35	50	60
% in 1850 or 1860 census	83	90	75
% in 1850 and 1860 censuses	43	34	20
% Slaveowners	97	69	51
% Property owners	100	100	82
Average age	34.1	36.9	34.3
Average no. of slaves	9.8	4.0	1.6
Average value of property ($)	9,497	4,329	2,702

Source: Record Group 28, Mississippi Department of Archives and History; U.S. Census, 1850 and 1860, Population and Slave Schedules, Amite County.

TABLE A.5. Carroll County: All County and Precinct Candidates, 1849–1860

Total Candidates	310
% in 1850 or 1860 census	87
% in 1850 and 1860 censuses	41
% Slaveowners	70
% Property owners	84
Average years of residency	9.9
% Slaveowners among male heads of household in entire county, 1850	62
% Slaveowners among male heads of household in entire county, 1860	67

Source: Record Group 28, Mississippi Department of Archives and History; U.S. Census, 1850 and 1860, Population and Slave Schedules, Carroll County.

TABLE A.6. Carroll County: County Candidates by Office, 1849–1860

	Representative	Sheriff & Treasurer	Clerks & Assessor	Ranger, Coroner & Surveyor
Total Candidates	16	15	23	24
% in 1850 or 1860 census	100	100	91	79
% in 1850 and 1860 censuses	63	73	48	46
% Slaveowners	81	87	76	58
% Property owners	100	93	86	79
Average age	36.3	39.0	33.8	39.7
Average no. of slaves	15.7	7.3	3.4	.9
Average value of property ($)	20,094	9,107	4,690	1,902

Source: Record Group 28, Mississippi Department of Archives and History; U.S. Census, 1850 and 1860, Population and Slave Schedules, Carroll County.

TABLE A.7. Carroll County: Precinct Candidates by Office, 1849–1860

	Board of Police	Justice of the Peace	Constable
Total Candidates	40	88	102
% in 1850 or 1860 census	88	90	83
% in 1850 and 1860 censuses	45	47	24
% Slaveowners	89	78	52
% Property owners	94	90	75
Average age	41.5	37.0	33.3
Average no. of slaves	13.1	5.8	2.8
Average value of property ($)	12,742	5,539	2,411

Source: Record Group 28, Mississippi Department of Archives and History; U.S. Census, 1850 and 1860, Population and Slave Schedules, Carroll County.

TABLE A.8. Harrison County: All County and Precinct Candidates, 1849–1860

Total Candidates	177
% in 1850 or 1860 census	68
% in 1850 and 1860 censuses	24
% Slaveowners	39
% Property owners	84
Average years of residency	8.9
% Slaveowners among male heads of household in entire county, 1850	33
% Slaveowners among male heads of household in entire county, 1860	25

Source: Record Group 28, Mississippi Department of Archives and History; U.S. Census, 1850 and 1860, Population and Slave Schedules, Harrison County.

candidates. I calculated property owners in the same manner, counting any-one who held real estate or slaves as a property owner.

Age: The age at which a candidate first ran for an office.

Number of slaves: Based on either the 1850 or 1860 slave schedules. If a man appears in both censuses, I pro-rated his slaveholding to correspond to the year in which he ran for office. If, for example, he ran for sheriff in 1855 and recorded ten slaves in 1850 and twenty in 1860, I credited him with fifteen slaves the year he ran for office.

Value of property: This figure was calculated in the same manner as the number of slaves owned, including pro-rating for men who appear in both censuses. In addition, the 1850 census includes real but not slaves in the "property" column. To adjust for this fact, I assigned each slave an average

TABLE A.9. Harrison County: County Candidates by Office, 1849–1860

	Representative	Sheriff & Treasurer	Clerks & Assessor	Ranger, Coroner & Surveyor
Total Candidates	7	25	18	27
% in 1850 or 1860 census	71	72	50	56
% in 1850 and 1860 censuses	71	28	17	22
% Slaveowners	100	44	42	27
% Property owners	100	94	67	60
Average age	36.2	35.7	33.7	37.9
Average no. of slaves	7.8	2.4	1.4	.5
Average value of property ($)	8,800	4,133	2,017	1,037

Source: Record Group 28, Mississippi Department of Archives and History; U.S. Census, 1850 and 1860, Population and Slave Schedules, Harrison County.

TABLE A.10. Harrison County: Precinct Candidates by Office, 1849–1860

	Board of Police	Justice of the Peace	Constable
Total Candidates	34	41	27
% in 1850 or 1860 census	79	76	70
% in 1850 and 1860 censuses	29	23	26
% Slaveowners	48	39	11
% Property owners	93	90	74
Average age	42.7	40.6	36.3
Average no. of slaves	4.6	.8	.3
Average value of property ($)	3,320	1,769	726

Source: Record Group 28, Mississippi Department of Archives and History; U.S. Census, 1850 and 1860, Population and Slave Schedules, Harrison County.

TABLE A.11. Hinds County: All County and Precinct Candidates, 1849–1860

Total Candidates	285
% in 1850 or 1860 census	87
% in 1850 and 1860 censuses	38
% Slaveowners	69
% Property owners	91
Average years of residency	9.7
% Slaveowners among male heads of household in entire county, 1850	67
% Slaveowners among male heads of household in entire county, 1860	76*

Source: Record Group 28, Mississippi Department of Archives and History; U.S. Census, 1850 and 1860, Population and Slave Schedules, Hinds County.
  *Estimated total.

TABLE A.12. Hinds County: County Candidates by Office, 1849–1860

	Representative	Sheriff & Treasurer	Clerks & Assessor	Ranger, Coroner & Surveyor
Total Candidates	24	16	21	19
% in 1850 or 1860 census	92	88	86	89
% in 1850 and 1860 censuses	54	50	43	32
% Slaveowners	86	79	72	47
% Property owners	95	93	94	76
Average age	40.9	40.1	29.0	32.2
Average no. of slaves	21.8	9.5	5.1	3.5
Average value of property ($)	27,476	7,578	5,361	5,060

Source: Record Group 28, Mississippi Department of Archives and History; U.S. Census, 1850 and 1860, Population and Slave Schedules, Hinds County.

TABLE A.13. Hinds County: Precinct Candidates by Office, 1849–1860

	Board of Police	Justice of the Peace	Constable
Total Candidates	30	72	60
% in 1850 or 1860 census	93	88	77
% in 1850 and 1860 censuses	64	38	22
% Slaveowners	82	81	41
% Property owners	93	92	80
Average age	41.1	37.8	34.2
Average no. of slaves	19.0	7.1	1.4
Average value of property ($)	22,764	7,440	1,847

Source: Record Group 28, Mississippi Department of Archives and History; U.S. Census, 1850 and 1860, Population and Slave Schedules, Hinds County.

TABLE A.14. Jasper County: All County and Precinct Candidates, 1849–1860

Total Candidates	204
% in 1850 or 1860 census	87
% in 1850 and 1860 censuses	35
% Slaveowners	57
% Property owners	93
Average years of residency	9.4
% Slaveowners among male heads of household in entire county, 1850	43
% Slaveowners among male heads of household in entire county, 1860	46

Source: Record Group 28, Mississippi Department of Archives and History; U.S. Census, 1850 and 1860, Population and Slave Schedules, Jasper County.

TABLE A.15. Jasper County: County Candidates by Office, 1849–1860

	Representative	Sheriff & Treasurer	Clerks & Assessor	Ranger, Coroner & Surveyor
Total Candidates	10	15	23	20
% in 1850 or 1860 census	100	93	91	80
% in 1850 and 1860 censuses	60	73	30	20
% Slaveowners	90	93	57	69
% Property owners	100	100	95	81
Average age	39.9	35.9	34.9	41.1
Average no. of slaves	16.8	2.6	2.2	3.2
Average value of property ($)	15,004	4,442	3,618	3,447

Source: Record Group 28, Mississippi Department of Archives and History; U.S. Census, 1850 and 1860, Population and Slave Schedules, Jasper County.

TABLE A.16. Jasper County: Precinct Candidates by Office, 1849–1860

	Board of Police	Justice of the Peace	Constable
Total Candidates	40	58	37
% in 1850 or 1860 census	93	88	70
% in 1850 and 1860 censuses	48	29	32
% Slaveowners	65	45	38
% Property owners	92	88	77
Average age	36.9	36.9	32.5
Average no. of slaves	5.1	2.2	1.0
Average value of property ($)	6,817	3,413	1,570

Source: Record Group 28, Mississippi Department of Archives and History; U.S. Census, 1850 and 1860, Population and Slave Schedules, Jasper County.

value of $500. Thus, a man who owned ten slaves in 1850 was credited with $5,000 worth of property in addition to the real estate he reported.

Family and Property: I counted the slaves owned and value of property held by their parents for men who were still living at home. These men made up a very small part of the sample, just under 1.5 percent.

Extreme Outliers. A small number of men were omitted from the calculations in tables A.3 thru A.16 because of extreme variation. For example, there were thirty-seven candidates for constable in Jasper County, of whom twenty-six were located in the census. One man was seventy-six years old when he ran for office. As no other candidate was over sixty years old, including him would have increased the average age by 2.8 years; I therefore excluded him as an extreme outlier. Exclusions of this kind amounted to approximately 1.5 percent of the total sample.

Election Officials. Data on these men were correlated in the same manner as those for voters and candidates. All biographical information included in the text comes from the manuscript schedules of the federal census in 1850 and/or 1860, unless otherwise cited.

Categorization of Offices. The grouping of county offices was based on average turnout and on apparent interest among voters. Sheriff, treasurer, assessor, and court clerks typically drew the most attention from voters; other county offices were more often uncontested or less competitive, resulting in lower turnout. Sheriff and treasurer also required candidates to post the largest bonds for surety. For all these reasons, I grouped the offices before making any comparative calculations of average wealth, residency, or slave ownership of candidates.

Conclusion

The figures shown in tables A.1–A.16 should be considered estimates only; they do, however, accurately reflect the hierarchy of public offices in Mississippi.

Notes

The following abbreviations are used in the notes and bibliography.

MDAH   Mississippi Department of Archives and History, Jackson, Mississippi.
SHC   Southern Historical Collection, University of North Carolina, Chapel Hill, North Carolina.
Duke   Perkins Library, Duke University, Durham, North Carolina.
BHMM   *Biographical and Historical Memoirs of Mississippi*, 2 vols. Chicago, 1891.
PMHS   *Publications of the Mississippi Historical Society*
AHR   *American Historical Review*
APSR   *American Political Science Review*
JAH   *Journal of American History*
JER   *Journal of the Early Republic*
JIH   *Journal of Interdisciplinary History*
JMH   *Journal of Mississippi History*
JSH   *Journal of Southern History*
WMQ   *William and Mary Quarterly*

Introduction

1. The incident is outlined in a letter from Thomas J. Humphries to J. F. H. Claiborne (hereafter JFHC), Nov. 15, 1855, JFHC Collection, MDAH.

2. I found no record of a duel; if a confrontation occurred, it was not fatal: Seal lived until 1907, and Saffold attended the 1857 Democratic Party convention in Jackson. *BHMM*, 2: 732; *Mississippian and State Gazette*, July 1, 1857.

3. On the psychological transformation that accompanied a shift from personal to institutional relationships, see Norbert Elias, *The Civilizing Process: The Development of Manners, Changes in the Code of Conduct and Feeling in Early Modern Times*, trans. Edmund Jephcott (Basel, Germany, 1939; reprint, New York, 1978), 191–205 and *passim*. Elias uses the term *personality structure* to describe the interaction of individual psychology with social forms or institutions in which the former is

shaped by the latter. See also Kristen B. Neuschel, *Word of Honor: Interpreting Noble Culture in Sixteenth-century France* (Ithaca, 1989), 103–131, 186–208; David Warren Sabean, *Power in the Blood: Popular Culture and Village Discourse in Early Modern Germany* (Cambridge, 1983), 30–36, 174–213; and Joanne Freeman, "Dueling and Politics: Reinterpreting the Burr-Hamilton Duel," WMQ 52 (1996): 289–318. European historians have surpassed Americanists in recognizing the importance of dueling and politics. Among others, see Kevin McAleer, *Dueling: The Cult of Honor in Fin-de-Siècle Germany* (Princeton, 1994); James Kelly, *That Damn'd Thing Called Honour: Dueling in Ireland, 1570–1860* (Cork, 1995); and Robert A. Nye, *Masculinity and Male Codes of Honor in Modern France* (New York, 1993).

4. William L. Barney, *The Secessionist Impulse: Alabama and Mississippi in 1860* (Princeton, 1974), 191.

5. For works that take a similar approach, see J. Mills Thornton III, *Politics and Power in a Slave Society: Alabama, 1800–1860* (Baton Rouge, 1978); and Stephanie McCurry, *Masters of Small Worlds: Yeoman Households, Gender Relations, and the Political Culture of the Antebellum South Carolina Low Country* (New York, 1995).

6. Ronald P. Formisano, "Deferential-Participant Politics: The Early Republic's Political Culture," APSR 68 (1974): 473–87, esp. 483–85. Earlier studies of antebellum Mississippi concluding that parties became widely accepted by the late 1830s include M. Philip Lucas, "The Development of the Second Party System in Mississippi, 1817–1846" (Ph.D. diss., Cornell University, 1983); Dale Prentiss, "Economic Progress and Social Dissent in Michigan and Mississippi, 1837–1861" (Ph.D. diss., Stanford University, 1990); Bradley Bond, *Political Culture in the Nineteenth-century South: Mississippi, 1830–1910* (Baton Rouge, 1995); and Barney, *Secessionist Impulse*.

7. With varying emphasis, this argument can be traced in: Eugene D. Genovese, *The Political Economy of Slavery* (New York, 1965); Michael P. Johnson, *Toward a Patriarchal Republic: The Secession of Georgia* (Baton Rouge, 1977); James Oakes, *The Ruling Race: A History of American Slaveholders* (New York, 1982); Steven Hahn, *The Roots of Southern Populism: Yeoman Farmers and the Transformation of the Georgia Upcountry, 1850–1890* (New York, 1983); and Barney, *Secessionist Impulse*.

8. Thornton, *Politics and Power*; Prentiss, "Economic Progress and Social Dissent"; Samuel C. Hyde Jr., *Pistols and Politics: The Dilemma of Democracy in Louisiana's Florida Parishes, 1810–1899* (Baton Rouge, 1996); Lacy K. Ford, *Origins of Southern Radicalism: The South Carolina Upcountry, 1800–1860* (New York, 1988).

9. William Cooper, Jr., *Liberty and Slavery: Southern Politics to 1860* (New York, 1983); Eric Walther, *The Fire-Eaters* (Baton Rouge, 1992); William Freehling, *The Road to Disunion*, vol. 1, *Secessionists at Bay, 1776–1854* (New York, 1990); Thornton, *Politics and Power*. Thornton concludes that secession was ultimately popular but was managed by politicians working within Alabama's Jacksonian political culture; disunion was, he argues, a popular response conditioned over the years by southern parties and politicians (291–306, 312–313, 457). Bond, in *Political Culture*, argues that Mississippi voters chose secession (a populist movement) to ensure access to their version of success and good citizenship (their political economy) and to prevent a loss of liberty. Unlike other studies, Bond finds that 1850s Mississippians embraced progressive economic development. McCurry, in *Masters of Small Worlds*,

concludes that secession was popular (296–98), but also notes planters' anxieties and suggests that they manipulated the final crisis (255–57, 278–83).

10. George C. Rable, *The Confederate Republic: A Revolution Against Politics* (Chapel Hill, 1994), esp. 10–38; Kenneth Greenberg, *Masters and Statesmen: The Political Culture of American Slavery* (Baltimore, 1985), 107–146, esp. 125, 134–35; Thornton, *Politics and Power*; J. William Harris, *Plain Folk and Gentry in a Slave Society: White Liberty and Black Slavery in Augusta's Hinterlands* (Middletown, Conn., 1985), 132–33, 137. Harris also emphasizes internal class conflict and whites' fears of racial annihilation, which are also featured in Barney, *Secessionist Impulse*; and Steven Channing, *Crisis of Fear: Secession in South Carolina* (New York, 1970).

11. Michael F. Holt, *The Political Crisis of the 1850s* (New York, 1978), esp. 230–52, 255–58. His recent work more firmly asserts that secession can only be explained through party politics, see *Political Parties and American Political Development from the Age of Jackson to the Age of Lincoln* (Baton Rouge, 1992), esp. 10–15. See also Daniel W. Crofts, *Reluctant Confederates: Upper South Unionists in the Secession Crisis* (Chapel Hill, 1989); Percy Lee Rainwater, *Mississippi: Storm Center of Secession 1856–1861* (New York, 1938); and Thomas Alexander, "The Civil War as Institutional Fulfillment," *JSH* 47 (1981): 3–32.

12. William E. Gienapp, *The Origins of the Republican Party, 1852–1856* (New York, 1987); Ronald P. Formisano, *The Birth of Mass Political Parties: Michigan, 1827–1861* (Princeton, 1971).

13. Ronald P. Formisano, *The Transformation of Political Culture: Massachusetts Parties, 1790s–1840s* (New York, 1983), 3–5; Paul F. Bourke and Donald DeBats, *Washington County: Politics and Community in Antebellum America* (Baltimore, 1995); Samuel P. Hays, "Society and Politics; Politics and Society," *JIH* 15 (1985): 481–99. On political discourse and how it is grounded in and must be assessed as part of the "material existence" and "the collective and value-laden assumptions of the people," see Jay M. Smith, "No More Language Games: Words, Beliefs, and the Political Culture of Early Modern France," *AHR* 102 (1997): 1439 (quote), 1413–40. Political scientists who emphasize attitudes or "evaluational and affective orientations" draw especially on the work of Gabriel Almond and Sidney Verba, *The Civic Culture: Political Attitudes and Democracy in Five Nations* (Princeton, 1963; reprint, Boston, 1965). The tradition in political history that concentrates on national elections, parties, elites, and ideology is well represented by Eric Foner, *Free Soil, Free Labor, Free Men: The Ideology of the Republican Party before the Civil War* (New York, 1970); Michael Morrison, *Slavery and the American West: The Eclipse of Manifest Destiny and the Coming of the Civil War* (Chapel Hill, 1997); Anthony Gene Carey, *Parties, Slavery and the Union in Antebellum Georgia* (Athens, Ga., 1997).

14. Clifford Geertz, *The Interpretation of Cultures: Selected Essays* (New York, 1973), 412–53; Frank O'Gorman, "Campaign Rituals and Ceremonies: The Social Meaning of Elections in England," *Past and Present* 135 (1992): 79–115, esp. 81; Norma Basch, in "A Challenge to the Story of Popular Politics," *JAH* 84 (1997), cogently calls for more careful consideration of what politics, specifically the act of voting, meant to most voters (903). Mary Ryan, among others, has argued repeatedly for a broadened concept of political, or public, culture as the means to a new synthesis of American history; see her *Civic Wars: Democracy and Public Life in the American City During the Nineteenth Century* (Berkeley, 1997).

15. A vast literature details the relationship between individual opinion and group norms or cultural ethics, often describing it as the "map of opinions and personality" that shapes each person's political attitudes. Political discourse and voting behavior, then, can be used to uncover the "map" of past "inarticulate" persons. See, e.g., M. Brewster Smith, "Opinions, Personality, and Political Behavior," *APSR* 52 (1958): 1–25: "'*Public* opinion' implies not so much the contrast between public vs. private circumstances of expression, as the existence of *consensually defined issues* in the social group whose opinions are under consideration" (15). See also M. Brewster Smith, Jerome S. Bruner, and Robert W. White, *Opinions and Personality* (New York, 1956); Robert E. Lane, *Political Ideology: Why the American Common Man Believes What He Does* (New York, 1962); Murray Edelman, *The Symbolic Uses of Politics* (Urbana, 1964); Frank J. Sorauf, *Political Parties in the American System* (Boston, 1964); and Bernard Berelson, Paul Lazarsfeld, and William N. McFee, *Voting* (Chicago, 1954). Lazarsfeld and his colleagues emphasize the importance of primary-group identification, while subsequent scholars detail the "cross-pressures" that conflict it, as well as the force of other reference groups to which a person may or may not belong. On the importance of "reference group theory," see esp. Robert K. Merton, *Social Theory and Social Structure* (Glencoe, Ill., 1957). One study of southern history, linguistics, and oratory that takes the same position is Dickson D. Bruce Jr., *Violence and Culture in the Antebellum South* (Austin, 1979), chap. 8.

For the opposing point of view—that newspaper editors and politicians "shaped more than presented public opinion"—see Carey, *Parties, Slavery, and the Union*, 145; Barney, *Secessionist Impulse*, 81, although he sometimes implies the opposite (e.g., 196); and, to some extent, Thornton, *Politics and Power*, 227, 235.

16. Reuben Davis, *Recollections of Mississippi and Mississippians* (Boston and New York, 1890), 397–98 (emphasis added).

17. Kirsten E. Wood, "'One Woman So Dangerous to Public Morals': Gender and Power in the Eaton Affair," *JER* 17 (1997): 275. On the household as a basis for "gendered" political history, see McCurry, *Masters of Small Worlds*, esp. 5–22, 92–93, 235–38 (including nn. 54–56). Others who consider gender in political history include Laura Edwards, *Gendered Strife and Confusion: the Political Culture of Reconstruction* (Urbana, 1997); and Rebecca Edwards, *Angels in the Machinery: American Party Politics from the Civil War to the Progressive Era* (New York, 1997).

18. David Gilmore, *Manhood in the Making: Cultural Concepts of Masculinity* (New Haven, 1990), 1. On women in antebellum politics, see Elizabeth Varon, *We Mean to Be Counted: White Women and Politics in Antebellum Virginia* (Chapel Hill, 1998); and, for Mississippi, Christopher Olsen, "Respecting 'the wise allotment of our sphere': White Women and Politics in Mississippi, 1840–1860," *Journal of Women's History* 11 (1999): 104–125.

19. Ute Frevert, "Bourgeois Honour: Middle-Class Duellists in Germany from the Late Eighteenth to the Early Twentieth Century," in *The German Bourgeoisie: Essays on the Social History of the German Middle Class from the Late Eighteenth to the Early Twentieth Century*, ed. David Blackbourn and Richard J. Evans (London, 1991), 269; Julian Pitt-Rivers, "Honour," in *International Encyclopedia of the Social Sciences*, 17 vols., ed. David L. Sills, (New York, 1968), 6: 503–511; Bertram Wyatt-Brown, *Southern Honor: Ethics and Behavior in the Old South* (New York, 1983); Edward Ayers, *Vengeance and Justice: Crime and Punishment in the Nine-*

teenth-century American South (New York, 1984). On language and honor, see esp. Steven M. Stowe, *Intimacy and Power in the Old South: Ritual in the Lives of the Planters* (Baltimore, 1987); and Neuschel, *Word of Honor*, x–xii, 115–31, 192–96.

20. David Gilmore, *Honor and Shame and the Unity of the Mediterranean* (Washington, D. C., 1987), 3. The clearest and most careful examination of how these issues of honor, family, and class evolved within one southern community is Orville Vernon Burton, *In My Father's House Are Many Mansions: Family and Community in Edgefield, South Carolina* (Chapel Hill, 1985).

21. Kenneth Greenberg, *Honor and Slavery: Lies, Duels, Noses, Masks, Dressing as a Woman, Gifts, Strangers, Humanitarianism, Death, Slave Rebellions, the Proslavery Argument, Baseball, Hunting, and Gambling in the Old South* (Princeton, 1996), xii–xiv (quote), 24–50; Orlando Patterson, *Slavery and Social Death: A Comparative Study* (Cambridge, Mass., 1982).

22. Similarly, studies that, like this one, rely more on actual voting returns and census data tend to emphasize residence and kinship as the paramount factors in voting. See Daniel W. Crofts, *Old Southampton: Politics and Society in a Virginia County, 1834–1869* (Charlottesville, Va., 1992); Bourke and DeBats, *Washington County*; Robert C. Kenzer, *Kinship and Neighborhood in a Southern Community: Orange County, North Carolina, 1849–1881* (Knoxville, 1987).

23. Joel Silbey, *The American Political Nation, 1838–1893* (Stanford, 1991), 31, 33. See also William E. Gienapp, "'Politics Seem to Enter into Everything': Political Culture in the North, 1840–1860," in *Essays on American Antebellum Politics, 1840–1860*, ed. Stephen E. Maizlish and John J. Kushma (College Station, Texas, 1982), 14–69. For the Upper South and the evolution of a partisan political culture that relegated antipartyism to the margins, see Crofts, *Reluctant Confederates*; William G. Shade, *Democratizing the Old Dominion: Virginia and the Second Party System, 1824–1861* (Charlottesville, 1996); Harry Watson, *Jacksonian Politics and Community Conflict: The Emergence of the Second American Party System in Cumberland County, North Carolina* (Baton Rouge, 1978); and Thomas E. Jeffrey, *State Parties and National Politics: North Carolina, 1815–1861* (Athens, Ga., 1989).

Studies that emphasize partisanship throughout the entire South include Silbey, *American Political Nation*, 41; and William J. Cooper, *The South and the Politics of Slavery 1828–1856* (Baton Rouge, 1978).

24. The classic study of colonial political culture, much of which also applies to antebellum Mississippi, remains Charles S. Sydnor, *Gentlemen Freeholders: Political Practices in Washington's Virginia* (Chapel Hill, 1952). See also Alan Taylor, "'The Art of Hook and Snivey': Political Culture in Upstate New York During the 1790s," *JAH* 90 (1993): 1371–95; and John Kolp, *Gentlemen and Freeholders: Electoral Politics in Colonial Virginia* (Baltimore, 1998). Studies of antebellum southern communities that trace the importance of kin networks and neighborhoods in politics include Christopher Morris, *Becoming Southern: The Evolution of a Way of Life, Warren County and Vicksburg, Mississippi, 1770–1860* (New York, 1995); Burton, *In My Father's House*; Kenzer, *Kinship and Neighborhood*; and Crofts, *Old Southampton*.

Chapter 1

1. Kirby quoted in Robert Haynes, "Law Enforcement in Frontier Mississippi," *JMH* 22 (1960): 34; John Q. Anderson, ed., "The Narrative of John Hutchins," *JMH* 20 (1958): 29.

2. John C. Burrus, "My Recollections of the Early Days of Bolivar County," in *History of Bolivar County, Mississippi, Compiled by Florence Warfield Sillers*, ed. Wirt A. Williams (Jackson, Miss., 1948), 102–104; John H. Lang, *History of Harrison County Mississippi* (Gulfport, Miss., 1936), 15–16; and Duncan McKenzie (hereafter DMcK) to Duncan McLaurin (hereafter DMcL), June 6, 1843, Duncan McLaurin Papers (hereafter DMP), Duke.

3. Burrus, "My Recollections," 102, "Mrs. Rosina Culp McGuire," 564–65, and "Archibald McGehee and Family," 474–77, all in Williams, ed., *Bolivar County*; John and Polly Colvin, quoted in Oakes, *Ruling Race*, 86; William Lowndes Lipscomb, *A History of Columbus Mississippi during the Nineteenth Century* (Birmingham, Ala., 1909), 37–38; Everett Dick, *The Dixie Frontier: A Comprehensive Picture of Southern Frontier Life before the Civil War* (New York, 1948; reprint, New York, 1964), 211.

4. Bond, *Political Culture*, 29–30; "Roads in Bolivar County," 63–65, Burrus, "My Recollections," 102–103, "Autobiographical Sketch of W. H. (Tony) Arnold," 393–401, and Ethel Burrus Sutherland, "Judge John Crawford Burrus and Family," 412, all in Williams, ed., *Bolivar County*; John H. Napier III, "Piney Woods Past: A Pastoral Elegy," in *Mississippi's Piney Woods: A Human Perspective*, ed. Noel Polk (Jackson, Miss., 1986), 16.

5. Lipscomb, *Columbus Mississippi*, 37–38; J. F. H. Claiborne, "A Trip Through the Piney Woods," *PMHS* 9 (1906): 490, 491. For the transformation of Vicksburg and the importance of roads, see Morris, *Becoming Southern*, esp. 103–155; William C. Davis, *A Way through the Wilderness: The Natchez Trace and the Civilization of the Southern Frontier* (New York, 1995); and Thomas Battle Carroll, *Historical Sketches of Oktibbeha County* (Gulfport, Miss., 1931), 52–53.

6. Joseph G. Baldwin, *The Flush Times of Alabama and Mississippi: A Series of Sketches*, introduction and notes by James H. Justus (New York, 1853; reprint, Baton Rouge, 1987), 88–89, 107–108.

7. Robert W. Dubay, *John Jones Pettus: Mississippi Fire-Eater: His Life and Times* (Jackson, Miss., 1975), 112; Professor Ferris quoted in Napier, "Piney Woods Past," 17. See also Joseph Holt Ingraham, *The South-West By a Yankee*, 2 vols. (New York, 1835), 2: 171–72.

8. Claiborne, "Piney Woods," 514–17; William Henry Sparks, *The Memories of Fifty Years* (Philadelphia, 1872), 331; Lipscomb, *Columbus Mississippi*, esp. 38–56.

9. Claiborne, "Piney Woods," 510 (quote); see also 491, 512, 520, 529.

10. Horace S. Fulkerson, *Random Recollections of Early Days in Mississippi* (Vicksburg, 1885; reprint, Baton Rouge, 1937), 12. For frontier Mississippi, see also "Autobiography of Gideon Lincecum," *PMHS* 8 (1904): 443–519; Bond, *Political Culture*, esp. 14–20; Thomas D. Clark and John D. Guice, *Frontiers in Conflict: The Old Southwest, 1795–1830* (Albuquerque, 1989); and David J. Libby, "Plantation and Frontier: Slavery in Mississippi, 1720–1835," (Ph.D. diss., University of Mississippi, 1997).

11. William Faulkner, *Absalom, Absalom!* (New York, 1986), 30; Sutherland, "Judge John Crawford Burrus and Family," in Williams, ed., *Bolivar County*, 412. See also Davis, *Through the Wilderness*, 47–50, 242–54; and Anderson, "Narrative of John Hutchins." On masculinity and hunting, see esp. Ted Ownby, *Subduing Satan:*

Religion, Recreation, and Manhood in the Rural South, 1865–1920 (Chapel Hill, 1990); Bruce, *Violence and Culture,* chap. 9.

12. Jesse M. Wilkins, "Early Times in Wayne County," *PMHS,* 6 (1902): 269; Lincecum, "Autobiography," 467; E. Anthony Rotundo, *American Manhood: Transformations in Masculinity from the Revolution to the Modern Era* (New York, 1993), 2–3. On the importance of relying on other men in the community to maintain order, especially through vigilante violence, see Christopher Waldrep, *Roots of Disorder: Race and Criminal Justice in the American South, 1817–80* (Urbana, 1998), esp. chaps. 2–3. Waldrep argues that antebellum Mississippians fostered a culture of community violence through their hostility to the institutional legal system.

13. Fulkerson, *Random Recollections,* 15. See also Wyatt-Brown, *Southern Honor,* pt. 2; Morris, *Becoming Southern,* 87–89; and Paul Escott, *Many Excellent People: Power and Privilege in North Carolina, 1850–1900* (Chapel Hill, 1985), 22–23.

14. Kenneth Stampp, *The Peculiar Institution: Slavery in the Ante-Bellum South* (New York, 1956), chap. 4; Frank F. Steel to "My dear Sister," Dec. 15, 1859, Frank F. Steel Letters, SHC; Christopher Morris, "An Event in Community Organization: The Mississippi Slave Insurrection Scare of 1835," *Journal of Social History* 22 (1988): 93–111; Libby, "Plantation and Frontier," 196–201, 251–87. Many scholars argue that these traits of aggressive masculinity and violence toward slaves were exaggerated in the Old Southwest. See Joan Cashin, *A Family Venture: Men and Women on the Southern Frontier* (Baltimore, 1991), 101–118.

15. Lyman Johnson and Sonya Lipsett-Rivera, eds., *The Faces of Honor: Sex, Shame, and Violence in Colonial Latin America* (Albuquerque, 1998), 3–5, and Mark Burkholder, "Honor and Honors in Colonial Spanish America," 18–44. This collection insightfully demonstrates honor's subtleties and its variations by class, gender, and region.

16. Citizens of North Mt. Pleasant to Governor Foote, Nov. 1852, Governor's Correspondence, MDAH. On manliness and physical form, see esp. Nicole Etcheson, "Manliness and the Political Culture of the Old Northwest, 1790–1860," *JER* 15 (1995): 61–68; Greenberg, "The Nose, the Lie, and the Duel in the Antebellum South," *AHR* 95 (1990): 57–74; Elliot J. Gorn, "'Gouge and Bite, Pull Hair and Scratch': The Social Significance of Fighting in the Southern Backcountry," *AHR* 90 (1985): 18–43.

17. On the early evangelical challenge to southern elites, see esp. Rhys Isaac, *The Transformation of Virginia, 1740–1790* (Chapel Hill, 1982); and Donald Mathews, *Religion in the Old South,* Chicago History of American Religion, ed. Martin E. Marty (Chicago, 1977), 10–38, 66–80.

18. Mathews, *Religion in the Old South,* 43 (quote), 41–46, 66–184, esp. 111–25. See also Mitchell Snay, *Gospel of Disunion: Religion and Separatism in the Antebellum South* (Cambridge, 1993), chap. 3; Eugene Genovese and Elizabeth Fox-Genovese, "The Religious Ideals of Southern Slave Society," *Georgia Historical Quarterly* 70 (1986): 1–16; Bertram Wyatt-Brown, "God and Honor in the Old South," *Southern Review* 25 (1989): 283–96; Edward Crowther, "Holy Honor: Sacred and Secular in the Old South," *JSH* 58 (1992): 619–36. On evangelical Christianity and secular hierarchy between men and women and between white men, see esp. McCurry, *Masters of Small Worlds, passim.*

19. Gilmore, *Manhood in the Making*, 14 (quote), and chap. 1, esp. 10–20; David Leverenz, *Manhood and the American Renaissance* (Ithaca, 1989), esp. 3–18, 34–52, 73–81, 108–109; and Michael Kimmel, *Manhood in America: A Cultural History* (New York, 1996), 7. See also Wallace Hettle, "The 'Self-Analysis' of John C. Rutherfoord: Democracy and Manhood of a Virginia Secessionist," *Southern Studies* 5 (1992): 81–116; and John Mayfield, "'The Soul of a Man': William Gilmore Simms and Myths of Southern Manhood," *JER* 15 (1995): 477–500. Southern and northern concepts of masculinity diverged in the nineteenth century. Yankee men increasingly emphasized work and the ability to provide financially, placing less value on physical prowess or loyalty. Coincident with urbanization and an autonomous society, this change tipped the balance toward individual and private considerations, especially self-control. See Rotundo, *American Manhood*, esp. 19–24. Elliot Gorn elucidates the changes in northern mainstream, middle-class manliness by contrasting it with an "underground" working-class model that looked much like the southern notion; see his "'Good-Bye, Boys: I Die a True American': Homicide, Nativism, and Working-class Culture in Antebellum New York City," *JAH* 74 (1987): 388–410.

20. Claiborne, "Piney Woods," 521–22; Gilmore, *Manhood in the Making*, 221.

21. Baldwin, *Flush Times*, xlvi, 190–91.

22. Wyatt-Brown, *Southern Honor*, 61; Rotundo, *American Manhood*, 14–17.

23. Fulkerson, *Random Recollections*, 16. The close relationship between hierarchy and honor in slave societies is detailed by Patterson, *Slavery and Social Death*; and Greenberg, *Honor and Slavery*. Two recent studies that emphasize the impact of slavery on household and gender relations, and on those between free men, are Morris, *Becoming Southern*, esp. 23–102, and McCurry, *Masters of Small Worlds*, esp. chap. 3.

24. Susan Dabney Smedes, *Memorials of a Southern Planter*, edited with an introduction and notes by Fletcher M. Green (New York, 1965), 53; James Byrne Ranck, *Albert Gallatin Brown: Radical Southern Nationalist* (New York, 1937), 31–32. See also Oakes, *Ruling Race*, esp. 69–95.

25. The early neighborhoods of Warren County, which was in the vanguard of socioeconomic development, presaged later growth in much of the state. See Morris's detailed discussion in *Becoming Southern*, esp. chaps. 2, 5–9; and Cashin, *Family Venture*, chap. 4. Neighborhoods often evolved in the same way among settlers to the rural Northwest. See John Mack Faragher, *Sugar Creek: Life on the Illinois Frontier* (New Haven, 1986), esp. 64–75, 130–70.

26. Charles Lowery, "The Great Migration to the Mississippi Territory, 1798–1819," *JMH* 30 (1968): 177–86; Porter L. Fortune, "The Formative Period," and John Edmond Gonzales, "Flush Times, Depression, War, and Compromise," both in *A History of Mississippi*, 2 vols., ed. Richard Aubrey McLemore (Hattiesburg, Miss., 1973), 1: 251–83, 284–309; Dunbar Rowland, *History of Mississippi: The Heart of the South*, vol. 1 (Chicago, 1925), 579–89; Hugh G. Brady, "Voting, Class and Demography in Antebellum Mississippi," (Master's thesis, Northern Illinois University, 1977), chap. 1; John Hebron Moore, *The Emergence of the Cotton Kingdom in the Old Southwest: Mississippi, 1770–1860* (Baton Rouge, 1988), 118; and Clark and Guice, *Frontiers in Conflict*, 161–83.

27. DMcK to DMcL, Feb. 25, 1838, June 20, 1842; Hugh Stewart (hereafter HS) to DMcL, Dec. 4, 1835, DMP; Morris, *Becoming Southern*, 88–89.

28. DMcK to Charles Patterson, Apr. 7, 1833; DMcK to John McLaurin (hereafter JMcL), May 11, 1834 DMP; Clark and Guice, *Frontiers in Conflict*, 181; Miss Mary J. Welsh, "Recollections of Pioneer Life in Mississippi," *PMHS* 4 (1901): 343. See also Dick, *Dixie Frontier*, 23–37, 63–77; and Faragher, *Sugar Creek*, 56–60, 144–55.

29. Welsh, "Recollections," 344; Dick, *Dixie Frontier*, 125–31, 199–201; Clark and Guice, *Frontiers in Conflict*, 191–99, 202–203; and Gregory Nobles, *American Frontiers: Cultural Encounters and Continental Conquest* (New York, 1997), 110–14.

30. Jonathan P. Stewart (hereafter JPS) to DMcL, June 20, 1831, Aug. 6, 1834; and Allan Stewart (hereafter AS) to DMcL, July 26, 1831, DMP.

31. Escott, *Many Excellent People*, 15–19; Kenzer, *Kinship and Neighborhood*, 12–13; Albert Ogden Parker, *County Government in Virginia: A Legislative History, 1607–1904* (New York, 1907), 182–87; Ralph Wooster, *The People in Power: Courthouse and Statehouse in the Lower South, 1850–1860* (Knoxville, 1969), 20–46, 82–111.

32. Edwin Arthur Miles, *Jacksonian Democracy in Mississippi* (Chapel Hill, 1961), 34–35; John W. Winkle, *The Mississippi State Constitution: A Reference Guide* (Westport, Conn., 1993), 5–7; Hon. R. H. Thompson, "Suffrage in Mississippi," *PMHS* 1 (1898): 25–49.

33. Rowland, *Mississippi*, 565–74; Miles, *Jacksonian Democracy*, 36–43; JPS to DMcL, Nov. 29, 1831, Aug. 9, 1843, DMP; *Mississippian*, June 29, 1849.

34. Miles, *Jacksonian Democracy*, 34; D. Clayton James; *Antebellum Natchez* (Baton Rouge, 1968); Charles Sackett Sydnor, *A Gentleman of the Old Natchez Region, Benjamin L. C. Wailes* (Durham, N.C., 1938); Rowland, *Mississippi*, 1: 507–564.

35. Miles, *Jacksonian Democracy*, 18–28.

36. Fortune, "Formative Period," 274–78; Gonzales, "Flush Times," 286–88; Miles, *Jacksonian Democracy*, 70–116; *Clinton Gazette*, Oct. 17, 1835.

37. Miles, *Jacksonian Democracy*, 32 (quote) 28–32.

38. J. W. Hardwick to Col. W. B. Campbell, Dec. 9, 1835, Campbell Family Papers; *Clinton Gazette*, Oct. 10, 1835; Lucas, "Second Party System," 84–86.

39. Lucas, "Second Party System," 18–19 (quote), 8–20; Miles, *Jacksonian Democracy*, 115. Robert May similarly attributes John Quitman's defeat in 1846 to his "ineptitude as a Jacksonian Era politician"; see his *John Anthony Quitman: Old South Crusader* (Baton Rouge, 1985), 129.

40. Lucas, "Second Party System," 389 (quote), 270–73, 325–89. See also Miles, *Jacksonian Democracy*: the convention system "had triumphed by 1839" (163).

41. *Mississippi Creole*, Oct. 23, 1841; and *Spirit of the Times*, May 15, 1841. Manuscript election returns are in Record Group 28 (Secretary of State), Mississippi Department of Archives and History, Jackson. A detailed guide to returns is included in the bibliography.

42. *Clinton Gazette*, Oct. 10, Oct. 17, 1835. See also DMcK to JMcL, Nov. 13, 1836, DMP.

43. "A Journey Through the South in 1836: Diary of James D. Davidson," *JSH* 1 (1935): 355. Rapacity and greed is also the central theme in Davis, *Through the Wilderness*.

44. Miles, *Jacksonian Democracy*, 130–45; Brady, "Voting, Class and Demography," 66–68.

45. Claiborne, "Piney Woods," 528, 518–19, 491; Orr, "A Trip from Houston to Jackson, Mississippi, in 1845," *PMHS* 9 (1906): 174; JPS to DMcL, July 30, 1840, Aug. 31, 1842.

46. *Independent Democrat*, Oct. 1, 1842; Rowland, *Mississippi*, 599–605; 611–25; Miles, *Jacksonian Democracy*, 146–56; Bond, *Political Culture*, 82–4.

47. *Mississippi House Journal*, 1841, quoted in Miles, *Jacksonian Democracy*, 156; J. A. P. Campbell, "Planter's and Union Bank Bonds," *PMHS* 3 (1901): 493–97.

48. *Vicksburg Daily Whig*, Sept. 14, 1843; JPS to DMcL, July 22, 1841, DMP. Bradley Bond argues that repudiation helped create the second party system in Mississippi, although it did not last as a partisan controversy. More important, he concludes, was the broader issue of establishing and maintaining liberty — economic and personal independence and virtue — and thereby avoiding "submission," a struggle which primarily defined the state's political economy. See *Political Culture*, 84–89, and *passim*.

49. DMcK to DMcL, Oct. 26, 1841, DMP; *Port-Gibson Correspondent*, Sept. 20, 1939; *Southron*, Nov. 1, 1843. See also JPS to DMcL, Dec. 10, 1841; DMcK to DMcL, July 31, 1842; JPS to DMcL, Mar. 24, 1842, DMP; *Vicksburg Daily Whig*, Sept. 2, 1845; *Hinds County Gazette*, May 28, 1845.

50. William K. Scarborough, "Heartland of the Cotton Kingdom," in McLemore, ed., *Mississippi*, 1:310–51; Prentiss, "Economic Dissent, 77–87. Prentiss argues severe depression destroyed people's confidence in the future, even after good times had returned. "Prosperity was . . . hoped for but neither to be expected nor trusted. The pace of change surprised nearly everyone, delighted almost no one" (54). This uneasy sentiment fostered a spirit of social dissent during the 1850s, one that, Prentiss concludes, helped the fire-eaters to play upon popular fears of economic change and lead the state out of the Union under the false issue of a threat to slavery. Bond, in *Political Culture*, argues more convincingly that Mississippians embraced the market and scrambled to accommodate internal improvements.

51. *Port-Gibson Herald*, July 17, 1845.

Chapter 2

1. Cleo Hearon, "Mississippi and the Compromise of 1850," *PMHS* 14 (1914): 45–60; *Mississippian*, Mar. 16, Apr. 20, 1849; and *Herald and Correspondent*, Apr. 27, 1849.

2. *Mississippian*, July 20, Sept. 28, 1849. See also *Gazette*, Nov. 15, 1850; and *Mississippian*, June 15, 1849.

3. *Mississippian*, Oct. 5 and 12, 1849; and *Vicksburg Daily Whig*, June 30, 1849.

4. *Herald and Correspondent*, Apr. 6, 1849.

5. *Canton Creole*, quoted in *Herald and Correspondent*, May 11, 1849; and *Vicksburg Daily Whig*, May 15, 1849.

6. *Herald and Correspondent*, June 8 and 29, 1849; *Vicksburg Weekly Whig*, May 1, 1849; and *Vicksburg Daily Whig*, May 15, 1849.

7. *Mississippian*, July 20, 1849. See also May, *Quitman*, 220–25; *Herald and Correspondent*, July 20, Aug. 10 and 17, and Sept. 14, 1849.

8. *Vicksburg Daily Whig*, Feb. 4, 1841; *Mississippian*, June 29, 1843; *Vicksburg Tri-Weekly Whig*, June 17, 1843; *Yazoo City Whig and Political Register*, Oct. 17, 1845; Brady, "Voting, Class and Demography," 90–95; *Mississippian*, Aug. 6, 1845;

Vicksburg Tri-Weekly Whig, Aug. 9 and Sept. 6, 1845; *Vicksburg Daily Whig*, Sept. 6, 1845.

9. *Vicksburg Tri-Weekly Whig*, Sept. 30, 1847; *Vicksburg Daily Whig*, Oct. 19 and 20, 1847; Benjamin Dill to John A. Quitman, Sept. 7, 1847, JFHC Collection.

10. *Herald and Correspondent*, June 8, 1849.

11. *Mississippian*, June 15, 1849; Feb. 23 and Apr. 13, 1849.

12. *Mississippian*, May 4 and Aug. 17. See also Davis, *Recollections*, 300–304.

13. *Mississippian*, June 22, Sept. 7 and 21, 1849.

14. *Herald and Correspondent*, Mar. 1 and 8, 1850; *Flag of the Union*, May 9, 1851; *Monroe Democrat*, Apr. 26, 1850.

15. H. A. Cooke to James E. Cooke, Jan. 11, 1851, H. A. Cooke Letters, MDAH; *Herald and Correspondent*, Sept. 6, 1850; Andrew Hutchinson et. al. to Charles D. Fontaine (hereafter CDF), Apr. 5, 1851, CDF Papers, MDAH; "A Southern Rights Whig," *Mississippi Palladium*, Oct. 17, 1851; *Mississippian*, Apr. 18, 1851. See also J. McDonald to John A. Quitman, March 9, 1851, JFHC Collection.

16. *Flag of the Union*, Nov. 22, 1850; Mary Floyd Summers, "Politics in Tishomingo County, 1836–1860," *JMH* 28 (1966): 144; *Herald and Correspondent*, Nov. 29, 1850, July 11, 1851.

17. *Southern Standard*, Feb. 1, 1851. See also *Monroe Democrat*, Oct. 2 and 9, 1850.

18. Many State-Rights leaders preferred Jefferson Davis to Quitman. Quitman was elected in 1849 but resigned before his term expired because the federal government had indicted him for filibustering in Cuba. Cleared of those charges, Quitman thought he deserved a chance to redeem himself. The party's platform, moderate compared to Quitman's own, reflected Davis's influence. See May, *Quitman*, 236–65.

19. Henry S. Foote, *Casket of Reminiscences* (Washington, D. C., 1874), 356; Davis, *Recollections*, 317.

20. Jason Niles Diary, July 2, 1851, June 14, 1851, SHC; Richard C. Glenn to Henry St. George Harris, Aug. 1, 1851, Henry St. George Harris Papers, Duke; Hugh McInnis to DMcL, May 14, 1851, DMP. See also John W. C. Watson to Gen. David Campbell, Sept. 5, 1851, Campbell Family Papers, Duke.

21. Powhatan Ellis to Margaret Keeling Ellis, Oct. 8, 1851, Munford-Ellis Family Papers, George W. Munford Division, Duke. See also May, *Quitman*, 253–64.

22. *Southern Standard*, Oct. 18, 1851.

23. *Primitive Republican*, Apr. 3, 24, and June 12, 1851; *Flag of the Union*, May 2, July 23, 1851; *Mississippi Palladium*, July 11, 1851.

24. Kenneth McKenzie (hereafter KMcK) to DMcL, Apr. 13, 1851, DMP.

25. Albert G. Brown, "A Letter to His Constituents," May 13, 1850, and "Speech at Ellwood Springs," Nov. 2, 1850, in *Speeches, Messages, and Other Writings of the Hon. Albert G. Brown, A Senator in Congress from the State of Mississippi*, ed. M. W. Cluskey (Philadelphia, 1859), 188, 189 (quotes), 178–90, 246–61; *Organizer*, June 9, 1849; Quitman's proclamation, Sept. 26, 1850, Governor's Correspondence, MDAH.

26. *Organizer*, June 9, 1849; *Monroe Democrat*, Oct. 20, 1851; KMcK to DMcL, Apr. 13, 1851, DMP.

27. *Mississippian*, March 1, 1851; *Monroe Democrat*, Oct. 20, 1851, Apr. 2, 1851.

28. *Mississippi Free Trader*, July 11, 1851, reprinted in *The Papers of Jefferson Davis*, vol. 4, 1849–1852, ed. Lynda Lasswell Crist, Mary Seaton Dix, and Richard E. Beringer (Baton Rouge, 1983), 209; *Organizer*, June 23, 1849, Nov. 2, 1850.

29. Cluskey, ed., *Hon. Albert G. Brown*, 250; Crist, Dix, and Beringer, eds., *Papers of Jefferson Davis*, 4: 207, 212.

30. *Organizer*, Nov. 2, 1850; *Constitution*, July 12, 1851. See, e.g., Davis's speech at Raymond, Aug. 5, 1851, quoted in *Mississippian*, Aug. 8, 1851.

31. *Vicksburg Weekly Whig*, Apr. 2, 1851. See also *Columbus Democrat*, March 8, 1851.

32. *Herald and Correspondent*, Oct. 11, 1850; *Vicksburg Weekly Whig*, July 9, 1851; *Hinds County Gazette*, Sept. 11, 1851. See also *Holly Springs Gazette*, Nov. 15, 1850; *Columbus Democrat*, Apr. 4, 1851; *Vicksburg Weekly Whig*, Oct. 16, 1850.

33. *Southern Standard*, May 10, 1851; Cluskey, ed., *Hon. A. G. Brown*, 235, 180–85. See also *Mississippi Palladium*, July 25, 1851.

34. *Columbus Democrat*, July 12, 1851.

35. *Vicksburg Weekly Whig*, July 23, 1851; *Primitive Republican*, July 17, 1851; *Holly Springs Gazette*, Nov. 15, 1850.

36. The preeminent study of Christianity, sectionalism, and southern national-ism is Snay, *Gospel of Disunion*; see chap. 5 and "Conclusion." See also Wyatt-Brown, *Southern Honor*, 88–114. J. G. Peristiany and Julian Pitt-Rivers distinguish between the "honor of precedence" associated with elites and defined by power over others and the "honor of virtue" for everyone else; the latter includes honesty, loyalty, and a concern for moral turpitude (Peristiany, ed., *Honour and Shame: The Values of Mediterranean Society* [Chicago, 1966]). Pitt-Rivers refined the distinction in a subsequent work coedited with Peristiany, *Honor and Grace in Anthropology* [Cam-bridge, 1992]). In it, he contrasts "honor owed to God" and "honor owed to other men." The former, as defined by the church, centers in a guilt-free conscience (honor in the eyes of God only), while the latter includes "the pecking order," physi-cal courage, and masculinity.

37. *Southern Standard*, May 31, 1851; *Mississippian*, July 20, 1849; *Organizer*, June 9, 1849.

38. *Mississippian*, Oct. 12, 1849; Crist, Dix, and Beringer, eds., *Papers of Jeffer-son Davis*, 4: 280.

Chapter 3

1. Shade, *Democratizing the Old Dominion*, 82; Gienapp, *Origins*, 365. Two recent discussions summarize and give shape to the debate over antipartyism in nine-teenth-century America. See Stuart Blumin and Glenn Altschuler, "Limits of Politi-cal Engagement in Antebellum America: A New Look at the Golden Age of Partici-patory Democracy," *JAH* 84 (1997): 855–85, and the several comments that follow. Blumin and Altschuler question the widespread acceptance, even the importance, of parties in all of antebellum America. See also "Round Table: Alternatives to the Party System in the 'Party Period,' 1830–1890," *JAH* 86 (1999): 93–166. In this discus-sion, both Ronald Formisano, "The 'Party Period' Revisited," and Mark Voss-Hub-bard, "The 'Third-party Tradition' Reconsidered: Third Parties and American Public Life, 1830–1900," emphasize the persistent antiparty rhetoric and behavior common to nineteenth-century America, especially in municipal and local elections and in

periodic "insurgencies" (100–102, 108 [and n. 31], 110 [and n. 40], 138–39). One good example of a local political culture based in antipartyism is described in Philip Ethington, *The Public City: The Political Construction of Urban Life in San Francisco* (Cambridge, 1994), esp. 66–85, 114–27, 167–69. Perhaps the most complete discussion of antiparty theory and rhetoric, which argues for their central role in the political culture and even in the creation of parties, is Gerald Leonard's "Partisan Political Theory and the Unwritten Constitution: The Origins of Democracy in Illinois," (Ph.D. diss., Univ. of Michigan, 1992).

2. "Party Spirit," *Oakland College Magazine* (hereafter *OCM*), Jan. 1858, Oakland College Papers (hereafter OCP), MDAH; "The Demagogue," *OCM*, July 1856; DMcK to DMcL, July 5, 1845, DMP; *Port-Gibson Herald*, Aug. 28, 1845.

3. *Prairie News*, May 26, 1859; *Fort Adams Item*, Jan. 20, 1855; *Piney Woods Planter and Amite Union Literary Reflector*, Jan. 25, 1840; *Southern Pioneer*, Oct. 16, 1841.

4. *Clinton Gazette*, Oct. 17, 1835; *Prairie News*, Sept. 16, 1858.

5. *Guard*, July 10, 1845. "Dull, plodding job" comes from Greenberg, *Masters and Statesmen*. See also *Hinds County Gazette*, Apr. 27, 1853; *American Citizen*, June 11, 1853. Among several studies that highlight the institutional weakness of the South and its justice system, see Ayers, *Vengeance and Justice*; Waldrep, *Roots of Disorder*; and Michael Stephen Hindus, *Prison and Plantation: Crime, Justice, and Authority in Massachusetts and South Carolina, 1767–1878* (Chapel Hill, 1980).

6. Voss-Hubbard, "'Third-party Tradition'," 124 (and n. 8), 130–31.

7. J. F. H. Claiborne, *Life and Correspondence of John A. Quitman* (New York, 1860), 161–62; *Herald and Correspondent*, Sept. 28, 1849. See also May, *Quitman*, 264–69; Thomas H. Woods to Ellis Malone, Jan. 18, 1852, Ellis Malone Papers, Duke; John A. Quitman to C. R. Clifton, Nov. 18, 1853, JFHC Collection; and DMcK to DMcL, Aug. 6, 1843, DMP.

8. Address before the Odd Fellows, Collegiate High School at Columbus, Mississippi, Oct. 1852 or Aug. 1853, Meek Family Papers, MDAH; *BHMM*, 2: 424–26.

9. "Ambition," *OCM*, Mar. 1858, 9–11; "Our Country," *OCM*, Nov. 1856, OCP.

10. William R. Cannon to Jefferson Davis, Dec. 12, 1855, in *Papers of Jefferson Davis*, vol. 5, *1853–1855*, ed. Lynda Lasswell Crist and Mary Seaton Dix (Baton Rouge, 1985), 145. See also Hiram Cassedy to JFHC, July 17, 1855, JFHC Collection.

11. J. McDonald to Richard Griffith, Sept. 6, 1854, Griffith Papers, MDAH. See also DMcK to DMcL, June 20, 1842, Aug. 29, 1842, Sept. 23, 1843, DMP.

12. "The Demagogue," *OCM*, July 1856, OCP; *Flag of the Union*, Oct. 8, 1852.

13. *Monroe Democrat*, Aug. 6, 1851.

14. *Yazoo City Whig and Political Register*, May 2, 1845; Colin S. Tarpley to Jefferson Davis, May 6, 1853, in Crist and Dix, eds., *Papers of Jefferson Davis*, 5: 12–14; Hiram S. Van Eaton to William Nicholas Whitehurst, Sept. 10, 1858, Whitehurst Papers, MDAH; *BHMM*, 2: 943–44; *Vicksburg Daily Whig*, May 1, 1849.

15. *Port Gibson Reveille*, Aug. 3, 1853; *Constitution*, Apr. 26, 1851. See also *Columbus Democrat*, July 14, 1849, Apr. 21, 1848; *Commonwealth*, Apr. 7, 1855; *Flag of the Union*, Feb. 11, 1853.

16. *Statesman*, Sept. 16, 1843; *Columbus Democrat*, July 7, 1849 (emphasis added). See also *Yazoo Democrat*, Nov. 19, 1845; July 20, 1853; *Eastern Clarion*, Aug. 3, 1859.

17. *Southern Standard*, July 2, 1853 (emphasis added); *Wilkinson Advertiser*, Mar. 31, 1858; on the 1843 disaffection, see the *Louisville Messenger*, Apr.–July; JPS to DMcL, Aug. 9, 1843, DMP.

18. *Vicksburg Weekly Whig*, May 22, 1850. See also *Vicksburg Daily Whig*, July 29, 1847, July 2, 1849; *Yazoo Weekly Whig*, Apr. 1, 1853.

19. *Yazoo City Weekly Whig*, July 22, 1853; *American Citizen*, June 11, 1853; *Port-Gibson Correspondent*, Nov. 8, 1845.

20. *Vicksburg Daily Whig*, Nov. 17, 1849. On tickets, see also *Hinds County Gazette*, Sept. 14, 1849.

21. *Yazoo City Weekly Whig*, Mar. 23, 1853; *Hinds County Gazette*, Feb. 11, 1856; *Weekly American Banner*, Mar. 21, 1856.

22. *Port Gibson Reveille*, July 20, 1853; *Mississippian*, Oct. 22, 1847; *Vicksburg Daily Whig*, Nov. 10, 1843.

23. *Columbus Democrat*, Aug. 4, 1849; *Democratic Flag*, Mar. 31, 1852; *Brandon Republican*, July 19, 1853; exchanges between "Senex" and "Q in the Corner," in the *Organizer*, Apr. and May, 1850 (quote from May 11). See also *Yazoo Democrat*, Aug. 20, 1845; *Southern Tribune*, Sept. 6, 1843; *Woodville Republican*, July 12, 19, and 26, 1851, Oct. 15, 1852; *Port Gibson Reveille*, Apr. 13, Oct. 26, and Nov. 2, 1853; *Port-Gibson Correspondent*, June 25, 1845.

24. See, e.g., *Fayette Watch-Tower*, Oct. 9 and 16, 1857; *Lauderdale Republican*, Aug. 7 and Oct. 30, 1855; *Empire Democrat*, Mar. 3, 1855; *Commonwealth*, Mar. 1 and Sept. 1, 1855. A debate over which party had a better claim to be the "antiparty party" appeared in the *Weekly American Banner*, June 29, 1855. On Know Nothings in Mississippi, see Cecil S. Hilliard Ross, "Dying Hard, Dying Fast: The Know-Nothing Experience in Mississippi," (Ph.D. diss., University of Notre Dame, 1982); W. Darrell Overdyke, *The Know-Nothing Party in the South* (Baton Rouge, 1950).

25. *Hinds County Gazette*, Nov. 8, 1854, May 23, 1855; *Southern Mercury*, Sept. 11, 1855.

26. *Tri-Weekly Mercury*, June 23, 1855. See also *Yazoo City Weekly Whig*, Dec. 15, 1854, Jan. 12 and Nov. 10, 1855; *Hinds County Gazette*, May 23, 1855, Apr. 29, 1857; *Weekly Conservative*, June 23, 1855.

27. *Mississippian and State Gazette*, July 1, 1857.

28. See the editorial by Benjamin F. Dill in the *Organizer*, Jan. 5, 1850.

29. *Weekly Independent*, Nov. 19, 1853; *Dollar Democrat*, July–Oct., 1845.

30. *Vicksburg Sentinel*, quoted in the *Monroe Democrat*, May 29, 1850; *Houston Patriot*, May 22, 1850; *Organizer*, Apr. 27, 1850. Proposals to change the method of representation in state conventions also often set Democrats against one another. See the *Southern Standard*, Feb. 12 and 26, 1853; and a report of the typically rancorous proceedings of the 1857 state convention in the *Mississippian and State Gazette*, July 1, 1857.

31. *Dollar Democrat*, Apr. 11, 1843 (see also July 30, 1842); *Commonwealth*, May 23, 1857.

32. Wiley P. Harris, "Autobiography of Wiley P. Harris," in *Courts, Judges, and Lawyers of Mississippi, 1798–1935*, ed. Dunbar Rowland (Jackson, Miss., 1935), 301;

Democrat, Mar. 16, 1853; *Southron*, July 20, 1841; *Liberty Advocate*, June 28, 1845; *Ripley Advertiser*, May 19, 1858. See also Blumin and Altschuler, "Limits of Political Engagement," 858–65.

33. Gordon Wood, *The Creation of the American Republic, 1776–1787* (Chapel Hill, 1969), 371 (quote), 189–91, 369–72. Kenneth Greenberg, in *Masters and Statesmen*, maintains that southerners — in his case, South Carolinians — distrusted parties and feared professional politicians. They wanted independent statesmen who would follow the dictates of their own conscience and not the shackles of party ideology. Mississippians may have wanted statesmen, too, but most decided that they were unlikely to get them. So, as parties and politicians could never be trusted, it was better to force partisan representatives to toe the line. One editorial urging more independent statesmen appeared in the *Holly Springs Gazette*, Aug. 12, 1841. Historian Daniel Dupre similarly identifies the problem of "trust" as foremost among early voters in Huntsville, Alabama, although he argues that the solution of candidates' pledges helped divide political factions in "an emerging partisan political culture"; see his *Transforming the Cotton Frontier: Madison County, Alabama, 1800–1840* (Baton Rouge, 1997), 197.

34. *Jefferson Journal*, June 25, 1858.

35. Crist, Dix, and Beringer, eds., *Papers of Jefferson Davis*, 4: 135, 300, also 191–93, 205–206. See also *Papers of Jefferson Davis*, vol. 3, *July 1846–December 1848*, ed. James T. McIntosh, Lynda L. Crist, and Mary S. Dix (Baton Rouge, 1981), 3–5. On the delicate job of assuming a certain "passivity" toward public power, see Greenberg, *Masters and Statesmen*, 3–41.

36. *Herald and Correspondent*, June 7, 1850; *Port-Gibson Correspondent*, Apr. 12, 1839.

37. *Mississippian*, June 6, 1851. See also *Dollar Democrat*, Mar. 12, 1841; *Herald and Correspondent*, June 23, 1852; *Constitution*, Apr. 19, 1851; James Lusk Alcorn to Amelia Alcorn, Nov. 26, 1850, Alcorn Family Papers, SHC.

38. *Flag of the Union*, Feb. 7 and 14, 1851; *Vicksburg Weekly Whig*, Sept. 11, 1850.

Chapter 4

1. Frank Montgomery, *Reminiscences of a Mississippian in Peace and War* (Cincinnati, 1901), 38.

2. My calculations are the result of step-wise ecological regression, encompassing state and national elections held between 1851 and 1860. The aggregate unit was the county (N = 57), and election returns were collected from *The Tribune Almanac* and *Mississippian*, 1851–1860. The results are presented simply as evidence of the uncertainty that characterized the electorate in state and national (partisan) elections — this uncertainty was caused, primarily, by geographic mobility and demographic change. The complete data are presented in Christopher J. Olsen, "Community, Honor, and Secession in the Deep South: Mississippi's Political Culture, 1840s–1861," (Ph.D. diss., University of Florida, 1996), 142–49. For further discussion of the technique, see Gienapp, *Origins*, esp. 475–81, and J. Morgan Kousser, "Ecological Regression and the Analysis of Past Politics," *JIH* 4 (1973): 237–62. For a critique, see William H. Flanigan and Nancy H. Zingale, "Alchemist's Gold: Inferring Individual Relationships from Aggregate Data," *Social Science History* 9 (1985):

73–91. In his new study of voting patterns in Civil War Texas, historian Dale Baum — using several types of regression analysis — also concludes that nonvoters were a critical factor in antebellum party elections and that staying home was much more important than switching. See *The Shattering of Texas Unionism: Politics in the Lone Star State during the Civil War Era* (Baton Rouge, 1999).

3. See, e.g., "Young Men Attach Yourself to the Democracy," *Eastern Clarion*, Dec. 4, 1858.

4. Dramatically lower rates of turnout after 1856 mean that many men who appear as nonvoters probably participated in some earlier elections but skipped the previous contest used in the equation. In other words, men listed as nonvoters late in the decade were less likely to be recent arrivals or twenty-one-year-olds than stable residents who were becoming part-time voters.

5. William L. Sharkey to CDF, May 28, 1855; Benjamin F. Dill to CDF, July 6, 1852, CDF Papers; Wiley P. Harris to JFHC, Aug. 30, 1855, JFHC Collection. See also the *Southron*, Nov. 1, 1843.

6. Among many studies of party organization that reach a similar conclusion, a classic is Frank J. Sorauf, *Party Politics in America* (Boston, 1968).

7. *Vicksburg Daily Whig*, Oct. 6, 1849; Hiram S. Van Eaton to William Nicholas Whitehurst, Aug. 18, 1858, Whitehurst Papers.

8. H. H. Tyson to CDF, June 20, 1853. See also Joseph Leake to CDF, Sept. 23, 1853. All the correspondence relating to this election are in the CDF Papers, box 2, folders 8 and 9.

9. Democrats of DeSoto to CDF, Oct. 12, 1853; Democrats of Tishomingo to CDF, Oct. 22, 1853; J. F. Cushman to CDF, Nov. 5, 1853.

10. —— [?] Terrell to CDF, Aug. 26, 1853; J. H. Brown to CDF, June 22, 1853.

11. R. S. Rozelle to CDF, Sept. 23, 1853; William R. Allen to CDF, Nov. 10, 1853.

12. *Vicksburg Whig*, Nov. 20, 1849, July 15, 1851; *Herald and Correspondent*, Nov. 2, 1849; *Southern Standard*, Oct. 18, 1851 and Mar. 26, 1853, editorial, "The Political Judiciary"; *Mississippian*, Aug. 17, 1858.

13. *Mississippi Creole*, July 31, 1841; *Louisville Messenger*, Sept. 23, Nov. 11, 1843. On parties in the Mississippi legislature, see Lucas, "Development of the Second Party System."

14. *Mississippian*, Mar. 12, 1845; *Port-Gibson Herald*, July 23, 1845 (quoting the *Yazoo Democrat*); *Port-Gibson Correspondent*, June 25, 1845. Some Vicksburg Whigs occasionally urged the party to nominate candidates for municipal offices; see *Vicksburg Daily Whig*, Nov. 10, 1843, Feb. 27, Mar. 3, 6, and 22, 1849.

15. *Hinds County Gazette*, July 4 (quotes), 25, Aug. 8, 1845.

16. *Southron*, July 23, Nov. 12, 1845; *Hinds County Gazette*, Nov. 7, 1845.

17. *Mississippi Democrat*, Jan. 29, Apr. 16, May 7, Nov. 12, 1845.

18. *Columbus Democrat*, July 28, July 21, 1849. See also June 30, July 7, and 14, 1849, ibid.

19. *Organizer*, May 26, June 9, 16, and 23, 1849. Unfortunately, election returns from Lafayette are spotty. Those from 1849 provide only a list of winners with no vote totals. Returns from 1845 and 1847 were apparently lost, and those from 1851 and 1853 include no precinct figures.

20. Sumners, "Politics in Tishomingo County," 141–42.

21. *Southern Tribune*, Nov. 10, 1843; *Yazoo Democrat*, Nov. 12, 1845; *Holly Springs Gazette*, Aug. 26, 1841, Apr. 28, 1843. See also the *Southron*, Nov. 1, 1843; *Vicksburg Daily Whig*, Nov. 10, 1843; *Mississippi Creole*, Sept. 11, 1841; *Mississippi Democrat*, Jan. 29, Apr. 16, May 7, Oct. 15, 1845.

22. *Independent Democrat*, Nov. 4, 1843; *Ripley Advertiser*, Mar. 31, 1858.

23. Several decades ago political scientists Dean Burnham, Jerrold Rusk, and Philip Converse laid out the major lines of the debate about the importance of behavioral and institutional factors that affect turnout and voting behavior. Their controversy can be traced through several exchanges. It started with Burnham, "The Changing Shape of the American Political Universe," APSR 59 (1965): 7–28; Rusk, "The Effect of the Australian Ballot Reform on Split Ticket Voting, 1876–1908," APSR 64 (1970): 1220–38; and continued in conversations in two later issues of the APSR: 65 (1971): 1149–57, and 68 (1974): 1002–1023.

24. *Empire Democrat*, Mar. 23, 1855.

25. Anderson Hutchinson, *Code of Mississippi: Being an Analytical Compilation of the Public and General Statutes of the Territory and State with References to the Local and Private Acts, From 1798 to 1848* (Jackson, 1848), 160.

26. *Woodville Republican*, Oct. 14, 1851; *Yazoo City Whig and Political Register*, Nov. 13, 1843. See also *Holly Springs Gazette*, Oct. 25, 1845.

27. *Mississippi Creole*, Oct. 23, 1841; *American Citizen*, Oct. 18, 1851.

28. *Prairie News*, Aug. 19, 1858; *Weekly Panola Star*, Sept. 8, 1858; *Yazoo City Weekly Whig*, May 11, 1855.

29. Perry McD. Collins et al. to [Democratic editors], July 18, 1849, Governor's Correspondence, MDAH.

30. Tippah and Leake county Democratic tickets, and John J. McRae et. al. to [Democratic editors], Oct. 1, 1855, in "Broadsides Collection 1825–1870," MDAH. See also *Liberty Advocate*, Aug. 5, 1843. Other discussions of tickets and their impact on the electoral process include W. Wayne Smith, "Jacksonian Democracy on the Chesapeake: The Political Institutions," *Maryland Historical Magazine* 62 (1967): 381–93, which suggests that Maryland tickets were strictly partisan by the 1840s; and Kenneth J. Winkle, "Ohio's Informal Polling Place: Nineteenth-century Suffrage in Theory and Practice," in *The Pursuit of Public Power: Political Culture in Ohio, 1787–1861*, ed. Jeffrey Brown and Andrew R. L. Cayton (Kent, Ohio, 1994), 169–84.

31. *Weekly Southron*, Oct. 29, 1847; *Democrat*, Nov. 4, 1843.

32. *Mississippi Democrat*, Nov. 3, 1845; *Columbus Democrat*, Nov. 3, 1849 (emphasis added); *Weekly American Banner*, Oct. 26, 1855; *Holly Springs Gazette*, Nov. 10, 1843.

33. William L. Sharkey et al., *The Revised Code of the Statute Laws of the State of Mississippi* (Jackson, 1857), 92; *Daily Free Trader*, Sept. 10, 1858.

34. *Hinds County Gazette*, Sept. 26, 1860.

35. Bourke and DeBats, *Washington County*, 201–204; Burnham, "American Political Universe," 7–28. My rates of roll-off are calculated from aggregate figures, not individual-level polling data (see Appendix).

36. Rusk, "Effect of the Australian Ballot," 1222–23, 1237.

37. *Hinds County Gazette*, Sept. 30, 1857; *Weekly Panola Star*, Oct. 21, 1857.

38. *Hinds County Gazette*, Oct. 8, 1858.

39. See, e.g., Burton, *In My Father's House*; Kenzer, *Kinship and Neighborhood*; Bourke and DeBats, *Washington County*, esp. chap. 4; Morris, *Becoming Southern*; Burton W. Folsom II, "Party Formation and Development in Jacksonian America: The Old South," *Journal of American Studies* 7 (1973): 217–29. The opposing view, that national issues and presidential elections brought men to the polls, is epitomized by Richard P. McCormick, *The Second American Party System: Party Formation in the Jacksonian Era* (Chapel Hill, 1966).

40. *Mississippian*, July 18 and 25, Aug. 8, 1851.

41. *Flag of the Union*, May 30, 1851. The greatest exceptions to local nonpartisanship, however, came during the Know-Nothing years (discussed in chap. 7).

42. *Ripley Advertiser*, Mar. 24, 1858.

43. Formisano, *Transformation of Political Culture*, parts two and three; Alan Tully, *Forming American Politics: Ideals, Interests, and Institutions in Colonial New York and Pennsylvania* (Baltimore, 1994), 316–430.

44. Robert M. Ireland, *Little Kingdoms: The Counties of Kentucky, 1850–1891* (Lexington, 1977), 43; also Ireland, *The County Courts in Antebellum Kentucky* (Lexington, 1972), esp. chap. 4; Thomas E. Jeffrey, "'Free Suffrage' Revisited: Party Politics and Constitutional Reform in Antebellum North Carolina," *North Carolina Historical Review* 59 (1982): 24–48; *Ripley Advertiser*, May 19, 1858.

45. Crofts, *Old Southampton*, 167; Shade, *Democratizing the Old Dominion*, 2–5, 76–82. See also Richard G. Lowe, "The Republican Party in Antebellum Virginia, 1856–1860," *Virginia Magazine of History and Biography* 81 (1973), 259–79. Crofts, in *Reluctant Confederates* (esp. chap. 2), summarizes the literature on Upper South politics.

46. Whitman Ridgway, *Community Leadership in Maryland, 1790–1840: A Comparative Analysis of Power in Society* (Chapel Hill, 1979); W. Wayne Smith, "Jacksonian Democracy on the Chesapeake: The Political Institutions," *Maryland Historical Magazine* 62 (1967): 381–93 (385, on bribery); Jeffrey, *State Parties*; Watson, *Jacksonian Politics and Community Conflict*; Marc Kruman, *Parties and Politics in North Carolina, 1836–1865* (Baton Rouge, 1983); Jean H. Baker, *The Politics of Continuity: Maryland Political Parties from 1858 to 1870* (Baltimore, 1973); Paul H. Bergeron, *Antebellum Politics in Tennessee* (Lexington, 1982); Paul E. McAllister, "Missouri Voters, 1840–1856: An Analysis of Ante-Bellum Voting Behavior and Party Politics," (Ph.D. diss., University of Missouri-Columbia, 1976); James M. Woods, *Rebellion and Realignment: Arkansas's Road to Secession* (Fayetteville, Ark., 1987).

47. Leonard, "Partisan Political Theory," 436 (quote), 242–349, 388–448.

48. Bourke and DeBats, *Washington County*, 166–67, 202–209, 315–16; Walter L. Buenger, *Secession and the Union in Texas* (Austin, 1984), 61; Nicole Etcheson, *The Emerging Midwest: Upland Southerners and the Political Culture of the Old Northwest, 1787–1861* (Bloomington, Ind., 1996); For a similar description of party activists leading groups of followers to the polls, see Winkle, "Ohio's Informal Polling Place," 169–73.

49. JPS to DMcL, July 10, 1845, DMP.

Chapter 5

1. Benjamin L. C. Wailes Diary, Nov. 6, 1860, Benjamin L. C. Wailes Collection, Duke.

2. A summary of these studies and their critics is Darret Rutman, "Assessing the Little Communities of Early America," *WMQ* 43 (1986): 163–78.

3. Don Harrison Doyle, "Social Theory and New Communities in Nineteenth-century America," *Western Historical Quarterly* 8 (1977): 151–65; idem, *The Social Order of a Frontier Community: Jacksonville, Illinois 1825–1870* (Urbana, 1978); Richard S. Alcorn, "Leadership and Stability in Mid-Nineteenth-century America: A Case Study of an Illinois Town," *JAH* 61 (1974): 685–702. The classic theoretical articulation of this position is Allan G. Bogue, "Social Theory and the Pioneer," *Agricultural History* 34 (1960): 21–34.

4. See Robert Wiebe, *The Search for Order, 1877–1920* (New York, 1967). He contends that America was still a nation of stable "island communities" late in the nineteenth century but does not directly address the issue of mobility. A classic statement of the unifying force of a national value framework within changing local identities is Louis Hartz, *The Liberal Tradition in America: An Interpretation of American Political Thought since the Revolution* (New York, 1955).

5. The effects of mobility on local politics — especially community leadership, class relations, and participation — are still only partly understood and not always addressed by historians. See Kenneth J. Winkle, *The Politics of Community: Migration and Politics in Antebellum Ohio* (Cambridge, 1988); idem, "The Voters and Lincoln's Springfield: Migration and Political Participation in an Antebellum City," *Journal of Social History* 25 (1992): 596–611; Bourke and DeBats, *Washington County*.

6. Darrett Rutman offers a framework for evaluating American communities over time. Rutman's model, taken from sociology, includes "vertical" and "horizontal" linkages as the key variables. The former are extracommunity connections, such as political parties, that transcend neighborhood boundaries; the latter are relations of neighbors or extended kin that remain within the locality. See his "Assessing the Little Communities," 176–78. See also Gerald D. Suttles, *The Social Construction of Communities* (Chicago, 1972), who argues for the critical role of territoriality, which includes vertical and horizontal linkages, in the construction of "natural communities." On the evolutionary nature of community and its shared history, see Sabean, *Power in the Blood*, 27–30 and *passim*.

7. Citizens of North Mt. Pleasant to Governor Foote, Nov. 1852, Governor's Correspondence, MDAH (emphasis added).

8. This problem was addressed by the "new political historians" of the 1960s and 1970s. They examined seriously for the first time "who voted for whom" and attempted to infer individual motivation from aggregate voting returns. Two summaries of this literature are Ronald P. Formisano, "Toward a Reorientation of Jacksonian Politics: A Review of the Literature, 1959–1975," *JAH* 63 (1976), and "The New Political History," *International Journal of Social Education* 1 (1986): 5–21. Since the 1980s, historians have employed more sophisticated quantitative methodologies — in particular ecological regression — to infer individual behavior. Individual-level voting data found in poll books that recorded actual votes are most promising sources. See Paul F. Bourke and Donald A. DeBats, "Identifiability of Voting in Nineteenth-Century America: Toward a Comparison of Britain and the United States before the Secret Ballot," *Perspectives in American History* 11 (1977): 259–88; idem, "Individuals and Aggregates: A Note on Historical Data and Assumptions," *Social Science History* 4 (1980): 229–50.

9. Ranck, *Albert Gallatin Brown*, 27–31; Carroll, *Oktibbeha County*, 66–67; David N. Young, "The Mississippi Whigs, 1834–1860," (Ph.D. diss., University of Alabama, 1968), 77–82.

10. Thomas Alexander et al., "Who Were the Alabama Whigs?" *Alabama Review* 16 (1963): 5–19; idem, "The Basis of Alabama's Ante-Bellum Two-party System," ibid. 19 (1966): 243–76. Both articles are elaborations on Marvin Meyers, *The Jacksonian Persuasion: Politics and Belief* (Stanford, 1957). Other studies reaching this conclusion to a greater or lesser degree include Watson, *Jacksonian Politics*; Thornton, *Politics and Power*; Crofts, *Reluctant Confederates*; Dupre, *Cotton Frontier*.

11. For the South, see, e.g., Thornton, *Politics and Power*; Watson, *Jacksonian Politics*; Dupre, *Cotton Frontier*. For the North, see Foner, *Free Soil, Free Labor, Free Men*.

12. *Monroe Democrat*, Mar. 31, 1852; *Democratic Flag*, Mar. 24, Sept. 8, 1852; Board of Police Minutes, Panola County, 1858. On the market orientation of antebellum Mississippi farmers and their support for internal improvements, see Bond, *Political Culture*, pt. 1.

13. The potency of neighborhood voting is widely acknowledged. Among many others, see Kenzer, *Kinship and Neighborhood*; Morris, *Becoming Southern*; Jeffrey, *State Parties*; Thornton, *Politics and Power*. Historians differ on the relative importance of such ideological and nonideological factors: was it parties or family, history, and community tradition? Daniel Crofts's *Old Southampton* especially demonstrates the difficulty of sorting out the effects of ideology from other factors. He concludes that residence was the paramount determinant (125–30), but often suggests that some sort of partisan ideology affected voters' outlook as well (52, 73–74, 105, 107–117). See also Lawrence Kohl, "The Virginian as American," review of Shade, *Democratizing the Old Dominion*, in *RAH* 26 (1998): 375–80.

14. Morris, *Becoming Southern*, 132–55. Historians of the nation's first party system note that early partisan divisions also arose from "highly local" rivalries "within towns and cities, counties and states." Alfred F. Young, *The Democratic Republicans of New York: The Origins, 1763–1797* (Chapel Hill, 1967), 570, quoted in Formisano, "Deferential-Participant Politics," 476. Jeffrey argues that ethnocultural conflict from the colonial years, reinforced by early-national-period issues, determined Whig-Democratic divisions in North Carolina (*State Parties*, 25–30).

15. Lang, *Harrison County*, 6–9; Williams, ed., *Bolivar County*, 16; Carroll, *Oktibbeha County*, 27–28; James Ruffin et al. to Governor Lynch, May 9, 1836, Governor's Correspondence, MDAH. See also *Prairie News*, July 22, 1858; and Board of Police Minutes for Harrison County, 1841–1860, Bolivar County, 1836–1855, Carroll County, 1844–1854.

16. Harris, "Autobiography," 287; Fulkerson, *Random Recollections*, 94; Montgomery, *Reminiscences*, 6–11. Nearly every study by historians and political scientists concludes that the greatest influence on partisanship is family tradition. Among many others, see Jean Baker, *Affairs of Party: The Political Culture of Northern Democrats in the Mid-Nineteenth Century* (Ithaca, 1983); Eleanor E. Maccoby, Richard E. Matthews, and Alton S. Morton, "Youth and Political Change," in *Political Behavior: A Reader in Theory and Research*, ed. Heinz Eulau, Samuel J. Eldersveld, and Morris Janowitz (Chicago, 1956), 299–307; Paul F. Lazarsfeld, Bernard Berelson, and Hazel Gaudet, *The People's Choice* (New York, 1952).

17. *Southern Standard*, Aug. 7, 1852; *BHMM*, 1: 793–94.

18. The best account of this process in an Upper-South state is Jeffrey, *State Parties*, 12–90 and *passim*.

19. *Yazoo City Weekly Whig*, May 20, 1853. Morris, in *Becoming Southern*, demonstrates that voters passed their local voting patterns on to the party era. "When state government became more important, and elections for governor became more contested, neighborhoods extended their idiosyncratic patterns to state [partisan] elections" (144). On the isolation of most rural neighborhoods well into the 1850s, see Kenzer, *Kinship and Neighborhood*, 10–13, 58, and chap. 3; see also *Fort Adams Item*, Nov. 12, 1853, Nov. 10, 1855.

20. On women and children at party functions, see Varon, *We Mean to Be Counted*; Jayne Crumpler DeFiore, "COME, and Bring the Ladies: Tennessee Women and the Politics of Opportunity during the Presidential Campaigns of 1840 and 1844," *Tennessee Historical Quarterly* 51 (1992): 197–212; Olsen, "'Respecting the wise allotment of our sphere,'" 108–111.

21. *Hinds County Gazette*, July 20, 1853; Aug. 21, 1851, June 19, 1851.

22. *Democratic Banner*, Aug. 5, 1853; Davis, *Recollections*, 197. See also *Yazoo City Weekly Whig*, July 14, 1854; Daniel Dupre, "Barbecues and Pledges: Electioneering and the Rise of Democratic Politics in Antebellum Alabama," *JSH* 60 (1994): 479–512.

23. Joseph Beckham Cobb, *Mississippi Scenes: or, Sketches of Southern and Western life and adventure, humorous, satirical, and descriptive, including the legend of Black Creek* (Philadelphia, 1851), 152–53.

24. *American Citizen*, Sept. 11, 1852.

25. Jefferson J. Birdsong Diary, Nov. 4, 1856, MDAH; *BHMM*, 1: 388.

26. *Hinds County Gazette*, Sept. 10, 1845, May 11, 1848, Mar. 2, 1853.

27. *Hinds County Gazette*, Mar. 2, 16, and June 8, 1859.

28. Davis, *Recollections*, 66–70.

29. DMcK to DMcL, Sept. 23, 1843, DMP.

30. *Liberty Advocate*, Nov. 11, 1843. See also Morris, *Becoming Southern*, esp. 91, 138–45.

31. Alexander Stringer to Governor Runnels, Sept. 9, 1834; W. W. Newman et al. to Governor McNutt, Nov. 8, 1839, Governor's Correspondence, MDAH.

32. HS to DMcL, Dec. 4, 1835, DMP.

33. *Southron*, Sept. 17, 1847.

34. These figures are still much lower than what Bourke and DeBats discovered for 1850s Oregon, where precinct roll-off ranged between 22 and 37 percent (*Washington County*, 202).

35. *Hinds County Gazette*, Nov. 23, 1853 (quote), Mar. 14, 1855; or *Fayette Watch-Tower*, July 11, 1856.

36. *Hinds County Gazette*, Apr. 18, 1855.

37. *Fayette Watch-Tower*, Aug. 28, 1857. See also ibid., Feb. 26, 1858; *Jefferson Journal*, Mar. 5, 1858.

38. *Jefferson Journal*, Nov. 13 and 20, Dec. 4, 1857.

39. Ibid., Dec. 18 and 25, 1857; Jan. 1, 8, 15, and 29, Feb. 5 and 11, Mar. 12, 1858.

40. Ibid., Mar. 5, 1858. The debate went on through March and April and into May. On the divisive possibilities of toll bridges, see *Port-Gibson Herald*, Aug. 28, Sept. 4, 11, and 18, 1845.

41. *Hinds County Gazette*, Sept. 16, 1857.

42. *Eastern Clarion*, Mar. 30 (quote), Mar. 23, 1859 (BOP vote). See also ibid., Apr. 6, 13, 1859.

43. Ibid., Apr. 20, 1859. See also W. J. Morris to Absalom F. Dantzler, Nov. 9, 1859, and J. C. Welborn to Absalom F. Dantzler, Nov. 17, 1859, Absalom F. Dantzler Papers, Duke.

44. Ibid., May 11, June 8, and Sept. 7, 1859; *BHMM*, 1: 614–15, 1145.

45. *Eastern Clarion*, May 4, June 1 and 8, Aug. 17 and 31, Sept. 7, 14, and 21, 1859. For other examples of county factionalism and state legislative races, see also *Port-Gibson Correspondent*, Sept. 13, 1839, and the 1839 and 1841 campaigns generally; *Yazoo City Whig and Political Register*, Apr. 25, 1845.

46. The law actually read that citizens "shall divide their respective counties into five districts, from each of which the qualified electors of the district shall elect one member" (Hutchinson, *Code of Mississippi*, 710). The issue was discussed in various newspapers (see, e.g., *Mississippian*, Sept. 24, 1845), and created confusion that caused several groups to appeal to the governor for clarification. See Henderson Williams to Governor Runnels, Dec. 10, 1835, and (no heading) Dec. 14, 1835, Governor's Correspondence, MDAH.

47. Each board appointed road overseers in similar fashion, typically during the spring term. See, e.g., BOP Minutes, Claiborne County, Mar. 1853, and Harrison County, Apr. 1860; *Fayette Watch-Tower*, May 1, 1857.

48. Robert Kenzer draws the same conclusion about county patronage and personal networks in Orange County, North Carolina, in *Kinship and Neighborhood*, 55. These characterizations of patronage again parallel those of historians of the first party system. See Carl E. Prince, *New Jersey's Jeffersonian Republicans: The Genesis of an Early Political Machine, 1789–1817* (Chapel Hill, 1967); Formisano, "Deferential-Participant Politics," esp. 479–80.

49. BOP Minutes, Claiborne County, Nov. 1853.

50. Murdo J. MacLeod, "The Primitive Nation State, Delegation of Functions, and Results: Some Examples from Early Colonial Central America," in *Essays in the Political, Economic, and Social History of Colonial Latin America*, ed. Karen Spalding (Newark, Del., 1982), 53–69; Peter Marzahl, "Creoles and Government: The Cabildo of Popayan," *Hispanic American Historical Review* 54 (1974): 636–56; Victor Nunes Leal, *Coronelismo: The Municipality and Representative Government in Brazil*, trans. June Henfrey (Rio de Janeiro, 1948; reprint, Cambridge, 1977), 16, 100–103, and *passim*.

51. BOP Minutes, Claiborne County, Aug. 1849 and Jan. 1858; *Claiborne County, Mississippi: The Promised Land*, compiled by Katy McCaleb Headley (Port Gibson, Miss., 1976), 204–205; BOP Minutes, Carroll County, Jan. 1859.

52. BOP Minutes, Carroll County, June 1858 and Jan. 1859.

53. BOP Minutes, Carroll County, Dec. 1859.

54. Sharkey et al., *Revised Code*, 193; *Southern Standard*, Oct. 31, 1852.

55. Sharkey et al., *Revised Code*, 198; *Hinds County Gazette*, Nov. 23, 1849.

Chapter 6

1. See O'Gorman, "Campaign Rituals and Ceremonies," 79–84; David I. Kertzer, *Ritual, Politics, and Power* (New Haven, 1988); Sally F. Moore and Barbara

Meyeroff, eds., *Secular Ritual* (Amsterdam, 1977); Jean Baker, "The Ceremonies of Politics: Nineteenth-Century Rituals of National Affirmation," in *A Master's Due: Essays in Honor of David Herbert Donald*, ed. William Cooper, Michael Holt, and John McCardell (Baton Rouge, 1985), 161–78; Steven M. Stowe, *Intimacy and Power*; idem, "The 'Touchiness' of the Gentleman Planter: The Sense of Esteem and Community in the Ante-Bellum South," *Psychohistory Review* 8 (1979): 6–17.

2. Many current scholars in ritual studies emphasize the active role of rituals in negotiating power relations rather than simply reflecting elite hegemonic power. This approach sees the message of ritual as contested, not imposed by elites. See e.g., Catherine Bell, *Ritual Theory, Ritual Practice* (New York, 1992), 3–29, 69–93, 98–117. Two recent studies applying this notion of ritual to American history focus on public celebrations and nationalism: Simon Newman, *Parades and the Politics of the Streets: Festive Culture in the Early American Republic* (Philadelphia, 1997); David Waldstreicher, *In the Midst of Perpetual Fetes: The Making of American Nationalism, 1776–1820* (Chapel Hill, 1997).

3. Daniel R. Hundley, *Social Relations in Our Southern States*, ed. William J. Cooper Jr. (Baton Rouge, 1979); Frederick Law Olmsted, *The Cotton Kingdom: A Traveller's Observations on Cotton and Slavery in the American Slave States*, ed. Arthur M. Schlesinger (New York, 1953); Wilbur J. Cash, *The Mind of the South* (New York, 1941); Eugene Genovese, *The Political Economy of Slavery; The World the Slaveholders Made: Two Essays in Interpretation* (New York, 1969); idem, "Yeoman Farmers in a Slaveholders' Democracy," in *Fruits of Merchant Capital: Slavery and Bourgeois Property in the Rise and Expansion of Capitalism*, ed. Eugene Genovese and Elizabeth Fox-Genovese (New York, 1983), 249–64. Summaries of these debates and literature up to 1987 are Randolph B. Campbell, "Planters and Plain Folks: The Social Structure of the Antebellum South," and Drew Faust, "The Peculiar South Revisited: White Society, Culture, and Politics in the Antebellum Period, 1800–1860," both in *Interpreting Southern History: Historiographical Essays in Honor of Sanford W. Higginbotham*, ed. John Boles and Evelyn Thomas Nolen (Baton Rouge, 1987), 48–77, 78–119. C. Vann Woodward, ed., *Mary Chesnut's Civil War* (New Haven, 1981), 204–205; James B. Smith to Jefferson Davis, Feb. 2, 1849, in Crist, Dix, and Beringer, eds., *Papers of Jefferson Davis*, 4: 10.

4. Patron-client systems, however, should not be confused with feudalism or serfdom; clients remained free to move, both geographically and socially, and the relationship was voluntary. See S. N. Eisenstadt and Louis Roniger, "Patron-Client Relations as a Model of Structuring Social Exchange," *Comparative Studies in Society and History* (1980): 42–77. A classic study of a patron-client political culture, although in a society with greater inequality and dependence, is Nunes Leal, *Coronelismo*. See also Neuschel, *Word of Honor*, 13–15 and *passim*; on consensual governance, see Jesse L. Byock, *Medieval Iceland: Society, Sagas, and Power* (Berkeley, 1988), chap. 6; Sabean, *Power in the Blood*; on hegemony, see T. J. Jackson Lears, "The Concept of Cultural Hegemony: Problems and Possibilities," *AHR* 90 (1985): 574; David Forgacs, ed., *An Antonio Gramsci Reader: Selected Writings, 1916–1935* (New York, 1988).

5. Snay, *Gospel of Disunion*, 216. On religion as hierarchical, see Genovese and Fox-Genovese, "Religious Ideals"; idem, "The Divine Sanction of Social Order"; McCurry, *Masters of Small Worlds*, esp. 147–238; for egalitarianism, see Oakes, *The*

Ruling Race, chap. 4; Isaac, *Transformation of Virginia*. For a review of the huge literature on southern class relations and community values, see Jane Turner Censer, "Planters and the Southern Community: A Review Essay," *Virginia Magazine of History and Biography* 94 (1986): 387–408. Local studies that detail the economic, social, and religious "ligaments of society," include Harris, *Plain Folk and Gentry*; Burton, *In My Father's House*; Morris, *Becoming Southern*; Kenzer, *Kinship and Neighborhood*; and McCurry, *Masters of Small Worlds*. All these works note the "double-edged sword" of white male supremacy based on the inviolability of property rights. McCurry emphasizes that the sword (along with evangelical religion) not only made planters superior to slaves and women but also evoked yeomen's respect and deference for their superior resources.

6. The historian most often associated with the egalitarian position is James Oakes. In his first book, *The Ruling Race*, Oakes places mobility at the heart of a "slaveholding world view" that "equated upward mobility with westward migration" (68). This all-consuming pilgrimage destroyed existing ties of friendship and neighborhood and rendered impossible a cultural system based on face-to-face relationships. The latter, he asserts, composed a "dying tradition" of "patriarchal family values" and hereditary status, all of which crumbled beneath "the entrepreneurial slaveholding culture of the antebellum South" (203). In *Slavery and Freedom: An Interpretation of the Old South* (New York, 1990), he extends the argument that status equals wealth. Among slaveholders in particular, patriarchal values became largely obsolete, undermined by partible inheritance, the migratory impulse, and bourgeois capitalism. Many yeomen, however, still valued communal and patriarchal values, and this distinction highlights Oakes's argument that the line between slaveholder and nonslaveholder was more rigid than he painted it in the earlier work. Slavery, he contends, undermined community solidarity and a reciprocal economy, isolating plantations and driving a wedge between two different cultures. A number of studies contend that Oakes may have overstated rates of mobility and argue that they were lower in the South than elsewhere. See Kenzer, *Kinship and Neighborhood*, 22–23, 164–65; Censer, "Planters and Southern Community," 396. Bond finds persistence rates of about one-third in antebellum Mississippi, perhaps somewhat higher in the 1850s, *Political Culture*, 64–65.

7. Richard Graham, *Patronage and Politics in Nineteenth-Century Brazil* (Stanford, 1990), 101. See also Winkle, *Politics of Community*, 86–87, 117–28; Thornton, *Politics and Power*, 156–61; McCurry, *Masters of Small Worlds*, 270–71.

8. The voting process is described in Sharkey et al., *Revised Code*, 90–93, which is virtually unchanged from the earlier Hutchinson, *Code of Mississippi*, 160–62. Quotations are from Sharkey et al.

9. See *Piney Woods Planter and Amite Union Literary Reflector*, Oct. 19, 1839; or the *Mississippian*, 1840–1860.

10. *Eastern Clarion*, Oct. 23, 1858; Hugh McDonald to Governor Runnels, Mar. 4, 1834, Governor's Correspondence, MDAH.

11. Drury Glover and Charles Grauss [?] to Governor McNutt, Nov. 7, 1839. Other protests include Citizens of Tunica County to Governor Tucker, Nov., 1843, and Alexander McCaskill to Governor Runnels, Mar. 27, 1834, Governor's Correspondence, MDAH; *House Journal*, 1854, 147–48; ibid., 1842, 359–63.

12. *BHMM*, 1: 769–70, 309–312.

13. Williams, ed., *Bolivar County*, 10–11, 128–29, 475.

14. Charles Bolton, *Poor Whites of the Antebellum South: Tenants and Laborers in Central North Carolina and Northeast Mississippi* (Durham, N.C., 1994), 112–26, 180–83. Bolton argues that intimidation was the central fact of political life for tenants. The notion of a relatively pure democracy is usually found in studies focusing not on local power relations between the elite and ordinary voters but rather on party ideology. See, e.g., Harry Watson "Conflict and Collaboration: Yeomen, Slaveholders, and Politics in the Antebellum South," *Social History* 10 (1985): 273–98: "Elections were free and frequent, political participation was nearly universal among eligible voters, outright coercion or bribery of voters was almost unknown" (274). Bourke and DeBats detail the importance of neighborhood voting and the potential for intimidation in Oregon, but conclude by favoring the existence of some sort of frontier democracy. They note the presence of coercion during viva voce elections, but argue that it declined with the advent of printed ballots; they also contend that 1850s Oregon was a "preclass environment" that had "stratification by wealth" but also a "lack of political content in those distinctions." See their *Washington County*, 282 (quotes), 283, 295; idem, "Identifiable Voting," esp. 283, 286; and idem, "Charles Sumner, the London Ballot Society, and the Senate Debate of March 1867," *Perspectives in American History*, New Series 1 (1984): 344–45.

15. William J. Rorabaugh, "Rising Democratic Spirits: Immigrants, Temperance, and Tammany Hall, 1854–1860," *Civil War History* 22 (1976): 138–57; Escott, *Many Excellent People*, 15–22; Crofts, *Old Southampton*, esp. 187; Smith, "Jacksonian Democracy on the Chesapeake," 381–93; Winkle, "Ohio's Informal Polling Place," 169 (quote), 172–74; Richard P. McCormick, *The History of Voting in New Jersey: A Study of the Development of Election Machinery, 1664–1911* (New Brunswick, N.J., 1953), 122–23, 131–32; Ethington, *The Public City*, 74–75. Formisano, *Transformation of Political Culture*, 140–48 and *passim*, and Winkle, *Politics of Community*, chaps. 3–5, detail how elite influence ebbed and flowed, surviving legal changes and the movement to printed ballots. Nonetheless, parties and the state were steadily eroding the personal, noninstitutional, antiparty political culture.

16. Bourke and DeBats, *Washington County*, 194; Winkle, *Politics of Community*, chap. 5.

17. On slaveholding as a mark of honor, see Patterson, *Slavery and Social Death*, esp. chap. 3; Greenberg, *Honor and Slavery*. In *Ruling Race*, Oakes argues that southerners cared nothing for "display" or public demonstrations of wealth. Yet, he says, they were obsessed with buying more land and more slaves, which, however varied their motives, provided the most obvious mark of status.

18. DMcK to DMcL, Nov. 2, 1845, DMP.

19. Clark and Guice, *Frontiers in Conflict*, 202. On local bureaucratic and military posts as marks of honor, see Burkholder, "Honor and Honors in Colonial Spanish America," 27–34.

20. The following discussion is based on a relatively large sample of about two thousand men from seven counties. Over 1,500 of them were located in the 1850 or 1860 manuscript census schedules and county tax rolls (see Appendix for discussion of methodological issues). The typically disparate nature of local election returns accentuates the problems of using idiosyncratic biographical data from the census, tax rolls, and local histories; the information is simply not regular or standardized

enough for easy presentation. The data in Tables A.2 through A.16 and in Figures 6.1 through 6.3 should therefore be considered estimates, although they do convey a clear sense of the hierarchy of public offices. The aggregate data, of course, can not provide quite the same sense as all of those two thousand contests. It is like trying to choose representative excerpts from several thousand letters and diaries.

21. Herbert Weaver, *Mississippi Farmers, 1850–1860* (Nashville, 1945), 61. See also Moore, *Emergence of the Cotton Kingdom*, 139–40; Wooster, *People in Power*, 82–105; Holt, *Political Crisis*, 229.

22. Williams, ed., *Bolivar County*, 483–84; Anna Alice Kamper, "A Social and Economic History of Ante-Bellum Bolivar County, Mississippi," (Master's thesis, University of Alabama, 1942), 85–87.

23. Lang, *Harrison County*, 8; Williams, ed., *Bolivar County*, 10–11, 37–38.

24. *Commonwealth*, June 23, 1855.

25. Sharkey et al., *Revised Code*, 120–50.

26. Oakes, *Ruling Race*, 57–68.

27. Hutchinson, *Code of Mississippi*, 374–466; Sharkey et al., *Revised Code*, 120–28, 131–33.

28. Albert E. Casey, assisted by Frances Powell Otken, *Amite County, Mississippi, 1699–1865*, 2 vols. (Birmingham, Ala., 1948; reprint, Liberty, Miss., 1961), 1: 224, 228–29, 237.

29. JPS to DMcL, Aug. 6, 1834 and May 17, 1837; HS to DMcL, Dec. 4, 1835, DMP.

30. Sharkey, *Revised Code*, 146–47; John Blalock to Joseph Mathews, Apr. 17, 1848, Governor's Correspondence, MDAH.

31. *Prairie News*, Feb. 18, 1858; *Weekly American Banner*, Oct. 19, 1855.

32. In Harrison County, for example, about two-thirds of all men owed taxes of only 40 cents, the rate for one adult poll. Harrison County Tax Rolls, 1855, 1858; Hutchinson, *Code of Mississippi*, 687–93.

33. Anderson Hutchinson, *Manual of Judicial, Ministerial and Civil Forms, Revised, Americanized, and Divested of Useless Verbage* (Jackson, Miss., 1852), 41.

34. Hutchinson, *Code of Mississippi*, 694–95.

35. Carroll County, personal tax rolls, 1855.

36. Casey, *Amite County*, 1: 602.

37. Special and municipal election returns are filed with regular elections in RG 28, MDAH (see bibliography).

Chapter 7

1. *Hinds County Gazette*, Aug. 15, 1855; Tyler Anbinder, *Nativism and Slavery: The Northern Know Nothings and the Politics of the 1850s* (New York, 1992), 20–31; Overdyke, *Know-Nothing Party*, 34–44.

2. Davis, *Recollections*, 345. On northern surprise victories, see Gienapp, *Origins*, 92, 100–101; Formisano, *Birth of Mass Political Parties*, 238–50.

3. Wiley P. Harris to JFHC, Oct. 8, 1855, JFHC Collection.

4. On Unionism, southern Whiggery, and Know-Nothings, see Overdyke, *Know-Nothing Party*. For Mississippi, see Donald Rawson, "Party Politics in Mississippi, 1850–1860," (Ph.D. diss., Vanderbilt University, 1964); Ross, "Dying Hard, Dy-

ing Fast," 191–95, 235–43; idem, "Charles D. Fontaine: A Mississippi Know-Nothing Leader," *JMH* 48 (1986): 105–118.

5. *Fort Adams Item,* June 9, 1855; DMcK to DMcL, Dec. 8, 1854, DMP. On Know-Nothings and antipartyism, see Michael F. Holt, "The Politics of Impatience: The Origins of Know Nothingism," *JAH* 60 (1973): 309–331; Formisano, *Birth of Mass Political Parties,* 238–50; Gienapp, *Origins,* 96–98; Jean H. Baker, *Ambivalent Americans: The Know-Nothing Party in Maryland* (Baltimore, 1977); John David Bladek, "'Virginia Is Middle Ground': The Know Nothing Party and the Gubernatorial Election of 1855," *Virginia Magazine of History and Biography* 106 (1998): 35–70.

6. Wiley P. Harris to JFHC, Oct. 8, 1855, JFHC Collection.

7. DMcK to DMcL, Dec. 8, 1854, DMP.

8. Overdyke, *Know-Nothing Party,* 73, 42–43.

9. Wyatt-Brown, *Southern Honor,* 55.

10. Gienapp, *Origins,* 182–87 (1855), 261–62, 330–34, 343–46 (1856 convention), and 305–448 (1856 election); Anbinder, *Nativism and Slavery,* 167–72 (1855), 194–209 (1856 convention), 212–45 (1856 election); Overdyke, *Know-Nothing Party,* 127–42, esp. 131–33.

11. *Fort Adams Item,* Sept. 2, 1854; *Tri-Weekly Mercury,* June 23, 1855.

12. *Oxford Signal,* Oct. 9, 1856; *Democratic Flag,* May 26, 1855.

13. *Commonwealth,* Sept. 1, 1855; Cluskey, ed., *Hon. Albert G. Brown,* 395; see Overdyke, *Know-Nothing Party,* 120, 292–95; Ross, "Dying Hard, Dying Fast," 113–16.

14. William L. Sharkey to CDF, May 28, 1855; Erasmus L. Acee to CDF, 1855, CDF Papers. See also Ross, "Dying Hard, Dying Fast," 145–61.

15. Ross, "Dying Hard, Dying Fast," 161–62.

16. Ross provides the most complete analysis of Mississippi nativism and emphasizes the number of Protestant clergymen who campaigned for the party and against popery. See ibid., esp. 117–38, 234–36. See also idem, "Pulpit and Stump: The Clergy and the Know Nothings in Mississippi," *JMH* 48 (1986): 271–82. Overdyke, *Know-Nothing Party,* downplays the party's anti-Catholicism: "Only to a limited and qualified extent could the party be labeled as anti-Catholic" (239).

17. *Weekly American Banner,* Nov. 14, 1856; Colin S. Tarpley to JFHC, Aug. 3, 1855, JFHC Collection.

18. See *Fort Adams Item,* "Catholicism and Liberty," Oct. 28, 1854, and "Self-Protection" (against foreigners and Jews), May 26, 1855. Oakland College, a Presbyterian institution in Claiborne County, also felt the effects of nativism. In November of 1855, students delivered orations on "Romanism versus Republicanism" and "The Huguenots," which celebrated Protestant heroes who fought Catholicism. OCP.

19. See various 1855 issues of the *Sun* (Attala), *Marshall Democrat* and *Empire Democrat, Ripley Advertiser* (Tippah), *Fort Adams Item* (Wilkinson), *Lauderdale Republican* and *Weekly American Banner* (Yazoo). Two other studies imply that the Know-Nothings held more conventions than Whigs and that the new party injected "ideology" into politics, but do not explore the implications. See Thornton, *Politics and Power,* 19, n.3; Kenzer, *Kinship and Neighborhood,* 63–64.

20. *Marshall Democrat,* Sept. 1 and Oct. 27, 1855.

21. *Ripley Advertiser,* Oct. 11 and Nov. 1, 1855.

22. *Lauderdale Republican,* June 11, Aug. 28, Sept. 25, 1855. See also Joseph Slade to Richard Griffith, Nov. 11, 1855, Griffith Papers, MDAH.

23. *Weekly American Banner*, June 13 (quote), Oct. 5, Nov. 9, 1855, June 6, 1856.

24. *Empire Democrat*, Nov. 25, 1854.

25. JFHC to John A. Quitman, Nov. 25, 1855, and Feb. 3, 1856 (quote), Quitman Family Papers, MDAH. See also E. H. Holliman to JFHC, July 9, Aug. 6, Aug. 27, 1855, JFHC Collection.

26. D. W. Owen to CDF, May 14, 1855, CDF Papers; Wiley P. Harris to JFHC, Aug. 30, 1855, JFHC Collection.

27. *Fort Adams Item*, Apr. 14, 1855 (also "Who Knows," May 5, 1855); *Weekly American Banner*, June 15, 1855; *Yazoo City Weekly Whig*, Oct. 20, 1854.

28. *Vicksburg Daily Whig*, Mar. 21, 1855.

29. *Commonwealth*, Dec. 1, 1855; Mar. 6, 1857.

30. *Yazoo City Weekly Whig*, Apr. 20, 1855.

31. *Weekly American Banner*, Mar. 14, 28, April 11 and 18, 1856.

32. Ibid., Nov. 3, 10, 1855.

33. The totals for assessor also matched the baseline, while the races for ranger and surveyor had only one candidate each. There was a recording error in the sheriff's race, which makes comparisons impractical. More examples of the Know-Nothings' impact on county elections are in Olsen, "Community, Honor, and Secession," chaps. 4 and 7.

34. Overdyke, *Know-Nothing Party*, 271; Ross, "Dying Hard, Dying Fast," 224–29. See also *Weekly Panola Star*, July 15, 1857 (and throughout the campaign); Rawson, "Party Politics in Mississippi," 228–33.

35. *Mississippian*, Feb. 17, Mar. 10, 1858; *Prairie News*, Feb. 25, 1858.

36. *Jefferson Journal*, Sept. 13, Feb. 26, Mar. 19, 1858; *Kemper Democrat*, Apr. 8, 1858; *Mississippian*, Apr. 14, June 9, 23, 1858.

37. *Commonwealth*, Nov. 14 and 28, 1857, Mar. 27, 1858.

38. Ibid., Mar. 13 and 20, 1858, Dec. 12, 1857. See also ibid., Mar. 13, 20, Apr. 10, Aug. 21, 1858.

39. Ibid., Jan. 14, 30, Feb. 6, 13, 1858.

40. Ibid., Feb. 20, 27, Mar. 6, 13, 27, 1858.

41. Ibid., Oct. 2, 1858.

42. See esp. the 1860 votes for assessor and coroner.

43. I did not find precinct totals for Tippah County in 1853 or 1858.

44. *Ripley Advertiser*, Nov. 15, 29, 1855.

45. Ibid., Mar. 3, 24 (quote), 1858.

46. Ibid., Mar. 24, 1858.

47. Ibid., Mar. 24, May 12, 1858.

48. *Mississippian*, June 9, Aug. 11, 1858; *Natchez Daily Courier*, Oct. 12, 1858. Democrats in Noxubee and Lafayette also nominated some candidates, although not a complete slate, but I failed to find election returns.

49. *Mississippian*, Oct. 27, 1858.

50. *Mississippi Democrat* and *Kemper Democrat*, both quoted in *Mississippian*, Oct. 27, 1858; *Mississippian*, Oct. 9, 1860.

Chapter 8

1. *Woodville Republican*, Aug. 9, 1853.

2. Stephen Oates, *With Malice toward None: A Life of Abraham Lincoln* (New York, 1977), 62.

3. Percy Lee Rainwater, ed., "The Autobiography of Benjamin Grubb Humphreys," *Mississippi Valley Historical Review* 21 (1934): 245. On the same connection between honor and secession within one southern community, see Burton, *In My Father's House*, esp. 225–26. The association between individual and community is particularly strong in rural, honor-bound societies. Conversely, in atomistic modern America, group identity is low. "[T]he personal, individual identity of the [contemporary] common man is relatively strong . . . while the social identity, the sense of self deriving from group membership, is pitifully weak" (Lane, *Political Ideology*, 382).

4. *Eagle*, June 1, 1855, quoted in Grady McWhiney, "Ethnic Roots of Southern Violence," in *A Master's Due*, ed. Cooper, Holt, and McCardell, 125–26; *Mississippian*, Aug. 23 and 30, 1854; Benjamin L. C. Wailes Diary, June 6, 7, 1860, Benjamin L. C. Wailes Collection, Duke; Jason Niles Diary, Dec. 12, 1850, SHC.

5. Horace V. Redfield, *Homicide, North and South: Being a Comparative View of Crime Against the Person in Several Parts of the United States* (Philadelphia, 1880); Bruce, *Violence and Culture*, 242. Bruce argues that a state's age was the crucial factor, suggesting that frontier conditions contributed heavily to violence. Other studies of southern violence include John Hope Franklin, *The Militant South, 1800–1861* (Cambridge, Mass., 1956); Sheldon Hackney, "Southern Violence," *AHR* 74 (1969): 906–925; Raymond D. Gastil, "Homicide and a Regional Culture of Violence," *American Sociological Review*, 36 (1971): 412–27; John Shelton Reed, "Below the Smith and Wesson Line: Southern Violence," in *One South: An Ethnic Approach to Regional Culture* (Baton Rouge, 1982), 139–53; James Denham, *A Rogue's Paradise: Crime and Punishment in Antebellum Florida, 1821–1861* (Tuscaloosa, Ala., 1997).

6. Lyon quoted in McWhiney, "Ethnic Roots of Southern Violence," 125–26; Bruce, *Violence and Culture*, 7.

7. *Prairie News*, Aug. 12, 1858.

8. The connection between slavery and violence is explored in, among others, Ayers, *Vengeance and Justice*; Greenberg, *Honor and Slavery*.

9. Prentiss quoted in Wyatt-Brown, *Honor and Violence*, 145; *Whig Advocate*, Feb. 23, 1839; Williams, *Dueling*, 55. See also Greenberg, *Masters and Statesmen*, 23–41; Wyatt-Brown, *Southern Honor*, 350–61; Bruce, *Violence and Culture*, 21–43; Stowe, *Intimacy and Power*, 1–49; Frevert, "Bourgeois Honour," 256–57, 269–70.

10. *Mississippian*, Nov. 4, 1853, May 26, 1854; Wilmuth S. Rutledge, "Dueling in Antebellum Mississippi," *JMH* 26 (1964): 190–91.

11. Gorn, "'Gouge and Bite,'" 21–22, 36, 39–42. See also Tom Parramore, "Gouging in Early North Carolina," *North Carolina Folklore Journal* 22 (1974); Wyatt-Brown, *Southern Honor*, 25–61, and pt. 3; Rutledge, "Dueling in Antebellum Mississippi," 185–91. Ritual violence was also prevalent in all social classes of other honor-bound societies; see, e.g., Nye, *Masculinity and Male Codes*, 28–30.

12. *Weekly American Banner*, May 16, 1856.

13. Davis, *Recollections*, 111.

14. On ritual words in an oral culture, see Stowe, *Intimacy and Power*, 15–30 and *passim*; Wyatt-Brown, *Honor and Violence*, 142–52; Greenberg, *Masters and Statesmen*, 38; Gorn, "Gouge and Bite," 19, 27–28; Lawrence Levine, *Black Culture and Black Consciousness: Afro-American Folk Thought from Slavery to Freedom* (New

York, 1977); Bruce, *Violence and Culture*, 3–113; McWhiney, "Ethnic Roots of Southern Violence," 129, 137.

15. Neuschel, *Word of Honor*, 103–104; Sharkey et al., *Revised Code*, 385, 631. Neuschel summarizes the work of several scholars on the implications of words in past and present societies. See esp. 103–118 (including nn. 1, 10, 14).

16. Nye, *Masculinity and Male Codes*, 191, 200, also 15–28. See also Neuschel, *Word of Honor*, 16, 194; Kelly, *Damn'd Thing Called Honour*, 130–32, 139–45, 277; McAleer, *Dueling*; George Armstrong Kelly, "Duelling in Eighteenth-Century France: Archaeology, Rationale, Implications," *Eighteenth Century* 21 (1980): 236–54.

17. See Elias, *Civilizing Process, passim*; Patrick H. Hutton, "The History of Mentalities: The New Map of Cultural History," *History and Theory* (1981): 237–59.

18. *Southern Standard*, May 8, 1852; Journal of S. M. Meek, July 22, 1857, S. M. Meek Papers.

19. *Vicksburg Weekly Whig*, Oct. 22, 1851.

20. Rutledge, "Dueling in Antebellum Mississippi," 187. On dueling, personal leadership, and weak institutions, see also Ethington, *Public City*, 78–83; Bertram Wyatt-Brown, "Andrew Jackson's Honor," *JER* 17 (1997): 1–36; William Rorabaugh, "The Political Duel in the Early Republic," ibid., 15 (1995): 1–23, esp. 15–22; Burton, *In My Father's House*, 71–73, 91–93; Joanne Freeman, "Slander, Poison, Whispers, and Fame: Jefferson's 'Anas' and Political Gossip in the Early Republic," *JER* 15 (1995): 25–57. Freeman asserts that "when a politician defended his honor, he was defending his ability to claim political power, promoting himself and his 'particular friends' while dishonoring political rivals" ("Dueling as Politics," 297). Williams paraphrases John Hope Franklin's comment (*The Militant South*, 38, 50) that in Mississippi, "as late as 1850," one rarely achieved much political success without demonstrating his masculinity in a duel (*Dueling in the Old South*, 16).

21. *Prairie News*, July 29, 1858, Jan. 27, 1859; Dec. 2, 1858 (quote). See also ibid., June 30, July 22, Nov. 11, 1858.

22. Williams, *Dueling in the Old South*, 32–33; Frederic Hudson, *Journalism in America* (New York, 1873), 762–64; *Port-Gibson Herald*, Sept. 22, 1848; William Oliver Stevens, *Pistols at Ten Paces: The Story of the Code of Honor in America* (Boston, 1940), 83–84.

23. *Prairie News*, Aug. 25, 1859; *Weekly Mississippian*, Aug. 7, 1859; *Natchez Daily Courier*, Oct. 13, 1859.

24. Christopher Olsen, "'Molly Pitcher' of the Mississippi Whigs: The Editorial Career of Mrs. Harriet N. Prewett," *JMH* 58 (1996): 237–54.

25. *Weekly American Banner*, Oct. 10, 17, Sept. 5, Nov. 7, Dec. 12, 1856.

26. Montgomery, *Reminiscences*, 35–36; resolutions quoted in Horace S. Fulkerson, *A Civilian's Recollections of the War Between the States* (Baton Rouge, 1939), 12. On the evolution of southern nationalism as rooted in slavery, and the ideological gulf it created, see John McCardell, *The Idea of a Southern Nation: Southern Nationalists and Southern Nationalism, 1830–1860* (New York, 1979).

27. Rainwater, *Storm Center*, 72–85 (quote, 83); Barney, *Secessionist Impulse*, 144. See also Oakes, *Ruling Race*, 37–41; Holt, Political Crisis, 229; Crofts, *Reluctant Confederates*, 193–94.

28. Edward Mayes, *Lucius Q. C. Lamar: His Life, Times, and Speeches, 1825–1893* (Nashville, 1896), 625; *Senate Journal*, 1856, 567. Mitchell Snay similarly argues

that religion unified southerners' objections to Republicanism, which included fear of race war, the threat to white supremacy, and loss of western territory. See his *Gospel of Disunion*, 214–18 and *passim*.

29. On the special importance of the word *equality* in the lexicon of honor, see esp. Stowe, "Touchiness of the Gentleman Planter," 14–15, and *Intimacy and Power*, 13–15, 25–49.

30. Woods, *Rebellion and Realignment*, 114 (quote), 115–17.

31. Gienapp, *Origins*, 357–65 (quotes, 363). See also Joel Silbey, "The Surge of Republican Power: Partisan Antipathy, American Social Conflict, and the Coming of the Civil War," in *Essays on American Antebellum Politics*, ed. Maizlish and Kushma, 216, 217.

32. *Fayette Watch-Tower*, July 31, 1857; Cluskey, ed., *Hon. Albert G. Brown*, 597.

33. *Weekly Democratic Advocate*, May 5, 1859. The argument that slavery was mostly a symbolic issue, of course, has a long history. Avery Craven emphasized southern notions of honor and Republican declarations of northern moral superiority in *The Repressible Conflict, 1830–1861* (Baton Rouge, 1939), and *The Growth of Southern Nationalism, 1848–1861* (Baton Rouge, 1953). See also Bertram Wyatt-Brown, "Honor and Secession," in *Yankee Saints and Southern Sinners* (Baton Rouge, 1985), 183–213. J. Mills Thornton notes the moral implications of Free Soil, which "came to be seen as the primary symbol of second-class citizenship" (*Politics and Power*, 221). Alabamians, he argues, responded with such vehemence because Free Soil "involved obvious and demeaning governmental discrimination against the South" (221). Fire-eaters made "two interlocking appeals, one to freedom and the ideal of individual autonomy, and one to equality and the alleged threat to manhood and self-respect" (213). Actual access to new slave territory remained relatively unimportant, compared to the symbolic force of Free Soil as a moral insult (225–26). Michael Holt also concludes that "without question the most persistent theme in secessionist rhetoric" was not the immediate threat of abolition or long-term consequences of Free Soil, "but the infamy and degradation of submitting to the rule of a Republican majority" (*Political Crisis*, 242). Even William Cooper, who most clearly places the tangible threat to slavery at the center of southern politics and secession, acknowledges that Republicanism was also "an unforgivable slander" to southerners, for whom "good name and reputation were the personal hallmarks of free and honorable men" (*Liberty and Slavery*, 257).

34. Albert Gallatin Brown to JFHC, Feb. 4, 1856, JFHC Collection; Powhatan Ellis to Charles Ellis, June 19, 1860, Munford-Ellis Family Papers, George W. Munford Division.

35. Powhatan Ellis to Powhatan Ellis Jr., Dec. 25, 1860, Munford-Ellis Family Papers, George W. Munford Division; Cluskey, ed., *Hon. Albert G. Brown*, 594, 595. On the importance of the religious foundation of the proslavery argument, see Drew Gilpin Faust, ed., *The Ideology of Slavery: Proslavery Thought in the Antebellum South, 1830–1860* (Baton Rouge, 1981); Snay, *Gospel of Disunion*, chap. 2.

36. Gov. Pettus's speech to the legislature, Nov. 26, 1860, Governor's Executive Journal, 1856–1866; Mayes, *Lamar*, 628. On Christianity and disunion, see Snay, *Gospel of Disunion*, chap. 5 and *passim*.

37. Cluskey, ed., *Hon. Albert G. Brown*, 596; House resolutions quoted in Claiborne, *John A. Quitman*, 340.

38. *Free Trader*, May 13, 1858; *Mississippian*, Jan. 15, 1858, quoting *True Southron*; *Mississippian*, Mar. 31, 1858, quoting *Port Gibson Herald*; Rainwater, *Storm Center*, 48–49.

39. *Prairie News*, Apr. 22, Mar. 11 and 18, 1858, Feb. 3, 1859. See also *American Citizen*, Oct. 1, 1859.

40. *Prairie News*, July 1, 1858.

41. Ibid., Aug. 5, 12, Sept. 23, 1858.

42. Rainwater, *Storm Center*, 96–102.

43. *Mississippi Free Trader*, Mar. 11, 1858; Barney, *Secessionist Impulse*, 190.

44. *Mississippian*, Dec. 11, Dec. 4, 1860.

45. Ibid., Nov. 13, Dec. 18, 1860. See also Rainwater, *Storm Center*, 144–49.

46. All quoted in Rainwater, *Secessionist Impulse*, 150, 151, 149.

47. *Brandon Republican*, Dec. 6, 1860.

48. *Hinds County Gazette*, Sept. 26, 1860. See also Barney, *Secessionist Impulse*, 214–15.

49. *Jackson News*, quoted in the *Brandon Republican*, Dec. 6, 1860. William Freehling emphasizes the importance of this sort of "tribal cry" that had united southerners throughout the antebellum years. It was successful again, he concludes, when Lower South secessionists rallied the voters "against taunting Yankees." Later, after Lincoln's call for troops, "the old tribal fury swept the Middle South." See his "The Divided South, Democracy's Limitations, and the Causes of the Peculiarly North American Civil War," in *Why the Civil War Came*, ed. Gabor S. Boritt (New York, 1996), 150–51, 170–72.

50. Broadsides Collection, Oct. 17, 1860, MDAH; Rainwater, *Storm Center*, 140–41 n. 15, 135–60; Barney, *Secessionist Impulse*, 56–162. On the relationship between the presidential contest and various elections for convention delegates and on the commitment to secession among Breckinridge voters, see Peyton McCrary, Clark Miller, and Dale Baum, "Class and Party in the Secession Crisis: Voting Behavior in the Deep South, 1856–1861," *JIH* 8 (1978): 429–57.

51. Brooke quoted in Barney, *Secessionist Impulse*, 199; *Mississippi Free Trader*, Aug. 27, Dec. 28, 1860 (also the *Mississippian*, July–Nov., 1860); Montgomery, *Reminiscences*, 36.

52. *Brandon Republican*, Dec. 6, 1860; Rainwater, *Storm Center*, 164, 161–75; Barney, *Secessionist Impulse*, 191–215.

53. Barney, *Secessionist Impulse*, 61–62, 78, 153–80; Rainwater, *Storm Center*, 109–114, 127–28. See also Snay, *Gospel of Disunion*, chap. 5, where he demonstrates the important role of secessionist ministers and their emotional appeals to defend southern Christianity.

54. Rainwater, *Storm Center*, 117; Barney, *Secessionist Impulse*, 205. See also Holt, who concludes that Democratic leaders in the Lower South who supported secession "were just as likely to be followers as leaders" (*Political Crisis*, 222).

55. Rainwater, *Storm Center*, 173; Lowndes County Unionists, Nov. 16, 1860, Broadsides Collection, MDAH; Barney, *Secessionist Impulse*, 216, 163–88, 207–230.

56. Barney, *Secessionist Impulse*, 237–45, 268–69; Rainwater, *Storm Center*, 177–79, 207–208; Bolton, *Poor Whites*, 138–80. Only Bolton argues that intimidation was a significant factor (among tenant farmers) in the support for secession.

57. Barney, *Secessionist Impulse*, 231.

58. *House Journal*, 1860, 14; Barney, *Secessionist Impulse*, 205–219.

59. Harris quoted in Rainwater, *Storm Center*, 193–94; Broadsides Collection, MDAH, Dec., 1860. Several studies argue that more Bell supporters than others abstained from the convention election; see McCrary, Miller, and Baum, "Class and Party."

60. Fulkerson, *Civilian's Recollections*, 8; Davis, *Recollections*, 402.

61. Fulkerson, *Civilian's Recollections*, 5, 8; Gov. Pettus's speech to the legislature, Nov. 26, 1860, Governor's Executive Journal, MDAH. See also Thomas H. Woods, "A Sketch of the Mississippi Secession Convention of 1861 — Its Membership and Work," *PMHS* 6 (1902): 91–104. Woods was a delegate from Kemper County.

62. John A. Campbell to Franklin Pierce, Dec. 19, 1860, quoted in Barney, *Secessionist Impulse*, 215. See Burton, *In My Father's House*; Harris, *Plain Folk and Gentry*; Greenberg, *Masters and Statesmen*.

Appendix

1. A good introduction to these issues is Kenneth Winkle, "The U.S. Census as a Source in Political History," *Social Science History* 15 (1991): 565–77. Probably the most skeptical assessment of the census figures and evidence of high voter turnout is Gerald Ginsburg, "Computing Antebellum Turnout: Methods and Models," *JIH* 16 (1986): 579–611.

Bibliography

Archival Sources

Mississippi Department of Archives and History, Jackson, Mississippi

Adams (Simeon Roe) and Family Papers
Birdsong (Jefferson J.) Diary
Broadsides File
Brown (Albert Gallatin) Papers
Burrus (John C.) Papers
Charles–Crutcher–McRaven Papers
Claiborne (J. F. H.) Collection
Cooke (H. A.) Letters
Crutcher–Shannon Papers
Fontaine (Charles D.) and Family Papers
Griffith (Richard) Papers
Howze (Isham Robertson) Family Papers
Meek (Samuel M.) and Family Papers
Oakland College Papers
Priestly (William) Papers
Quitman Papers
Quitman (John Anthony) and Family Papers
Wailes (Benjamin L. C.) Collection
Whitehurst (William Nicholas) Papers

Perkins Library, Special Collections, Duke University, Durham, North Carolina

Campbell Family Papers
Carpenter (G.) Letter

Dantzler (Absalom F.) Papers
Kirkpatrick (Pauline) Letters
Malone (Ellis) Papers
McDowell (James) Papers
McLaurin (Duncan) Papers
Munford-Ellis Family Papers
Pope-Carter Family Correspondence
St. George Harris (Henry) Papers
Scarborough Family Papers
Stapp (Joseph D.) Papers
Wailes (Benjamin L. C.) Collection

Southern Historical Collection, University of North Carolina, Chapel Hill, North Carolina

Alcorn (James Lusk) Papers
Lea Family Papers
McLaurin (William) Papers
Meek (S. M.) Papers

Niles (Jason) Diary
Orr (Jehu Amaziah) Papers
Steel (Frank F.) Letters
Wright-Herring Papers

Federal Census

MS Population Schedules, Amite County, 1850, 1860.
MS Population Schedules, Bolivar County, 1850, 1860.
MS Population Schedules, Carroll County, 1850, 1860.
MS Population Schedules, Claiborne County, 1850, 1860.
MS Population Schedules, Harrison County, 1850, 1860.
MS Population Schedules, Hinds County, 1850, 1860.
MS Population Schedules, Jasper County, 1850, 1860.
MS Population Schedules, Marshall County, 1850, 1860.
MS Population Schedules, Rankin County, 1850, 1860.
MS Population Schedules, Tishomingo County, 1850, 1860.
MS Slave Schedules, Amite County, 1850, 1860.
MS Slave Schedules, Bolivar County, 1850, 1860.
MS Slave Schedules, Carroll County, 1850, 1860.
MS Slave Schedules, Claiborne County, 1850, 1860.
MS Slave Schedules, Harrison County, 1850, 1860.
MS Slave Schedules, Hinds County, 1850, 1860.
MS Slave Schedules, Jasper County, 1850, 1860.

State Records

Mississippi Department of Archives and History, Jackson, Mississippi

Map Collection
Levy Boards, RG 20

Governor's Correspondence, 1835–1861, Record Group 27

Secretary of State, Record Group 28, Manuscript Election Returns 1843–1860, vols. 23a–34b

Volume 23a (general election, state offices, 1843).

Volume 23b (general election, state offices, 1843).

Volume 24a (general election, state offices, 1845).

Volume 24b (general election, governor, 1845).

Volume 26a (general election, November, 1847, Adams County through Yallobusha County).

Volume 27b (general election, November, 1847, Lowndes County through Yazoo County).

Volume 28a (general election, November, 1849).

Volume 28b (local and special elections, 1849, Adams County through Lowndes County).

Volume 28c (local and special elections, 1849, Madison County through Yazoo County).

Volume 29a (special convention election, September, 1851; general election, November, 1851, Adams County through Pontotoc County).

Volume 29b (general election, November, 1851, Rankin County through Yazoo County).

Volume 30b (general election, November, 1853, Adams County through Panola County).

Volume 31a (general election, November, 1853, Perry County through Yazoo County; local and special elections, 1854–1855, Adams County through Harrison County).

Volume 31b (local and special elections, 1854–1855, Hinds County through Yazoo County).

Volume 31c (general election, November, 1855).

Volume 32a (general election, November, 1857).

Volume 33a (general election, October, 1858, Adams County through Madison County).

Volume 33b (general election, October, 1858, Marshall County through Yazoo County; local and special elections, 1858).

Volume 33c (general election, November, 1859; local and special elections, 1859).

Volume 34a (general election, November, 1860, Adams County through Panola County).

Volume 34b (general election, November, 1860, Perry County through Yazoo County).

County Records

Mississippi Department of Archives and History, Jackson, Mississippi

Adams County Records

Board of Police Minutes, 1849–1851

Amite County Records

Personal Tax Rolls, 1856, 1858, 1859

Bolivar County Records
    Board of Police Minutes, 1847–1856
    Tax Rolls, 1855, 1858
Carroll County Records
    Board of Police Minutes, 1848–1860
    Personal Tax Rolls, 1855, 1856, 1857, 1858
Claiborne County Records
    Board of Police Minutes, 1844–1858
Covington County Records
    Board of Police Minutes, 1854–1860
Harrison County Records
    Board of Police Minutes, 1841–1860
    Personal Tax Rolls, 1853, 1856, 1858
Hinds County Records
    Board of Police Minutes, 1854–1860
Panola County Records
    Board of Police Minutes, 1857–1860
Rankin County Records
    Personal Tax Roll, 1855

Newspapers

American Citizen (Canton), 1851–1859
Brandon Republican, 1859
Chickasaw Union (Pontotoc), 1837
Clinton Gazette, 1835
Columbus Democrat, 1848–1853
Commonwealth (Canton), 1855–1857
Constitution (Oxford), 1851
Democratic Advocate (Lexington), 1856
Democratic Banner (Holly Springs), 1853
Democratic Flag (Oxford), 1852, 1855
Dollar Democrat (Oxford, Coffeeville), 1841–1845
Eagle of the South (Jackson), 1859
Eastern Clarion (Paulding), 1858–1859
Empire Democrat (Holly Springs), 1854–1855
Fayette Watch-Tower, 1855–1857
Flag of the Union, 1850–1853
Fort Adams Item, 1854–1855
Fort Adams Times, 1853
Gallatin Argus, 1858
Guard, The (Holly Springs), 1843–1845
Herald of the South (Brandon), 1859
Hinds County Gazette (Raymond), 1848–1855
Holly Springs Gazette, 1841–1847, 1849–1850, 1853
Hornet, The (Carrollton), 1843
Independent Democrat (Canton), 1842–1844
Mississippian (Jackson), 1843–1861

Jefferson Journal (Fayette), 1857–1858

Kemper Democrat (DeKalb), 1858

Lauderdale Republican (Marion), 1854–1856

Lexington Advertiser, 1851

Liberty Advocate, 1843–1846

Louisville Messenger, 1842–1843

Marshall Democrat (Holly Springs), 1855

Marshall Jeffersonian (Holly Springs), 1851–1852

Mercury (Jackson), 1854–1855

Mississippi Creole (Clinton), 1841

Mississippi Democrat (Carrollton), 1845–1847

Mississippi Free Trader (Natchez), 1849–1859

Mississippi Intelligencer and General Advertiser for the New Counties (Pontotoc), 1838–1839

Mississippi Palladium (Holly Springs), 1851–1852

Mississippi Times (Holly Springs), 1856

Mississippi Union and State Gazette (Jackson), 1853–1856

Monroe Democrat (Aberdeen), 1850–1852

Natchez Daily Courier, 1852–1854

North Mississippi Union (Eastport, Jacinto), 1851, 1854

Oxford Signal, 1856

Piney Woods Planter and Amite Union Literary Reflector (Liberty), 1838–1840

Port-Gibson Correspondent, 1838–1845

Port-Gibson Herald, 1842–1848

Port Gibson Herald and Correspondent, 1849–1851

Prairie News (Okolona), 1858–1859

Primitive Republican (Columbus), 1851–1852

Ripley Advertiser, 1855–1856

Sea Coast Democrat (Mississippi City), 1857

Southern Marksman (Clinton), 1838–1839

Southern Pioneer (Carrollton), 1840–1841

Southern Reveille (Port Gibson), 1851–1854, 1858–1859

Southern Standard (Columbus), 1851–1853

Southern Star (Jackson), 1852

Southern Sun (Jackson), 1840

Southern Tribune (Pontotoc), 1842–1845

Southron (Jackson), 1840–1848

Spirit of the Times (Pontotoc), 1841

Statesman (Jackson), 1843

Sunny South (Aberdeen), 1857–1858

True Democrat (Paulding), 1845–1847

Vicksburg Whig, 1844–1860

Weekly American Banner (Yazoo City), 1855–1856

Weekly American Times (Vicksburg), 1857

Weekly Conservative (Aberdeen), 1854–1855

Weekly Independent (Aberdeen), 1850–1853

Western Statesman, The (Carrollton), 1844

Wilkinson Gazette (Woodville), 1858
Woodville Republican, 1850–1855, 1858
Yazoo City Weekly Whig, 1851—1854
Yazoo Democrat (Yazoo City), 1850–1854, 1859

Published Documents

Biographical and Historical Memoirs of Mississippi. 2 vols. Chicago, 1891.

Campbell, J. A. P., Amos R. Johnston, and Amos Lovering, eds. *The Revised Code of the Statute Laws of the State of Mississippi*. Jackson, 1871.

Claiborne, John Francis Hamtramck. *Life and Correspondence of John A. Quitman*, vol. 2. New York, 1860.

Cluskey, M. W., ed. *Speeches, Messages, and Other Writings of the Hon. Albert Gallatin Brown, A Senator in Congress from the State of Mississippi*. Philadelphia, 1859.

Crist, Lynda Lasswell, Mary Seaton Dix, and Richard E. Beringer, eds. *The Papers of Jefferson Davis*, vol. 4, 1849–1852. Baton Rouge, 1983.

Crist, Lynda Lasswell, and Mary Seaton Dix, eds. *The Papers of Jefferson Davis*, vol. 5, 1853–1855. Baton Rouge, 1985.

————. *The Papers of Jefferson Davis*, vol. 6, 1856–1860. Baton Rouge, 1989.

DeBow, James D. B. *The Seventh Census of the United States, 1850: An Appendix*. Washington D.C., 1853.

————. *Statistical View of the United States: Compendium of the Seventh Census*. Washington D.C., 1854.

Hutchinson, Anderson. *Code of Mississippi: Being an Analytical Compilation of the Public and General Statutes of the Territory and State, with Particular References to the Local and Private Acts, from 1798–1848*. Jackson, 1848.

Journal of the Convention of the State of Mississippi, and the Act Calling the Same; with the Constitution of the United States, and Washington's Farewell Address. Jackson, 1851.

Kennedy, Joseph C. G. *Population of the United States in 1860*. Washington D.C., 1864.

————. *Agriculture of the United States in 1860*. Washington D.C., 1864.

Mayes, Edward. *Lucius Q. C. Lamar: His Life, Times, and Speeches, 1825–1893*. Nashville, 1896.

McIntosh, James T., Lynda L. Crist, and Mary S. Dix, eds. *The Papers of Jefferson Davis*, vol. 3, *July 1846–December 1848*. Baton Rouge, 1981.

New York Tribune Association. *A Political Text-Book for 1860: Comprising a Brief View of Presidential Nominations and Elections: Including All the National Platforms Ever Yet Adopted*. Compiled by Horace Greeley and John F. Cleveland. New York, 1868.

————. *The Tribune Almanac: For the Years 1838 to 1868, Inclusive: Comprehending the Politician's Register and the Whig Almanac*. 2 vols. New York, 1868.

Sharkey, William L., Samuel S. Boyd, Henry T. Ellett, and William L. Harris. *The Revised Code of the Statute Laws of the State of Mississippi*. Jackson, 1857.

Thorndale, William, and William Dollarhide, eds. *Map Guide to the U. S. Federal Censuses, 1790–1920*. Baltimore, 1987.

United States Government. *Compendium of the Enumeration of the Inhabitants and Statistics of the United States, as Obtained at the Department of State, from the Returns of the Sixth Census*. Washington D.C., 1842.

Wiltshire, Betty Couch. *Marriages and Deaths from Mississippi Newspapers*, vol. 4, 1850–1860. New York, 1990.

Published Travel Accounts, Reminiscences, Contemporary Articles, and Diaries

Anderson, John Q., ed. "The Narrative of John Hutchins." *JMH* 20 (1958): 1–29.

Baldwin, James G. *Flush Times of Alabama and Mississippi: A Series of Sketches*. Introduction and notes by James H. Justus. Baton Rouge, 1987.

Bettersworth, John Knox, ed. *Mississippi in the Confederacy: As They Saw It*. Baton Rouge, 1961.

Carroll, Thomas Battle. *Historical Sketches of Oktibbeha County*. Gulfport, Miss., 1931.

Claiborne, John Francis Hamtramck. "Rough Riding Down South." *Harper's New Monthly Magazine* 25 (June 1862).

———. "A Trip through the Piney Woods." *PMHS* 9 (1906): 487–538.

Claiborne County, Mississippi: The Promised Land. Compiled by Katy McCaleb Headley. Port Gibson, Miss., 1976.

Cobb, Joseph Beckham. *Mississippi Scenes: or, Sketches of Southern and Western Life and Adventure, Humorous, Satirical, and Descriptive, including the Legend of Black Creek*. Philadelphia, 1851.

Davis, Reuben. *Reminiscences of Mississippi and Mississippians*. Cambridge, 1889.

Foote, Henry Stuart. *Casket of Reminiscences*. Washington D.C., 1874.

Fulkerson, Horace S. *A Civilian's Recollections of the War between the States*. Baton Rouge, 1939.

———. *Random Recollections of Early Days in Mississippi*. Vicksburg, 1885.

Harris, Wiley P. "Autobiography of Wiley P. Harris." In *Courts, Judges, and Lawyers of Mississippi, 1798–1935*, ed. Dunbar Rowland. Jackson, 1935.

Hudson, Frederic. *Journalism in America*. New York, 1873.

Ingraham, Joseph Holt. *The South-West By a Yankee*, 2 vols. New York, 1835.

"A Journey through the South in 1836: Diary of James D. Davidson." *JSH* 1 (1935): 1–35.

Lincecum, Gideon. "Autobiography of Gideon Lincecum." *PMHS* 8 (1904): 443–519.

Lipscomb, Dr. William Lowndes. *A History of Columbus Mississippi During the Nineteenth Century*. Birmingham, Ala., 1909.

Montgomery, Frank A. *Reminiscences of a Mississippian in Peace and War*. Cincinnati, 1901.

Olmsted, Frederick Law. *A Journey in the Back Country, 1853–1854*. Williamstown, Mass., 1972.

Rainwater, Percy Lee, ed. "The Autobiography of Benjamin Grubb Humphreys." *Mississippi Valley Historical Review* 21 (1934): 231–55.

———. "The Autobiography of James H. Maury." *JMH* 5 (1943): 87–102.

Smedes, Susan Dabney. *Memorials of a Southern Planter*. Edited with introduction by Fletcher M. Green. New York, 1965.

Sparks, William Henry. *The Memories of Fifty Years*. Philadelphia, 1850; reprint, Macon, 1872.

Warren, Harris Gaylord. "Vignettes of Culture in Old Claiborne." *JMH* 20 (1958): 125–45.

Welsh, Miss Mary J. "Recollections of Pioneer Life in Mississippi." *PMHS* 4 (1901): 343–56.

Wilkins, Jesse M. "Early Times in Wayne County." *PMHS* 6 (1902): 260–72.

Williams, Wirt A., ed. *History of Bolivar County, Mississippi, Compiled by Florence Warfield Sillers*. Jackson, 1948.

Woods, Thomas H. "A Sketch of the Mississippi Secession Convention of 1861 — Its Membership and Work." *PMHS* 6 (1902): 91–104.

Books and Articles

Alcorn, Richard S. "Leadership and Stability in Mid-Nineteenth-century America: A Case Study of an Illinois Town." *JAH* 61 (1974): 685–702.

Alexander, Thomas. "The Civil War as Institutional Fulfillment." *JSH* 47 (1981): 3–32.

Alexander, Thomas B., Peggy Duckworth Elmore, Frank M. Lowery, and Mary Jane Pickens Skinner. "The Basis of Alabama's Ante-Bellum Two-party System: A Case Study in Party Alignment and Voter Response in the Traditional Two-party System of the United States by Quantitative Analysis Methods." *Alabama Review* 19 (1966): 243–76.

Alexander, Thomas B., Kit C. Carter, Jack R. Lister, Jerry C. Oldshue, and Winfred G. Sandlin. "Who Were the Alabama Whigs?" *Alabama Review* 16 (1963): 5–19.

Almond, Gabriel, and Sidney Verba. *The Civic Culture: Political Attitudes and Democracy in Five Nations*. Princeton, 1963; reprint. Boston, 1965.

Altschuler, Glenn C., and Stuart M. Blumin, "Limits of Political Engagement in Antebellum America: A New Look at the Golden Age of Participatory Democracy," *JAH* 84 (1997): 855–910.

Anbinder, Tyler. *Nativism and Slavery: The Northern Know Nothings and the Politics of the 1850s*. New York, 1992.

Ayers, Edward. *Vengeance and Justice: Crime and Punishment in the Nineteenth-century American South*. New York, 1984.

Baker, Jean H. *Affairs of Party: The Political Culture of Northern Democrats in the Nineteenth Century*. Ithaca, 1983.

———. "The Ceremonies of Politics: Nineteenth-century Rituals of National Affirmation." In *A Master's Due: Essays in Honor of David Herbert Donald*, ed. William Cooper, Michael Holt, and John McCardell, 161–78. Baton Rouge, 1985.

———. *The Politics of Continuity: Maryland Political Parties From 1858 to 1870*. Baltimore, 1973.

Barney, William L. *The Secessionist Impulse: Alabama and Mississippi in 1860*. Princeton, 1974.

Basch, Norma. "A Challenge to the Story of Popular Politics." *JAH* 84 (1997): 900–903.

Baum, Dale. *The Shattering of Texas Unionism: Politics in the Lone Star State During the Civil War Era*. Baton Rouge, 1999.

Beeman, Richard. "Robert Munford and the Political Culture of Frontier Virginia." *American Studies* 12 (1971): 169–83.

Bell, Catherine. *Ritual Theory, Ritual Practice*. New York, 1992.

Berelson, Bernard, Paul Lazarsfeld, and William N. McFee. *Voting*. Chicago, 1954.

Bergeron, Paul H. *Antebellum Politics in Tennessee*. Lexington, 1982.

Bladek, John David. "'Virginia Is Middle Ground': The Know Nothing Party and the Gubernatorial Election of 1855." *Virginia Magazine of History and Biography* 106 (1998): 35–70.

Bogue, Allan G. "Social Theory and the Pioneer." *Agricultural History* 34 (1960): 21–34.

Bolton, Charles. *Poor Whites of the Antebellum South: Tenants and Laborers in Central North Carolina and Northeast Mississippi*. Durham, N.C., 1994.

Bond, Bradley. *Political Culture in the Nineteenth-Century South: Mississippi, 1830–1900*. Baton Rouge, 1995.

Boritt, Gabor S., ed. *Why the Civil War Came*. New York, 1996.

Bourke, Paul F., and Donald A. DeBats. "Identifiability of Voting in Nineteenth-Century America: Toward a Comparison of Britain and the United States before the Secret Ballot." *Perspectives in American History* 11 (1977): 259–88.

————. "Individuals and Aggregates: A Note on Historical Data and Assumptions." *Social Science History* 4 (1980): 229–50.

————. *Washington County: Politics and Community in Antebellum America*. Baltimore, 1995.

Braden, Waldo W., ed. *Oratory in the Old South, 1828–1860*. Baton Rouge, 1970.

Bruce, Dickson D., Jr. *Violence and Culture in the Antebellum South*. Austin, 1978.

Buenger, Walter L. *Secession and the Union in Texas*. Austin, 1984.

Burnham, Walter Dean. "The Changing Shape of the American Political Universe." *APSR* 59 (1965): 7–28.

Burton, Orville Vernon. *In My Father's House Are Many Mansions: Family and Community in Edgefield, South Carolina*. Chapel Hill, 1985.

Burton, Orville Vernon, and Robert C. McMath, eds. *Class, Conflict, and Consensus: Antebellum Southern Community Studies*. Westport, Conn., 1982.

Byock, Jesse L. *Medieval Iceland: Society, Sagas, and Power*. Berkeley, 1988.

Caire, R. J., and Katy Caire. *History of Pass Christian*. Pass Christian, Miss., 1976.

Campbell, Randolph B. "Planters and Plain Folks: The Social Structure of the Antebellum South." In *Interpreting Southern History: Historiographical Essays in Honor of Sanford W. Higginbotham*, ed. John Boles and Evelyn Thomas Nolen, 48–77. Baton Rouge, 1987.

Carey, Anthony Gene. *Parties, Slavery, and the Union in Antebellum Georgia*. Athens, Ga., 1997.

Casey, Albert E., assisted by Frances Powell Otken. *Amite County, Mississippi, 1699–1865*, 2 vols. Birmingham, Ala., 1948.

Cashin, Joan. *A Family Venture: Men and Women on the Southern Frontier*. Baltimore, 1991.

Censer, Jane Turner. "Planters and the Southern Community: A Review Essay." *Virginia Magazine of History and Biography* 94 (1986): 387–408.

Channing, Steven A. *Crisis of Fear: Secession in South Carolina*. New York, 1970.

Clark, Thomas D., and John Guice. *Frontiers in Conflict: The Old Southwest, 1795–1830*. Albuquerque, N.M., 1989.

Converse, Philip E. "The Nature of Belief Systems in Mass Politics." In *Ideology and Discontent*, ed. David E. Apter, 206–261. New York, 1964.

Cooper, William J., Jr. *Liberty and Slavery: Southern Politics to 1860*. New York, 1983.

———. *The South and the Politics of Slavery, 1828–1856*. Baton Rouge, 1978.

Cooper, William J., Jr., Michael F. Holt, and John McCardell, eds. *A Master's Due: Essays in Honor of David Herbert Donald*. Baton Rouge, 1985.

Craven, Avery. *The Growth of Southern Nationalism, 1848–1861*. Baton Rouge, 1953.

———. *The Repressible Conflict, 1830–1861*. Baton Rouge, 1939.

Crenshaw, Ollinger. *The Slave States in the Presidential Election of 1860*. Baltimore, 1945.

Crenson, Matthew A. *Neighborhood Politics*. Cambridge, 1983.

Crofts, Daniel W. *Old Southampton: Politics and Society in a Virginia County, 1834–1869*. Charlottesville, Va., 1992.

———. *Reluctant Confederates: Upper South Unionists in the Secession Crisis*. Chapel Hill, 1989.

Crowther, Edward. "Holy Honor: Sacred and Secular in the Old South." *JSH* 58 (1992): 619–36.

Davis, William. *A Way through the Wilderness: The Natchez Trace and the Civilization of the Southern Frontier*. New York, 1995.

DeFiore, Jayne Crumpler. "COME, and Bring the Ladies: Tennessee Women and the Politics of Opportunity during the Presidential Campaigns of 1840 and 1844." *Tennessee Historical Quarterly* 51 (1992): 197–212.

Denham, James. *A Rogue's Paradise: Crime and Punishment in Antebellum Florida, 1821–1861*. Tuscaloosa, Ala., 1997.

Dick, Everett. *The Dixie Frontier: A Comprehensive Picture of Southern Frontier Life before the Civil War*. New York, 1948; reprint. New York, 1964.

Doyle, Don Harrison. *The Social Order of a Frontier Community: Jacksonville, Illinois, 1825–1870*. Urbana, 1978.

———. "Social Theory and New Communities in Nineteenth-century America." *Western Historical Quarterly* 8 (1977): 151–65.

Dubay, Robert W. *John Jones Pettus: Mississippi Fire-Eater: His Life and Times*. Jackson, 1975.

Dupre, Daniel. "Barbecues and Pledges: Electioneering and the Rise of Democratic Politics in Antebellum Alabama." *JSH* 60 (1994): 479–512.

———. *Transforming the Cotton Frontier: Madison County, Alabama, 1800–1840*. Baton Rouge, 1997.

Edelman, Murray. *The Symbolic Uses of Politics*. Urbana, 1964.

Edwards, Laura. *Gendered Strife and Confusion: the Political Culture of Reconstruction*. Urbana, 1997.

Edwards, Rebecca. *Angels in the Machinery: American Party Politics from the Civil War to the Progressive Era*. New York, 1997.

Eisenstadt, S. N., and Louis Roniger. "Patron-Client Relations as a Model of Structuring Social Exchange." *Comparative Studies in Society and History* 1980: 42–77.

Elias, Norbert. *The Civilizing Process: The Development of Manners, Changes in the Code of Conduct and Feeling in Early Modern Times*. Translated by Edmund Jephcott. Basel, Germany, 1939; reprint. New York, 1978.

Escott, Paul D. *Many Excellent People: Power and Privilege in North Carolina, 1850–1900*. Chapel Hill, 1995.

Etcheson, Nicole. *The Emerging Midwest: Upland Southerners and the Political Culture of the Old Northwest, 1787–1861*. Bloomington, Ind., 1996.

————. "Manliness and the Political Culture of the Old Northwest, 1790–1860." *JER* 15 (1995): 59–77.

Ethington, Philip J. *The Public City: The Political Construction of Urban Life in San Francisco, 1850–1900*. Cambridge, 1994.

Faulkner, William. *Absalom! Absalom!* New York, 1986.

Faust, Drew Gilpin, ed. *The Ideology of Slavery: Proslavery Thought in the Antebellum South, 1830–1860*. Baton Rouge, 1981.

————. "The Peculiar South Revisited: White Society, Culture, and Politics in the Antebellum Period, 1800–1860." In *Interpreting Southern History: Historiographical Essays in Honor of Sanford W. Higginbotham*, ed. John Boles and Evelyn Thomas Nolen, 78–119. Baton Rouge, 1987.

Flanigan, William H., and Nancy H. Zingale. "Alchemist's Gold: Inferring Individual Relationships from Aggregate Data." *Social Science History* 9 (1985): 73–91.

Folsom, Burton W. II. "Party Formation and Development in Jacksonian America: The Old South." *Journal of American Studies* 7 (1973): 217–29.

Foner, Eric. *Free Soil, Free Labor, Free Men: The Ideology of the Republican Party before the Civil War*. New York, 1970.

Ford, Lacy K. Jr. *Origins of Southern Radicalism: The South Carolina Upcountry, 1800–1860*. New York, 1983.

Forgacs, David, ed. *An Antonio Gramsci Reader: Selected Writings, 1916–1935*. New York, 1988.

Formisano, Ronald P. *The Birth of Mass Political Parties: Michigan, 1827–1861*. Princeton, 1971.

————. "Deferential-Participant Politics: The Early Republic's Political Culture." *APSR* 68 (1974): 473–87.

————. "The New Political History." *International Journal of Social Education* 1 (1986): 5–21.

————. "The 'Party Period' Revisited." *JAH* 86 (1999): 93–120.

————. "Toward a Reorientation of Jacksonian Politics: A Review of the Literature, 1959–1975." *JAH* 63 (1976): 42–65.

————. *The Transformation of Political Culture: Massachusetts Parties, 1790s–1840s*. New York, 1983.

Franklin, John Hope. *The Militant South, 1800–1861*. Cambridge, Mass., 1956.

Freehling, William. *The Road to Disunion*, vol. 1, *Secessionists at Bay, 1776–1854*. New York, 1990.

Freeman, Joanne. "Dueling as Politics: Reinterpreting the Burr-Hamilton Duel." *WMQ* 53 (1996): 289–318.

————. "Slander, Poison, Whispers, and Fame: Jefferson's 'Anas' and Political Gossip in the Early Republic." *JER* 15 (1995): 25–47.

Frevert, Ute. "Bourgeois Honour: Middle-Class Duellists in Germany from the Late
    Eighteenth to the Early Twentieth Century." In *The German Bourgeoisie: Es-
    says on the Social History of the German Middle Class from the Late Eighteenth
    to the Early Twentieth Century*, ed. David Blackbourn and Richard J. Evans,
    255–92. London, 1991.

Garner, James W. "The First Struggle over Secession in Mississippi." *PMHS* 4 (1901):
    89–104.

Gastil, Raymond. "Homicide and a Regional Culture of Violence." *American Socio-
    logical Review* 36 (1971): 412–27.

Gee, Mrs. O. K. *History of Middleton, Carroll County, Mississippi*. Winona, Miss.,
    1961.

Geertz, Clifford. *The Interpretation of Cultures; Selected Essays*. New York, 1973.

Genovese, Eugene D. "Marxian Interpretations of the Slave South." In *Toward a
    New Past: Dissenting Essays in American History*, ed. Barton Bernstein. New
    York, 1968.

———. *The Political Economy of Slavery: Studies in the Economy and Society of the
    Slave South*. Toronto, 1961.

———. *The World the Slaveholders Made: Two Essays in Interpretation*. New York,
    1969.

Genovese, Eugene D., and Elizabeth Fox-Genovese. "The Divine Sanction of Social
    Order: Religious Foundations of the Southern Slaveholders' World View." *Jour-
    nal of the American Academy of Religion* 55 (1987): 211–33.

———. "The Religious Ideals of Southern Slave Society." *Georgia Historical Quar-
    terly* 70 (1986): 1–16.

———. "Yeoman Farmers in a Slaveholders' Democracy." In *Fruits of Merchant
    Capital: Slavery and Bourgeois Property in the Rise and Expansion of Capital-
    ism*, ed. Elizabeth Fox-Genovese and Eugene D. Genovese, 249–64. New York,
    1983.

Gienapp, William E. *The Origins of the Republican Party, 1852–1856*. New York,
    1987.

Gilmore, David D. *Manhood in the Making: Cultural Concepts of Masculinity*. New
    Haven, 1990.

Gilmore, David D., ed. *Honor and Shame and the Unity of the Mediterranean*.
    Washington, D.C., 1987.

Ginsburg, Gerald. "Computing Antebellum Turnout: Methods and Models." *JIH* 16
    (1986): 579–611.

Gorn, Elliot. "'Good-Bye Boys, I Die a True American': Homicide, Nativism, and
    Working-Class Culture in Antebellum New York City." *JAH* 74 (1987): 388–410.

———. "'Gouge and Bite; Pull Hair and Scratch': The Social Significance of Fight-
    ing in the Southern Backcountry." *AHR* 90 (1985): 18–43.

Graber, Doris A. *Verbal Behavior and Politics*. Urbana, 1976.

Graham, Richard. *Patronage and Politics in Nineteenth-century Brazil*. Stanford,
    1990.

Greenberg, Kenneth. *Honor and Slavery: Lies, Duels, Noses, Masks, Dressing as a
    Woman, Gifts, Strangers, Humanitarianism, Death, Slave Rebellions, the Pro-
    slavery Argument, Baseball, Hunting, and Gambling in the Old South*.
    Princeton, 1996.

———. *Masters and Statesmen: The Political Culture of American Slavery*. Baltimore, 1985.

———. "The Nose, the Lie, and the Duel in the Antebellum South." *AHR* 95 (1990): 57–74.

Hackney, Sheldon. "Southern Violence." *AHR* 74 (1969): 906–925.

Hahn, Steven. *The Roots of Southern Populism: Yeoman Farmers and the Transformation of the Georgia Upcountry, 1850–1890*. New York, 1983.

Harris, J. William. *Plain Folk and Gentry in a Slave Society: White Liberty and Black Slavery in Augusta's Hinterlands*. Middletown, Conn., 1985.

Harris, Marvin. *The Rise of Anthropological Theory: A History of Theories of Culture*. New York, 1968.

Hartz, Louis. *The Liberal Tradition in America: An Interpretation of American Political Thought since the Revolution*. New York, 1955.

Haynes, Robert. "Law Enforcement in Frontier Mississippi." *JMH* 22 (1960): 27–42.

Hays, Samuel P. "Society and Politics: Politics and Society." *JIH* 15 (1985): 481–99.

Hearon, Cleo. "Mississippi and the Compromise of 1850." *PMHS* 14 (1914): 7–229.

Hermann, Janet Sharp. *Joseph E. Davis: Pioneer Patriarch*. Jackson, 1990.

Hettle, Wallace. "The 'Self-Analysis' of John C. Rutherfoord: Democracy and Manhood of a Virginia Secessionist." *Southern Studies* 5 (1992): 81–116.

Hindus, Michael Stephen. *Prison and Plantation: Crime, Justice, and Authority in Massachusetts and South Carolina, 1767–1878*. Chapel Hill, 1980.

Holt, Michael F. *The Political Crisis of the 1850s*. New York, 1978.

———. *Political Parties and American Political Development from the Age of Jackson to the Age of Lincoln*. Baton Rouge, 1992.

———. "The Politics of Impatience: The Origins of Know Nothingism." *JAH* 60 (1973): 309–331.

Howe, Daniel Walker. *The Political Culture of the American Whigs*. Chicago, 1979.

Huckfeldt, Robert, Eric Plutzer, and John Sprague. "Alternative Contexts of Political Behavior: Churches, Neighborhoods, and Individuals." *Journal of Politics* 55 (1993): 365–81.

Hutton, Patrick H. "The History of Mentalities: The New Map of Cultural History." *History and Theory* (1981): 237–59.

Hyde, Jr., Samuel. *Pistols and Politics: The Dilemma of Democracy in Louisiana's Florida Parishes, 1810–1899*. Baton Rouge, 1996.

Hymes, Dell. "Linguistic Aspects of Comparative Method." In *The Methodology of Comparative Research*, ed. Robert T. Holt and John E. Turner, 295–342. New York, 1970.

Inscoe, John C. *Mountain Masters, Slavery, and the Sectional Crisis in Western North Carolina*. Knoxville, 1989.

Ireland, Robert M. *The County Courts in Antebellum Kentucky*. Lexington, 1972.

———. *Little Kingdoms: The Counties of Kentucky, 1850–1891*. Lexington, 1977.

Isaac, Rhys. *The Transformation of Virginia, 1740–1790*. Chapel Hill, 1982.

James, D. Clayton. *Antebellum Natchez*. Baton Rouge, 1968.

Jeffrey, Thomas E. "'Free Suffrage' Revisited: Party Politics and Constitutional Reform in Antebellum North Carolina." *North Carolina Historical Review* 59 (1982): 24–48.

————. *State Parties and National Politics: North Carolina, 1815–1861.* Athens, Ga., 1989.

Johnson, Michael P. *Toward a Patriarchal Republic: The Secession of Georgia.* Baton Rouge, 1977.

Kelly, George Armstrong. "Duelling in Eighteenth-Century France: Archaeology, Rationale, Implications." *Eighteenth Century* 21 (1980): 236–54.

Kelly, James. *That Damn'd Thing Called Honour: Duelling in Ireland, 1570–1860.* Cork University Press, 1995.

Kenzer, Robert C. *Kinship and Neighborhood in a Southern Community: Orange County, North Carolina, 1849–1881.* Knoxville, 1987.

Kertzer, David I. *Ritual, Politics, and Power.* New Haven, 1988.

Kimmel, Michael. *Manhood in America: A Cultural History.* New York, 1996.

Kolp, John. *Gentlemen and Freeholders: Electoral Politics in Colonial Virginia.* Baltimore, 1998.

Kousser, J. Morgan. "Ecological Regression and the Analysis of Past Politics." *JIH* 4 (1973): 237–62.

Kruman, Marc. *Parties and Politics in North Carolina, 1836–1865.* Baton Rouge, 1983.

Lane, Robert E. *Political Ideology: Why the American Common Man Believes What He Does.* New York, 1962.

Lang, John H. *History of Harrison County Mississippi.* Gulfport, Miss., 1936.

Lazarsfeld, Paul, Bernard Berelson, and William N. McFee. *The People's Choice.* New York, 1944.

Leal, Victor Nunes. *Coronelismo: The Municipality and Representative Government in Brazil.* Translated June Henfrey. Rio de Janeiro, 1948; reprint. Cambridge, 1977.

Lears, T. J. Jackson. "The Concept of Cultural Hegemony: Problems and Possibilities." *AHR* 90 (1985): 567–93.

Leonard, Gerald. "The Ironies of Partyism and Antipartyism: Origins of Partisan Political Culture in Jacksonian Illinois." *Illinois Historical Journal* 87 (1994): 21–40.

Leverenz, David. *Manhood and the American Renaissance.* Ithaca, 1989.

Levine, Lawrence. *Black Culture and Black Consciousness: Afro-American Folk Thought from Slavery to Freedom.* New York, 1977.

Lippmann, Walter. *Public Opinion.* New York, 1922.

Lowe, Richard G. "The Republican Party in Antebellum Virginia, 1856–1860." *Virginia Magazine of History and Biography* 81 (1973): 259–79.

Lowery, Charles. "The Great Migration to the Mississippi Territory, 1798–1819." *JMH* 30 (1968): 177–86.

Lucas, M. Philip. "Beyond McCormick and Miles: The Pre-Partisan Political Culture of Mississippi." *JMH* 44 (1982): 329–48.

Maccoby, Eleanor, Richard E. Matthews, and Alton S. Morton. "Youth and Political Change." In *Political Behavior: A Reader in Theory and Research,* ed. Heinz Eulau, Samuel J. Eldersveld, and Morris Janowitz, 299–307. Chicago, 1956.

MacLeod, Murdo J. "The Primitive Nation State, Delegation of Functions and Results: Some Examples from Early Colonial Central America." In *Essays in the*

Political, Economic and Social History of Colonial Latin America, ed. Karen Spalding, 53–67. Newark, Del., 1982.

Maizlish, Stephen E., and John J. Kushma, eds. *Essays on American Antebellum Politics, 1840–1860*. College Station, Texas, 1982.

Malinowski, Bronislaw. *Magic, Science, and Religion and Other Essays*. Boston, 1948.

Marzahl, Peter. "Creoles and Government: The Cabildo of Popayan." *Hispanic American Historical Review* 54 (1974): 636–56.

Mathews, Donald. *Religion in the Old South*. Chicago History of American Religion, ed. Martin E. Marty. Chicago, 1977.

May, Robert E. *John A. Quitman: Old South Crusader*. Baton Rouge, 1985.

Mayfield, John. "'The Soul of a Man': William Gilmore Simms and Myths of Southern Manhood." *JER* 15 (1995): 477–500.

McAleer, Kevin. *Dueling: The Cult of Honor in Fin-de-Siècle Germany*. Princeton, 1994.

McCain, William D. *The Story of Jackson: A History of the Capital of Mississippi, 1821–1951*. Jackson, 1953.

McCardell, John. *The Idea of a Southern Nation: Southern Nationalists and Southern Nationalism, 1830–1860*. New York, 1979.

McCormick, Richard P. *The History of Voting in New Jersey: A Study of the Development of Election Machinery, 1664–1911*. New Brunswick, N.J., 1953.

———. *The Second American Party System: Party Formation in the Jacksonian Era*. Chapel Hill, 1966.

McCrary, Peyton, Clark Miller, and Dale Baum. "Class and Party in the Secession Crisis: Voting Behavior in the Deep South, 1856–1861." *JIH* 8 (1978): 429–57.

McCurry, Stephanie. *Masters of Small Worlds: Yeoman Households, Gender Relations, and the Political Culture of the Antebellum South Carolina Low Country*. New York, 1995.

———. "The Two Faces of Republicanism: Gender and Proslavery Politics in Antebellum South Carolina." *JAH* 78 (1992): 1245–64.

McKee, James W. "William Barksdale and the Congressional Election of 1853 in Mississippi." *JMH* 34 (1972): 129–58.

McLemore, Richard Aubrey, ed. *A History of Mississippi*, vol. 1. Hattiesburg, Miss., 1973.

McWhiney, Grady. "Ethnic Roots of Southern Violence." In *A Master's Due: Essays in Honor of David Herbert Donald*, ed. William Cooper, Michael Holt, and John McCardell, 112–37. Baton Rouge, 1985.

Merton, Robert K. *Social Theory and Social Structure*. Glencoe, Ill., 1957.

Meyers, Marvin. *The Jacksonian Persuasion: Politics and Belief*. Stanford, 1957.

Miles, Edwin Arthur. *Jacksonian Democracy in Mississippi*. Chapel Hill, 1960.

———. "The Mississippi Press in the Jackson Era, 1824–41." *JMH* 19 (1957): 1–20.

Moore, John Hebron. *Agriculture in Ante-Bellum Mississippi*. New York, 1971.

———. *The Emergence of the Cotton Kingdom in the Old Southwest: Mississippi, 1770–1860*. Baton Rouge, 1988.

———. "Local and State Governments of Antebellum Mississippi." *JMH* 44 (1982): 104–134.

Moore, Sally F., and Barbara Meyeroff, eds. *Secular Ritual*. Amsterdam, 1977.

Morris, Christopher. *Becoming Southern: The Evolution of a Way of Life: Warren County and Vicksburg, Mississippi, 1770–1860.* New York, 1995.

———. "An Event in Community Organization: The Mississippi Slave Insurrection Scare of 1835." *Journal of Social History.* 22 (1988): 93–111.

Morrison, Michael. *Slavery and the American West: The Eclipse of Manifest Destiny and the Coming of the Civil War.* Chapel Hill, 1997.

Napier, John H., III. "Piney Woods Past: A Pastoral Elegy." In *Mississippi's Piney Woods: A Human Perspective,* ed. Noel Polk, 12–24. Jackson, Miss., 1986.

Neuschel, Kristen B. *Word of Honor: Interpreting Noble Culture in Sixteenth-Century France.* Ithaca, 1989.

Newman, Simon. *Parades and the Politics of the Streets: Festive Culture in the Early American Republic.* Philadelphia, 1997.

Nobles, Gregory. *American Frontiers: Cultural Encounters and Continental Conquest.* New York, 1997.

Nye, Robert A. *Masculinity and Male Codes of Honor in Modern France.* New York, 1993.

Oakes, James. *The Ruling Race: A History of American Slaveholders.* New York, 1982.

———. *Slavery and Freedom: An Interpretation of the Old South.* New York, 1990.

Oates, Stephen. *With Malice toward None: A Life of Abraham Lincoln.* New York, 1977.

O'Gorman, Frank. "Campaign Rituals and Ceremonies: The Social Meaning of Elections in England, 1780–1860." *Past and Present* 135 (1992): 79–115.

Olsen, Christopher. "'Molly Pitcher' of the Mississippi Whigs: The Editorial Career of Mrs. Harriet N. Prewett." *JMH* 58 (1996): 237–54.

———. "Respecting 'the wise allotment of our sphere': White Women and Politics in Mississippi, 1840–1860." *Journal of Women's History* 11 (1999): 104–125.

Overdyke, W. Darrell. *The Know-Nothing Party in the South.* Baton Rouge, 1950; reprint. Gloucester, Mass., 1968.

Ownby, Ted. *Subduing Satan: Religion, Recreation, and Manhood in the Rural South, 1865–1920.* Chapel Hill, 1990.

Owsley, Frank Lawrence. *Plain Folk of the Old South.* Baton Rouge, 1949; reprint. Chicago, 1965.

Parramore, Tom. "Gouging in Early North Carolina." *North Carolina Folklore Journal* 22 (1974): 55–62.

Parsons, Talcott. *Politics and Social Structure.* New York, 1969.

Patterson, Orlando. *Slavery and Social Death: A Comparative Study.* Cambridge, 1982.

Pereyra, Lillian A. *James Lusk Alcorn: Persistent Whig.* Baton Rouge, 1966.

Peristiany, Jean G., ed. *Honour and Shame: The Values of Mediterranean Society.* Chicago, 1966.

Pillar, James J. *The Catholic Church in Mississippi, 1837–65.* New Orleans, 1964.

Pitt-Rivers, Julian. "Honour." In *International Encyclopedia of the Social Sciences,* 17 vols., ed. David L. Sills, 6: 503–511. New York, 1968.

Pitt-Rivers, Julian, and J. G. Peristiany. *Honor and Grace in Anthropology.* Cambridge, 1992.

Porter, Albert Ogden. *County Government in Virginia: A Legislative History, 1607–1904.* New York, 1947.

Prince, Carl E. *New Jersey's Jeffersonian Republicans: The Genesis of an Early Politi-cal Machine, 1789–1817.* Chapel Hill, 1967.

Pugh, David G. *Sons of Liberty: The Masculine Mind in Nineteenth-century America.* Westport, Conn., 1983.

Rable, George C. *The Confederate Republic: A Revolution against Politics.* Chapel Hill, 1994.

Rainwater, Percy Lee. *Mississippi: Storm Center of Secession, 1856–1861.* New York, 1938.

Ranck, James Byrne. *Albert Gallatin Brown: Radical Southern Nationalist.* New York, 1937.

Redfield, Horace V. *Homicide, North and South: Being a Comparative View of Crime Against the Person in Several Parts of the United States.* Philadelphia, 1880.

Reed, John Shelton. *One South: An Ethnic Approach to Regional Culture.* Baton Rouge, 1982.

Ridgway, Whitman. *Community Leadership in Maryland, 1790–1840: A Comparative Analysis of Power in Society.* Chapel Hill, 1979.

Riesman, David, and Nathan Glazer. "The Meaning of Opinion." *Public Opinion Quarterly* 12 (1948–1949): 633–48.

Rorabaugh, William. "The Political Duel in the Early Republic." *JER* 15 (1995): 1–23.

———. "Rising Democratic Spirits: Immigrants, Temperance, and Tammany Hall, 1854–1860." *Civil War History* 22 (1976): 138–57.

Rosenbaum, Walter A. *Political Culture.* New York, 1975.

Ross, Cecil S. Hilliard. "Charles D. Fontaine: A Mississippi Know-Nothing Leader." *JMH* 48 (1986): 105–118.

———. "Pulpit and Stump: The Clergy and the Know Nothings in Mississippi." *JMH* 48 (1986): 271–82.

Rotundo, E. Anthony. *American Manhood: Transformations in Masculinity from the Revolution to the Modern Era.* New York, 1993.

Rowland, Dunbar, ed. *Courts, Judges, and Lawyers of Mississippi, 1798–1935.* Jackson, 1935.

Rowland, Dunbar. *History of Mississippi: The Heart of the South,* vol. 1. Chicago, 1925.

Rowland, Mrs. Dunbar. *History of Hinds County Mississippi: 1821–1922.* Jackson, 1922.

Rusk, Jerrold. "The Effect of the Australian Ballot Reform on Split Ticket Voting, 1876–1908." *APSR* 64 (1970): 1220–38.

Rutledge, Wilmuth S. "Dueling in Antebellum Mississippi." *JMH* 26 (1964): 181–91.

Rutman, Darrett. "Assessing the Little Communities of Early America." *WMQ* 43 (1986): 163–78.

Ryan, Mary P. *Civic Wars: Democracy and Public Life in the American City during the Nineteenth Century.* Berkeley, 1997.

Sabean, David Warren. *Power in the Blood: Popular Culture and Village Discourse in Early Modern Germany.* Cambridge, 1983.

Shade, William G. *Democratizing the Old Dominion: Virginia and the Second Party System, 1824–1861.* Charlottesville, Va., 1996.

Shalhope, Robert. "Toward a Republican Synthesis: The Emergence of an Understanding of Republicanism in American Historiography." WMQ 29 (1972): 49–80.

Shore, Laurence. Southern Capitalists: The Ideological Leadership of an Elite, 1832–1885. Chapel Hill, 1986.

Silbey, Joel. The American Political Nation, 1838–1893. Stanford, 1991.

———. "The Surge of Republican Power: Partisan Antipathy, American Social Conflict, and the Coming of the Civil War." In Essays on Antebellum American Politics, 1840–1860, ed. Stephen Maizlish and John J. Kushma, 199–229. College Station, Texas, 1982.

Skates, John Ray. Mississippi: A Bicentennial History. New York, 1979.

Smith, Jay M. "No More Language Games: Words, Beliefs, and the Political Culture of Early Modern France." AHR 102 (1997): 1413–40.

Smith, M. Brewster. "Opinions, Personality, and Political Behavior." APSR 52 (1958): 1–25.

Smith, M. Brewster, Jerome S. Bruner, and Robert W. White. Opinions and Personality. New York, 1956.

Smith, W. Wayne. "Jacksonian Democracy on the Chesapeake: The Political Institutions." Maryland Historical Magazine 62 (1967): 381–93.

Snay, Mitchell. Gospel of Disunion: Religion and Separatism in the Antebellum South. Cambridge, 1993.

Sorauf, Frank J. Party Politics in America. Boston, 1968.

———. Political Parties in the American System. Boston, 1964.

Stampp, Kenneth. The Peculiar Institution: Slavery in the Ante-Bellum South. New York, 1956.

Stevens, William Oliver. Pistols at Ten Paces: The Story of the Code of Honor in America. Boston, 1940.

Stowe, Steven M. Intimacy and Power in the Old South: Ritual in the Lives of the Planters. Baltimore, 1987.

———. "The Touchiness of the Gentleman Planter: The Sense of Esteem and Continuity in the Ante-Bellum South." Psychohistory Review 8 (1979): 6–17.

Sumners, Mary Floyd. "Politics in Tishomingo County, 1836–1860." JMH 28 (1966): 133–51.

Suttles, Gerald D. The Social Construction of Communities. Chicago, 1972.

Sydnor, Charles Sackett. A Gentleman of the Old Natchez Region: Benjamin L. C. Wailes. Durham, N.C., 1938.

———. Gentlemen Freeholders: Political Practices in Washington's Virginia. Chapel Hill, 1952.

Taylor, Alan. "'The Art of Hook and Snivey': Political Culture in Upstate New York during the 1790s." JAH 90 (1993): 1371–95.

Thompson, Hon. R. H. "Suffrage in Mississippi." PMHS 1 (1898): 25–49.

Thornton, J. Mills, III. Politics and Power in a Slave Society: Alabama, 1800–1860. Baton Rouge, 1978.

Tully, Alan. Forming American Politics: Ideals, Interests, and Institutions in Colonial New York and Pennsylvania. Baltimore, 1994.

Turner, Victor. The Ritual Process: Structure and Anti-Structure. Chicago, 1969.

Van Gennep, Arnold. *The Rites of Passage*. Edited by Monika Vizedom and Gabrielle Caffee. Chicago, 1960.

Varon, Elizabeth. "Tippecanoe and the Ladies, Too: White Women and Party Politics in Antebellum Virginia." *JAH* 82 (1995): 494–521.

———. *We Mean to Be Counted: White Women and Politics in Antebellum Virginia*. Chapel Hill, 1998.

Voss-Hubbard, Mark. "The 'Third-party Tradition' Reconsidered: Third Parties in American Public Life, 1830–1900." *JAH* 86 (1999): 121–50.

Waldrep, Christopher. *Roots of Disorder: Race and Criminal Justice in the American South, 1817–80*. Urbana, 1998.

Waldstreicher, David. *In the Midst of Perpetual Fetes: the Making of American Nationalism, 1776–1820*. Chapel Hill, 1997.

Walther, Eric. *The Fire-Eaters*. Baton Rouge, 1992.

Warren, Roland L. *The Community in America*. Chicago, 1963.

Watson, Harry L. *Jacksonian Politics and Community Conflict: The Emergence of the Second American Party System in Cumberland County, North Carolina*. Baton Rouge, 1981.

———. "Conflict and Collaboration: Yeomen, Slaveholders, and Politics in the Antebellum South." *Social History* 10 (1985): 273–98.

Weaver, Herbert. *Mississippi Farmers, 1850–1860*. Nashville, 1945.

Wiebe, Robert. *The Search for Order, 1877–1920*. New York, 1967.

Williams, Jack Kenny. *Dueling in the Old South: Vignettes of Social History*. College Station, Texas, 1980.

Williams, Wirt A., ed, *History of Bolivar County, Mississippi*. Jackson, 1948; reprint. Spartanburg, S.C., 1976.

Winkle, John W. *The Mississippi State Constitution: A Reference Guide*. Westport, Conn., 1993.

Winkle, Kenneth J. "Ohio's Informal Polling Place: Nineteenth-century Suffrage in Theory and Practice." In *The Pursuit of Public Power: Political Culture in Ohio, 1787–1861*, ed. Jeffrey P. Brown and Andrew R. L. Cayton, 169–184. Kent, Ohio, 1994.

———. *The Politics of Community: Migration and Politics in Antebellum Ohio*. Cambridge, 1987.

———. "The U.S. Census as a Source in Political History." *Social Science History* 15 (1991): 565–77.

———. "The Voters and Lincoln's Springfield: Migration and Political Participation in an Antebellum City." *Journal of Social History* 25 (1992): 596–611.

Wood, Gordon. *The Creation of the American Republic 1776–1787*. Chapel Hill, 1969.

Wood, Kirsten. "'One Woman So Dangerous to Public Morals': Gender and Power in the Eaton Affair." *JER* 17 (1997): 237–75.

Woods, James M. *Rebellion and Realignment: Arkansas's Road to Secession*. Fayetteville, Ark., 1987.

Wooster, Ralph A. *The People in Power: Courthouse and Statehouse in the Lower South, 1850–1860*. Knoxville, 1969.

Wyatt-Brown, Bertram. "God and Honor in the Old South." *Southern Review* 25 (1989): 283–96.

————. *Honor and Violence in the Old South*. New York, 1986.
————. *Southern Honor: Ethics and Behavior in the Old South*. New York, 1982.
————. *Yankee Saints and Southern Sinners*. Baton Rouge, 1985.
Young, Alfred F. *The Democratic Republicans of New York: The Origins, 1763–1797*.
    Chapel Hill, 1967.

Dissertations and Unpublished Material

Anderson, Rachel Roach. "A History of Madison County, Mississippi." Master's the-
    sis: Mississippi College, 1967.
Brady, Hugh G. "Voting, Class and Demography in Antebellum Mississippi." Mas-
    ter's thesis: Northern Illinois University, 1977.
Green, Gabriel Collins. "Jasper County: A Prospect 1833–1968." Master's thesis: Mis-
    sissippi College, 1968.
Kamper, Anna Alice. "A Social and Economic History of Ante-Bellum Bolivar
    County, Mississippi." Master's thesis: University of Alabama, 1942.
Johnson, Christopher Stephen. "Poverty and Dependency in Antebellum Missis-
    sippi." Ph.D. diss.: University of California at Riverside, 1988.
Leonard, Gerald Flood. "Partisan Political Theory and the Unwritten Constitution:
    The Origins of Democracy in Illinois." Ph.D. diss.: University of Michigan, 1992.
Libby, David J. "Plantation and Frontier: Slavery in Mississippi, 1720–1830." Ph.D.
    diss.: University of Mississippi, 1997.
Lucas, Melvin Philip. "The Development of the Second Party System in Mississippi,
    1817–1846." Ph.D. diss.: Cornell University, 1983.
McAllister, Paul. "Missouri Voters, 1840–1856: An Analysis of Ante-Bellum Voting Be-
    havior and Party Politics." Ph.D. diss.: University of Missouri-Columbia, 1976.
McCulloch, James Victor. "A History of Jasper County, Mississippi." Master's thesis:
    Mississippi State College, 1954.
Oldshue, Jerry C. "A Study of the Influence of Economic, Social, and Partisan Char-
    acteristics on Secession Sentiment in the South, 1860–1861: A Multiple and
    Partial Correlation Analysis Employing the County as the Unit of Observation."
    Ph.D. diss.: University of Alabama, 1975.
Olsen, Christopher J. "Community, Honor, and Secession in the Deep South: Mis-
    sissippi's Political Culture, 1840s–1861." Ph.D. diss.: University of Florida, 1996.
Prentiss, Dale R. "Economic Progress and Social Dissent in Michigan and Missis-
    sippi, 1837–1860." Ph.D. diss.: Stanford University, 1990.
Rawson, Donald M. "Party Politics in Mississippi, 1850–1860." Ph.D. diss.: Vander-
    bilt University, 1964.
Ross, Cecil S. Hilliard. "Dying Hard, Dying Fast: The Know-Nothing Experience in
    Mississippi." Ph.D. diss.: Notre Dame University, 1982.
Ruff, Hazel Shelton. "The History of Hinds County, Mississippi before 1860." Mas-
    ter's thesis: Duke University, 1941.
Smith, Earl J. "The Free, Foreign-Born Population of Mississippi in the 1850s."
    Ph.D. diss.: Vanberbilt University, 1974.
Volz, Harry August, III. "Party, State, and Nation: Kentucky and the Coming of the
    American Civil War." Ph.D. diss.: University of Virginia, 1982.
Young, David N. "The Mississippi Whigs, 1834–1860." Ph.D. diss.: University of Ala-
    bama, 1968.

Index